Necroclimatism in a Spectral World (Dis)order?

Rain Petitioning, Climate and Weather Engineering in 21st Century Africa

Edited by

Artwell Nhemachena & Munyaradzi Mawere

Langaa Research & Publishing CIG
Mankon, Bamenda

Publisher:
Langaa RPCIG
Langaa Research & Publishing Common Initiative Group
P.O. Box 902 Mankon
Bamenda
North West Region
Cameroon
Langaagrp@gmail.com
www.langaa-rpcig.net

Distributed in and outside N. America by African Books Collective
orders@africanbookscollective.com
www.africanbookscollective.com

ISBN-10: 9956-550-46-9

ISBN-13: 978-9956-550-46-3

© Artwell Nhemachena & Munyaradzi Mawere 2019

List of Contributors

Artwell Nhemachena holds a PhD in Social Anthropology; MSc in Sociology and Social Anthropology, BSc Honours Degree in Sociology. In addition to having a good mix of social science and law courses in his undergraduate studies, he also has a Certificate in Law and a Diploma in Education. He has lectured in Zimbabwe before pursuing his PhD studies in South Africa. His current areas of research interest are Knowledge Studies; Development Studies; Environment; Resilience; Food Security and Food Sovereignty; Industrial Sociology; Agnotology, Sociology and Social Anthropology of Conflict and Peace; Transformation; Sociology and Social Anthropology of Science and Technology Studies, Democracy and Governance; Relational Ontologies; Decoloniality and Anthropological/Sociological Jurisprudence. He has published over 80 book chapters and journal articles in accredited and peer-reviewed platforms. He has also published over fourteen books in accredited and peer reviewed platforms. At the University of Namibia, he chairs the Faculty of Humanities and Social Sciences Seminar Series on Researching, Writing and Publishing. Artwell Nhemachena is also a Research Fellow in the College of Humanities of the University of South Africa. He is also an active member of the Council for the Development of Social Science Research in Africa (CODESRIA).

Munyaradzi Mawere is a Professor and Research Chair in the Simon Muzenda School of Arts, Culture and Heritage Studies at Great Zimbabwe University, in Zimbabwe. He holds a PhD in Social Anthropology from the University of Cape Town, South Africa; three Masters Degrees namely: Master of Arts Degree in Social Anthropology; Master of Arts Degree in Philosophy; Master of Arts Degree in Development Studies; a BA (Hons) Degree in Philosophy, and a number of certificates across disciplines. He is an author of more than 70 books and over 300 book chapters and peer-reviewed academic journals with a focus on Africa straddling the following areas: poverty and development, African philosophy, society and culture, democracy, human rights, politics of food production, humanitarianism and civil society organisations, indigenous knowledge systems, urban anthropology, existential anthropology, cultural philosophy, environmental anthropology, society and politics, decoloniality and African studies. Professor Mawere's research acumen has earned him prestigious international honours such as the Wenner-Gren Research Fellowship (2011-2014) and recently (2017), the much coveted Association of African Studies (ASA) Presidential Fellowship Award. He is a Senior Editorial Board Member and peer-reviewer for a number of publishing houses and journals, and has been involved in several research projects across disciplines. Some of his recently published (authored and edited/co-edited) books include: *Humans, Other Beings and the Environment: Harurwa (Edible stinkbugs) and Environmental Conservation in South-eastern Zimbabwe*; *Theory, Knowledge, Development and Politics: What Role for the Academy in the Sustainability of Africa?*; *Democracy, Good Governance and Development in Africa: A Search for Sustainable Democracy and Development*; *Culture, Indigenous Knowledge and Development in Africa: Reviving Interconnections for Sustainable Development*; *Myths of Peace and Democracy? Towards Building Pillars of Hope, Unity and Transformation in Africa*; *Harnessing Cultural Capital for Sustainability: A Pan Africanist Perspective*; *Divining the Future of Africa: Healing the Wounds, Restoring Dignity and Fostering Development*; *African Cultures, Memory and Space: Living the Past Presence in Zimbabwean Heritage*; *Violence, Politics and Conflict Management in Africa: Envisioning Transformation, Peace and Unity in the Twenty-First Century*; *African Philosophy and Thought Systems: A Search for a Culture and Philosophy of Belonging*; *Africa at the Crossroads: Theorising Fundamentalisms in the 21st Century*; *Colonial Heritage, Memory and Sustainability in Africa: Challenges, Opportunities and Prospects*; *Underdevelopment, Development and the Future of Africa*; *Theorising Development in Africa: Towards Building an African Framework of Development*; and *Human Trafficking and Trauma in the Digital Era: The Ongoing Tragedy of the Trade in Refugees from Eritrea*.

Takavafira Masarira Zhou holds a PhD in Environmental History. He is an environmental historian, a Lemba, trade unionist, and Human Rights defender. He is a holder of B.A. General, B.A. Special Honours in History, Masters in African History, Graduate Certificate in Education, and D. Phil in Environmental History from the University of Zimbabwe. He was a Teaching Assistant in the History Department at the University of Zimbabwe (1991-1995), a History

Lecturer at Mutare Teachers' college (2002-2004), and a part-time History Lecturer at Africa University (2002-2004). As a History Lecturer at Great Zimbabwe (2004-2008) he helped to transform the history subject area into the Department of History and Development Studies. He was a technical advisor (researcher) in Zimbabwe Constitution Select Committee (2010-2011) that produced Zimbabwe's new Constitution in 2013. He was also a member of the National Education Advisory Board (2009-2013) that among other things helped the then Ministry of Education, Sports, Arts and Culture in strategic planning, resource mobilisation and policy formulation during the period of Inclusive Government. Currently he is the president of the Progressive Teachers' Union of Zimbabwe, and treasurer of the Non Aligned Teachers' Unions of Southern Africa (ANTUSA). He has presented various papers at conferences in Zimbabwe, Africa, Europe and Asia. He has also published on African agriculture; white settler farming; environmental impact of mining in Zimbabwe; peace and security in Africa; History curricula changes in Zimbabwe; post-2016 Africa's development; teacher education; poverty, natural resources and underdevelopment in Africa; poverty, conflict and vulnerability in Africa; and general history and politics of Zimbabwe.

Wisdom Sibanda is currently a PhD candidate in Geography at the University of the Free State, South Africa. He holds a Master of Science in Environmental Policy and Planning (UZ); Bachelor of Science in Politics and Administration (UZ); Diploma in Water and Sanitation; Certificates in Monitoring and Evaluation; Participatory Rural Appraisal; Rural Development; Participatory Health and Hygiene; Geographical Information System. Sibanda, a former Assistant District Administrator in the Local Government of Zimbabwe and Projects Officer at Culture Fund Zimbabwe Trust, has a vast experience of serving in the public service as well as in local and international NGOs in a wide range of programmes including Monitoring and Evaluation and emergency Water, Sanitation and Hygiene (WASH). His research interests include community participation; Development and appraisal; Demand-led WASH programs; Water resources management; Environmental management; Climate change and disaster risk management.

Fortune Sibanda holds a Ph.D. He is an Associate Professor in the Department of Philosophy and Religious Studies, Simon Muzenda School of Arts, Culture and Heritage Studies, Great Zimbabwe University. He has widely published articles in refereed journals and book chapters on various themes from a religious perspective, which include the Environment and Climate Change, New Religious Movements, Land Question, Indigenous Ways of Knowing, Human rights issues and Power dynamics in the African context. He co-edited: *Power in Contemporary Zimbabwe* (2018). Prof Sibanda is a member of the African Consortium for Law and Religion Studies (ACLARS), African Theological Institutions in Southern and Central Africa (ATISCA), Association for the Study of Religion in Southern Africa (ASRSA) and African Association for the Study of Religion (AASR).

Semie M. Sama is a Post-Doctoral fellow at McGill University and at the Centre for International Governance Innovation (CIGI), Canada, where she researches in the field of international environmental law, including climate law and policy. She is also a member of the McGill Centre for Human Rights and Legal Pluralism and The Tshepo Institute for the Study of Contemporary Africa. Her research focuses on legal and policy solutions to environmental issues. Her areas of interest include environmental law, climate change, sustainable development, constitutional law, human rights, investment law, and public policy. Dr. Sama holds a Ph.D. in law from the University of Ottawa; an LL.M. in global sustainability and environmental law from the University of Ottawa; an M.Sc. in ecotechnology and sustainable development from Mid Sweden University and Stockholm University; and an LL.B. from the University of Buea. Before joining the Centre for International Governance and McGill University, Dr. Sama was a UN Global Environment Outlook Fellow (during which she contributed to the Sixth *Global Environment Outlook GEO-6: Healthy Planet, Healthy People*). She also worked for the University of Ottawa, Oxfam Canada and the Foundation for Environment and Development. Dr. Sama has received numerous awards and honours, including the Social Sciences and Humanities Research Council (SSHRC) of Canada Award, the IUCN Academy of Environmental Law Scholarship, the

University of Ottawa's International Admission Scholarship and the Minister of Higher Education Honours Prize of the Government of Cameroon.

Ignatius Gutsa is currently a Senior Lecturer in the Department of Sociology at the University of Zimbabwe. He holds a PhD in Anthropology from the University of the Witwatersrand in South Africa, an MSc in Sociology and Social Anthropology and BSc (Hons) Sociology from the University of Zimbabwe. His research interests are in ageing, climate change, local knowledge systems, livelihoods and rural development.

Olúwọlé Tẹ́wọ́gboyè Òkéwándé has been lecturing in the Department of Linguistics and Nigerian Languages, University of Ilorin, Ilọrin, Nigeria since 1998. His research interests include the fields of African religions, semiotics, stylistics and culture. His Doctoral Thesis, "A Semiotic Investigation of Links between *Ifá, Ìbejì* and *Ayò Ọlọ́pọ́n*" is a study that establishes *Ifá's* relationship with *Ayò Ọlọ́pọ́n* and *Ìbejì* around codes, symbols, icons and indices. He has published in reputable local, national and international journals.

Nancy Mazuru is a lecturer in the Department of History, Archaeology and Development Studies at Great Zimbabwe University. She holds a Master of Science degree in Development Studies from Women's University in Africa. Currently, she is a Development Studies PhD candidate at the University of the Witwatersrand, Johannesburg, South Africa.

Aaron Rwodzi holds a PhD in History. He is currently a lecturer in the Department of History under the Faculty of Humanities and Social Sciences at the Catholic University of Zimbabwe. His areas of research interest include political and social history, democracy, ethnicity and culture.

Nkwazi Mhango is a PhD candidate at the University of Manitoba, in Canada. He is the author of *Saa yaUkombozi, Nyuma ya Pazia, Souls on Sale, Born with Voice, Africa Reunite or Perish, Psalm of the Oppressed, Africa's Best, Worst President: How Neocolonialism and Imperialism*

Maintained Venal Rules in Africa, 'Is It Global War on Terrorism' or Global War over Terra Africana?: The Ruse Imperial Powers Use to Occupy Africa Militarily for Economic Gains, Africa's Dependency Syndrome: Can Africa Still Turn Things around for the Better? How Africa Developed Europe: Deconstructing the His-story of Africa, Excavating Untold Truth and What Ought to Be Done and Known. Also, Mhango has contributed many chapters to various scholarly books and he is a poet, teacher, columnist, Journalist, Peace and Conflict Scholar, and member of Writers' Association of Newfoundland and Labrador (WANL), St. John's, NL, Canada and an alumnus of Universities of Dar es Salaam (Tanzania), Menno Simons College at the University of Winnipeg and Arthur V. Mauro Centre at St. Paul College of Manitoba (Canada).

Edmore Dube holds a PhD and he is a senior lecturer in the Department of Philosophy and Religious Studies, Great Zimbabwe University, Mashava Campus. He currently lectures in ethics in African indigenous religions, and has keen interest on how such ethics can lead to human flourishing. He shares a general interest on inter-religious dialogue envisaged by the contemporary world as a panacea to the problems of religious imperialism, as demonstrated by missionaries who disregarded indigenous taboos with utter impunity. He is convinced that genuine dialogue can enhance peace, stability and mutuality. He also has research interests on how religion may enhance public health as well as strengthen institutions of justice bent on serving the common good.

Beatrice Lantern is senior lecturer in the Department of African Languages and Culture at Great Zimbabwe University, Masvingo in Zimbabwe. She holds a Master of Arts Degree in African languages and culture from Midlands State University. Currently, she is studying for a PhD with the University of South Africa (UNISA). Her research interests are in language planning, onomastics, translation studies and indigenous knowledge systems.

Alex Munyonga is a philosophy of science education lecturer at Mkoba Teachers College and also a lecturer for ethics at The Catholic University of Zimbabwe's Humanities Department. He holds an MA in Philosophy, Special Honours Degree in Philosophy, B.A. (Philosophy and Religious Studies) and a Postgraduate Diploma in Education all from the University of Zimbabwe. Munyonga is an Ambassador of Peace with the IIFWP. His areas of interest are education in contemporary African society, applied ethics with special reference to environmental, social, business, political and clergy ethics. He is also interested in African metaphysics and the indigenous knowledge systems. His latest publication is a book chapter on the death penalty law in the context of xenophobic attacks in South Africa, 2008 and 2015; edited by Mangena *et al* and published by the Verom Press, USA in 2018.

Revd. Martin Mujinga holds a Ph.D. He is an Ordained Minister of the Methodist Church in Zimbabwe. He has taught at several theological institutions and Universities in Zimbabwe and South Africa. Dr. Mujinga is the author of three books. He has contributed articles in peer-reviewed journals. He has reviewed articles for journals. Mujinga has also written chapters for book publications. His research interest is in the healing ministry, African Spirituality, Methodist history and theology and the role of religion in transforming societies. He can be contacted at martinmujinga@gmail.com +263 772 207 033; +263 716 402 119

Tom Tom is a Doctoral Research Fellow under the South African Research Chair Initiative- Chair in Social Policy, College of Graduate Studies at the University of South Africa (UNISA); and Lecturer in the Department of Development Studies, Faculty of Applied Social Sciences, Zimbabwe Open University (ZOU). He is a sociologist whose research, publications and teaching focus on development sociology and social policy. His work revolves around enhancing people's wellbeing. He is an active member of Young African Researchers in Agriculture (YARA) Network and the South African Sociological Association (SASA).

Clement Chipenda is a Doctoral Research Fellow under the South African Research Chair Initiative- Chair in Social Policy, College of Graduate Studies at the University of South Africa (UNISA). Having worked for the Government of Zimbabwe and several NGOs, he has accumulated extensive hands-on community practice and experience in research and publication in social policy, human rights and development. He is widely published in journals and books on empirically-informed development practice. He is a member of Young African Researchers in Agriculture (YARA) Network and the South African Sociological Association (SASA).

Table of Contents

Foreword xv

Chapter One
Fast-Tracking Africa to Climate Apocalypse (FATACA)?
An Introduction to Decolonising Climate
and Weather Issues 1
Artwell Nhemachena & Munyaradzi Mawere

Chapter Two
The Historiography and Politicisation
of Droughts in Colonial Africa 69
Takavafira Masarira Zhou

Chapter Three
Climate Change and the Future of Africa:
Impacts on Water Resources in Eastern
and Southern Africa.. 109
Wisdom Sibanda & Fortune Sibanda

Chapter Four
Chipping and Refashioning the Soapstone?
A Symbolic Re-appraisal of the Colonial
Wresting of Weather and Climate Control
from African Spirit Mediums 133
Edmore Dube

Chapter Five
Rain Petitioning in African Indigenous
Knowledge Systems: Insights from Ifa
among the Yoruba People of Nigeria 155
Oluwole Tewogboye Okewande

Chapter Six
Perceptions and Experiences of Climate
Change in Rural Zimbabwe:
The Case of Elderly Women in
Goromonzi District 179
  Ignatius Gutsa

Chapter Seven
Neoimperial Engineering of Droughts
and Famine on Post-Colonial Zimbabwe?
Knowledge Systems and the Politics of
Land Repossession in Africa.. 209
  Beatrice Lantern

Chapter Eight
Climatological Anomalies, Food Politics
and the Poor in Africa 231
  Aaron Rwodzi

Chapter Nine
Climate Change in Zimbabwe:
Challenges and Prospects for Rural
Women in Bikita District 255
  Nancy Mazuru

Chapter Ten
Towards an Ecotheology?
A Postcolonial Analysis of the Ecological
Depletion at Kwenda Mission of the
Methodist Church in Zimbabwe....................................... 277
  Martin Mujinga

Chapter Eleven
Land (Dis)possession and Environmental
Destruction in Zimbabwe: A Critical Reflection
of Events since the Beginning of the 21st Century 301
  Alex Munyonga

Chapter Twelve
A Benchmaking Framework to Boost
Africa's Standards to Reduce Emissions
from the Transportation Sector..327
    Semie M. Sama

Chapter Thirteen
Global Warming and Climate
Colonialism/Imperialism:
Appraising Decolonisation...351
    Nkwazi Nkuzi Mhango

Chapter Fourteen
Moving Beyond Neoimperial
Lamentations over Decolonising
African Land and Environments:
The Model of Zimbabwe as the Future 371
    Tom Tom & Clement Chipenda

Foreword

The figures of ghosts have always been useful to empires particularly because ghosts make their spectral errands in the middle of the nights whereof indigenous victims of the spectral deconstruction wake up to find their autonomy, freedom, liberty, sovereignty, livelihoods, material possessions, sleep, health, limbs and even some lives have disappeared. Although spectrality, hauntology, zombie politics, zombie economies, spectral-geographies and zombie environmentalism have been popularised since about the 1990s, it is useful to note that enslavement and colonial eras were also eras of the spectrality, hauntings and deconstructions of African kingdoms, queendoms, and chiefdoms together with their institutions viz politics, cultures, societies, religions, economies and legal institutions. Empire has used the agency of humans as well as the agency of nonhuman horses, microorganisms and pieces of technology to launch spectral deconstructions of African institutions since the enslavement and colonial eras. Infusing and suffusing humans and nonhumans with artificial intelligence, neoempire is equipping itself with proxies whose spectral deconstructive agency/vitality/performativity/actions will be handy in deconstructing the sovereignties and autonomies of states and societies at the margins of the world. The idea is to prepare for the insurrections of cosmopolitics, including nature as a force multiplier. Symptomatic of environmental escapism, in the insurrections, the targeted states are accused of dominating or colonising nature: in the discourses, colonial/imperial states seek to evade demands for reparations, restitutions and restorations for enslaving and colonising Africans and other indigenous peoples by accusing the indigenous peoples and their states of dominating/colonising animate nature/nonhumans. The aim is to then spectrally turn nature/nonhumans against indigenous people who demand reparations, restitution and restoration for enslavement and colonisation. In the discourses, indigenous people are not supposed to demand reparations, restoration and restitution for enslavement and colonisation – they should simply be resilient or the animate nonhumans that they have supposedly also colonised and dominated will turn [or more accurately will be conjured] against them and begin to also demand reparations.

Departing from humanistic Derridean deconstructionism, the book pays attention to ways in which nature/nonhumans, including climate are relied upon in spectral hauntology and in deconstructing the sovereignties and autonomies of the colonised indigenous people. In the context of celebrations of the agency, vitality, performativity, propensities and actions of nature/nonhumans, the book anticipates cataclysmic apocalypses originating from various forms of spectrality and hauntological deconstructions of sovereignties and autonomies in the margins of the world. Thus, just as the spectre or ghost complicates and disrupts linearity of time and binaries between the past and the present, neoimperialism is also about confounding binaries or distinctions between the past empire and the present empire such that there is the past in the present of indigenous people – the ghosts of the past visit the ecologies of the present. In some academies of contemporary era, there is the celebration of the spectral "colonial comeback". Of course spectres are shapeshifters and tricksters; they defy their shapes as much as they defy binaries between the dead and the living, good and evil, moral and immoral, human and animal, nature and culture, the human and nonhuman and so on. The mark of the spectre is disruption of order, of conventions, of normativity and normality, of morality, ethics, humanity, cultures, politics, economies, societies and environments; and in all these disruptions spectres may not leave traces of their footprints because they always want to monopolise spectrality and deconstruction. In a world that is replete with spectrality, it may be necessary to shift emphasis from preoccupation with critiquing domination, order, structures, hierarchies, hegemonies, dictatorships and authoritarianism to ways in which spectral performances disrupt and deconstruct normalcy, normativity and cosmic order all of which are germane to contemporary climate change/global warming discourses. In fact, spectres are averse to structures, order, life and so on, which they disrupt and deconstruct in their spectral errands. To become a spectre is to assume a surreptitious deconstructive and disruptive figure.

In the light of the foregoing, it is necessary to ask why environmental degradation and pollution discourses focus on the physical environment while ignoring the ways in which spectres pollute social, human, cultural, moral, legal and political environments. Mixing up and defying binaries between the clean and unclean, the dirty and the clean, the living and the dead, spectres understandably visit pollution and various forms of degradation on human environments yet discourses on degradation and pollution have been eluded by the figure of the spectre that makes deconstructive errands in the middle of the night. Equally, while discourses on environmental degradation have condemned shifting cultivation and various forms of transhumance, this book wonders why the other shifting, wandering, disruptive, deconstructive and hauntological spectres are not also considered to be risky to environmental stability and normativity. Spectres shift or move between huge swathes of land even between the worlds of the dead and the worlds of the living yet their shiftings are hardly considered in the discourses on shifting cultivation as a cause of environmental degradation. As spectres, it may be understandable that they escape the radars of the most advanced tracking devices in the world. Perhaps spectres defy extinction as much as they defy the radars of tracking devices. When human radars fail to track spectres, the human tendency is to engage in various forms of denialism – to deny the existence of the spectres and to discount the spectral errands to the human world.

Eurocentric science on climate change is also pitted in sterile crevices between denialism and avowalism yet the scientists hardly ask themselves how far their science has also become spectral. One can think of the spectrality of colonial/imperial race science involving eugenic experiments on the colonised peoples. One can think of spectral colonial/imperial science that was used to manufacture various kinds of chemical and biological organisms with which to perpetrate genocide on indigenous peoples; similarly, one can consider colonial/imperial spectral science that was used in apartheid South Africa, Rhodesia, Namibia, Angola and other countries to subjugate the colonised and enslaved; equally one can consider poisonous chemicals that were used to douse food given to indigenous peoples suffering colonisation. Perhaps science has become not only spectral but a form of necroscience. Perhaps when colonised and enslaved peoples deny some forms of science, they are not narrowly rejecting or denying the present form but they are also denying its history, that is, the spectrality of science in a world where binaries between the past and the present, the safe and the unsafe, the humanely and unhumanely have vanished. In addressing denialism and avowalism, it is necessary to take context into cognisance – that is, to consider the spectrality of the forms of science including how they have shifted between the worlds of the past and the present, the worlds of the dead and the living and so on.

The idea might be to establish a normal science, which is sensitive to indigenous peoples' contexts, so that the normal science can redress the abnormalities in climate and global warming. A form of science that carries abnormalities of the imperial and colonial race science cannot redress the abnormalities of climate change and global warming. A form of science that rejects and ignores the cultural, social, political, economic and religious contexts of indigenous people cannot cleanse abnormalities in climate change/global warming because the science itself carries abnormalities that have not been cleansed. In other words, colonial/imperial race science polluted science and now science itself is suffering from greenhouse effect originating from race science – climate science is heating up in the context of denialism. Science needs to be sensitive to the logics of sacrifice in the colonial and imperial contexts; it has to be sensitive to inequalities in the world that is embedded in an imperial/colonial context which suffers denialism. Science has to be sensitive to its historical context where it has been imperially used to justify and naturalise the dispossession, genocide, exploitation and subjugation of indigenous people. In this vein, science has to be as sensitive to context as to team up with indigenous mediums that are responsible for rain petitioning. This is particularly necessary in a context where Eurocentric correspondence theories of truth are troubled; where matters of causality, including cause and effect relationships are being criticised. The contemporary era is one of spectrality and complexity wherein science has to admit its own spectrality – the age of coming out from the closets is also an age of being cleansed as part of a ritual of exiting from the colonial/imperial closets: put in other words, it is an age wherein there should be admission that there is not only one science but several sciences including the indigenous sciences, technology and mathematics that were destroyed by colonialists at precolonial African universities like the University of Timbuktu, in Mali.

The hunt for the Creator, the prime mover, *primum movens*, unmoved mover, primary cause or first cause or mover of all things does not have to end with the Nietzschean supermen, of science. It has to go beyond them and their world because in a spectral epoch, there should be movements between different worlds. Redressing climate change requires attention to the logics of spectrality, including the spectral absence presence of victims of enslavement and colonial dispossession and genocide who are activating and animating the cosmos into anomalous global warming/climate change. They are also accusing and cursing living humans of centuries-old denialism to compensate in order to restore normalcy in the world. The question here is why, on the one hand, the abnormalities of the enslavement and colonisation of indigenous peoples are not being addressed yet, on the other hand, the abnormalities of climate change and global warming do not even wait for centuries to be addressed? Why is it that the United Nations pushes so hard for global attention to abnormalities in climate change and global warming issues but it does hardly anything to push for the redress of the abnormalities of enslavement and colonisation for which indigenous people deserve reparations, restitution and restoration? Might the United Nations be biased towards transnational corporations with which it has signed the Global Compact – some of which corporations were complicit in the enslavement and colonisation of indigenous people? Might the contemporary drive towards the catastrophic extinction of indigenous people be meant to be a final solution to evade reparations, restitution and restoration of what is due? Has it not been argued already that reparations for enslavement cannot be paid because all the direct victims have died? Might it not similarly be argued, after the extinction, that all the direct victims of colonisation are dead so reparations, restitution and restorations are not possible/necessary? Might this not be what is meant by some scholars' current postulations about "emancipatory catastrophism"?

It is also important to take into cognisance the vengeance of indigenous people's early colonial heroes/mediums/guardians who were killed by colonialists; some of the heroes/mediums/guardians' skulls and sacred objects are still detained in Euro-American museums even as indigenous people are struggling to perform rain petitioning ceremonies which require those sacred objects. Skulls of African mediums/heroes/guardians from states such as Namibia, Zimbabwe, Angola and others are still lying in Euro-American museums despite African demands for their return. If Africans are to have effective rain petitioning ceremonies, it means the Euro-Americans should first return the skulls and other skulls of African mediums/guardians/heroes who they unjustly killed during the era of colonial robbery. In addition to the skulls, it is necessary for Euro-Americans to return the sacred objects and artefacts which they collected, or more accurately stole, from Africans at the inception of colonialism – African rain petitioning rituals will not have much effectiveness when the skulls, sacred objects and artefacts of their cultural, political, spiritual and social heroes are still detained in Euro-America. Of course missionaries and other colonialists, including their scientists, have derided African rain petitioning ceremonies as ineffective "rain making" ceremonies but the paradox is that it is the same missionaries and other colonialists who stole African artefacts, sacred objects, desecrated African shrines and divided Africans such that they would not be able to work together in the ceremonies. In addition, colonialists who were homosexuals such as Cecil John Rhodes mischievously chose to be buried at Matopo Hills' Malindidzimu, in Zimbabwe, where precolonial Africans from what is now Zambia, Botswana, Zimbabwe, Mozambique and South Africa would make trips to hear God's voice. In the light of such desecration of the African shrines, it is not surprising that climate change is happening and that African rain petitioning rituals are no longer very effective. Euro-American scholars, thinkers and institutions would promote and encourage homosexuality/queers, which they celebrate as a challenge to normativity or as a deconstruction of heteronormativity but paradoxically they decry the deviation of climate from the norm. They celebrate challenges to normativity but they also lament the climatic deviation from normativity. They celebrate social, cultural, political, sexual and religious dissidents operating in Africa and other excolonies yet when climate also deviates and becomes a "dissident" the same Euro-Americans would want to coerce the excolonies to sign and ratify treaties on ways to resolve the climatic abnormalities. When crises happen in Africa, such as in Robert Mugabe's Zimbabwe, they are quick to blame and even "smartly" sanction individual African leaders but when [climatic] crises happen globally, they are simply described as anthropogenic, without tracking and "smartly" sanctioning the specific individuals responsible for such global crises.

Artwell Nhemachena & Munyaradzi Mawere

Chapter One

Fast-Tracking Africa to Climate Apocalypse (FATACA)? An Introduction to Decolonising Climate and Weather Issues

Artwell Nhemachena & Munyaradzi Mawere

Introduction

Discourses that critique human domination and control over nature and the environment have themselves ironically become dominant over humanity and nature. While dismissing the Universalist, hierarchial, moralist, humanistic, transcendental and orderly God of Creation ex nihilo who is accused of being dominating, hegemonic and hierarchical, some Eurocentrists are now evangelising and universalising their discourses on critique of domination, control and hierarchy in ways that are turning them into Supermen replacing the God of Creation. Deconstructing domination and control is one way that is being used to reject God, who is criticised not only for Creationism but also for dominating and controlling humanity and nature. The issue here is that those that do the laborious work of deconstructing God often do so not merely for the sake of deconstruction but for the sake of replacing those, including God, who they deconstruct. The colonial deconstruction of African precolonial states, economies, epistemologies, cultures and societies was followed up with replacement of the precolonial establishments with colonial establishments; the Darwinist deconstruction, in the 1800s, of the God of Creation and morals was followed up with the replacement of the supremacy of God of Creation with the supremacy of empire which thrived on violence, chaos, the Big Bang and postcreationism. Similarly, the Nietzschean (1887) deconstruction of the binaries between good and evil was followed up with the replacement of Godly goodness with imperial evilness in Africa. The colonial deconstruction of African humanity was followed up with discourses that animalised Africans portraying them

1

as indistinct from animals and beasts of burdens for empire. In the contemporary era, there is not only deconstruction of binaries between humans and animals, culture and nature, good and evil, death and life, safe and unsafe, God and Devil; but there are also discourses that deconstruct humanity, God and Anthropos. The problematique here is that those that sponsor deconstruction hide their own wills to power and to domination, and such wills to power begin with deconstruction itself – deconstruction is already an expression of possession of power and the will to use that power to dominate. The point is that those that sponsor deconstruction are often spectral, not only in the sense of ghostly deconstructing and destabilising Godly order but also in the sense of wanting to establish their own order, hierarchies, transcendentalism, domination and hegemony – they do not deconstruct simply for deconstruction's sake.

It is also necessary to note that decolonisation is not synonymous with Eurocentric and neoimperial deconstruction and destabilisation. The enslavement and colonisation processes were indeed about deconstruction of the institutions of the enslaved and colonised – so contemporary scholars should not mistake the deconstruction of the institutions of the neocolonised for decolonisation. When Eurocentric science has long deposed God, it becomes hypocritical for the Eurocentric scholarship to attempt to employ the logics of moral panics, including in contemporary climate change discourses. Moral panics would require the existence of God as the source of the morals around which any panics can be generated. Having deposed God and then disfigured African societies, cultures, religions and spirituality in an attempt to exterminate the same, Eurocentric scientists paradoxically generate moral panics and confusion in a world where sources of morals have been effaced and deposed. In a world where African human beings are regarded as indistinct from animals/nonhumans, it is cause for wonder where morals would come from. Similarly, in a world where African societies and cultures are destroyed, it is cause for wonder where morals would come from. The point here is that moral panics around climate change, climate catastrophism, and climate apocalypse would require clear and convincing morals or what Emile Durkheim (Hamilton, 1995) would call conscience collective – which itself presupposes the existence of

2

clear and convincing societies and social facts. Neoimperialism and neocolonialism are in essence about theft, robbery, looting, plunder and exploitation on a planetary scale – they are not about morality, ethics, etiquette or maintaining conscience collective of societies.

In a context where human beings are encouraged to breach God's contract and ancestral taboos, morals, ethics, laws and etiquette, it is not clear where the morals in the climate apocalypse are coming from. The morals around climate apocalypse moral panics could be coming from some sort of malicious civil religion, in Bellah's (2005) sense, wherein Euro-America has become god and is hence setting morals, ethics, laws and etiquette for all human beings in the world. However, the deposition of God can be argued to be as sacrilegious as to cause climate change, including climate apocalypse itself. The point is that, in a world marked by supposed complexity, climate change could be a result of the deposition of God who has been denied by Eurocentric scientists. Paradoxically Eurocentric scientists, who have denied God, condemn human beings that deny and resist their climate science. In other words, Eurocentric scientists who have denied God, ironically, do not want other human beings to deny their own climate science. The argument is, if scientists do not want other human beings to deny their science, the same scientists must not deny the existence and power of God in the first instance – scientists are the prototype denialists because they needlessly deny the existence of God, including a place to God in the climate change equation. But even as they deny the existence of God and associated morals, the same scientists would want to create moral panics around climate change catastrophism.

While for climate change scientists, climate change is the greatest catastrophe humanity is witnessing, for religious adherents, the greatest catastrophe lies in the scientists' denial of the existence of God and associated morals. Put differently, while climate scientists would want to create moral panics and pandemonium around climate change, religious adherents would create moral panics and launch moral crusades around climate scientists' denial of God and morals. In this regard, dangerous folk devils (Dunbar *et al*, 2015) are not found among those that deny climate change but they are among those that deny the existence of God and associated morals. Thus, Frederick Nietzsche's announcement that 'God is dead'; that Godly

3

transcendental morals and ethics were dead and; that supermen had replaced God (Nietzsche, 1887; Halilovic, 1998; Chakra *et al*, 2018) constitutes dangerous folk devilish behaviour that would attract moral crusades and moral panics. The question then would be whether what is called climate change is not in fact a manifestation of God's wrath on His deposition; might climate change including droughts, famine, floods, landslides and heat waves not be a sign of God's wrath and anger against His deposers? Why must scientists' anger with climate change denialists be justified in a world that denies the anger of God? Why must human anger with denialists be justified in a world that denies the anger of God — must human beings including human conjurations and anger be given pre-eminence in such instances?

The major problem in the foregoing is that Eurocentrists, including scientists, have deposed God and they have replaced God's transcendence with the global transcendence of elitist human beings. They have replaced Godly transcendence with the neoimperial transcendence of humans that paradoxically delight in denying the existence of God while at the same time manifesting intolerance with human beings who deny their climate science. Thus, aiming to construct a new revolutionary order, a global aristocracy, grounded in radical atheism and not in Divine right, Nietzsche and Feuerbach (Neumann, 1982; Schrift 2001) pronounced the death of God and the rise of Supermen who supposedly replaced Him. After pronouncing God as dead, Nietzsche then announced the disappearance of truth and the erosion of the distinction between truth and falsehood in a context where the Supermen's will to power was celebrated (Nietzsche, 2002). Arguing that the will to deception and craven self-interest should be accorded a higher and more fundamental value for all life, Nietzsche (2002) proposed that the binary between good and evil be devalued. Nietzsche opined that there were connections, relations and links between good and evil such that it was futile to conceive them as binaries or dichotomies — his effort was to erode and cloud the distinctions between good and evil, truth and falsehood. Thus, for Nietzsche (2002), the falsity of judgements or assertions was not itself an objection — the question, for him, was how far an assertion or judgement preserves and promotes [colonial] life whether good or evil. In this sense, even the

4

falsest judgements or assertions are indispensable to Westerners who prize the falsification of the world partly through numbers. So, Nietzsche argued that 'a renunciation of false judgements would be a renunciation of [neocolonial] life, a negation of [neoimperial] life' (Nietzsche, 2002: 7). Nietzsche (2018) argued thus:

> The falseness of an opinion is not for us any objection to it: it is here, perhaps, that our new language sounds most strangely. The question is, how far an opinion is life-furthering, life-preserving, species-preserving, perhaps species-rearing, and we are fundamentally inclined to maintain that the falsest opinions…are the most indispensable to us, that without a recognition of logical fictions, without a comparison of reality with the purely IMAGINED world of the absolute and immutable, without a constant counterfeiting of the world by means of numbers, man could not live, that the renunciation of false opinions would be a renunciation of life, a negation of life.

In line with Nietzsche's deposition of God, morality and ethics, Africans have been depicted since the colonial era, as without transcendental God, morals and ethics – Africans were conveniently depicted, by colonial scholars and thinkers, as animists without a transcendental God, morals, ethics and even laws. The elimination of transcendental God, morals, ethics and laws in colonial depictions of precolonial Africans was deliberate. This was meant to pave the way for the crimes of colonisation, including robbery, theft, looting, rape, plunder and exploitation of Africans – of course in ways that would anger God and bring about famines, droughts, landslides and floods. Thus, at the inception of colonialism, that denied the transcendence of God, morals and ethics in Africa, there were recurrent and intense droughts, famines, landslides, heat waves and floods as will be explained in this book. Consistent with Nietzsche's denial of the binary between good and evil, Africans were robbed, dispossessed and exploited in ways that attracted the anger of God who then visited droughts, famines and floods to the matrix of colonisation. Of course, the emphasis that Nietzsche placed on connections, relations or ties between good and evil was meant to cancel out binaries between God and the Devil in the early colonial context wherein colonialists sought to perpetrate various kinds of heinous, inhuman, and unGodly crimes on Africans and other colonised people. To legitimise the perpetration of unGodly crimes, it was necessary for colonialists to depose God, including by cancelling off the binaries between good and evil, moral and immoral. In this regard, we argue that contemporary calls to deconstruct binaries are merely replicating and in fact advancing the Nietzschean edicts to deconstruct binaries between good and evil, between God and the Devil. The same holds for contemporary calls to popularise relationality, relational ontologies and connections, which in our view, merely replicate Nietzschean calls about relations between good and evil, between God and the Devil.

Because colonialists worked with a Nietzschean model that denied the existence of binaries between good and evil, between the moral and immoral, between God and the Devil, neoimperial rationality was so devoid of morality that it was considered rational to colonise, dispossess, rob, rape and exploit other people including in ways that angered God. Contemporary climate change could be a result of Eurocentric forms of criminal (not merely instrumental) rationality (Merchant, 2008) which deny the existence of Godly morality and binaries between good and evil. In other words, we argue that the problem is not simplistically about the existence of "instrumental" or "materialistic" rationality including "materialistic" consumer culture but the major problem lies in the denial of binaries between good and evil, between the moral and immoral, and between God and the Devil. In other words, we argue that colonial/imperial rationality was not merely instrumental or materialistic but it was criminal rationality, including criminal (not merely materialistic) consumer culture. God does not punish human beings who are instrumental or materialistic in bringing about the good and moral things but He punishes them for being instrumental in bringing about the immoral and evil things. Put in other words, God would in fact punish human beings for not being instrumental or materialistic in bringing about the good and moral things. Thus, God would not punish humanity for being materialistic in moral ways. The point therefore is that deconstruction of binaries/dichotomies between humans and animals, good and evil, moral and immoral would not resolve the problem of climate change because God enjoins humanity to draw distinctions between good and evil, between the moral and immoral and the human and animal. As with the Nietzschean project, it is Darwinist and Hobbesian theories of the state of nature and survival of the fittest that would erode distinctions between the moral and immoral, the good and evil, and the Godly and Devilish. Instead of theorising life in terms of the state of nature, Hobbes should have theorised it in terms of state of Godliness; equally instead of theorising life in terms of survival of the fittest, Charles Darwin should have theorised it in terms of survival of the moralest or survival of the Godliest. Unfortunately, theories on the state of nature and survival of the fittest, which are mistaken to be rational when in fact they are devilish, reduced human beings to the level of animals wherein what mattered was not morality, distinction between good and evil, moral and immoral but what mattered most was nature and survival by any means, moral or immoral. In this sense Nietzcheanism, Hobbesianism and Darwinism explain the immoralities, unGodliness and criminality of the enslavement and colonisation perpetrated on Africans – in this sense, they explain the wrath of God who visited droughts, famines and floods particularly since the beginning of the atrocities and holocausts on Africans.

This book exposes the nefarious logics behind the Euro-American projects premised on the Nietzschean model, Darwinian and Hobbesian theories – projects which were all meant to erode and undo binaries/distinctions/dichotomies between God and the Devil, the good and the evil, and the moral and the immoral. As such, the book is an effort to decolonise climate and weather discourses as they are manipulated by Euro-America in its endeavour to replace God with the Nietzschean supermen.

The Problematiques of Contemporary Climate Change Discourses

One problem with contemporary climate change discourses is that they do not inform us what we should do with the theories about the state of nature and survival of the fittest, which theories undergird the planetary robbery, dispossession, theft, looting and plunder without regard to morals, ethics, justice and laws to the original owners bestowed by God. In fact, the scientists themselves are cast in a state of nature wherein they compete for survival in ways that hardly speak to transcendental Godly morality. The problem is also that where some human beings define and proselytise their own inhuman and unGodly morality, such morality would be used to cap, control, disable and "greenhouse" other humans. In so far as Eurocentric epistemologies prevent the neocolonised peoples from reaching Godly perfections, Kingdom, endowments, transcendentalism and morality, the Euro-Americans can be understood as greenhousing the neo-colonial subjects and preventing them to share in the Godly morality, endowments and transcendentalism. The point here is that the greenhouse effect must not be narrowly defined in terms of physical climatic conditions because there is also greenhouse effect in the moral sense wherein Africans are trapped in neocolonial and neoimperial morally suffocating conditions marked by extreme heat and moral droughts. When Eurocentric scientists get preoccupied with global warming, droughts and floods, the assumption is that global warming, droughts and floods occur only in the form of physical atmospheric states or processes; the global warming, even heating of morals, ethics and rectitude are ignored by those that want to narrow global warming to physical atmospheric conditions as if such global warming happens in moral vacuum. When indigenous people explain climate change and global warming in terms of loss of morals, ethics, etiquette including the proliferation of prostitution, homosexuality, murder, incest, bestiality, adultery and so on, they should be understood as refusing parochialism. Morals heat up in the same way there is global warming – and so humanity must be worried as much about the heating up and loss of morality as they are worried about global warming and climate change in the physical sense. In this sense, we concur with scholars like Francis Nyamnjoh (2012) who argue that the resilient colonial education has a greenhouse effect on Africans. Thus, we contend that when neocolonised subjects deny Eurocentric epistemologies, they are not necessarily denying the greenhouse effect but they are protesting against the broader greenhouse effect of the neo-colonial education, including western scientism that is premised on hopelessly narrow versions of [physical] greenhouse effects. Africa and other colonised peoples are experiencing not only the physical forms of global warming but they are also experiencing broader versions of global heating up with respect to neo-colonial education, neo-colonial cultures, neo-colonial epistemologies, neo-colonial plunder, dispossession, looting, robbery and other immoral, illegal, unjust depredations all of which are ample evidence of greenhouse effects in a wider sense of the term.

The time that Nietzsche wrote his book, *Beyond good and evil* in the 1800, the colonisation of much of Africa was also happening and this colonisation was marked by droughts, floods and famine that killed Africans in their numbers. The era of the colonisation of Africa was marked by droughts, floods and famines not only in the physical senses but also in the moral, epistemological, legal, ethical, justice, social, political and social senses – colonialists/imperialists brought various forms of droughts, floods and famines some of which are hardly being researched on or marked as deserving civil protection and disaster management interventions. There were as much physical droughts and floods as there were social, cultural, legal, moral, ethical, epistemological droughts, famines and floods. Thus, during the colonial era and following Nietzsche, Hobbes and Darwin, the binary between good and evil was rejected at the same time the binary between African human beings and animals was rejected by colonialists. The rejection of binaries between God and the Devil was done at the same time the binary between African human beings and animals was rejected. The rejection of God was made at the same time Africans and their goodness were rejected by colonialists. Paradoxically, after having rejected Godly morality and distinction between good and evil, colonialists proceeded to generate moral panics about Africans whom they described as barbaric, savages, atavistic, backward, pre-logical, beastly and dangerous animals, and so on. The moral panics were deployed to the convenience of the colonialists who, while rejecting the existence and omnipresence of God and Godly morals, ironically sought to launch moral crusades against Africans – whatever the source of colonial "morals" was.

It is for the above reason that we argue, contemporary climate change and related natural disasters are also being used to create moral panics around African states that would refuse to sign climate change protocols – such that those that refuse to sign are described as dangerous folk devils (Rohloff, 2012; 2011; 2013). While Africans and their states are forced to become subjects to the international criminal courts and to climate change protocols, some Euro-

American states and institutions are exempt from such international protocols and courts yet they are the major polluters of the atmosphere. Thus, in the same way, colonialists who were the major robbers, looters, plunderers and murderers were exempt from accountability for the crimes they committed, and indeed continue to commit in Africa, contemporary climate change discourses replicate the Nietzschean logics of beyond good and evil – that is neoimperialists are beyond the distinction between good and evil; they are beyond accountability in so far as crimes perpetrated on Africans are concerned. It is only Africans and other colonised peoples that supposedly constitute folk devils to be bonded using neoimperial global moral crusades and moral panics which paradoxically depose and discount the transcendental Godly morals, ethics, laws and justice.

When the global media, scholars and institutions are looking for the Devil, they always come to Africa where they always find supposed folk devils for human rights abuses, for breaches of democracy, for lack of accountability, for breaches of the rule of law, for backwardness, for refusal to sign climate change protocols, for impunity, for refusal to become subjects of the international criminal court and for lack of subjection to the Earth Tribunal or Earth court. Even as the west is busy dumping its toxic e-waste in Africa (Anyinam, 1991; UN Environment, 30 January 2018; Sirleaf, 2018; Kanamugire, 2017), the western convention has been to look for folk devils in Africa (Cunneen, 2008) – empire is beyond the binaries between good and evil so it is assumed that it cannot be blamed and African humanity should not look for folk devils in the west even when the west dumps its waste on the African continent.

Even as the west has disrupted African indigenous knowledge systems and practices that helped redress climate change including droughts, famines and floods, the west with its compatriot, America, has condemned African epistemologies and practices as ineffective and unscientific. While defiling African sacred places, vilifying African ancestors and describing them as demons; mocking African spirit mediums as backward and irrational, Euro-America has blamed African systems as ineffective in countering droughts and redressing famines. In other words, those that disrupted and destroyed African systems are also the ones that blame African systems for supposed failures. Those that have colonised, dispossessed, robbed and exploited Africans are the same ones that accuse Africans of failing and incapability. Those that have destroyed African granaries are the very same people that are blaming Africans for failure and mocking Africans as prone to hunger, starvation and famine. In the light of colonial disruptions and destructions of African epistemologies and practices, it is not surprising that the colonial era was marked by massive droughts, famine and epidemics across the continent (Weiss, 2003; Chigodora, 1997). If in the cosmos there are connections, as some scholars are arguing, it must be evident that there are connections between institutions such as marriage and family, religion, politics, spirituality, culture and economy with the phenomena including droughts, famines and floods. Bearing in mind the connections, we argue that colonial disruptions of African marriages, families, cultures, spirituality, religions, polities and economies caused the droughts, famines, floods and epidemics during the neo-colonial era. Apart from displacing Africans from the well-watered and fertile soiled Highveld areas (Chigodora, 1997), colonialists disrupted and destroyed African cosmologies because cosmic harmony was based on harmony within African institutions including families, marriages, cultures, religions, polities and economies. In this sense, we argue that colonialists did not only depose and displace Africans from the physical Highveld areas but they also displaced them from the fertile and well-watered Highveld areas in moral, social, political, spiritual, religious, legal, epistemological, political, social, and economic senses. In a colonial context where colonialists protected and promoted witchcraft, homosexuality, adultery, incest, prostitution, theft, robbery, murder and friction among Africans who were divided into "tribes" and "ethnic" groups, it is not surprising that God and the *mhondoro* guardians visited massive droughts, famines, floods and epidemics on colonial Africa. Crimes and practices like witchcraft, incest, murder, theft, prostitution, suicide, adultery, infanticide and abortion (Nhlapo, 2017; Gelfand, 1959; Bourdillon, 1979; Schofeleer, 1979; van der Broght, 2009; Humbe, 2018) are known to bring down the vengeance of God and *mhondoro* that withdraw rain, and bring famine and floods as well as epidemics across the continent.

Whereas Africans and their states and governments protest against Euro-America's promotion and encouragement of homosexuality, incest, prostitution, adultery and witchcraft on the continent of Africa (Chicago Tribune, 9 June 2004; Humbe, 2018; Nhemachena & Warikandwa, 2019), Euro-Americans who seek to profit from the disorder and adversities on the continent do not heed African calls for morality and etiquette. African explanations of droughts, famine and floods in terms of prevalence of immorality including homosexuality, prostitution, incest, murder, infanticide, abortion and witchcraft are not necessarily irrational or mystical or mythological or fictions as alleged by biased westerners (Chicago Tribune, 9 June 2004; Humbe, 2018) and Americans who perceive themselves as scientific. Biased Euro-Americans dismiss African explanations because they profit from African problems, including from famines, floods, droughts and disorder on the African continent. The presence of disorder and problems, whether real or imagined, creates opportunities for Euro-American interventionisms including the ongoing recolonisation of Africa. Slave drivers and colonialists had to invent problems on the African continent so as to legitimise their projects of enslaving and colonising Africans – slave drivers and neocolonisers gain foothold by pretending to be helping to solve problems, which may be real or imagined, natural or neoimperially created. In this regard, if African families, marriages, religions, polities, cultures, economies and legal systems were to continue to work efficiently and harmoniously, colonialists would have no chances of intervening and recolonising Africa. African problems including about famines, droughts and floods create opportunities for neocolonisers hence, African preventive mechanisms are often summarily dismissed as irrational, spiritist, mythological and mystical even as neoimperialists work irrationally and mystically to recolonise Africa. Neocolonisation and neoimperialism are themselves not rational and so it is irrational for them to dismiss African epistemologies and preventive measures as irrational. Thus, when Africans connect homosexuality, incest, prostitution, adultery, defilement, wanton defloration and witchcraft and sorcery to droughts, famine and floods, the explanations must not be dismissed by those that have irrationally enslaved and colonised Africa in the first place. Those that have acted as

12

irrationally as to enslave and colonise other people cannot automatically become the gatekeepers and referees of rationality in the world – they cannot be allowed to eat their cakes and have them.

Further to the foregoing, even in western science, it is known that there can be hidden or latent variables which can explain things. The issue here is that God and *mhondoro* guardians are also hidden variables that explain famine, droughts and floods in the world. The world has got implicate order and explicate order metaphysics both of which explain reality or events. The implicate order metaphysics include the real but hidden order which is invisible to mundane human perception – it comprises the hidden variables (Geis, 2010; Bohn, 1985; Adams, 1991). It is the implicate order that makes possible human beings' structured explicate order including the visible and manifest order that is amenable to ordinary human perception.

This is to say that, even when Pope Benedict and other people including in Africa and U.S.A suggested that LGBTQ are to blame for hurricanes and for climate change (Independent 6, September 2017; The Times, 23 December 2008; Newsweek, 3 September 2017; Dynes, 2016; Agane, 2013), they should be understood as having been speaking about implicate order metaphysics that scientists, who privilege explicate order or ocular senses, would not be eager to understand. Denial of the implicate order metaphysics including the invisible is part of the tradition of imperialism which denied the existence of an invisible transcendental God of morality, justice, law and ethics in precolonial Africa. However, we argue that neoimperialists themselves were and are also an invisible variable or force even in contemporary Africa where they invisibly and spectrally meddle and cause conflicts, manipulate African political, legal, cultural, social, religious and economic systems. The era of independence in Africa does not mean that empire vanished from the continent – empire simply assumed invisibility and it became an invisible variable operating on the logics of implicate order metaphysics. Neoempire is well aware that once invisible forces or variables become accepted as part of the explananda of what is happening in Africa, Africans will begin to explain their suffering more in terms of invisible neoimperial forces than in terms of the visible, local, personal and micro-level variables. Put in other words, neoempire has increasingly assumed the role of the invisible unmoved mover on Africa and, for this, it does not want Africans to explain their travails in terms of invisible forces because this would expose neoempire as an invisible force that explains droughts, floods, and famines on the continent of Africa. If invisible forces become conventionally and formally accepted as explananda of droughts, floods, and famine, the risk is that it becomes clear to the populace that climate change is something other than climate change – it is a tool used by neoempire to destroy African order and to model Africa towards the neoimperial New World Order or a Euro-American ruled One World Government.

Haunting postindependence Africa invisibly and from a distance, neoempire has assumed the figure of a spectre and a sorcerer hurling deconstructive curses on the African suitors that rejected it by demanding independence. Because of the prevalence of spectrality, sorcery and witchcraft wherein neoempire assumed the figure of the spectre to haunt and deconstruct the excolonies, there is a growing body of literature on spectrality, hauntology, sorcery, becomings, vitality, agency, action, performativity and witchcraft (de Pilar Blanco *et al*, 2013; Deleuze and Guattari, 1987; Zukauskaite, 2013; 2015; Moro, 2018; Weber, 2006; Giroux, 2010; Braidotti, 2012; Cameron, 2015; Krawczak, 2018; Fu, 2018). Spectral hauntings confound the linearity of time such that postindependence Africa is haunted by the figures of the past in ways that negate distinctions between the colonial past and the postcolonial present; by using its media, education systems, "international" policies, religions and laws to haunt postindependence Africa, neoempire has lingering absence presence in Africa; neoempire reincarnates and becomes, in postindependence Africa, by ideologically and spiritually taking possession of the mental faculties of Africans who it wittingly and unwittingly mobilises and enrols into the spectral game of deconstructing their own African states, cultures, societies and religions. Neoempire is also increasingly scientifically and technologically mobilising and enrolling nature/nonhumans whose agency/vitality/performativity/propensity/action/animacy Eurocentric scholars are increasingly celebrating (Zukauskaite, 2013; 2015; Kurzweil, 2005; Wolfe, 17 January 2005). By mobilising and enrolling both human beings and nature that are infused and suffused

14

with neoimperial ideologies, spirituality, intelligence, vitality, essence, agency and propensities, neoempire is not only human in the sense of using human agency but it is also becoming animal or nonhuman in the sense of mobilising, enrolling, assuming and shapeshifting into nonhuman figures in order to play the game of spectrality or hauntology. In other words, by mobilising and using both human and nonhuman agency, vitality, actions and propensities, neoempire is increasingly becoming an imperceptible/indiscernible/ambiguous absence presence; a sorcerous shapeshifter; or a living dead in its game of spectrally deconstructing excolonies. Thus, underscoring the borderline positions of deconstructive neoimperial spectrality, Deleuze and Guattari (1987:246) argue:

> Sorcerers have always held anomalous positions, at the edge of the fields or woods. They haunt the fringes. They are at the borderline of the village, or between villages…The sorcerer has a relation of alliance with the demon as power of the anomalous.

Resonating with Deleuze and Guattari, Douglas (1966: 5-8) observes that:

> Witchcraft, then, is found in the non-structure. Witches are social equivalents of beetles and spiders who live in the cracks of the walls and wainscoting. They attract the fears and dislikes which other ambiguities and contradictions attract in other thought structures, and the kind of powers attributed to them symbolise their ambiguous inarticulate status…Sorcery is another matter. As a form of harmful power which makes use of spells, words, actions and physical materials, it can only be used consciously and deliberately…Sorcery is found in the structural interstices where we have located witchcraft, as well as the seats of authority.

Much as colonialists did not want Africans to blame the invisible imperial system for their suffering, the contemporary New World Order will be increasingly reliant on ideologies of animism and posthumanism which serve to conceal the invisible neoimperial transcendental systems that explain suffering in Africa. Neoempire would prefer to see Africans only blaming themselves and their states for the suffering they have experienced or are experiencing. When Africans begin to blame the spectral invisible neoimperial system, including the One World Government, empire is quick to allege that there is scapegoating, irrationality, mythologisation and absence of science on the part of Africans that will be pointing out the invisible machinations of neoempire. Thus, empire does not want Africans to see the evil that invisible forces conjure up; they would not want Africans to blame magical conjurations, including sorcery and witchcraft perpetrated by invisible evil persons and institutions (Van Wyk 2004) – this is because neoempire is itself part of the invisible beings that conjure magical and sorcerous practices on Africans. The idea for neoempire is to protect evil invisible transcendental persons and beings because it is part of such beings. This is one reason why African convictions in sorcery and witchcraft were vilified by empire. Vilifying African convictions that evil invisible beings conjure trouble on the continent, Eurocentric scholars and thinkers argue that Africans believe in scapegoating; that they always want to identify evil individuals ultimately responsible for catastrophes in life; that whenever there is evil, Africans would want to identify witches who would be removed from society (Van Wyk, 2004). The point here is that since neoimperial conjurations are essentially similar to sorcery and witchcraft, empire is prone to legitimising, protecting and promoting sorcery and witchcraft that include creating natural hazards such as privations, droughts, famine and floods.

Witchcraft and sorcery are about forms of individualism and even collectivism that deconstruct and subvert the moral and normal rules as decreed by God and *mhondoro* guardians. In this sense, homosexuality and the queer are promoted and encouraged by neoimperial forces that are keen to subvert the normal moral order in Africa so as to cause anarchy. Thus, during the colonial era, colonialists also protected and promoted witchcraft and sorcery that were relied upon to subvert the normal and moral precolonial order in Africa. Witchcraft and sorcery were handy to colonialists and neoimperialists because they were relied upon to subvert precolonial order, structures and hierarchy. Colonialists and imperialists have always wanted to monopolise order and this is why they have sponsored disorder and subversive activities against precolonial African order. Sponsoring and creating [cosmic] disorder and anarchy among Africans would weaken African resistance to (re)colonisation. Those that oppose empire would die in the disorder and anarchy created by (neo)colonialists.

Much as colonial era droughts, famines, floods and epidemics predominantly affected Africans and their livestock, contemporary climate change or global warming is noted as affecting mainly Africans and other colonised, dispossessed and exploited peoples. Earmarked for extinction via climate change; targeted in contemporary resurgence of scientific eugenics and scientific racism; affected negatively by contemporary genomics, postgenomics and biotechnology (Beaton, 2007; Evans, 2 March 2018; El-Haj, 2007), Africans are re-experiencing colonial comeback wherein they are targeted in eugenic science that earmarks them for extinction. As part of eugenics and exposing Africans to extinction, the west dumps toxic waste in Africa and then it also profits from the medicalisation of those Africans that become ill (Schmidt, 2006; Endfield, 2018) – dumping waste in Africa presupposes racial superiority and the assumption that Africans are fit to live on the basis of consuming western waste or detritus.

Already, in the context of discourses about reducing world population from about 7 billion to about 1 billion (Lovelock, 2007), there are also discourses that argue that colonialists managed to reduce world temperatures in 1600 by killing over 55 million indigenous people through spreading diseases, via murder and genocide in the so-called Great Dying (The Guardian, 31 January 2019; Koch *et al.*, 2019). It is argued that the Great Dying resulted in an anomalous decrease in atmospheric carbon dioxide at that time and this is noted to have caused a decrease in global surface air temperatures (Koch *et al.*, 2019). Thus, while Lovelock (1988; 2007) argues for feeding the world's poor with toxic genetically modified food even as the global elites feed on safe organic real food, other scholars argue that it is indigenous people, in poor, remote, fragile locations, who will be disproportionately affected by climate change (Nursey-Bay *et al.,* 2018; Belfer *et al,* 2017). The problem in the argument that the indigenous people are in remote and fragile locations is that it does not historicise the locations of indigenous people who were in fact colonially displaced to marginal, remote and fragile environments. If indigenous people die because they were

17

displaced to fragile and remote locations, we contend that it is the resilient colonial structures of land ownership and control that have exposed and killed off indigenous people. In essence, what is catastrophised as climate change should be catastrophised as colonial dispossession and robbery which rendered indigenous people vulnerable in the first place. Instead of merely catastrophising climate change and global warming, it is necessary to also catastrophise colonial land ownership patterns that have seen indigenous people being dispossessed and pushed to fragile, dry and remote locations. Neocolonisation is meant to fast track Africans to extinction via the facades of climate change that is supposed to engender the Great Dying of indigenous people in 21st century and thereafter.

While empire is so keen on developing and popularising tracking devices for human beings, cars, livestock and so on, we notice absence of keenness to track the real sources or origins of what is called climate change which is simplistically attributed to "anthropogenic" causes as if all human beings are equally responsible for the problem. We argue that it is not economic growth, productivity, economic size or consumerism that are causing climate change. In fact, while American and other western scientists and scholars would want the world to believe that their economies have seen phenomenal growth, productivity and massive consumerism, we argue following Nhemachena & Warikandwa (2019) that if Euro-American economies really grew and operated productively, then Euro-America should have been able to compensate African victims of enslavement and colonisation. As Nhemachena & Warikandwa (2019) argue, if Euro-American economies really grew productively then they should have been able to compensate African victims of their enslavement and colonisation – Euro-American economies are based more on plunder, looting, robbery and exploitation than on growth and productivity and this explains why they cannot let go of Africans that are being sucked since the enslavement and colonial eras. Climate change can be argued to be a result of neoimperial theft, robbery, dispossession and exploitation. Instead of attributing it to economic growth, overproductivity, overconsumption and African population growth, climate change and global warming must be correctly seen as resulting from plunder, looting, theft, robbery and dispossession of resources belonging to indigenous people. In this

18

sense, what needs to be abated is not growth, productivity or consumption, but what needs cessation is planetary plunder, robbery, looting, dispossession and exploitation of resources belonging to indigenous peoples.

The question is why the Euro-American world is quick to catastrophise climate change and global warming while on the other hand they do not want to admit the hotness of global apartheid that explains the travails of dispossessed, robbed and exploited indigenous people across the world? In other words, the hotness of global apartheid has been present for centuries, and even before the scientists discovered climate change or global warming, yet such global apartheid is not catastrophised even though it has reached unbearable temperatures and heat waves for indigenous peoples. Why does Euro-America including the United Nations worry more about global warming and not at all about the hotness of global apartheid which is killing indigenous peoples in the world? Preoccupation with physical environmental pollution and greenhouse effect neglects the broader version of the pollution and greenhousing of indigenous cultures, societies, polities, moral sensibilities, sexualities and spiritualities which pollution partly results from illegitimate [neocolonial/neoimperial] contacts/combinations/conflation/mixing between things – there are entities that must be kept separate to avoid pollution and greenhousing indigenous people's institutions (Forth, 2018; Nagle, 2009).

Our neologisms "necroclimatism" is used herein to refer to the killing or the death of indigenous people and other colonised, deemed "disposable" and "dispensable surplus" people, due to "climate change" and global warming. Like necropolitics, necroeconomies and necrocapitalism (Nhemachena & Warikandwa, 2019), necroclimatism primarily targets indigenous people that are deemed to be disposable, dispensable and surplus people in a world marked by global apartheid and the criminality associated with global theft, plunder, robbery, dispossession and exploitation of the indigenous people. Those that are vulnerable to necroclimates are precisely those that are also vulnerable to necropolitics, necrocapitalism and necroeconomies – the intersection is that all these necros thrive on the death of indigenous people. Like necrocapitalism, necroeconomies and necropolitics, "necroclimatism" profits from the death of other people particularly the death of those that are made vulnerable by the "necroimperialist" corporations, states and institutions that are generating global warming and climate change. Like sorcery, witchcraft and sacrifice, necroclimatism is about the conjurations or geoengineering of weather and climate in ways that render the indigenous and other colonised peoples vulnerable not only to existential threats and ontological insecurity but to death itself. Because necroclimatism is depicted as a modality to reconfigure the economies, politics and societies, we note here that such necroclimatism is also a way of performing necropolitics and necroeconomies. Since direct or overt genocide is no longer tolerable in international law, neoempire has designed necroclimatism so that the genocide of indigenous and other colonised peoples would be performed less by direct murder, poisoning, assassinations or massacres than by covert means including deploying nature as an agent or actor. For this reason, necroclimatism encompasses the attribution of agency/action, vitality, performativity and propensities to nature. Just as empire used human proxies or agents to perpetrate assassinations, genocide and massacres on indigenous people, in the contemporary era, neoempire would engage the agency/action, propensities, performativity and vitality of nature to achieve the same end of genocide. The idea is to precipitate another Great Dying similar to but on a larger scale than the Great Dying that occurred in early colonial America, as explained above.

Like in necropolitics, necrocapitalism and necroeconomies, necroclimatism does not seek to attribute agency to climate itself but to human beings or conjurers who seek to [magically] mobilise the agency, vitality or performativity of nature to cause the death of others. In so far as it uses the agency or actions of nature to cause the Great Dying of neocolonised peoples, necroclimatism is a subset of what we call necroenvironmentalism - the subjection of human beings, who are deemed to be disposable, to death by manipulating the environment, including the food they eat. The issue here is that neoempire seeks to conceal the agency or actions of human beings desiring to profit from the death of others by animistically attributing supreme, autonomous agency/action to nature or machines. The

20

contemporary popularisations of deconstructions of binaries or dichotomies between nature and culture, humans and nonhumans, evil and good, reality and falsehood, truth and falsehood, objectivity and subjectivity, natural and unnatural should be understood in the context of neoimperial quests to "naturalise" the death of others who become victims of necroclimatism and associated conjurations. Thus, in necroclimatism, the victims of "climate" induced deaths are made to think that the problem is with the climate, which supposedly autonomously and agentially acts. The agency or actions of human beings is foreshadowed in attributions of agency or action to climate and nature more broadly. However, human beings conjure climate change in order to profit from the death of other human beings that are considered to be disposable surplus beings.

Necroclimatism is not about denialism of the changes associated with climate but it makes it possible to see ways in which human conjurers of climate are shielded in a zone beyond "good and evil", and more generally beyond binaries between nature and culture, human and nonhuman forces. Once shielded in the zone beyond good and evil, it becomes difficult, if not impossible, to prosecute human criminals who cause genocide through covertly conjuring changes to climate and weather. In other words, it becomes difficult if not impossible to tell whether deaths are occurring through natural or human causes. Similarly, it becomes difficult if not impossible to tell whether changes in climate are occurring because of Godly causes or covert human conjurations or through the Devil's interventions. Thus, after having rejected the existence of God, scientists believe that the universe, created through the Big Bang, would come to an end at about 100 trillion years (Ani, 2016). This is similar to the apocalyptic provisions in the Bible but what is not clear in secular science is whether it is God or the Devil that will cause the universe to come to an end at 100 trillion years. If God is dead, as Nietzsche postulated in the 1800s, the question is whether the Devil is still alive and whether it is the Devil that then causes the universe to come to an end via the envisaged climate apocalypse and the associated catastrophism.

As noted above, the era when Nietzsche wrote about the death of God and beyond good and evil, in the 1800s (Nietzsche, 1887), saw the colonisation of Africans, massive dispossession, genocide

21

against indigenous people and exploitation of Africans. It was an era when God was pronounced as dead and so the era saw the triumph of evil perpetrated against African colonial victims. Although Nietzsche is noted as having been against transcendental structures, the era when he wrote on the death of God saw the rise of transcendental colonial and imperial structures that supplanted African structures and Godly hierarchies, morality, ethics and justice. In other words, the era after God was pronounced dead saw the triumph of colonial evils, despite the Nietzschean efforts to move beyond the binaries between good and evil. In the same way, contemporary efforts are being made to supplant African states and governments and replace their sovereignty with the sovereignty of a One World Government, colonialists also supplanted and replaced African states, social and cultural structures and hierarchies – colonialists destroyed African sovereignties and replaced them with the sovereignty of colonial states. Put otherwise, colonisation was about the rejection of the transcendence of precolonial African states and of Godly morality, law, ethics and justice which were replaced with the transcendence of imperialism – in the contemporary era, there is again the rejection of the transcendence of African states and of God which are being replaced with the transcendence of the Euro-American ruled One World Government.

In the contemporary era, there are efforts to impose a "global" carbon tax in order to constitute a transcendental One World Government, in the same way colonialists imposed taxes on Africans in order to establish the transcendence of colonial states. The One World Government constituted and ruled by a global secret society (Dice, 2010) is characterised by eugenics wherein the "disposable" and "surplus" colonised and dispossessed people will be fed on unhealthy GMOs while the global elite will eat organic, real, healthy foods and home cooked meals prepared by chefs and dieticians (*Ibid*). Writing about Gaia that, he argues, has power to kill millions of humans who he accuses of abusing the Earth, James Lovelock's (2007) logics are similar to Dice (2010). Lovelock (2007) argues that the world population of about 7 billion, who are abusing the earth, is too big to feed and sustain. For this reason, Lovelock further argues that there is need to feed that population with food that is synthesised by the chemical and biochemical industries from carbon dioxide, water and nitrogen so that the earth can be saved. For Lovelock, human beings must stop worrying about cancer that arises from the chemicals because human beings will die of cancer anyway since the air we breathe is already laden with carcinogen. Lovelock (2007: 169 - 72) argues thus:

> …we could synthesize all the food needed by eight billion people, and thereby abandon agriculture…The chemicals for food synthesis would come directly from the air, or more conveniently from carbon compounds sequestered from power-station effluent…What would be synthesised would not be intricate, natural chemicals we now eat as broccoli, olives, apples, steaks or, more probably hamburgers and pizzas. Rather, the large new food factories would make simple sugars and amino acids. This would be the feed stock for tissue cultures of meat and vegetables and for junk food made from any convenient organism that could be… eaten…Whatever form the future society takes it will be tribal, and hence there will be the privileged and the poor. This being so, there would in our high-tech world surely be a fashion among the rich for eating real food: vegetables grown in soil and cooked with meat and fish. We are in our present mess because the luxuries of whole-house heating and private transport by car have become necessities and far beyond the Earth's capacity to provide.

Sharing the Nietzschean logics in the thesis on the death of God, Lovelock (2007) celebrates the vengeance of Gaia that he argues will be doing the human culling to eliminate the human beings that are breaking her rules. Thus, arguing that it is the poor in the world who must eat the synthetic, unreal, nonorganic food and die away, Lovelock proposes returning to colonial eugenics and scientific racism premised on global food apartheid between those that eat real, organic, healthy food and those that eat the unhealthy synthetic GMO food and risk cancer and other such abnormalities. Much as Africans have suffered and died at the hands of the invisible hand of the market, which is granted agency and vitality by Eurocentric scholars, Lovelock similarly grants autonomous agency and vitality to Gaia, his earth goddess, that he argues will do the human culling through climate change, weather changes, earthquakes and volcanic eruptions (Smith, 2006; Lovelock, 2007). Underscoring the evilness of Gaia, Lovelock argues that human beings, and this can be understood as referring to the impoverished and dispossessed and exploited people of the earth, should not seek to extend their lives; they should die early because Gaia no longer has the capacity to provide for the 7 billion world population.

The problem with Lovelock's (2007) argument is that he ironically assumes that Gaia has no capacity to provide for the 7 billion world population while on the other hand Euro-Americans assume that Africans have got unlimited capacity to yield land and other resources for the Euro-American citizens, including neoimperialists. He is worrying more about the incapacity of Gaia yet Eurocentric scholars and thinkers do not worry about the incapacity of Africans to yield land and other resources to neoimperial forces. In fact, Africans are being dispossessed of their land in the contemporary transnational land grabs wherein carbon offsetting is used to justify the robbing of Africans. Imperialism, that has always assumed that Africans have unlimited capacity to provide not only material resources but also to provide labour power for imperial industries, paradoxically worries about the incapacities of Gaia to provide for humanity. It is naive and ironic to assume that Africans have an unlimited capacity to provide for neo-colonial and neoimperial settlers while at the same time arguing that Gaia has limited capacity to provide for humanity. If incapacity to provide for humanity justifies Gaia's human culling, the question is, must Africans' incapacity to provide for neocolonialists and neoimperialists also justify Africans' assassinations of neo-colonialists and neoimperialists who continue to press on Africans for more and more land and other resources?

The point in the foregoing is that neo-colonial settlers and neoimperialists have not only grown their economies on Gaia as Lovelock would assume; neocolonial and neoimperial economies have been grown on the backs of Africans [not on the back of Gaia as such] and so if Gaia's vengeance is justified, then it logically follows that African vengefulness is also justified such that degrowth and postgrowth movements must necessarily transfigure into deimperialist and decolonial movements. The point here is that neoimperialists would want to hide behind Gaia to legitimise their own vengeance towards African liberation efforts. If Gaia, or Euro-

Americans' Mother goddess, is justified in vengefulness for western exploitation, then why must Africans not be vengeful for enslavement and neocolonisation by the same westerners who are now ironically more worried about the vengefulness of their own Mother goddess/Gaia than they are worried about the vengefulness of those that they enslaved and colonised? If Gaia will kill the dispossessed, exploited and impoverished as is presumed in Eurocentric climate change discourses, the question is whether such Gaia is a goddess of justice or injustice? Why would such a goddess called Gaia not pay attention to the injustices suffered by Africans and other peoples that were enslaved and colonised? What kind of a Mother goddess would not pay attention to the historicity of injustices for enslaved and colonised Africans? Would a mother, in the real sense, not ensure that crimes of robbery, dispossession, looting, plunder and exploitation are made good? Why should humanity follow the logics of a Gaia goddess that has no sensibilities for morals, ethics, justice and laws including the need for restitution, restoration and compensation to those that were enslaved and colonised? In this sense, if Gaia is a goddess that does not pay attention to morals, ethics and legality in favour of those that were enslaved and colonised, might Gaia not be the same goddess that legitimised the enslavement and colonisation, including dispossession, exploitation and genocide of Africans over the past centuries? Why does Gaia not get worried when Euro-Americans dispossess Africans and when they dump their waste on the African continent?

In light of the foregoing, we also ask why Gaia does not get worried when Euro-Americans use weather and climate as weapons wherein they produce fog, floods, droughts, cyclones and famines on their enemies, such as when America used weather warfare over Vietnam (Smith, 2006). The ineffectiveness of Gaia in preventing weather and climate warfare explains the humanistic 1978 Convention on the Prohibition of Military or Any Other Hostile Use of Environmental Modification Techniques (ENMod Convention) which prohibits the use of techniques that would have widespread, long-lasting or severe effects through deliberate manipulation of natural processes and causing such phenomena as earthquakes, tidal waves and changes in climate and in weather patterns (Smith, 2006).

25

The point here is that Gaia has not had the capacity to prevent wars, genocide, colonisation and enslavement of Africans and other peoples. In this regard, if Gaia has no capacity to prevent colonisation and enslavement, then is it a moral, ethical and legal goddess that victims of centuries-old injustices can bank on? Or is Gaia a goddess that is biased towards the global elites including neoimperialists and neo-colonialists who take pleasure in sacrificing the colonised, the dispossessed, the impoverished and the exploited peoples of the world to their selfish goddess, Gaia, which lacks capacity for legality, morality, justice and ethics? In the light of contemporary emphases on deconstruction of binaries, we argue that Gaia is a western goddess beyond good and evil it is a goddess that supplants God in the Nietzschean sense of the death of God.

Ignoring not only inequalities, domination and injustices in the world but also ignoring crimes of genocide, dispossession, robbery, plunder, looting and exploitation of colonised peoples by the global elite, Gaia appears to be a blind and deaf goddess of destruction and death eager to further sacrifice the colonised and impoverished. In fact, the bias of Gaia towards the global elites betrays the fact that it is the global elites that are conjurating the figure of Gaia to do their bidding in depopulating the world as a way to defuse indigenous people's rising claims to restoration, restitution and reparations for enslavement and colonisation.

To conjurate Gaia, the U.S.A is noted as engaging in the High-Frequency Active Aural Research Program (HAARP) to geoengineer the weather and climate which it uses to control all continents, thereby causing floods, tsunamis, earthquakes, storms, hurricanes, famines and droughts as desired (Smith, 2003; Burks, 14 October 2018; Olsen, 2013; Freeland, 2014). Officially described as pure science research station, HAARP is the prototype for "Star Wars" weapons system that is used to control the weather through the mechanism of an "ionospheric heater" (Smith, 2003). Designed in a context where Eurocentric scholars are pushing to end the sovereignty of colonised states, HAARP is argued to be a military project for U.S.A full spectrum dominance to end all other nations by creating a One World Government which de-sovereignises all other states. Disguised as a civilian project, HAARP has seen many universities and institutes participating (Smith, 2006) towards the fulfilment of its goals. Possessing technologies which can be covertly used for beaming microwave or extremely low frequency radio waves at targeted populations, HAARP can be used to effect disorientation, illness, moods shifts, to disrupt human mental processes, jam all global communication, cause wildlife to change migration and to put words into people's heads (Smith, 2003; Begich *et al*, 2002; Freeland, 2014). Olsen (2013: 132-133) writes thus:

> The most notorious program is HAARP, the High-Frequency Active Aural Research Program. This technology can potentially trigger floods, droughts, hurricanes and earthquakes. The scientific idea behind HAARP is to "excite" a specific area of the ionosphere and observe the physical processes in that excited area with the intention of modifying ecological conditions. HAARP can also be used as a weapon system, capable of selectively destabilizing agricultural and ecological systems of entire regions. At a recent international symposium, scientists asserted that manipulation of climate through modification of cirrus clouds is neither a hoax nor a conspiracy theory, but in fact is fully operational…It can cause missile or satellite destruction, or modify weather patterns around the globe. HAARP can also cause worldwide brainwave pattern changes in the population with the flick of a switch. It was also developed for new weapon types: geophysical, weather and psychotropic…Some scientists in their laboratories are trying to device certain types of pathogens that would be ethnic specific so that they could just eliminate certain ethnic groups and races; others are designing or engineering some sort of insect that can destroy specific crops. Others are engaging even in an eco-type terrorism whereby they can alter the climate and set off earthquakes and volcanoes remotely through the use of electromagnetic waves.

Although some nations deny weaponising the weather, The US Airforce reported weather as a force multiplier and it stated that it would want to own, exploit and manipulate the weather by 2025 (Crone, 2017). Crone (2017: 83) write thus:

> …the idea was by 2025 we would be able to manipulate virtually every aspect of weather. The rationale for this is really the ultimate war: if you never have to fire a round and nobody ever knew who launched

the fight; this is what weather warfare offers militaries around the world...Fifty years from now geophysical manipulation of the planet could be the weapon of war. Where it is not bombs and bullets; it is earthquakes, its tidal waves, manipulation of weather systems. Those become the future of warfare. When we talk about weather warfare, we are talking about death technology. This has nothing to do with enhancing life. The aim of weather warfare is catastrophic environmental destruction and horrific loss of life.

In a world wherein binaries between nature and culture, human and nonhuman, good and evil, truth and falsehood, natural and artificial, life and death are deconstructed, it becomes possible for the global elites to hide behind nature such that they perpetrate genocide while hiding behind weather and climate change or nature's vitality/agency/performativity/propensity, more broadly. They make it difficult to disentangle the agency/actions or vitality of nature and the agency or actions of human beings launching weather and climate warfare. For this reason there are popularisations of environmental humanities and digital humanities that emphasise the connections, relations/relational ontologies between humans and nature, humans and technology. The point here is that in the post-truth societies that are being constituted, global elites would seek to produce as much ignorance as possible so that those targeted for genocide using weather and climate warfare would think they are dying of natural causes when in fact they are victims of covert weather and climate manipulation. Mainstream media silences voices attempting to expose secret weather and climate modification programmes (Freeland, 2014). Critical voices that try to expose secret and dangerous programmes like weather and climate modification, GMO foods, HAARP, chemtrails, and metallic pathogens (Freeland, 2014) are silenced. Members of the public that exposed dangerous electromagnetic radiation, who have exposed and opposed GMOs and glyphosate in Monsanto's Roundup have either died mysteriously or they have been threatened, hacked, slandered and terrorised by corporations, some of which have ties to intelligence, military and private security companies. The same fate has been suffered by the so-called developing countries of the world. If a developing country refuses to comply with the World Bank or International Monetary

Fund guidelines, they would use technology to send a flood or drought that would convince the leaders to reconsider their positions – the climate change projects which are in essence military projects are "outsourced" or privatised to universities and defence contractors (Freeland, 2014).

The challenge arising from the foregoing is that humanity is told that it's getting into the age of extinction or an apocalypse but then those that announce the arrival of such an age of extinction are quick to profess absence of binaries between truth and falsehood, between nature and culture, between human and nonhuman, between knowledge and ignorance, between science and fiction. Whether in the sciences or humanities, there are arguments about fuzziness and absence of binaries – there are inclinations toward complexity and quantum theories such that humanity is informed about impending extinction but the causes are supposedly neither natural nor cultural, but complex.

What is clear however, is that the extinction and death of humanity begins with the death of God projects such as those masterminded by Nietzsche, Hobbes and Darwin wherein the transcendence of God, truth, morality and ethics has been rejected at a time when the transcendence of Gaia is being celebrated. The rejection of the transcendence of God has been followed up with the rejection of the transcendence of African nation states which are currently under siege – thus, the age of extinction is also the age of the death of the sovereignty of African nation states. The age of extinction is also an age wherein God is dismissed as too distant to rule the world (Lovelock, 1988) even as the global elites are creating the One World Government which they use to rule distant colonised territories. Thus, the age of extinction is an era when the theological apocalypse of the New Testament is replaced with the apocalypse of climate change (Northcott, 2014; Fagan, 2017). The point we are making here is that there is no way God can be pronounced dead and human beings continue to live. Also, the problem, as far as the colonised peoples are concerned, is not the presence of Godly transcendence but the problem is with neoimperial theft, robbery, plunder, looting and dispossession sanctioned by absence of effective transcendental Godly morality, ethics and laws in a neo-colonial world. In fact, there is a paradox in that while Euro-Americans reject the transcendence of God, they are angling for a transcendental One World Government under their rule – this is enough evidence that resolving threats of extinction requires the transcendentalism of God, morality, ethics and natural laws and not merely the transcendence of Euro-Americans over the rest of the world.

Denial of Godly transcendence can be understood as evidence of a form of conspiracy to kill God. Similarly, the denial of sovereignty of African states is evidence of a form of conspiracy to kill or destroy African politics, freedom and independence. In fact, denial of sovereignty of African nation states constitutes evidence of conspiracy to recolonise Africans – colonisation also denies the sovereignty of the states of the precolonial victims. Denial of binaries between truth and falsehood, between knowledge and ignorance can be understood as conspiracy to generate not only ignorance but anarchy in the world. In a context where there are conspiracies to destroy African politics and the politics of other colonised peoples, there are already discourses about postpolitics and the disappearance/extinction of the political; there are discourses about the disappearance/extinction of dissensus, disappearance of divergent views, disappearance of divergent conflicting and alternative trajectories of the future (Swyngedouw, 2009; Asayama, 2015). In this sense, the postpolitical is also postdemocratic in the sense of the death or extinction of democracy. In such a postpolitical, postdemocratic and postGod world order marked by populism, there is invocation of a common condition or predicament, of the need for common human-wide action, of need for mutual collaboration and cooperation (Swyngedouw, 2009), and these invocations are meant to pull humanity towards the One World Government that Euro-America is envisaging and determined to control.

In the light of the foregoing, we argue that depictions of the contemporary world in terms of the risk society thesis by scholars like Ulrich Beck and Anthony Giddens (Beck, 2015; Nuth, 2007) are imprecise when looked at from the point of view of the colonised and enslaved peoples in the world. What Beck and Giddens call risk society is in fact a society in which other people – the neoenslaved and neocolonised – are sacrificed. In this sense, it would be more accurate to describe it in terms of sacrifice society. Modern society is in fact a sacrifice society that sacrifices the enslaved and colonised peoples – they are sacrificed in the interests of the market, capitalism, climate change, and in the interest of human organ extraction and trafficking, among other aspects. The first sacrifice was to reject the transcendence of God who is being replaced with Gaia; the second sacrifice has to do with neoenslavement and neocolonisation; third there has been sacrifice of African autonomy and sovereignty in an increasingly postpolitical world (dis)order. All these forms of sacrifice involved risks for the neoenslaved and neocolonised but not necessarily for the neocolonisers and neoslave drivers. There is more sacrifice, sacrifice of other people on a wider scale in the so-called global society where millions and billions of neoenslaved and neocolonised people are suffering due to exploitation, dispossession, robbery, plunder and looting on a planetary scale. The point is that the people are not just suffering risks but they are being subjected to sacrifice in the interest of global elites.

The logic of sacrifice in climate change discourses is clear in what is called emancipatory catastrophism and apocalyptic catastrophism. Emancipatory catastrophism naturally alludes to the fact that there are some people in the world who will benefit from the sacrifice of others in the age of climate change; apocalyptic catastrophism underscores the fact that there are some who will die or be sacrificed in the age of the climate change discourses. Thus, humanity faces the peril of mass extinction through species suicide, ecological devastation and planetary obligation and ecological disasters (Aravamudan, 2013). In this regard, there are some people who are now calling for human extinction; human beings are encouraged to commit suicide, to abandon humanism, to voluntarily practice human extinction [such as through human extinction movements], welcome the demise of human beings/species and to celebrate biocentrism, ecocentrism, earthcentrism, ecocriticism, ecosophy, ecophilosophy, ecopsychology (Aravamudan, 2013; Nhemachena & Warikandwa, 2019). In this sense, it is not only Gaia that is set to do human culling but there are already apocalyptic cults or para-religions which refuse order, tradition and normativity preferring nihilism and extinction of human beings – they represent the suspension of binaries between life and death, good and evil that underwrite the ultimate human extinction (Mukherjee, 2016). So, churches, such as the Church of Satan, Temple of Sets and Church of Euthanasia

31

(Moro, 2018; Mukherjee, 2016), have been established in America supposedly to establish ecological balance between humans and nonhumans partly by encouraging human beings to eat one another [and not eat animals]; the church encourages human beings to save the planet by killing themselves, to eat children and foetuses, to stop procreating, to engage in sodomy, to engage in bestiality and obscene sexual activity, abortion and cannibalism. The Church of Euthanasia works in the same line with the Gaia Liberation Front which also calls for extinction of humans (Mukherjee, 2016; Dery, 2015; Smith, 2019). The illogics of eating or cannibalising one another are being legitimised through discourses that collapse distinctions between human beings and animals – cannibalising other humans begins with simianisation, desocialisation, dehumanisation as is evident in tropes on animism, animalisation, animatism, posthumanism, transhumanism, postanthropocentrism and so on (Mail & Guardian, 26 February 2016; Hund *et al*, 2015; Mills, 2015; Namibian, 18 July 2005; News24, 25 March 2014; Nhemachena & Kaundjua, 2018).

At ideological, ontological and epistemic levels, calls for human beings to cannibalise one another are being legitimised through calls to suspend binaries between humans and animals, between humans and nonhumans, death and life. Increasingly, Africans and other colonised peoples are depicted as animists and hence as indistinct from animals. Thus, just like during the enslavement and colonial eras, colonised peoples that are targeted for cannibalisation and extinction are depicted as indiscernible from animals; they are depicted as indistinct from apes, monkeys, baboons, dogs and other beasts – they are denied distinctively human attributes, they are denied polities, sovereignty, autonomy, statehood and they are depoliticised and deemed to be in a postpolitical era (Smith *et al*, 2015; Berglex *et al*, 2014; Kenis, 2018; Anshelm *et al*, 2014). Writing about post-political scenario, Wengel (2015: 2 - 18) notes thus:

> Several political theorists and philosophers debate about the emergence of a post-political and post-democratic condition, implying a state of consensus on a global scale…The consensus debate surrounding environmental issues is assumed to imply a repression of radical political discourse. Even though citizens assumingly get engaged in counteracting climate change evermore, the engagement is done in a

rather non-political manner...Post-politics refers to a global depoliticisation, the emergence of a politics of consensus and the abolishment of disagreements in the public sphere based on the acknowledgement of the neoliberal market logic in the post-crisis era.

The emphasis on suspending binaries and dichotomies and on generating consensus is meant to legitimise the envisaged One World Government which will usurp sovereignty from African states as well as from the states of other colonised peoples. The idea of a postbinary world order is to paralyse African politics and nation states that are demanding restitution, reparations and compensation for enslavement and colonisation. Thus, African states and leaders and academics that continue demanding restitution, restorations and compensation will more easily be accused of relying on binaries or dichotomies – they will be defused and depoliticised thereby. Africans that continue to seek justice from enslavers and colonisers will be accused of relying on binaries. The suspension of binaries or dichotomies include the binaries between slave and slave driver, between colonised and coloniser, between victim and offender – the effect of suspending such binaries would be to make the politics of restitution, restoration and compensation impossible – it would be to depoliticise politics of restitution, restoration and compensation. In this sense, a postbinary or postdichotomous world (dis)order is not necessarily a just world but it is a continuation of the Nietzschean society beyond good and evil; it catapults neoempire beyond justice and beyond law, morality and ethics of restitution and compensation.

In a world order wherein African states are terrorised by Euro-America through some NGOs and civil society organisations that bully African states using various pretexts; and in a world wherein the International Criminal Court focuses on prosecuting African leaders and in a world (dis)order wherein Euro-America securitises climate change even as it dumps toxic waste on Africa, the One World Government is being established on the basis of logics of sacrifice. Depicted as a grave threat causing conflicts, chaos, and destabilising countries, climate change is securitised such that extraordinary measures are legitimised; speakers on climate change calculate what metaphors and arguments are most likely to persuade the public to see climate change as a security issue (Warner et al, 2019). The problem in securitising climate change in the United Nations Security Council raises questions about why other issues that affect the colonised, dispossessed and exploited people are not securitised as well. It is cause for wonder why the ongoing transnational land grabs which are dispossessing African peasants are not also securitised. Africans are being subjected to a new scramble for Africa wherein African resources, including land, are being looted and plundered yet the United Nations Security Council decides to securitise climate change only. Similarly, Africans and other dispossessed and neocolonised people are losing jobs due to the development of industrial and humanoid robots (Harari, 2018; Nhemachean & Warikandwa, 2019), yet the United Nations chooses to securitise climate change only and ignore these other sources of insecurity that are affecting the neocolonised, dispossessed and exploited peoples in the world. Securitisation of climate change wrongly assumes that climate change or global warming is the only existential threat or ontological insecurity issue (Myers, 2014; Forest, n.d) yet there are many other issues that are not just warm, as global warming is, but there are global hot issues affecting indigenous peoples who have suffered centuries old enslavement and colonisation.

Much as thinkers and scholars are writing about climate catastrophism, from an indigenous people's perspective it is possible to talk about **dispossession catastrophism**; much as there is talk about climate apocalyptism, and it is possible to talk about **enslavement and neo-colonial apocalyptism**. Much as there is talk about climate catastrophism, it is also possible to talk about **unemployment catastrophism.** Also, while there is catastrophic terrorism, we note that African states are also being terrorised through the United Nations, to cede or hand over their sovereignty to a world body that is actually a Euro-American body seeking to establish a One World Government in the name of governing security threats in the world. The problem here is that foregrounding climate change is itself a form of denialism in the sense that it denies the equal importance of other security threats for instance arising from enslavement, colonisation, and contemporary new scramble for Africa and so on. Denialism is not only found among those that deny the existence of climate change, but denialism is also found among those that accept the existence of climate change in ways that signal denial of other security threats. Indigenous peoples have had their claims for restitution, restoration and compensation for enslavement and colonisation denied but the United Nations has not brought the deniers to book. There are also many among the Westerners who deny the severity of effects of enslavement and colonisation which they perpetrated against the indigenous people such as those of Africa.

The upshot of the above is that existential threats and ontological insecurity of Africans arise as much from resilient logics of enslavement and colonisation as from climate change. The point here is that it is not enough to worry solely about the need to normalise climate and weather issues in a world wherein indigenous people are encouraged to revolt against the normal structures within their cultural, moral, political and social fabrics. In this regard, the Euro-American world ironically promotes queers who are supposed to disrupt normativity, including heteronormativity in Africa, yet the same Euro-America would raise alarm when climate and weather become abnormal. The point is that Euro-American world promotes rebels against African cultures, societies, religions and states yet the same Euro-America would raise alarm when climate and weather become abnormal as well. In fact, the irony is that while Euro-America raises alarm about the diversion from normal climate and weather patterns, the same Euro-America encourages indigenous people to rebel in their personal lives, indigenous people are encouraged to rebel against their genes and elect to be childless; and they are encouraged to rebel against their political and social authorities even if the rebellions would cause extinction at social, political, cultural, religious, physical and epistemic levels (Barash, 2000; Bristow *et al*, 2016; Anshelm *et al*, 2014; Jamieson, 1996).

The Biases and Tyranny of Imperialism in Climate Discourses

The problem with colonialism/imperialism is that it asks indigenous people to adopt attitudes of self-denial even as it expects them not to deny or resist colonisation. Indigenous people are expected to adopt a form of self-denialism that engenders their extinction in the face of climate change but they are not expected to deny neoimperialism/neocolonialism. Already, human genetic material including DNA of supposedly disposable and dispensable indigenous people are being collected supposedly before they become extinct (Harry, 2000; Hamilton, 2000). Through biocolonialism, Euro-American corporations are not only collecting stories but also blood and genes from indigenous people who are set to become extinct, to vanish and disappear (Harry, 2000; Harry *et al*, 2005; Reardon, 2008; Lone, 1999). Instead of protecting indigenous people from the ongoing new scramble for Africa, the ongoing transnational land grabs, from the geoengineering that is creating weather and climate changes, Euro-America chooses to protect the genes, blood and biomes of the indigenous people; their idea is arguably to patent indigenous life and to produce clones, in the future, that would not remember the original imperial sin of enslavement, subjugation and colonisation. In this sense, when postmodernists argue that there is nothing original anymore, that all we have are copies of originals, that there is no distinction between nature and culture, the natural and the artificial, they must be understood to be referring to the patenting of indigenous life through genomics and cloning, frivolous science, which entail the production of patented copies of original human beings. Contemporary discourses about extinction through global warming and climate change would assist the corporate projects to patent indigenous people's lives in ways that would underwrite Euro-American owners of patents as supermen in the Nietzschean sense.

While indigenous people have rejected Euro-American depictions that they are becoming extinct, contemporary discourses on climate change are hideously repeating the assertions that indigenous people will become extinct. Much as colonialists justified looting of indigenous people's artefacts and possessions, by claiming that they were becoming extinct, contemporary climate change discourses are used to cause panic (Pottage, 1998; Lone, 1999) among the human race so that they agree to the nefarious science of GMOs, genomics and cloning. Instead of resolving the problem of dispossession and exploitation, of indigenous people, by transnational institutions and corporations, the human genome diversity projects simply collect the genes and blood of the indigenous people on the pretext that they are becoming extinct (Cann, 1998; Amani *et al*, 2005; Doson *et al*, 1999; Hamilton, 2000).

Indigenous human inhabitants are bioprospected in ways that generate profits for the transnational corporations engaged in Western bioimperialism wherein scientists promise to immortalise samples by the Human Genome Diversity Project.

Underlying the Human Genome Diversity Projects and the discourses on the extinction of indigenous people is the presupposition that indigenous people are disposable, valueless and dispensable such as was the case during enslavement and colonisation (Mignolo, 2009). Furthermore, if to be disposable or dispensable is a function of statelessness and lack of citizenship (Mignolo, 2009), we would argue that the One World Government which destroys African states' sovereignty would worsen the disposability and dispensability of Africans and other indigenous people who thereby become stateless. Loss of state sovereignty results in more vulnerability to the depredations and lootings of the global elite. Africans who have been constituted as disposable and dispensable through enslavement and through dispossession, robbery, theft, looting, plunder and exploitation, will be more vulnerable to dispossession and the looting of transnational corporations if the One World Government is constituted, as is evident in the discourses of climate catastrophism. Indigenous people who have been considered disposable, dispensable and surplus people for centuries are still considered to be human waste, surplus population and destined for extinction with climate change and global warming (Mignolo, 2009; De Gregori *et al*, 1987; Wenzel, 2018; Yee, 2000; Calina, 2015).

Having been dispossessed of their land located in well-watered and fertile soils, it is indigenous people who are suffering climate change and global warming more than other people; displaced to hot low-lying areas, it is indigenous people who are suffering the heat waves more; displaced to overcrowded reserves or communal lands, it is indigenous people who are suffering pollution and infectious disease more; displaced to drier areas, it is indigenous people who are suffering waterborne diseases more; displaced to dry areas, it is indigenous people who are suffering food insecurity more (Pitz *et al*, 2014; Serdeczny *et al*, 2015). What is more worrisome is the fact that after having dispossessed and exploited indigenous people, Euro-America is now condemning the indigenous people as unsustainable

37

and due for extinction. For this reason, there is proliferation of discourses on disposability and dispensability of surplus humans or human waste as they are called; there are discourses about the necessity of moving away from preoccupation with sustainability including from sustainable development, from sustainable natural resources use, from sustainable growth and human security (Gabel, 2015; Khan, 2002; Bluhdon, 2017; Bluhdon, 2011; Alfredsson *et al*, 2018; Bluhdon, 2013; Bostrom *et al*, 2018).

In the age of politics of unsustainability, disposability, dispensability and human waste, Africans face the real threat of being disconnected from the so-called humanitarian aid/assistance which have come to constitute their major basis of livelihood since the era when they were colonially dispossessed and robbed. Disconnecting indigenous people from humanitarian aid while at the same time covertly geoengineering and doctoring climate and weather patterns would be a sure way of ensuring the extinction, disposability and dispensability of the indigenous people. Disconnecting indigenous people from such humanitarian aid while at the same time manipulating weather and climate patterns would be a definite sign of the advent of the politics of unsustainability as instigated by Euro-America. The idea in the oncoming politics of unsustainability is to disconnect indigenous people from their roots and livelihoods and let them die (Cartwright, 1996; McLachlan, 2008; Rachels, 2001; McGee *et al*, 2019) in disarray. In this regard, it is contended that there is a difference between killing and preventing everyone from dying (McLachlan, 2008). Thus, Rachels (2001) argues:

> We allow people to die, for example, when we fail to contribute money to famine relief; but even if we feel somewhat guilty we do not consider ourselves murderers. Nor do we feel like accessories to murder when we fail to give blood, sign an organ donor card, or do any of the other things that could save lives. Common sense tells us that, while we may not kill people, our duty to give them aid is much more limited.

Letting indigenous people die makes no difference with mass killings of the indigenous people. It would allow for the establishment of full-spectrum dominance by Euro-America more

38

than was in the case of colonialism; via manipulation of weather and climate, Euro-America would destabilise, destroy enemy states' ecosystems, destroy agriculture of enemy states, disable communication systems of enemy states, to impoverish citizens of enemy states; the sad thing is that all these manipulations of weather and climate are not discussed in academies as well as in the United Nations (Global Research, 5 July 2018; House *et al*, 1996; Coles, n.d; Quayle, 2007; Daily Star, 7 January 2017).

Used in the Vietnam War during the 1960s, environmental warfare, weather warfare or geophysical warfare (Ananda, 19 October 2017; Von Werlhof, 28 November 2017; Ross, 1992; Goldblat, 1975; Coles, n.d), has been noted as a potent electromagnetic weaponry of mass destruction on a global scale that allows for hiding behind the cover of anthropogenic global warming. Ross (1992: 516- 520) writes thus:

> Environmental warfare refers to the manipulation of the environment for hostile military purposes. Throughout history, the environment has been a repeated victim of military strategy, often to frustrate advancing troops or to cause widespread damage to an enemy, in order to force the opposition into submission...The use of the environment as an implement of war is also not uncommon to the United States (US). In the U.S – Navaho wars of 1860 to 1864, the United States deliberately destroyed sheep and other livestock, as well as fruit orchards and other crops of the Navaho, as part of its successful strategy of subjugation...Future environmental warfare could involve atmospheric modifications, including fog and cloud dispersion or generation, hailstone production, release of materials which might alter the electrical properties of the atmosphere, generation and direction of destructive storms, rain or snowmaking, and control of lightning and climate modifications...One final option might be the use of animals in environmental warfare. This was the case in the first and second World Wars where weapons such as the "pigeon guided missile", napalm bats, and explosive dogs were the subject of experimentation.

While some scholars lament environmental terrorism and environmental warfare wherein forces of nature are used as weapons (Schofield, 1999) of mass destruction of indigenous peoples, other scholars celebrate the fact that the environment is no longer a passive "object" to be managed by some human beings (Clark, 2010). Scholars like Clark (2010) celebrate the deconstructive agency of nature or the environment, that is, they celebrate the multiple scales, invisibility, global scope, unpredictability, and alarming menace of climate change and associated nonhuman agencies. Whereas other scholars note that colonialists have always used nonhuman agencies, including diseases, flora, fauna, invasive pests and weeds, as proxies in colonial projects or in ecological imperialism designed to subjugate indigenous people (Crosby, 1986; Crosby *et al*, 2004; Foster *et al*, 2004), some scholars like Clark (2010) celebrate the deconstructive agency of nonhuman nature. Thus, noting ways in which empire is moving beyond Derridean humanistic deconstruction to a modality wherein nonhuman nature is also mobilised to deconstruct indigenous African states, societies and cultures, we argue that climate change is in fact a manifestation of Euro-American efforts to deconstruct African nationalism, nation states (Swyngedouw, 2010; Kelly, 2012; Jagerskog, 2011; Boeno, 2015; Dupont, 2018; Kurt, 2012; Marshall, 2015), societies and cultures that would otherwise pose problems for the constitution of the One World Government. Global capital would want to be free to move or flow across an open world and so discourses on climate change and on the need for a One World Government would serve global capital that also sponsors researches on climate change, catastrophism and apocalypse

Global governmentality or the One World Government would be constituted on the basis of the perceived need to control climate change and global warming on a global scale; in order to ensure that indigenous people relinquish control over and sovereignty and autonomy over their resources, ideologies that put human beings and nature at the same level or plane would be propagated such that human beings will have no claims to ownership and control over their local resources; in order to reverse indigenous people's sovereignty over their resources, ideologies around relationality and flat ontologies would be propagated (Hamilton, 2017; Simons, 2017; Smith, 2017; Nhemachena & Warikandwa, 2019; Nhemachena *et al*, 2019). In order to ban elections in a dictatorial One World Government, nature will be considered to be an agent and an actor in politics such that human beings cease to be the sole or privileged political actors – there are already discourses around the democratisation of objects, quasi-objects or things (Simons, 2017; Smith, 2017). In a context where human beings are considered to be at the same level with nature, it becomes possible to play politics of unsustainability, it becomes conceivable and tolerable to throw some human beings overboard as disposable, surplus, dispensable human waste or as sacrifice cargo – in the same way slaves were thrown overboard (Chassot, 2015; Scott, 1943).

Also, to legitimise the disposal and dispensability of some human beings in the face of climate change, there is popularisation of ideologies about postanthropocentrism, posthumanism, transhumanism, biocentrism, ecocentrism, earthcentrism, ecosophy, ecophilosophy, ecopsychology and ecocriticism (Buell, 2009; Smith, 2008; Hoving, 2003; Oppermann, 2016; Fagan, 2017; Johns-Putra, 2016; Li *et al*, 2016; Posthumus *et al*, 2014). The underlying idea in all these aspects is to suspend logics of human rights, by deconstructing the centrality of the human, so that it will become conceivable and tolerable to dispose of other human beings who are due to be thrown overboard the global spaceship in the era of extinction, the era of the Anthropocene and climate change. Once the human and human rights are no longer central, it becomes possible and conceivable to sacrifice indigenous people in the age of climate change so as to appease Gaia, in James Lovelock's (2007) sense.

Setting the stage for the disposability and dispensability of indigenous people, there are discourses about eco-nihilism in an age where the security of the human is deconstructed and the human is being called upon to sacrifice – to submit to an ethics of sacrifice that sacrifices ethics (Gibson, 2006; Fagan, 2017; Roberts, 2005). Human beings are being called upon to become nonethical, nonresponsible and to offer their lives as a gift without hope of return or return in time – giving oneself to death (Roberts, 2005).

In the age where God has been pronounced as dead, human beings sacrifice their lives to the Nietzschean supermen and to Gaia as the goddess of death. Already, drones are being depicted fetishistically and mystically as inhabiting a field of metaphysical theology, embodying dreams of transcendence and destruction and possessed of divine powers (Noys, 2015). Within the context of drone surveillance, fetishisation and mysticisation, there are discourses about the human duties to die - not merely the right to die but the duty to die (Choibi, 2010; Jecker, 2014; Hardwig, 2000; Arnett, 2002). Members of humanity including the ill, the aged, the dependent, those that are considered to be a burden to others, and those that have medical conditions are argued to have a duty to die (Choibi, 2010; Jacker, 2014; Hardwig, 2000; Tong, 2000; Feinberg, 1977; Arnett, 2002). In this regard, a new but malicious ethics is developing in which the worth of the individual and the security of human life are being rejected along with the rejection of binaries between right and wrong, good and evil, life and death, good and bad, ethical and unethical, moral and immoral, Godly and unGodly (Arnett, 2002). Some scholars are arguing that there is nothing special in being human, that killing is beneficent, that suicide is rational and that caring for the elderly is a burden, that humans must not be speciesist but should rather blur the distinctions between humans and animals (Arnett, 2002). In a postbinary or postdichotomy world (dis)order, there is the trivialisation of evil.

With evil trivialised, the misanthropism of neoMalthusianism is then foregrounded such that, for Africa, the Malthusian Anticipatory Regime for Africa (MARA) has been set up to promote extinction projects that blame the dispossessed and impoverished for climate change and global warming (Hartmann, 2014; Nhemachena *et al*, 2017; Vanderheiden, 2005; Independent, 18 May 2010; Bachram, 2004). The announcements calling upon the dispossessed and colonised to die are nothing new but an old story told in a different language because Africans have been made to die and sacrificed since the enslavement and colonial eras. In the contemporary era of the 21st century, there are renewed calls by Euro-Americans to recolonise Africans and other indigenous peoples (Gilley, 2017; Sorensen, 2016; Ludwig, 2018; Kursar, 2013; Augustin, 2017; Barnhizer, 2013). In the contemporary era, Africans are advised to valorise universalism and globalisation as opposed to their own interests, which are often depicted as parochial. What is forgotten is that colonialism also came in the guise of universalism and inclusiveness. What discourses on globalisation and universalism overlook is that there are no universal or global stomachs that are inclusive of indigenous people whose resources are being looted and plundered in the name of globalisation and universalism. Those that own and possess resources are better placed to deal with climate change such that addressing climate change should necessarily address resource ownership and control by indigenous people. Apart from ecological debts and debts for ecological imperialism (Foster *et al*, 2004; Murphy, 2009), Euro-America has a duty to ensure restitution, restoration and reparations to indigenous people of Africa and Asia.

Instead of calling for the voluntary extinction of indigenous people or calling for indigenous people to adopt the duty to die, Euro-America needs to ensure restitution, restoration, reparations and above all reciprocal justice so that indigenous people are better resourced to adapt and deal with the vagaries and challenges of climate change. Instead of focusing on climate catastrophism and apocalypse, Euro-America must meditate over catastrophism and apocalypses connected to enslavement and colonisation of indigenous people. Similarly, rather than focusing on fast-tracking indigenous people to climate catastrophism and apocalypse, Euro-America must fast-track indigenous people to restitution, restoration and reparations that are long overdue. Rather than sponsoring climate change and extinction movements, Euro-America thus must sponsor restitution, restoration and reparation movements that will benefit the indigenous peoples of the world.

Chapter outlines

In chapter two, Takavafira Masarira Zhou examines the intricate and contentious causes of droughts; he also examines the impacts of droughts during the colonial period in Africa. Both the colonial governments' intervention measures and African people's strategies to ameliorate the effects of droughts are interrogated. Zhou argues that the application of recent approaches in environmental history often reveals the logic and rationale of indigenous knowledge and organisation in natural resources management in contrast to received colonial western 'scientific' ideas which summarily blame Africans for environmental degradation. This chapter argues that neo-Malthusian environmental narrative which perceives climatic change and environmental degradation as products of increases of African populations and their supposedly poor farming practices are nothing but colonial hegemonic and totalising discourses justifying colonial

43

dispossession, control and use of African natural resources. The chapter, therefore, traces the politicisation of droughts in which placing blame on African farmers and pastoralists was a colonial strategy relied upon to justify colonial rule, centralisation of planning and control over African natural resources. The chapter stresses that while droughts occurred in pre-colonial Africa, their effects were minimal due to the existence of African coping practices acquired through experimentation and innovation over many years. Case studies from West Africa, East Africa, and Southern Africa will be used to unravel the history of droughts in colonial Africa.

Wisdom Sibanda & Fortune Sibanda's chapter three focuses on the Eastern and Southern African regions as typical case studies of areas that have been vulnerable to climate change because of their poverty, spatial and temporal diversity and because of the limited resources possessed by their population. Few studies have looked at impacts of climate change on water resources conflicts at local and regional scales. The chapter posits that the primary drivers of many aspects of climate change and related conflicts are largely anchored on anthropogenic factors whose remedy should emanate from responsible human actions. The chapter also draws insights from the Indigenous Knowledge Systems (IKS) to suggest possible solutions to the challenge of climate change. A case study approach of selected countries in Eastern and Southern African regions has been adopted. A desk review on the environmental effects of climate change on water, conflict, climate change patterns and severe droughts was done in order to ascertain the potential impact of climate variability.

In chapter four, Edmore Dube argues that the sustained sandwiching of African Indigenous Religion by western forces has discredited but has neither invalidated it nor effectively eliminated it from the hearts of indigenous Africans. Eurocentric education, including research, has been the most lethal weapon upon which western culture relied to emasculate Africans with regards weather control. On the political level, British theorist Lugard advised on indirect rule which left chiefs with nominal powers, insufficient to guide communities through cleansing rituals necessary for mastering the weather. In terms of sustained empirical research, clerical anthropologists like Tempels and von Sicard publicised the sources of indigenous power, exposing them to abuse by the colonial authorities and missionaries. All this went into 'chipping and refashioning' of indigenous cultures, loosening control over weather, and creating clone control in the hands of ineffective Christian pretenders who failed to completely wean Africans from rain petitioning or *mukwerera*. The end result has been the development of a marauding climate change eluding controls possibly due to continuous defilement of the covenant of Mwari (God).

Chapter five, which is authored by Oluwole Tewogboye Okewande argues that *Ifá,* the foundation on which the culture of the Yorùbá people of Nigeria rests, basically encapsulates the scientific and religious knowledge. Therefore, the chapter investigates the Yorùbá worldview through the *Ifá's* prescriptions about climate change, which is the latitude condition in the determination of heat or cold in regards to rain petitioning. Rain petitioning occurs when the hot climate seems unbearable to the extent that, the negative effects result in a lot of hazards such as famines, droughts, sicknesses and diseases. Semiotic approach is adopted because; symbolism is basic to *Ifá.* Relevant *Ifá* corpus that evinces on the rain petitioning are explored to establish the Yorùbá indigenous system of rain petitioning. The *Ifá's* corpuses suggest that the implementation order of rain petitioning is sanctioned by the spiritual forces mediated by *Ifá.* This is because, to the Africans generally and, the Yorùbá people in particular, the control of the physical and invisible aspects of the peoples' lives, including climate, depend on the ancestors, divinities, supernatural agents and spirits and human beings. It is found out from the study that, on one hand, among the Yorùbá, climate change in relation to rain petitioning is impossible without *Ifá* and on the other hand, rain petitioning is one of the means by which the Yorùbá people overcome or reduce the effects of climate change for their favourable and peaceful system of living.

In chapter six, Ignatius Gutsa explores the indigenous meteorological philosophy shared in a Zimbabwean village, to explain ongoing climate change. The central vernacular meteorological philosophy is explored focusing on *'kushanduka kwemwaka'* (seasonal change) and *'kushanduka kwemamiriro ekunze'* (change in the state of the environment/surroundings) in Gutsa village. Also explored are contestations regarding causality of the weather and climate changes. Climate change as presented in this chapter is *kushanduka kwemwaka* (change in seasons) and not *kushanduka kwemamiriro ekunze* (change in the state of the environment/surroundings) which could refer to the hourly, daily, weekly and monthly weather and not to seasonal changes. In exploring *kushanduka kwemwaka,* emphasis is on the changes in the seasons per se as well as changes in the characteristics which are found in the specific season. These are wind patterns, temperature and rainfall patterns together with their timing (commencement, length, cessation and frequency). Consequently *kushanduka kwemamiriro ekunze* is found in *kushanduka kwemwaka.* Shona, the language used in the study setting is an indigenous language spoken in Zimbabwe; it also refers to people who speak the Shona language.

Beatrice Lantern's chapter seven discusses what she calls the hegemonic tendencies of Euro-American imperialists on African indigenous knowledge systems in post-colonial Zimbabwe. For Lantern, weather and climate engineering is the means by which Euro-America exercises hegemony over Africa. Droughts and famines are partly a function of neo-imperial engineering over Africa. The chapter, therefore, discusses the history of droughts and famines in Zimbabwe, the land question, rain petitioning and rain making systems in both African and western traditions. The means and ends of drought and famine engineering in Zimbabwe are also examined. The chapter underscores the strategies that may be considered in fighting climate change and it urges Africans to revitalise territorial cults for the good of their societies.

In chapter eight, Aaron Rwodzi problematises the connections between weather, food politics and the rural poor in Africa generally, and Zimbabwe in particular. More specifically, the chapter teases out the politicisation of food handouts by politicians when elections and periods of droughts and famines coincide. It also teases out the politicisation of climatological anomalies by western agents who operate as foreign companies or non-governmental organisations (NGOs). Rwodzi argues that political parties such as Zimbabwe African National Union Patriotic Front (ZANU- PF) and the Movement for Democratic Change (MDC) among others, often prey on the indigent who hardly eke a mere subsistence from their land due to poverty and insufficient rainfall. The political parties provide essential food relief that is, however, dependent on party support. It

46

is argued in this chapter that in Zimbabwe, as elsewhere in Africa, the vulnerable people are the objects of a great deal of political and electoral manipulation; politics of the stomach takes precedence. The chapter argues that politicians must not ride roughshod over the poor. It argues that more rights education is required to prevent the use of food as an instrument of politics.

Nancy Mazuru's chapter nine focuses on the effects of climate change in Zimbabwe with particular reference to rural women. The chapter focuses on Bikita district. It examines several ways in which climate change is affecting rural women. The findings of the study revealed that Bikita district is experiencing low rainfall and this is leading to a decline in agricultural produce. The decline in agricultural produce is threatening food security in the district and it is women who largely bear the brunt because they are the ones who dominate farming activities. Agriculture is the major source of livelihood for women in this district. Mazuru argues that reduced crop yields affect food security and in this regard, it is women again who shoulder this burden because they are the ones who are responsible for preparing food for their families. At the same time, declining agricultural produce plunges rural women into poverty because they get income through selling surplus yields and home processed foods. The chapter also points out that the depletion of wild resources such as fruits, mopane worms, stink bugs and mushrooms affects rural women. Such depletion affects the dietary needs of the households; it also reduces income generated through the sale of these resources. Besides that, climate change is also leading to scarcity of local herbs for both human beings and livestock. Various herbs that are used for women's reproductive and maternal health are at the risk of extinction due to low rainfall patterns that are being experienced in the district. The chapter has also argued that low rainfall in Bikita is leading to scarcity of fuelwood and water sources.

Writing chapter ten from an ecotheological perspective, Martin Mujinga points out that the Methodist Church in Zimbabwe inherited land as the privileges of the colonisers' including missionary land grabbing. He notes that many mission farms, including Kwenda, are experiencing ecological challenges emanating from tenants and "squatters" seeking to reclaim their lost heritage. Mujinga argues that the Zimbabwean government's land redistribution, which started in the year 2000, provided an opportunity for the Black majority to regain their land that was stolen by the colonisers. Colonialists had stolen the fertile and well-watered land, and they pushed Black people to marginal land that was dry and infertile. The displacement of Africans to marginal areas is the cause of environmental degradation. For Mujinga, ecotheology arose to address the plundering of natural resources by "humanity". The chapter further argues that, by dispossessing Africans, colonialists are the ones that deprived and took Africans from the Garden of Eden and now they hypocritically blame Africans for the disappearance of the Garden of Eden that was stolen by the same colonialists and imperialists. Therefore, the author argues that environmental crisis presents the church with an evangelical opportunity.

In chapter eleven, Alex Munyonga notes that Zimbabwe is being haunted by climate change related challenges. Droughts and floods have increased their frequency. He notes that rivers, streams, ponds and wetlands are drying up. Debates surrounding the arrest of such environmental challenges have called for more ownership, control, sustainable environmental care and management. The chapter argues that the long history of lack of indigenous ownership and control of natural resources is responsible for improper environmental care and management. The general argument is that as long as the Africans, and Zimbabweans in particular, do not repossess their resources then there will be no incentive for them to care for the environment. If western neoimperialist forces continue to own and control African natural resources, then environmental plundering will persist; these forces are geared towards looting, stealing, grabbing and syphoning African resources in order to build overseas economies.

Focusing on measures to alleviate climate change, Semie M. Sama's chapter twelve informs transport policy in Canada's British Columbia and Sweden, two of the 15 jurisdictions that received the 2018 United Nations Momentum for Change Climate Action Award. With a focus on the transport sector, the aim is to offer a framework upon which Africa can translate laws to reduce emissions and strengthen national adaptive capacity into action in a way that will not compromise the prospects for holding global temperature increases well below 2° C. Sama notes that both governments have adopted the objective to make their territories one of the world's first fossil-free states. To that end, they have launched fossil-free initiatives and taken climate actions. Drawing from the experience of British Columbia and Sweden, the chapter argues that a successful climate policy should have the following elements: information on climate change impacts; data on emissions of greenhouse gases (GHGs) in the jurisdiction; ambitious GHG emissions targets against a baseline year, including a net-zero GHG emissions targets; and a climate action plan to implement audacious GHG reduction targets. It notes that pricing carbon pollution; promoting adoption of and innovation in clean vehicles and fuels; creating new clean tech jobs; and working to direct the development of dependable and safe transportation infrastructure that is constructed to withstand extreme weather events are significant pillars of their climate strategies. Sama further contends that if these strategies have put Sweden and British Columbia top of the list of jurisdictions that are doing the most to save the climate system, there's no excuse for failing to follow suit and pass climate laws to cut GHG emissions far beyond what other governments have done and yet still enjoy robust economic growth in Africa.

In chapter thirteen Nkwazi Nkuzi Mhango contends that global warming has not yet received deserved attention. His chapter argues that nothing can be achieved without decolonising the international status quo. He argues that if the international community is sincere and serious about global warming, the first step towards addressing and arresting it is for them to accept the blame for creating it. For Mhango, neocolonial powers created and benefited from global warming. The solution that he offers is for the international community to embark on decolonisation of the suffocating international superstructure. Because he sees the current environmental problems as emanating from neocolonisation, Mhango suggests the need for real decolonisation at the international level which is currently marked by resilient colonial structures. He points out that some powerful states are conducting nuclear experiments in other people's countries such as the Marshall Islands where the United States of America ran some harmful nuclear tests.

Tom Tom and Clement Chipenda's chapter fourteen contends that land is an essential component of the environment, including climate. They argue that policies pertaining to land reforms, and environment/ climate change are in essence social policies concerned with people and their wellbeing. The chapter considers Zimbabwe's land repossession in a broader context of a decolonial agenda in environment and climate discourses. The authors note that decoloniality has been blended with the Transformative Social Policy conceptual framework. Tom Tom & Clement Chipenda observe that TSP ties well with attempts to decolonise land tenure in Zimbabwe, and broadly the Global South. They argue that popular land movements by the Black masses underline their rejection of neo-colonialism. For this reason, they contend that the repossession of land in Zimbabwe was a correct move to address the imbalances in land tenure – the authors opine that this was a necessary move to decolonise land, space and livelihoods of indigenous Zimbabweans. For the authors, Zimbabwe overturned the bimodal land tenure that was skewed against the Black majority and it put in place a trimodal agrarian arrangement that is dominated by indigenous smallholder farmers.

References

Aane, A. (2013) Eating it Out: Cannibalism and Sexual Deviance in Nineteenth Century Travel Writing, in Fahs, B. *et al* (eds) *The Moral Panics of Sexuality*. Springer.

Ani, N. C. (2016) Does scientism Undermine Other Forms of Knowledge https://verbumetecclesia.org.za/index.php/ve/article/view1558

Adams, E, M. (1991) *The Metaphysics of Self and World: Towards a Humanistic Philosophy*. Temple University Press.

Alfredsson, E. *et al.* (2018) The Political Economy of Unsustainable Consumption and Production, Working Group Scoping Paper: Systems of Sustainable Consumption & Production, Future Earth Knowledge Action Network

Amani, B. *et al.* (2005) The Human Genome Diversity Project: the Politics of Patents at the Intersection of Race, Religion, and Research Ethics, in *Law & Polics* vol 27 (1): 152-188.

Ananda, R. (19 October 2017) Planetary Weapons and Military Weather Modification: Chemtrails, Atmospheric Geoengineering and Environmental Warfare in Global Research https://www.globalresearch.ca/military-weather-modification-chemtrails-atmospheric-geoengineering-and-environmental-warfare

Anshelm, J. *et al.* (2014) *Discourses of Global Climate Change: Apocalyptic Framing and Political Antagonisms.* Routledge.

Anshelm, J. *et al.* (2014) *Discourses of Global Climate Change: Apocalyptic Framing and Political Antagonism.* Taylor & Francis.

Anshelm, J. *et al.* (2014) The Lost Chance to Save the Planet? An Analysis of the Geoengineering Advocacy Discourse in *The Public Debate, in Environmental Humanities* vol 5: 101-113

Anyinam, C. A. (1991) Transboundary Movements of Hazardous Wastes: the Case of Toxic Waste Dumping in Africa, in *Int J Health Serv* vol 21 (4): 759-77.

Aravamudan, S. (2013) The Catachronism of Climate Change, in *Diacritics* vol 41 (3): 6-30.

Arnett, J. C. (2002) The Bioethics Movement: An Emerging Culture of Death, in *Hacienda Publishing,* 7 (2): 48-49.

Asara, V. (2015) Democracy without Growth: the Political Ecology of the Indignados Movement PhD Thesis. Universitat Autonomia de Barcelona.

Asayama, S. (2015) Catastrophism towards 'Opening Up' or 'Closing Down'? Going beyond the Apocalyptic Future and Geoengineering, in *Current Sociology* vol 63 (1): 89-93.

Augustin, M. (2017) How to Escape from the Dead End of Post-Democracy, in *Filosoficky Casopis* vol 1 (93)

Bachram, H. (2004) Climate Fraud and Carbon Colonialism: the New Trade in Greenhouse Gases, in *Capitalism Nature Socialism* vol 15 (4): 1-16.

Barash, D. P. (2000) Evolutionary Existentialism, Sociology, and the Meaning of Life, in *Bioscience* vol 50 (11): 1012-1017

Barnhizer, D. (2013) Through a Prism Darkly: Surveillance and Speech Suppression in the Post-Democracy Electronic State in Cleveland-Marshall Legal Studies Paper No 13-SSRN http://ssm.com/abstract=2328744258

Bassett, T. J. *et al.* (2015) Political Ecological Perspectives on Socioecological Relations, in *Natures Sciences Societies* vol 23 (2): 157-165.

BBC News (6 April 2007) Prison for SA 'Baboon Murderer' news.bbc.co.uk/2/hi/Africa/6532771.stm

Braidotti, R. *et al.* (eds) (2012) *Revisiting Normativity with Deleuze.* A & C Black.

Beaton, B. (2007) Racial Science Now: Histories of Race and Science in the Ages of Personalized Medicine, in *The Public Historian* vol 29 (3): 157-162.

Beck, U. (2015) Emancipatory Catastrophism: What Does it Mean to Climate Change and Risk Society? In *Current Sociology* vol 63 (1): 75-88

Begich, N. *et al.* (2002) *Angels Don't Play this HAARP: Advances in Tesla Technology.* Earthpulse Press.

Belfer, E. *et al.* (2017) Representation of Indigenous Peoples in Climate Change Reporting, in *Climate Change* vol 145 (1-2): 57-70.

Bellah, R. N. (2005) Civil Religion in America, in *Daedalus* vol 134 (4): 40 – 55.

Berglez, P. *et al* (2014) The Post-Political Condition of Climate Change: An Ideological Approach, in *Capitalism Nature Socialism* vol 25 (1): 54-71.

Berman, J. *et al.* (2012) Forensic Psychiatry in Care Psychology/Third Edition) https://www.scienceirect.com/topics/medicine-and-dentistry/automatism

Berry, R. B. (2012) Parasomnias, in Fundamentals of Sleep Medicine https://www.sciencedirect.com/topics/medicine-and-dentistry/automatism

Blanc, N. (2017) Environmental Humanities and New Materialisms: The Ethics of Decolonising Nature and Culture, A Most Preparator Conference for the 2017 World Humanities Conference

Bourdillon, M. F. C. (1976) *The Shona People.* Gwelo. Mambo Press.

Bluhdon, I. (2017) Post-capitalism, Post-growth, 'Post-Consumerism? Eco-political Hopes Beyond Sustainability, in *Global Discourse* vol 7: 42-61.

Bluhdorn, I. (2007) A Theory of Post-Ecological Politics in *Environmental Politics* vol 6 (3): 125-147.

Bluhdorn, I. (2011) The Politics of Unsustainability: COPIS, Post-Ecologism, and the Ecological Paradox, in *Organization & Environment* vol 20 (10): 1-20.

Bluhdorn, I. (2013) The Governance of Unsustainability: Ecology and Democracy after the Post-Democratic Turn, in *Environmental Politics* vol 22 (1): 16-36.

Boeno, R. (2015) Climate Change and Securitization: the Construction of Climate Deterrence https://www.researchgate.net/publication/305/45733-climate-change-and-securitization-the-construction-of-climate-deterrence

Bostrom, M. *et al.* (2018) *Environment & Society: Concepts & Challenges.* Palgrave MacMillan

Bostrom, M. *et al.* (2018) Introduction: Conceptualizing Environment-Society Relations, in Bostrom, M. *et al.* (eds) *Environment and Society: Concepts and Challenges.* Springer.

Bristow, T. *et al.* (2016) Climates of History, Cultures of Climate, in Bristow, T. *et al.* (eds) *A Cultural History of Climate Change.* London & New York. Routledge.

Buell, L. (2009) What is Called Ecoterrorism, in Gramma, *Journal of Theory and Criticism* vol 16: 153-166.

Burks, F. (14 October 2018) HAARP: Secret Weapon Used for Weather Modification, Electromagnetic Warfare, in Global Research https://www.globalresearch.ca/haarp-secret-weapon-used-for-weather-modification-electromagnetic-warfare/20407

Cardbury D. (1997) *The Feminisation of Nature: Our Future at Risk.* London: Penguin Books.

Cagirkan, B. (2016) Social Changes and Level of Ontological Insecurity or Senses of Risk, in *International E-Journal of Advances in Social Sciences* vol 2 (5): 447-484.

Calina, C. (2015) Disposable Life: the Literary Imagination and the Contemporary Novel, PhD Dissertation. Duke University, http://hd/:hadle.net/10161/9955

Cann, H. M. (1998) Human Genome Diversity, in *CR Aacd* 111 vol 321 (6): 443-6.

Cameron, E. (2008) Cultural Geography Essays: Indigenous Spectrality and the Politics of Postcolonial Ghosts Stories, in *Cultural Geographies* vol 15 (3)

Cartwright, W. (1996) Killing and Letting Die: A Defensible Distinction, in *British Medical Bulletin* vol 52 (2): 354-361

Chakra, M. A. *et al* (2018) Immediate Action is the Best Strategy when Facing Uncertain Climate Change, in *Nature Communications* vol 9 (2566).

Chamberlian, L. (7 February 2012) The Political Message of Nietzsche's God Is Dead", in The Guardian https://www.theguardian.com/commentisfree/belief/2012/feb/07/political-message-nietzsche-god-is-dead.

Chassot, J. (2015) Voyage through Death/to Life Upon these Shores: the Living Dead of the Middle Passage, in *Atlantic Studies* vol 12 (1): 90-108

Chigodora, J. (1997) Famine and Drought: The Question of Food Security in Zimbabwe, in *Drought Network News* (1994-2001) vol 9 (1): 1-6

Choibi, M. (2010) The Duty to Die and the Burdensomeness of Living, in *Bioethics*, 24 (8): 412-20.

Clark, T. (2010) Some Climate Change Ironies: Deconstruction, Environmental Politics and the Closure of Ecocriticism in *The Oxford Literary Review* vol 32 (1): 131-149.

Coles, T. J. (n.d) Weather Weapons: The Dark World of Environmental Warfare https://www.lobster.magazine.co.uk/free/lobster62/lob62-weather-wars.pdf

Crone, B. (2017) *The Final Countdown* vol 1. Lulu.Com

Crosby, A. W. (1986) *Ecological Imperialism: The Biological Expansion of Europe, 900-1900.* Cambridge University Press.

Crosby, A. W. (2004) *Ecological Imperialism: The Biological Expansion of Europe 900-1900.* Cambridge University Press.

Crouch, C. (2004) *Post-Democracy.* Polity

Cunneen, C. (2008) Riot, Resistance and Moral Panic: Demonising the Colonial Other, in University of New South Wales Faculty of Law Research Series vol 29 http://law.bepress.com/unswwps-flrps08/art29

Daily Star. (7 January 2017) US Super Weapon to Trigger Hurricanes, Blizzards and 'Own the Weather' for WW3 https://www.dailystar.co.uk/news/latest-news/575796/weather-modification-US-weapons-air-force-HAARP-operation-Popeye.

De Fretas, K. D. *et al.* (2015) Forensic Psychiatry and Forensic Psychology: Criminal Responsibility, in Encylopedia of Forensic and Legal Medicine https://www.sciencedirect.com/topic/medicien-and-dentistry/automatism

De Gregori, T. R. *et al.* (1987) Surplus People and Expendable Children The Structure of Apartheid and the Mortality Crisis in South Africa, in *The Review of Black-Political Economy* vol 15 (4): 47-62.

Del Pilar Blanco, M. *et al.* (eds) (2013) *The Spectralities Reader: Ghosts and Haunting in Contemporary Cultural Theory*. Bloomsbury.

Deleuze, G. and Guattari, F. (1987) *A Thousand Plateaus: Capitalism and Schizophrenia*. Minneaplois & London: University of Minnesota Press.

Derrida, J. (2008) *The Gift of Death*. Chicago & London: The University of Chicago Press.

Dery, M. (2015) *I Must Not Think Bad Thoughts: Drive-by Essays in American Dread*, American Dreams. Minnesota Scholarshiponline.

Dice, M. (2010) *The New World order: Facts and Fiction*. Mark Dice.

Dodson, M. *et al.* (1999) Indigenous Peoples and the Morality of the Human Genome Diversity Project, in *J. Med. Ethics* vol 25 (2): 204-8.

Douglas, M. (1966) *Purity and Danger: An Analysis of the Concepts of Pollution and Taboo*. London: Routledge & Kegan Paul.

Dotan, A. (2016) The Neoliberal Biopolitics of Climate Security: Resilience and the European Union's Securitization of Climate Change, in Simon Frazer University Institutional Repository Summit sfu.ca/item/16907

Dunbar, D. *et al.* (2015) The Devil Rejoiced: Volk, Devils and Moral Panic in White South Africa, 1978-1982, in *Journal of Historical Sociology* vol 28 (2) DOI:10.1111/jobs.112041

Dupont, C. (2018) The EU's Collective Securitization of Climate Change, in *West European Politics* vol 42 (1): 369-390.

Dynes, W. R. (2016) *Encyclopedia of Homosexuality* vol 2. Routledge.

El-Haj, N. A. (2007) The Genetic Reinscription of Race, in *Annu Rev Anthropol* vol 36: 283-300

Evans, G. (2 March 2018) The Unwelcome Revival of 'Race Science' https://www.theguardian.com/news/2018/mar/02/the-unwelcome-revival-of-race-sceicne

Fagan, M. (2017) Security in the Anthropocene: Environment, Ecology, Escape, in *European Journal of International Relations,* 23 (2): 292-314.

Fagan, M. (2017) Who's Afraid of the Ecological Apocalypse? Climate Change and the Production of the Ethical Subject, in *The British Journal of Politics and International Relations,* 19 (2): 225-244.

Feinberg, J. (1977) Voluntary Euthanasia and the Inalienable Right to Life. The Tanner Lecture on Human Values Delivered at the University of Michigan 1 April 1977.

Fetter, J. (17 December 2018) Conspiracy Theorists are Obsessed with the Wrong 'New World Order' in The Nation https://www.thenation.com/article/conspiracy-theory-climate-change-globalist-exxon

Forth, G. (2018) Purity, Pollution, and Systems of Classification DOI:10.1002/978118924396

Forest, J. J. F. (n.d) The Final Act: Ideologies of Catastrophic Terror https://www.ac/u.org/sites/default/files/field_document/AC LURM002778.pdf.

Foster, J. B. (2004) Ecological Imperialism: the Curse of Capitalism, in *Socialist Register*: 186-201

Foster, J. B. *et al.* (2004) Ecological Imperialism: The Curse of Capitalism, in *Socialist Register* https://socialistregister.com/index php/srv/article/download/5817/27131

Freeland, E. (2014) *Chemtrails, HAARP, and the Full Spectrum Dominance of Planet Earth*. Feral House.

Friedrichs, J. (2014) Who's Afraid of Thomas Malthus? In Mafredo, M. *et al.* (eds) *Understanding Society and Natural Resources*. Springer Derdrecht.

Fu, M. (2018) Fantastic Time as Para-History: Spectrality and Historical Justice in Mo Yan's Life and Death are Wearing Me Out, in *Comparative Literature* vol 2 (2): 73-87.

Gabel, M. (2015) Regenerative Development: Going 'Beyond Sustainability, in *Kosmos Journal for Global Transformation* https://www.kosmosjournal.org/article/regenerative-development-going-beyond-sustanability

Geis, J. W. (2010) *Physics, Metaphysics, and God – Third Edition: A Perspective on Physics.* Authorhouse.

Gelfand, M. (1959) *Shona Rituals with Special Reference to the Chaminuka Cult.* Cape Town: Juta.

Gibson, G. C. (2006) *Fossil Fuelled Federal Deficits: Blogged in the U.S.A.* Lulu.Com.

Gilley, B. (2017) The Case for Colonialism, in *Third World Quarterly* DOI:10.1080/01436597:2017.1369037

Giroux, H. A. (2010) Zombie Politics and Other Late Modern Monstrosities in the Age of Disposability*, in Policy Futures in Education, vol 8 (1)*

Global Research. (5 July 2018) The Ultimate Weapon of Mass Destruction: "Owning the Weather" for Military Use https://www.globalresearch.ca/the-ultimate-weapon-of-mass-destruction-owning-the-weather-for-military-use-2/5306386

Goering, L. (9 June 2004) Africa's Gays Persecuted as Cause of Ills, in *Chicago Tribune,* https://www.chicagotribune.com/news/et-xpm-2004-06-09-0406090188-story.html

Goldblat, J. (1975) The Prohibition of Environmental Warfare, in *Ambio* vol 4 (5/6): 186-190.

Hamblin, J. D. (2013) *Arming Mother Nature: The Birth of Catastrophic Environmentalism.* Oxford University Press.

Hamilton, C. (2000) The Human Genome Diversity Project and the New Biological Imperialism, in *Santa Clara Law Review* vol 41 (2)

Hamilton, P. (1995) *Emile Durkheim.* Taylor & Francis.

Hamilton, S. T. (2017) Governing Through the Climate: Climate Change, the Anthropocene and Global Governmentality, PhD Thesis: London School of Economics and Political Science.

Hanser, M. (2009) Killing, Letting Die and Preventing People from Being Saved, in *Utilitas* vol 11 (3): 277-295.

Harari, Y. N. (2018) *21 Lessons for the 21st Century.* London: Jonathan Cape.

Hardwig, J. (2000) *Is There a Duty to Die?: And Other Essays in Bio-Ethics.* Routledge.

Harry, D. (2000) Indigenous Peoples Critical of 'the Human Genome Project, in *IATP Institute for Agriculture & Trade Policy* https://www.iatp.org/news/indigenous-peoples-critical-of-the-human-genome-project.

Harry, D. (2014) Biocolonialism and Indigenous Knowledge in United Nations Discourse, in *Griffith Law Review* vol 20 (3): 702-728.

Harry, D. *et al.* (2005) Genetic Research: Collecting Blood to Preserve Culture? In *Cultural Survival Quarterly Magazine* https://www.culturealsurvival.org/publications/cultural-survival-quarterly/

Hartmann, B. (2014) Converging on Disaster: Climate Security and the Malthusian Anticipatory Regime for Africa, in *Geopolitics* vol 19 (4): 757-783.

House, T. J. *et al.* (1996) Weather as a Force Multiplier: Owning the Weather in 2025: A Research Paper Presented to Air Force 2025 Preklady o dlesa.sk/up-content/uploads/owning-the-weather-in-2025.pdf.

Hoving, I. (2013) Earthly Things: Ecocriticism, 'Globalization, and the Material Turn, in *Frame* vol 26 (2): 71-85.

Hultman, M. *et al.* (2017) *Masculinities of Global Climate Change: Exploring Ecomodern, Industrial and Ecological Masculinity in Rich Countries: Work, Public Policy & Action.* Taylor & Francis.

Humbe, B. P. (2018) Divisi Witchcraft in Contemporary Zimbabwe: Contest between Two Legal Systems as Incubator of Social Tensions among the Shona People, in Green, M. C. *et al.* (eds) *Religion, Law and Security.* Stellenbosch Conf RAP: 269-282

Hund, W. D. *et al.* (eds) (2015) *Simianization: Apes, Gender, Class and Race.* LIT Verlag Munster.

Independent. (18 May 2010) Eco-anarchists: A New Breed of Terrorists https://www.independent.co.uk/environemt/eco-anarchist-a-new-breed-of-terrorist-1975559.html.

Jamieson, D. (1999) Ethics and Intentional Climate Change, in *Climate Change* vol 33: 323-336.

Jecker, N. S. (2014) Against a Duty to Die, in American Medical Association, *Journal of Ethics* 16 (5): 390-394.

John-Putra, A. (2016) Climate Change in Literature and Literary Studies: From Cli-Fi, Climate Change Theatre and Ecopoetry to Ecocriticism a d Climate Change Criticism, in *WIRES Climate Change* vol 7 (2): 266-282.

Kanamugire, J. C. (2017) African Response to Transboundary Movement of Hazardous Waste, in *AUDJ* vol 13 (3): 121-133.

Kelly, E. (2012) Does Deconstruction Matter? Being 'at Home' in the Era of Climate Change, in *Journal of Media and Cultural Studies* vol 27 (1): 41-53.

Kenic, A *et al.* (n.d) Searching for "the Political' in Environmental Politics in Environmental Politics http://www.tandfonline.com/101/fenp20#.USWdqNJDuSo

Kenis, A. (2018) Post-Politics Contested: Why Multiple Voices on Climate Change Do Not Equal Politicisation, in *Environment and Panning C: Politics and Space* https://doi.org/10.1177/0263774x18807209

Khan, A. S. (2002) Earth on the Market: Beyond the Limits of Sustainable Growth in *Global Policy Forum* https://www.globalpolicy.org/component/content/article/225/32214.html

Kinnvall, C. *et al.* (2018) Introduction to 2018 Special Issue of European Security: 'Ontological (In)security in the European Union, in *European Security* vol 27 (3): 249-265.

Koch, A. *et al.* (2019) Earth System Impact of the European Arrival and Great Dying in the Americas after 1492, in *Quaternary Science Reviews* vol 207: 13-36.

Krawczak, M. (2018) The Spectrality of Nuclear Catastrophe: The Case of Chernobyl, Conference: Electronic Visualisation and the Arts http://dx.doi.org/10.14236/ewic/EVAC18.30

Kursar, T. (2013) In a Post-Democracy Trap, Paper for the 7th ECPR General Conference, Sept 4-7 Bordeaux

Kurtz, G. (2012) Securitization of Climate Change in the United Nations 2007-2010, in Hexagon Series on Human and Environmental Security and Peace Book Series vol 8

Kurzweil, R. (2005) *The Singularity is Near: When Humans Transcend Biology*. Penguin Books.

Li, C. *et al.* (2016) Reading Climate Change in the Anthropocene: Material Ecocriticism and Chinese Environmental Literature, in *Studies in Ecocriticism* vol 21 (2): 138-151.

Lifshey, A. (2010) *Specters of Conquest: Indigenous Absence in Transatlantic Literatures*. Fordham University Press.

Lone, D. L. (1998) Whose Genes are they? The Human Genome Diversity Project, in *Health Soc Policy* vol 10 (4): 51-66.

Lovelock, J. (1988) *The Ages of Gaia: A Biography of our Living Earth.* Oxford University Press.

Lovelock, J. (2007) *The Revenge of Gaia: Why the Earth is Fighting Back and How We Can Still Save Humanity.* London: Penguin Books.

Ludwig, G. (2018) Post-Democracy and Gender: New Paradoxes and Old Tensions, in *Distinktion: Journal of Social Theory* vol 19 (1): 28-46.

Mail & Guardian. (26 February 2016) Comparing Black People to Monkeys Has a Long, Dark Simian History, https://mg.co.za/article/2016-02-29-comparing-black-people-to-monkes-has-a-long-dark-simian-history

Mail & Guardian. (4 January 2016) Twitter Erupts after KZN Estate Agent Calls Black People 'Monkeys' https://mg.co.za/article/2016-01/04-twitter-erupts-after-kzn-estate-agent-calls-black-people-monkeys

Manelshagen, F. (2012) Climate Catastrophism: The Future of the History of Climate Change, in Janky, A. *et al.* (eds) *Historical Disasters in Context: Science, Religion, and Politics.* New York & London: Routledge.

Marchant, G. E. *et al.* (2016) The Short-Term Temptations and Long-Term Risks of Environmental Catastrophism, in *Jurimetrics* vol 56 (4)

Marshall, N. (2015) Environmental Migration in an Era of Accelerated Climate Change: Proposing a Normative Framework for International Migration Rights and Domestic Migration PhD University of Alberta.

McGee, A. *et al.* (2019) Withholding and Withdrawing Life-Sustaining Treatment and the Relevance of the Killing Versus Letting Die Distinction, in the *American Journal of Bioethics* vol 19 (3): 34-36.

McLachlan, H. V. (2008) The Ethics of Killing & Letting Die, in Becker, L. C. *et al* (eds) *Encyclopedia of Ethics* 2nd Edition. Routledge.

Merchant, C. (2008) The Violence of Impediments: Francis Bacon and the Origins of Experimentation, in *Critiques and Contentions* vol 99: 731-760

Mignolo, W. (2009) Dispensable and Bare Lives: Coloniality and the Hidden Political/Economic Agenda of Modernity in *Human Architecture: Journal of the Sociology of Self Knowledge* vol 2: 69-88

Mills, C. W. (2015) Bestial Inferiority: Locating Simianization within Racism, in Hund, W. D. *et al.* (eds) *Simianization: Apes, Gender, Class and Race.* LIT Verlag Munster.

Milman, O. (31 January 2019) European Colonization of Americas Killed So Many it Cooled Earth's Climate https://www.theguardian.com/environment/2019/jan/31/eur opean-colonization-of-americas-helped-cause-cliamte-change

Moro, P. A. (2018) Witchcraft, Sorcery, and Magic, in The International Encyclopedia of Anthropology https://doi.org/10.1002/9781118924396.wbiea/915

Mukherjee, S. R. (2016) Para-Religions of Climate Change: Humanity, Eco-Nihilism, Apocalypse, in Bristow, T. *et al.* (eds) *A Cultural History of Climate Change.* London & New York. Routledge.

Murphy, J. (2009) Environment and Imperialism: Why Colonialism Still Matters, in Sustainability Research Institute, University of Leeds SRI Papers ISSN 1753-1330 No 20.

Myers, T. C. (2014) Understanding Climate Change as an Existential Threat: Confronting Climate Denial as a Challenge to Climate Ethics, in *De Ethica: A Journal of Philosophical, Theological and Applied Ethics* vol 1 (1): 53-70.

Nagle, J. C. (2009) The Idea of Pollution, in *UC Davis Law Review* vol 43 (1)

Namibian. (18 July 2005) 'Baboon Shooting' Claims Return in Trial Over Farm Worker Killing https://www.namibian.com.na/index.php?.id=13648&page-archive

Neumann, H. (1982) Nietzsche's The Superman, The Will to Power and the Eternal Return, in *Ultimate Reality and Meaning*, 5 (4): 280-295.

News24. (25 March 2014) Farmer Istook Worker for Baboon https://www.news24.com/southafrica/news/farmer-mistook-worker-for-baboon-20140325?cpid=1

Nhemachena, A. & Kaundjua, M. (2018) Incorporated or Cannibalised by Posthuman Others? Sanctions and Witchcraft in

Contemporary Zimbabwe, in Nyamnjoh, F. B. (ed) *Eating and Being Eaten: Cannibalism as Food for Thought*. Bamenda: Langaa RPCIG.

Nhemachena, A. *et al.* (2017) Transnational Corporations Land Grabs and the Ongoing Second Mad Scramble for Africa: An Introduction, in Wariakndwa, T. V. *et al.* (eds) *Transnational Land Grabs and Restitution in an Age of the (De) Militarised New Scramble for Africa: A Pan African Socio-Legal Perspective*. Bamenda: Langaa RPCIG.

Nhemachena, A. & Warikandwa, T. V. (2019) *Grid-Locked African Economic Sovereignty: Decolonising the Neoimperial Socio-Economic & Legal Forcefields in the 21ˢᵗ Century*. Bamenda: Langaa RPCIG.

Nhlapo, T. (2017) Homicide in Traditional African Societies: Customary Law and the Question of Accountability, in *African Human Rights Law Journal* vol 17 (1)

Nietzsche, F. (1887) *The Gay Science*. Leipzig E. W. Fritzsch.

Nietzsche, F. (2002) *Nietzsche Beyond Good and Evil: Prelude to a Philosophy of the Future*. Cambridge University Press.

Nietzsche, F. (2018) *Beyond Good and Evil*, Classic Choice Books.

Northcott, M. (2014) *A Political Theology of Climate Change*. SPCK.

Noys, B. (2015) Drone Metaphysics, in *Culture Machine* vol 16: 1-22.

Nyamnjoh, F. B. (2012) Potted Plants in Greenhouses: A Critical Reflection of the Resilience of Colonial Education in Africa, in *Journal of Asian and African Studies* vol 47 (2): 129-154.

Nughton, P. (23 December 2008) Pope Accused of Stoking Homophobia after he Equates Homosexuality to Climate Change, in *The Times*, https://www.thetimes.co.uk/article/pope-accused-of-stoking-homophobia-after-he-equates-homosexuality-to-climate-change

Nursely-Bray, M. *et al.* (2018) County, Climate Change Adaptation and Colonisation: Insights from an Indigenous Adaptation Planning Process, Australia, in *Heliyon* vol 4

Nuth, M. J. (2007) Ontological Security and the Global Risk Environment: A Case Study of Risk and Risk Perception in the Tourist – Dependent Township of Akaroa, Masters Thesis University of Canterbury.

O'Halloran, K. (2017) *Posthumanism and Deconstructing Arguments: Corporate and Digital-Driven Critical Analysis*. Taylor & Francis.

Olsen, B. (2013) *Future Esoteric: The Unseen Realms.* 2nd Edition. CCC Publishing.

Oppermann, S. (2016) From Posthumanism to Posthuman Ecocriticism, in *Relations* vol 4 (1): 24-37

Patz, J. A. *et al.* (2014) Climate Change Challenges and Opportunities for Global Health, in *JAMA* vol 312 (15): 1565-1580.

Peters, K. (2018) Disasters, Climate Change, and Securitization: the United Nations Security Council and the United Kingdom's Security Policy, in *Disasters* vol 42 (2): 196-214.

Posthumus, S. *et al.* (2014) Reading Environment(s): Digital Humanities Meets Ecocriticism, in *Studies in Ecocriticism* vol 18 (3): 254-273.

Pottage, A. (1998) The Inscription of Life in Law: Genes, Patents, and Bio-Politics, in Brownsword, R. *et al.* (eds) *Law and Human Genetics: Regulating a Revolution.* Hart Publishing.

Quayle, S. (2007) *Weather Wars and Un-Natural Disasters.* Stephen Quayle.

Rachels, J. (2001) Killing and Letting Die, in Becker, L. C. *et al.* (eds) *Encyclopedia of Ethics*, 2nd Edition. Routledge.

Rasha-Robinson, L. (6 September 2017) Gay People to Blame for Hurricane Harvey, Say Evangelical Christian Leaders, in *Independent*,
https://www.independnt.co.uk/news/world/americas/gay-people-hurricane-harvey-blame-christian-leaders-texas-fooding

Reardon, J. (2008) Race without Salvation: Beyond the Science/Society Divide in Genomic Studies & Human Diversity, in Koenig, B. A. *et al.* (eds) *Revisiting Race in a Genomic Age.* Rutgers University Press.

Roberts, T. (2005) Sacrifice and Secularization: Derrida, de Vries, and the Future of Mourning, in Sherwood, Y. *et al.* (eds) *Derrida and Religion: Other Testaments.* Psychology Press.

Robock, A. (17 February 2015) The CIA Asked Me about Controlling the Climate – This is Why We Should Worry, in *The Guardian*
https://www.theguardian.com/commetisfree/2015/feb/17/cia-controlling-climate-geoengineering-climate-change.

Rohloff, A. (2011) Shifting the Focus? Moral Panics as Civilizing and Decivilizing Processes, in Hier, S. P. (ed) *Moral Panics and the Politics of Anxiety*. London: Routledge: 71-85

Rohloff, A. (2012) Climate Change, Moral Panics, and Civilization: on the Development of Global Warming as a Social Problem, PhD Thesis. Brunel University.

Rohloff, A. (2013) Moral Panics Civilizing and Decivilizing Processes? A Comparative Discussion in *Política y Sociedad* vol 50 (2): 483-500.

Ross, M. A. (1992) Environmental Warfare and the Persian Gulf War: Possible Remedies to Combat Intentional Destruction of the Environment, in *Penn State International Law Review* vol 10 (3): 515-539.

Saini, A. (22 January 2018) Racism is Creeping Back into Mainstream Science – We Have to Stop it, in *The Guardian*, https://www.thegaurdian.com/commentisfree/2018/jan/22/eugenics-racism-mainstream-sceince

Salter, W. M. 91915) Nietzsche's Superman, in *The Journal of Philosophy, Psychology and Scientific Methods*, 12 (16): 421-438.

Schmidt, C. W. (2006) Unfair Trade e-Waste in Africa, in *Environmental Health Perspectives* vol 114 (4): 232-5.

Schoffeleers, J. M. (ed) (1999) *Guardians of the Land: Essays on Central African Territorial Cults*. Gweru: Mambo Press.

Schofield, T. (1999) The Environment as an Ideological Weapon: A Proposal to Criminalize Environmental Terrorism, in *Boston College Environmental Affairs Law Review*, 26 (3)

Schrift, A. D. (2001) Rethinking the Subject or How One 'Becomes' Other than What One is, in Schacht, R. (ed) *Nietzsche's Postmoralism: Essays on Nietzsche's Prelude to Philosophy's Future*. Cambridge University Press.

Scott, H. H. (1943) The Influence of the Slave-Trade in the Spread of Tropical Disease in *Transactions of the Royal Society of Tropical Medicine and Hygiene* vol 37 (3)

Serdeczny, O. *et al.* (2015) Climate Change Impacts in Sub- Saharan Africa: from Physical Changes to Their Social Repercussion, in *Regional Environmental Change* vol 15 (8)

Shin, H. (2013) Dialectic of Spectrality: A Transpacific Study on Being in the Age of Cyberculture Ph.D. University of Stanford

Sibanda, F. (2012) The Impact of Rastafari Ecological Ethics in Zimbabwe: A Contemporary Discourse, in *The Journal of Pan African Studies* vol 5 (3): 59-76.

Simons, M. (2017) The Parliament of Things and the Anthropocene: How to Listen to Quasi-Objects, in *Techne-Research in Philosophy and Technology* vol 21 (2-3): 1-25.

Sinclair, H. (3 September 2017) Did Gay Sex Cause Hurricane Harvey or Was it Climate Change? Some on the Right Blame LGBT Americans (No Seriously) https://www.newsweek.co/gay-americans-are-blame-human-harvey-apparently

Sirleaf, M. V. S. (2018) Not Your Dumping Ground: Criminalization of Trafficking in Hazardous Waste in Africa, in *Wisconsin International Law Journal* vol 35 (2)

Smith, D. L. *et al* (2015) Aping the Human Essence Simianisation as Dehumanisation https://www.researcgate.net/publication/282359877.

Smith, J. E. (2003) *HAARP: The Ultimate Weapon of the Conspiracy.* Adventure Unlimited Press.

Smith, J. E. (2006) *Weather Warfare: The Military's Plan to Draft Mother Nature.* Adventure Press.

Smith, J. L. (2017) I, River? New Materialism, Riparian NonHuman Agency and the Scale in *Asian Pacific Viewpoint* vol 58 (1): 99-111.

Smith, K. C. (2019) Homo Reductio: Eco-Nihilism and Human Colonization of other World, in *Futures* https://doi.org/10/1016/j.futures.2019.02.005.

Smith, R. K. (2008) "Ecoterrorism"? A Critical Analysis of the Vilification of Radical Environmental Activists as Terrorists, in *Environmental Law* vol 38: 537-576.

Solomon, R. C. (26 January 2007) Pessimism vs Existentialism in the *Chronicle Review* https://www.chronicle.com/article/pesimismvsexisetntialism

Swyngedouw, E. (2009) The Antinomies of the Postpolitical City': in Search of a Democratic Politics of Environmental Production, in *International Journal of Urban and Regional Research* vol 33 (3): 601-20.

Swyngedouw, E. (2010) Apocalypse Forever? In *Theory, Culture & Society* vol 27 (2-3): 2113-232.

Tait, A. G. (2016) Representing Conflict and Environmental Crisis: Fragments from a Speculative Future, in *Studies in Ecocriticism* vol 21 (1): 78-90.

The Guardian. (5 January 2016) South African Woman Faces Criminal Charges over Racist Tweets https:www.thegaurdian.com/world/2016/jan/05/south-african-woman-faces-criminal-charges-racist-tweets

Tong, R. (2000) Duty to Die, in Humber, J. M. *et al* (eds) *Is There a Duty to Die? Biomedical Ethics Reviews*, Humanan Press Totowa, N. J;

UN Environment. (30 January 2018) https://wedocs.unep.org/bitstream/handle/20.500.11822/226 66/BamakoconventionCOP-2 Eng. Pdf?

Vahanian, G. (2009) *The Death of God: The Culture of Our Post-Christian Era*. WIPF & Stock Pub

Van der Broght, E. (2009) *The God-Given Land Religious Perspectives on Land Reform in South Africa* vol 2 Rozenberg Publishers Amsterdam.

Van Paaschen, C. (n.d) Biopolitics and ZoePolitics in a Post-Political Era: Hegemonic Struggle in the Swedish Debate on Foreign Terrorist-Fighters. Lund University

Van Wyk, W. W. C. (2004) African Witchcraft in Theological Perspective in *HTS* vol 60 (4): 1201-1228.

Vanderheiden, S. (2005) Eco-terrorism or Justified Resistance? Radical Environmentalism and the "War on Terror", in *Politics and Society* 33 (3): 425-447.

Von Werlhof, C. (28 November 2017) Earth as Weapon, Geo-engineering as War in Global Research https://www.globalresearch.ca/earth-as-weapon-geoengineering-as-war/5620460

Warde, P. *et al*. (2018) *The Environment: A History of the Idea*. JHU Press.

Warner, J. *et al*. (2017) Securitization of Climate Change: The Risk of Exaggeration, in *Ambiente & Sociedade* vol 20 (3): 203-224.

Warner, J. *et al*. (2019) Securitization of Climate Change: How Invoking Global Dangers of Instrumental Ends Can Back fire, in *Environment and Planning C: Politics and Space* https://doi.org/10.1177/2399654419834018

Weber, J. (2006) From Science and Technology to Feminists Technoscience, https://www.uni-bielefeld.de/ZIF/FG/2006Application/PDF/Weber_essay.pdf

Weiss, H. (2003) Migrations during Times of Drought and Famine in Early Colonial Northern Nigeria, in *Studia Orietnalia* vol 95: 1-29.

Wengel, L. (2015) *Post-Political Numbness of a Digital Society: The Political Condition of Environmental Activism on Twitter.* Jonkoping University.

Wenzel, J. (2018) 'We Have Been Thrown Away': Surplus People Projects and the Logics of Waste, in *Social Dynamics: A Journal of African Studies* vol 44 (2): 184-197.

Windfield, G. (2018) Climate and Colonialism, in *WIRES Climate Change* vol 9 (2)

Wolf, J. (17 January 2005) Pentagon Nixed Developing Gay Aphrodisiac: Pentagon Spurned Plan to Initiate Enemy Homosexuality https://www.chron.com/news/bizzare/aphrodisiac-1923818.php

Yee, D. (2000) *Disposable People: New Slavery in the Global Economy, Kevin Bales.* University of California Press.

Zukauskaite, A. (2013) Politics of Imperceptibility: Philosophy, PostFeminism and New Media Arts, in *Baltic Screen Media Review* vol 1: 67-79.

Zukauskaite, A. (2015) Deleuze and Beckett towards Becoming-Imperceptible, in Wilmer, S. E. *et al.* (eds) *Deleuze and Beckett.* London: Palgrave MacMillan

Chapter Two

The Historiography and Politicisation of Droughts in Colonial Africa

Takavafira Masarira Zhou

Introduction

This chapter examines the intricate and contentious causes of droughts and their impacts during the colonial period in Africa. Both the colonial governments' intervention measures and African people's strategies to ameliorate the effects of droughts are interrogated. The application of recent approaches in environmental history reveals the logic and rationale of indigenous knowledge and organisation in natural resources management in contrast to received colonial western 'scientific' ideas which summarily blame Africans for environmental degradation. The dominant colonial approach was steeped towards an anthropocentric concern with establishing direct relationships between droughts and human activities, particularly as causes of famines, migration and demographic changes. Against this backdrop, this chapter argues that neo-Malthusian environmental narrative which perceives climate change and environmental degradation as products of increases of African populations and their supposedly poor farming practices are nothing but colonial hegemonic and totalising discourses justifying colonial control and use of natural resources. The chapter, therefore, traces the politicisation of droughts in which placing blame on African farmers and pastoralists was a colonial strategy relied upon to justify colonial rule, dispossession, centralisation of planning and control over African natural resources. The chapter stresses that while droughts occurred in pre-colonial Africa, their effects were minimal due to the existence of African coping practices acquired through experimentation and innovation over many years. With the entrenchment of colonial rule, such knowledge and practices were effaced. Considering drought as part of a broader environmental historiography, the chapter hopes to weave the nuances of seasonality and long term adaptations to climatic crises into a coherent historical fabric that recognises local patterns and accommodates changes in ecologies during the colonial period. Case studies from West Africa, East Africa, and Southern Africa will be used to unravel the history of droughts in colonial Africa.

Drought/Climate Historical Background and Definitions

Views of the connection between climate and history in the historical canon have changed substantially since the 1970s. Ladurie's (1988: 1-2) interest in climate history developed as a natural result of work on agricultural and economic change. He argues strongly that climate's effect on human action must be mediated by climate's effect on the physical environment (harvests, forests, water resources, forage) and the subsequent effects on the human habitat, epidemiology, and demography. Bryson and Paddock (2016: 3-4) thrust this perception on human-climate connection further by postulating the principle of 'limiting factors' or the particular features of a given ecology that can be measured over time and that restrict human economic activity. Examples of key factors affecting agriculture and economic activity are temperature, rainfall, and sharp divisions of the seasons. Rainfall rather than temperature is the most relevant climatic limiting factor of food production in Africa. Not surprisingly, Glantz (1987: 15) argues that a meteorological drought is far less damaging than an agricultural drought, and defines an agricultural drought as "the lack of adequate soil moisture to sustain a crop's growth and production." The timing of rainfall and its particular relationship to the constellation of labour, cropping patterns, and capital requirements of specific African farming system is a critical but neglected aspect of both the historical and contemporary development of rural society and economy. Indeed, the patterns of seasonal rainfall trigger social and economic processes of labour, renewal of resources (food, seed, crops, and forage) and the shortage or abundance of harvests.

Climatic history in Africa is a comparatively recent phenomenon, stimulated largely by crises of food supply and perspectives of natural resource degradation since the 1970s (Nicholson, 1979; Webster,

1979). Historians of Africa writing on issues of climate have ventured ambitious conclusions on the basis of extremely weak historical data, drawing broad conclusions about effects of climate on economic, social and demographic change. A case in point is Miller's (1982: 20) work on the climate history of Angola which circumvents the lack of data on rainfall by arguing that:

> Drought is subjectively defined by its sufferers in terms of disappointed expectations of rain and his dissonant cognition of his circumstances. Thus subjective records of human responses to weather available for early centuries may be as useful for assessing the general significance of major droughts in West Central African history as the problematic instrumental record of more recent times.

On the contrary, Rasmussen (1987: 8) gives a more nuanced definition of drought as "an extended and significant negative departure in rainfall relative to the regime around which society has stabilized." As such, drought is a prolonged period of rain deprivation. Like any other natural disaster, a drought arises out of a combination of environmental, economic, social and political factors. The interplay of these factors determines to what extent a system will be disrupted by new and/or suddenly intensified stresses. In this chapter drought is also viewed as a symptom of underdevelopment, and incidentally as one of its causes.

Pre-Colonial African Economies

In order to do justice to the historiography and politicisation of droughts during the colonial period, it is important to examine pre-colonial economies of African communities. Pre-colonial African environmental management theory stressed judicious and efficient land use and holding it in trust for successive generations. According to Cheater (1990), Neocosmos (1987) and Nyambara (2001), 'communal tenure' in indigenous societies meant that because the land and its resources belonged to the community, every full member of such a community had an inalienable right to a reasonable share according to his/her requirements. While acknowledging the existence of political, economic and social differences in pre-colonial

Africa, it is noteworthy that such differences did not restrict a person's right to land more so because land was plentiful. Traditional leaders served as trustees who allotted land to new comers and ensured that its use was in harmony with the traditional land tenure formula as well as environmentally friendly. As succinctly put forward by a Nigerian herder quoted in Lane (1997:43), "Land belongs to a vast family of which many are dead, few are living and countless are still unborn." Zhou (2012:45-46) stresses that environmental consciousness was an expected part of the behaviour of traditional leaders as "people who were of ruling quality but were not able to respectfully preserve the land, the forests, rivers and marshes were not appropriate to become chiefs." Danjumba and Mohammed (2015: 1-4) have shown that indigenous practices such as Zai (ancestral planting pits) provide an effective way of improving the management of degraded lands and reduce soil erosion, vegetation loss and biodiversity as well as grain yields. Zai's importance has been best recorded in Burkina Faso and Niger Republic where people rehabilitated their degraded lands and increased production by many folds.

When faced with exhaustion of land under cultivation, declining yields, increasing labour requirements and pest attacks, African farmers responded by returning the field to nature, and carried on cultivation on another portion of land. A number of scholars, such as Ahn (1970), Nye and Greenland (1960), Hopkins (1974) and Richards (1985), have described the dynamics of 'shifting' cultivation, of which there were numerous systems. A typical Shona family in pre-colonial Zimbabwe would clear about one acre of virgin land by chopping down small trees leaving the trunks standing at a height of one metre, lopping branches off large trees, and later burning them. Many Bantu speaking agriculturalists employed this version of what was once rather loosely termed 'shifting cultivation', but which is better described by Allan's (1965: 6) phrase 'land rotation cultivation.' Moore and Vaughan (1994) have shown how, in the pre-colonial period, farmers in northeast Zambia practised *chitemene*, a system of seasonal land rotation agriculture that required large tracts of land but maximised scarce soil nutrients.

Land rotation cultivation provided ashes that were important in raising the fertility of the soil and improving its friability, while burning also destroyed small weeds and insects pests. Put succinctly, land rotation cultivation had advantages that included sustaining soil fertility, renewing soil texture, pest control and maintaining biodiversity. The nature of the soil and climate, and the nature of crops were crucial in determining the times needed to restore the fertility of a temporarily abandoned field. Be that as it may, most farmers were able to judge, from the appearance of the soil, and in particular the natural vegetation, when an area had become adequately restored for fresh use. Such rational cropping potential was undoubtedly relevant to successful and appropriate environmental land management. As such, land rotation agriculturalists had a rich fund of ecological knowledge of the various succession stages of tree regeneration, which they used to determine the fertility of the land for cropping and various cropping strategies employed on the land under cultivation. It was an adaptation to an environment of relatively sparse population and abundant land, which allowed the soil ample time to recover its fertility and also prevented soil erosion. Arguably, land management practices and indigenous agricultural innovation in pre-colonial Africa constituted sustainable use of natural resources, and encouraged the regeneration of vegetation.

Iliffe (2007) asserts that Africa's agricultural systems were historically mobile, in order to adapt to the environment and the climate rather than transforming them. Most livestock economies in Africa chose to follow the movement of moisture and pasture rather than stock-piling their animal's food supply. It is noteworthy that herders traditionally raised animals for their milk and hides, as drought insurance, and for the social status they conferred upon their owners. Herders' preferences to migrate droughts were translucently tuned judgements about species' needs for food and moisture, as well as their capacity to work and serve as a form of wealth. Yet, as usual, there has been an infinite set of variations and exceptions. McCann (1999: 274) shows that, in northern Ethiopia, farmers did not move with the seasons but rotated the planting of cereals peas and beans (pulses), and there was fallowing in the fashion finely tuned to the arrival and departure of summer rains followed by a long dry season. In eastern Sudan, camel-herding Hadendowa planted sorghum in moist riveran soils and then retreated with their animals to distant wet season pastures until the harvest was ready, eight months later. McCann (1999: 275) has further shown that the Maasai of East Africa historically followed pasture with their herds of cattle and goats, carefully avoiding full contact with thickets of acacia scrub infested with tsetse flies bearing deadly trypanosomiasis (sleeping sickness).

In light of the recursiveness of rainfall and harvest variability, it is not surprising that African communities were geared to environmental risk, and possessed adaptive flexibility and adjustment capability with respect to drought and oscillations in the availability of food. The existence of precarious environment gave rise in many peasant societies to a subsistence ethic predicated upon a safety-first or risk aversion principle. This involved a plethora of locally adapted cereal varieties, a preference for the consumable as opposed to the marketable, or reliance on historically established planting and intercropping strategies. The fundamental agronomic strategy consisted of intercropping of sorghums and millets, each characterised by contrasting moisture requirements. This complementarity was propped up by what Watts (1983: 29) calls "a complex orchestration of microenvironments involving variations in spacing, moisture availability, and soil type, all of which were conjoined through complicated sequential patterns of decision - dependent upon the onset, character, and duration of the rains." Such adaptive programs could be supplemented by other drought resistant crops, such as cassava, or the resort to foraging, hunting and gathering. Zhou (2012: 90-92) asserts that in pre-colonial Zimbabwe, the Shona and Ndebele guaranteed security from droughts by cultivating traditional crops such as sorghum, bulrush millet and finger millet that, through indigenous knowledge systems, could be stored for five to six years. Conversely, agricultural diversity and agronomic variation bred a systematic stability.

The subsistence ethic was also expressed through social activities and institutions that functioned, *inter-alia*, as guarantors of a minimal food supply. Shortage was essential to the preservation of a measure of self-sufficiency and permitted the long term constitution of reserves sufficient to cover seed requirements and grain during the period of pre-harvest hunger. During the wet season, when seasonal food shortages peaked, hardships could be partially alleviated by participation in communal work parties. However, central to the subsistence ethic and to the moral economy in general, was the 'logic of gift'; the reciprocal and redistributive qualities which bound peasant fabrics, and by which the possibility of accumulation found an institutional obligation to redistribute. The inflated emphasis on the role of kinship and descent grouping generally was one way in which risks were diffused and collective security instituted. In pre-colonial Zimbabwe, chiefs owned fields in every community whose products were harvested and placed in communal granaries, and only distributed to communities during times of scarcity (Zhou, 2012). All in all, in societies predicated upon absolute hierarchical segmentation between rulers and subjects, it is conceivable that the upper echelons of political authority in pre-colonial Africa were expected to act as the ultimate buffer for the village level redistributive operations. It was precisely colonialism and expanded commodity production, as will be shown below, that severed households from these reciprocal ties. This severance magnified vulnerability to droughts.

The Advent of Colonialism in Africa

At the Berlin Conference of 1884, European powers outlined the doctrine of effective occupation of Africa, which was a powerful stimulus to actual European invasion on the ground in order to make good the claims made on maps. Consequently, between 1885 and 1912 all the continent, with the exception of Ethiopia and Liberia, was overrun by European-led military forces and brought under European colonial rule (Zhou, 2018: 75-76). Colonialism integrated African economies within the orbit of the global capitalist economy. Colonialism transformed the social relation of production throughout Africa. Pre-capitalist farmers and herders' economic independence was eroded by colonial integration, their adaptive capability and margin of subsistence security accordingly changed for the worse. In the process African farmers and herders became less capable of responding to, and coping with, droughts and food shortages. It is within this framework that the politicisations of droughts by colonialists, or the labelling of African farming methods as poor and responsible for droughts and climate change, must be dismissed with the greatest contempt they deserve. Case studies from the Sahel region of West Africa, Kenya in East Africa and Zimbabwe in Southern Africa unravel the historiography and politicisation of droughts in colonial Africa.

The Sahel Region of West Africa

Murray (1989) defines the Sahel as the eco-climatic and bio-geographic zone of transition in Africa between the Sahara desert to the north and Savanna of the higher rainfall, termed the Sudanian zone, to the south. Having a semi-arid climate, it stretches across the south-central latitudes of Northern Africa between the Atlantic Ocean and the Red Sea. According to Huntington (1834: 287) the name is derived from the Arabic word *sahil* meaning 'coast' or 'shore' in a figurative sense (in reference to the southern edge of the vast Sahara), while the name in Swahili means 'coastal dweller' in a literal sense. The Sahel part of Africa includes (from west to east) parts of northern Senegal, southern Mauritania, central Mali, northern Burkina Faso, the extreme south of Algeria, Niger, the extreme north of Nigeria, central Chad, central and southern Sudan, the extreme north of South Sudan, Eritrea, Cameroon, Central African Republic and the extreme north of Ethiopia. However, this case study is largely confined to Sahel region of West Africa (including parts of Gambia). Historically, the western part of the Sahel was sometimes known as the Sudan region. This belt was roughly located between the Sahara and the coastal areas of West Africa.

Brief Pre-Colonial Sahel Economy

Pre-colonial economy of the Sahel region was fundamentally similar to the pre-colonial African economy outlined above. Fundamentally, people of the Sahel region developed complex farming and herding systems that were adapted to the environment. Farmers raised indigenous crops such as sorghum and millet in areas where there was sufficient rainfall. They developed patterns of land rotation cultivation that allowed soils to be replenished by fallow periods of up to twenty years. Dunsmore *et al.* (1976: 12, 19) have shown how other farmers irrigated crops in the floodplains of the major rivers such as the Niger, Senegal, and Gambia. Through this flood recession cultivation they were able to plant different crops as the water receded. Similarly, herders developed various pastoral systems. Some engaged in nomadic pastoralism in the northern areas bordering the Sahara. Others affianced in transhumant pastoralism often moved north in the rainy season and south during the dry season, and engaged in agro-pastoralism. Another traditional system of livestock farming, sedentary animal husbandry, developed in the southern, higher rainfall zones, but was less important compared to cultivation there. As put forward by Baier (1976), while at times there were tensions between the farmers and herders competing for limited resources, in large measure they had a mutually beneficial relationship in which the herders provided milk, manure, and other animal products to the farmers in exchange for food grains and use of crop residues after harvests. Much as both farmers and herders produced food primarily for their own subsistence, they also produced enough surplus to feed small non-agricultural populations as well as to survive periodic droughts.

Colonial Conquest of the Sahel Region

During the latter part of the 19th century, the French conquered much of the Sahel while Britain established control over Gambia. These changes disrupted traditional production systems. Under colonial rule, colonies were regarded as providers of raw materials to Europe; the colonies were also consumers of manufactured products. Once the French and British gained administrative control of the Sahel in the 1890s, they promoted export crops, especially groundnuts and cotton, damaged local artisan industries by giving favoured tax status to European goods, and forced rural people into the cash economy by demanding payment of taxes in cash. In the process African farmers and herders became less capable of responding to, and coping with droughts and food shortages. Traditional mechanisms and adjustments disappeared, the extension of cash cropping undermined self-sufficiency in foodstuffs, a dependence on volatile world commodity prices (for cotton and groundnuts) amplified an already high tax burden and households became increasingly vulnerable to environmental perturbations such as droughts and harvest shortfalls. This vulnerability and marginality is epitomised by periodic droughts and famines in the Sahel region, the major ones occurring in 1910 to 1914, 1927, 1930, 1940, 1942, 1944 and 1951 (Watts, 1983:30; Caldwell, 1975). The whole colonial period up to independence in 1958 for Senegal and 1960 for the other countries, the Sahel region experienced recurrent droughts.

Politicisation of Droughts in the Sahel Region

The French's politicisation of droughts or the blame of African farming methods for causing droughts and climate change during the colonial period was a product of colonial manipulation of reality and fertile imagination of colonial foresters. The process now called desertification emerged in West Africa in the 1920s, as a result of concerns by French colonial administrators, foresters and social scientists about the perceptible progressive drying out of large areas of their Sahelian colonies, and a presumed extension of the Sahara. In the 1930s these worries spread to English-speaking colonies. A forester from the Indian Forest Service, Stebbing, made a tour in 1934 through British and French colonies in West Africa and up across the Sahara, after which he propagated his findings and became very influential. As put forward by Stebbing (1937a:31):

> The present-day results of investigations would appear to prove that the Sahara is far from stationary on its Southern frontiers; that blown sand and desiccation are increasing in the colonies lying in juxtaposition to the desert, and that the present method of agricultural livelihood of the population living in these regions, with their unchecked action of firing the country side annually, and methods of pasturage – all tend to assist sand penetration, drying up of water supplies, and desiccation.

Stebbing (1938: 12-13) spelled out elaborately that in West Africa the advancing Sahara:

> ... owes its commencement to the system of farming the bush or degraded type of form of shifting cultivation. With an increasing population the same areas are refarmed at shorter intervals, with a consequent more rapid deterioration of the soil constituents, until a stage is reached when the soil is no longer sufficiently productive for

agriculture. It may then be made over for stock-raising. The grazing and browsing, accompanied by the universal practice of annually firing the countryside, reduces the quality, height and density and therefore forest or bush, and the soil becomes covered with sandy top, gradually increasing in depth. Once this stage has developed the rapidity in the degradation of the bush increases until it no longer affords sustenance to cattle; then the sheep disappears; and under the final exploitation by goat herds to feed their flocks the savannah succumbs and the desert has encroached and extended its boundaries.

It was Stebbing's (1937a: 33) conviction that the prime factors in the process of desertification were indigenous forms of land use, made more damaging by population growth resulting from the ending of "local warfare" and "improvements in health", resulting in a reduced area available for cultivation, and a large increase in animal numbers. He also posited that there was a feedback from damaging land use to reduced or more intermittent rainfall, though he did not spell out how this mechanism operated. Stebbing (1937b:24) gave one of the earliest estimates of the rate of southward advance of the desert, quoting a retired French colonial administrator who believed that in Mali and Niger the Sahara had advanced at an average of one kilometre a year during the previous three centuries. Stebbing (1938: 24) also reported that the desert was accelerating. His work was influential, and the main features of his analysis shaped succeeding writers on desertification. He also prodded the British and French into action.

Consequently, a joint Anglo-French Forestry Commission was established in 1936-7 for the express purpose of ascertaining the extent of desert encroachment across West Africa and the degree to which it was being accelerated by African farmers and herders. The Anglo-French Forestry Commission (1937: 8) discovered no instances of large-scale sand movement; on the contrary, it found that dunes had been largely stable since the desiccation of the Sahara in Late Quaternary times. It further noted that although there were clear signs of localised sand encroachment due to the cultivation of marginal soils, this was offset by evidence of countermovement in other areas. The Commission (1937: 7) observed that ground water levels did not suggest any general climatic desiccation in recent times, nor was there much evidence of receding woodlands: "there is no lack of natural regeneration and in some places it is even abundant."

A geographer and former member of the Anglo-French Commission, Stamp (1940) pointed to several shortcomings of Stebbing's analysis, including especially his assumption that Savanna vegetation was degraded forest. He lamented the lack of interdisciplinary analysis in what was essentially an ecological matter, and concluded that there was little evidence for desiccation as an autonomous mechanism, but that such a problem as existed was mainly one of soil erosion. In Stamps' (1940: 300) words:

> There now seems to be little doubt that the problem before West Africa is not the special one of Saharan encroachment but the universal one of man-induced soil erosion, which necessitates remedial measures comparable with those being adopted in other parts of the world but with special modification in view of the local agricultural system of bush fallowing and burning.

The findings of the Anglo-French Forestry Commission (1937) as well as Stamps' warning not to confuse the observed change in vegetation from forest to grassland, along a transect from wetter to drier areas with the process of progressive degradation at the drier end, was largely ignored. The debate on desertification along Stebbing's perception continued in the 1940s, 1950s, 1960s and thereafter.

Charney *et al.* (1975, 1977) give a bio-geophysical analysis behind the recurrence of droughts in the Sahel region. They argue that removal of vegetation by human activity such as deforestation and livestock grazing increased the reflectivity or albedo of the land surface and led to a reduction in the radiative heating of the atmosphere, causing enhanced subsidence and reducing the potential for convective rainfall. According to Lamprey (1975), the Sahara continued to advance in the north Kordofan region of Sudan after 1958. He further asserts that ecological degradation was largely due to past and current land use practices accelerated during periods of drought. Lamprey (1975: 16) argues that sand encroachment was "… the result of several thousand years of abuse of the fragile ecosystems which formerly existed in the Sahara and Nubia areas." In his conclusion Lamprey (1975: 20) remarked that there was a "… need to educate the rural population, particularly as many of the problems are due to traditional and hitherto unquestioned practices." Yet, as shown below, the real need was to educate the colonial government about the realities of development in a highly variable, semi-arid environment.

It is imperative to explain the politicisation of droughts during the colonial period or why the false assumption that African farmers and herders' supposedly poor systems of economy caused droughts and famine during the colonial period. Such assumptions remained topical despite lack of evidence. The Stebbing controversy of the 1930s, with its roots in French colonial botany of the previous decades, took place at a time when France, having recently completed the conquest of the Sahelian countries, was setting up and seeking to justify a large and highly centralised natural resource management bureaucracy on the French metropolitan model. The assumption that local herders and farmers had such inefficient systems of land use that they were destroying the land was, at the very least, a convenient one at such a moment. Periods of drought reinforced that perception for outsider observers unused to the inter-annual variability of the Sahelian climate. Outside observers were also closeted by Europeans and Americans' pre-occupation with the issue of desertification as a result of the Dust-bowl phenomenon in the United States (Anglo-French Forestry Commission, 1937). It is perhaps significant, as Swift (1996: 87) notes, that it was in general soldiers, administrators and foresters (the most military of civil servants in the French system) who argued the desertification case most strongly, and geographers, geologists and other scientists who were most sceptical.

Desertification justified increasing control by natural resource bureaucracies, such as the planning, forest and wildlife or national parks services, over land, and those within and without such services who benefitted by such arrangements were among the most vocal in support of national anti-desertification plans (Swift, 1996: 87). As such, colonial regimes in Africa used alarmist predictions of environmental crisis to legitimise state policies aimed at wresting control of natural resources from local communities for the benefit of outside interests. In the name of 'environmental protection', colonial governments and their corollary conservation groups

81

promoted regulations that came at the expense of local farmers, hunters, and forest-users whose livelihoods depended on natural resources. The desertification narrative provided colonial governments with an internationally accepted excuse to be nasty about and to pastoralists. Desertification was, therefore, used as a rationale for colonial governments to evict pastoralists from traditional grazing areas in the Sahel. All in all, the desertification narrative, with its implicit threat to the survival of whole dry land economies, was used to justify politically authoritarian colonial actions.

The assumption that indigenous land use practices had a detrimental effect on the Sahelian environment leading to land degradation and desertification was based to a large extent on the concept of carrying capacity. Mortimore (1998) provide evidence from parts of the Sahel and from other semi-arid parts of Africa that strongly challenges ideas that land degradation and desertification is the result of the approaching or breaching of carrying capacities. He provides evidence that shows that productivity and soil fertility have been maintained in parts of the Sahelian zones of northern Nigeria and Niger, despite reduced rainfall and increased population densities. Mortimore and Adams (2001) argue that successful adaptation to climatic desiccation in these areas was achieved through more intensive but small-scale agricultural practices involving higher livestock densities, soil and water conservation, crop diversification and integrated farm management approaches. Timmer *et al.* (1996) describe indigenous management techniques of trees in central Burkina Faso as having contributed to a sustainable use of tree resources. Fairhead and Leach (1996) have described how indigenous land management practices south of the Sahel in Guinea led to increases in forest density, refuting the view that Guinea forests are simply the remnants of continuous woodland that has been cleared for agriculture.

By and large, the evidence given above clearly associates large-scale observed changes in the Sahelian land surface to climatically-driven oscillations of the location of the transition zone from the semi-arid Sahel to the arid Sahara, and convincingly refutes perceptions that regional-scale changes in the Sahelian region coupled with land-atmosphere system were due to the systematic abuse of the land by African farmers and herders. Such assertions were nothing other than patent *obiter dicta* to justify colonial rule, central planning, and colonial control of rural resources. What has been interpreted as desertification in many instances was nothing other than the natural response of semi-arid landscapes and ecosystems to climatic variability. This is not to suggest that there were no challenges associated with over-exploitation of natural resources and more localised land degradation resulting from human activity, but that such scenarios were largely generated by colonialism rather than farmers and herders as reflected below.

Vulnerability to Droughts: African Farmers and Herders under Colonial Rule

By integrating African economies into the economic systems of the industrialised countries, colonialism progressively wrecked African ecosystems, increasing their vulnerability to droughts. Ball (1978: 276) argues that the entrenchment of colonial rule in West Africa in the late 1890s witnessed increased imports of European goods that virtually destroyed indigenous industries such as blacksmithing and weaving thereby causing the decline of caravanning – an important source of income, especially in drought years, for some pastoralists. Worse still the entrenchment of colonial rule also witnessed the promotion of crops which were useful to the French and British industries, primarily groundnuts and cotton. Not surprisingly, Wolof and Serer farmers in Senegal and Gambia dedicated more and more of their land and labour to peanut production in order to obtain cash needed to pay taxes and purchase the goods they no longer produced as well as new consumer goods. Colonial rulers also cleared new lands for groundnut cultivation by conscripting men into forced labour brigades, a practice that was not abolished until 1946 (Ball, 1978: 285). As such, the need to produce ever-increasing amounts of export crops led to intensification of production in more populated areas and to expansion of farming into areas with poorer soils and less regular and less abundant rainfall than the older agricultural regions.

The advent of colonialism witnessed growth without development due to the over-dependence on one or two exports.

Rodney (1972: 256) asserts that in Senegal and Gambia, groundnuts accounted for 85% to 90% of monetary earnings. Fundamentally, the two African colonies were forced to grow nothing but peanuts. The concentration on one or two cash-crops for sale abroad had many harmful effects, as sometimes; cash-crops were grown to the exclusion of staple foods – thus causing famines. Rodney (1972: 257) argues that in Gambia "rice farming was popular before the colonial era, but so much of the best land was transferred to groundnuts that rice had to be imported on a large scale to try and counter the fact that famine was becoming endemic." Yet the threat of famine was a small disadvantage compared to the extreme vulnerability and insecurity of mono-culture, which left African producers helpless in the face of capitalist manoeuvres. Conversely, an expansion of cash crops for export – particularly cotton and groundnuts – which was encouraged since the beginning of colonial period in Sahel region occurred to the detriment of food crops such as sorghum, millet and rice. The reduced emphasis on the local production of food crops, during the colonial period, together with a gradual erosion of the indigenous forms of food storage and distribution of surplus food via the local leaders meant that the rural population became increasingly vulnerable to food shortages.

With the expansion of the French oil industry after the Second World War, demand for groundnuts also increased. Ball (1978: 285) posits that the high levels of rainfall after 1951 encouraged northward movement of peasants into lands previously devoted to herding. The good weather conditions of this period helped to obscure the dangers inherent in this strategy. Increased population, without a concomitant intensification of peanut production, put pressure on the land in the Peanut Basin. Consequently, fallowing, the traditional means of restoring some fertility to the soil was curtailed, eventually giving rise to semi-continuous cultivation in some areas, and ultimately reducing fertility and yields. According to Grove (1973: 41) cultivators moved to new lands, at first good lands, but later increasingly marginal lands, sometimes disrupting the migratory patterns of the pastoralists; others moved to cities. He also points to loss of soil fertility in the old coastal groundnut-producing regions, such as Senegal. Caldwell (1975: 46) argues that the loss of fertility led to wind and rain erosion, and subsequent deterioration of the soil in the cotton growing regions, particularly Chad, and around large towns, especially Zinder in southern Niger. As put forward by DuBois (1973: 9-10), the clearing of land for groundnut and cotton production purposes and deforestation resulting from the need for firewood and timber contributed to erosion and, again, were noticeable around large towns. By and large, the opportunities for guarding against these harmful practices were limited as the emphasis during the colonial period was on increasing production of export crops, not on conservation.

In the pastoral areas, overgrazing was induced, to a large extent, by the alteration of the pastoral environment by colonialists. Pastoral economies had been shaped by the need to exist within an essentially hostile environment in pre-colonial Sahel region. The level of technology in a pastoral society was low, and its means of manipulating its natural environment were limited. An extensive knowledge of the soil, plant life, and water resources of the Sahel was built up over centuries. According to Laya (1975), methods designed to mitigate the harmful effects of climatic changes included migrations of varying lengths, changes in herd composition, controlled reproduction of animals, and caravanning. Attempts by the French to integrate the Sahelian livestock sector into a commercialised economic system during the colonial period worked to negate the impact of some of these indigenous means of combating droughts. Ball (1978: 286) posits that the freedom of movement of pastoralists was increasingly curtailed, first by the creation of colonial boundaries and the introduction of the *laissez-passer*, and subsequently by the definition of international borders. Equally important were restrictions on the use of river-flooded land, increasingly used for irrigated farming, which had hitherto provided important dry season grazing reserves.

Baier (1976: 8) is of the view that technical innovations in pastoral areas after 1950 disrupted the animal-water-fodder balance and must be blamed to a large extent for overgrazing. The proliferation of deep boreholes in some pastoral zones – each of which replaced several shallow wells because of the much larger volume of water produced – diminished the amount of pasture available to the animals, since the latter could only travel a limited distance away from their water supply to graze. Droughts greatly intensified the problems generated by the boreholes. As submitted by Laya (1975: 57), in the past deteriorating pastures had been preceded by wells running dry, so that herders were forced to leave for the south before pasture was completely degraded. However, the ready availability of water from boreholes long after pasture had seriously deteriorated upset the balance between the two resources, and the old signal to leave the arid lands no longer operated. Above all, boreholes functioned to trap herders in the desert. Laya (1976: 70-93) argues that near the large wells herders were making the two day trek to and fro; as conditions worsened, pasture deteriorated in a widening radius. Conversely, the areas surrounding the boreholes became increasingly overgrazed and during drought years livestock died in large quantities around the wells, not out of thirst but out of hunger and consequent exhaustion. After 1950, the availability of water was far out of balance with the condition of pasture thereby making herders vulnerable to droughts. All in all, the official encouragement of irrigated agriculture along river banks, the installation of wells and boreholes, restrictions on herders' movements combined during the colonial period to break down the very systems of pasture division, constructed and implemented by pastoralists themselves, that had been designed to minimise both overgrazing and conflict between pastoral groups.

By and large, the problems of ecological degradation that faced the Sahel zone in West Africa can be seen to have arisen partly from the implementation of colonial policies designed primarily to obtain immediate financial and material benefits by colonialists. Such investments as were made were localised and little attention was paid to their potentially harmful social and ecological impact. This emanated from colonialists' production for profit rather than for well-being of African community as a whole. The rational exploitation of natural resources over the long term in this situation was accorded low priority because it was difficult to place a monetary value on the protection of range land or the conservation of water, while a ton of groundnuts or piece of machinery had a definite price. Colonial administrators appear to have ignored warnings from colonial Veterinary Service and other groups that unless range management were pursued in conjunction with other improvements, severe ecological degradation was likely to occur.

Global Temperature Patterns and Effects on the Sahel Region

Modulation of the African Monsoon by regional and global patterns of sea-surface temperatures provides the best explanation for variation in Sahelian rainfall on multi-year to decadal timescales. Lamb (1978) points to a casual effect between lower-ocean surface temperatures in the Atlantic north of the equator and higher ones to the south as having been responsible for an overall global warming that ensued in the Sahel during the 20th century. Folland *et al.* (1986) argue that relationship between sea-surface temperature patterns and Sahelian rainfall are well established from statistically-based climatological analyses and have been used with some success in seasonal rainfall forecasts in the region. Follard *et al.* (1986) demonstrated that dry conditions in the Sahel have been associated with a particular configuration of global sea-surface temperature patterns characterised by positive (warm) anomalies in the southern hemisphere and northern Indian Oceans, and negative (cool) anomalies in the remaining northern hemisphere oceans. Giannini *et al.* (2003) further identifies sea-surface temperatures as the principal driver of Sahelian rainfall variability, which they model successfully for the period 1930-2000 using only sea-surface temperature forcing, and a model that also represents land-atmosphere interaction via moisture feedbacks. This may, therefore, explain the recurrent drought periods lasting one or two decades that have been a persistent feature of the Sahel over the past 520 years.

Therefore, desertification seems more attributable to global climatic processes than local African farmers and herders' actions. As such, ocean temperatures, especially the Hadley circulation in the North Atlantic, had a far greater role in determining rainfall patterns by affecting the position of the Inter Tropical Convergence Zone. Yet sound as this may appear, it must never close out the impact of land surface feedback that emanated from colonial policies designed primarily to obtain immediate financial and material benefits, as demonstrated above.

Politicisation of Drought in Kenya

The British Empire established the East Africa Protectorate in 1895, from 1920 known as the Kenya Colony. Colonial narratives portrayed the area occupied by Africans in Kenya as a crucible for a series of crises, including human and livestock epidemics, 'overgrazing', soil erosion, droughts, low productivity, underdevelopment, fuel wood shortage, biodiversity loss, and threatened wildlife. African farmers and herders in Kenya recounted a very different story in which land alienation, land hunger, and limits on mobility of people and their herds by the colonialists restructured the ecological and spatial order of their homeland, to the benefit of White settlers and the detriment of many Blacks. The history of crisis construction and resolution by outsiders, juxtaposed with the diverse experience of people within Kenya reflect the politicisation of droughts in order to justify colonialism and control of natural resources by colonialists.

The effects of drought were minimal on African societies in pre-colonial Kenya because of a number of factors. Fundamentally, their mixed economy of crop cultivation and pastoral activities shielded them from the whims of nature. African farmers grew sorghum, millet, maize, beans, sweet potatoes, bananas, squash, sugarcane, and other crops in addition to keeping livestock (cattle, goats, and sheep). As put forward by Ochieng (1988:23), persistent starvation (*midenyo*) was a colonial phenomenon as before "the whites came our people were better fed." When crops failed African farmers fell back on animals and fish products. It was rare that animals and crop diseases struck at the same time. Land and manpower were readily available and during land rotation cultivation and harvesting everybody was involved. Apart from cultivating drought resistant millets, such as *ochut, andiwo* and *kal*, and drought resistant traditional maize (*ndere*), the Kikuyu, Luo, Akamba and Luyia also relied a lot on wild vegetables which they fell back onto when drought and food shortages persisted. Brett (1973) argues that the Luo ate a variety of wild fruits in times of droughts and food scarcity. Apart from livestock, fish and birds, wild animal meat also constituted a regular source of protein for African communities in pre-colonial Kenya. Livestock and crop surpluses were rarely sold and every married man was obliged to have his food store (*mondo*) which was only used when the general family stores (*derè*) were depleted. Above all, the elastic kinship system of the extended family guaranteed redistribution of food during periods of droughts and starvation (*mindenyo*). According to Bernard and Thorn (1981), Lambert (1947) and Wailer (1985), a mix of private and common property rights, integrated crop-livestock systems, spatially separated holdings, flexible patterns of settlement and mobility, and mutual reciprocity arrangements served to limit vulnerability and provided mechanisms for coping with drought. Thus, unless there was a terrible natural calamity the African economy and social institutions guaranteed sufficient food for everybody.

The impact of colonialism on traditional Kenyan societies, cultures and economies was largely negative. Kennedy (1987) and Mosley (1983) argue that British Kenyan economic policy was very largely determined by the need to maintain the viability to maintain White settler agriculture. Various land and labour laws that were enacted in favour of settlers throughout the colonial period (1895-1963) were tailor-made to guarantee incentives to White settlers. Such land appropriation and labour demands contributed to land degradation and made African societies such as the Kikuyu Luo, Akamba, Luyia and Maasai vulnerable to droughts and famines. There were seven main colonial droughts and famines in Kenya in 1897-1900, 1906-7, 1917-19, 1928-29, 1931-34, 1942-43, 1951-52 and 1961.

During the early colonial period, human and cattle diseases were part of the crises identified by administrators and travellers in Kenya. Hardinge (1899) and Wamalwa (1989) argue that the 1890s saw the construction of the Uganda Railroad, which also contributed to the spread of rinderpest among cattle as well as the introduction of smallpox by European foreigners. These forces combined with a drought in the late 1890s to bring about the great famine of 1897-1901 (Ambler, 1988). Since cattle served as the main drought insurance, the results of combined drought and cattle disease were devastating. Viewing the devastation around them, colonial officials and observers, while recognising the epidemics, blamed African cattle-rearing practices as well as their supposedly 'primitive' standards of living for the magnitude of the disaster. Rocheleau *et al.*

(1995: 1040) assert that colonial observers identified several reasons for the African farmers and herders' supposedly low standard of living, accusing them of weakness of character, irrational attachment to their cattle, and inefficient and destructive cultivation practices. Assuming that famine resulted from African social and agricultural practices, colonial authorities defined a 'public health crisis' among the African societies. Blaming African farmers and herders for epidemics which plagued Kenyan societies during the 1890s reflected European experiences and prejudices; the epidemics themselves derived from contact with European people and livestock.

In Kenya, the bankruptcy of the Imperial East Africa Company following the construction of the Mombasa-Kisumu railway line between 1896 and 1901, led to extensive land seizure in the period 1901-1905 in order to promote settler settlement (Mosley, 1983). By seizing land, the Company achieved two things simultaneously. It provided Whites with land and it created conditions whereby landless Africans were impelled to work not just to pay taxes but also to survive. The colonial government also prevented Africans from growing cash crops so that they would survive by working for the Whites. According to Rodney (1972: 180) one of Kenya's White settlers, Colonel Grogan, put it bluntly when he said of the Kikuyu: "We have stolen his land. Now we must steal his limbs. Compulsory labour is the corollary of our occupation of the country." As early as 1906 the effect of labour migration began to tell among the Kikuyu, Luo, Akamba and Luyia. Goldsworthy (1982: 5-6) argues that death due to sleeping sickness early in the century and continued expatriation of African men to work outside their homelands greatly affected rural agricultural production. The grain surpluses (*mondo*) which the men used to store in the past were no more. A considerable number of cattle were sold to pay taxes, while others had been confiscated during colonial punitive expeditions. It followed, therefore, that Africans were more vulnerable to drought and famine as they no longer had surpluses to fall back on. Not surprisingly the failure of the 1906 November rains was followed by the 1907 famine which killed hundreds of people (Ochieng, 1988: 26-27). Despite the fact that the colonial government had precipitated the 1906-1907 famine, through their labour policies and neglect of African agriculture, it still politicised drought and famine by blaming African agriculturalists for cultivating in what it termed the 'usual superficial manner' (Ochieng, 1988: 26).

In Kenya, as in many parts of Africa, droughts have always catalysed famines, while the real causes of famines lie hidden in mistaken human policies and environmental deterioration. There were no fundamental changes in British labour and economic policies in the land of Kikuyu, Luo, Akamba and Luyia after the 1907 famine. Even though the colonialists encouraged Africans to grow cotton, simsim and maize as cash crops after 1907, by no means did this reduce African vulnerability to droughts and famines. During the First World War, large numbers of Africans were recruited for the Carriers Corps and colonial farms. According to Ogot (1967) and Ochieng (1985), by 1916 the methods of recruitment were very brutal so that many Africans living in the proximity of the Uganda protectorate crossed the boundary to reside in Uganda territory. Similarly, by 1920 thousands of Kikuyu, Luo, and Luyia in Kenya had settled on the coast to work in coconut or sisal plantations (Mosley, 1983; Berman and Lonsdale, 1992). With so many young men living outside their homelands, rural agricultural labour was depleted. Only women and old men remained in the villages. Not surprisingly, the limited rains at the end of 1917 turned into critical shortage of food from 1918 to 1919. Population pressure in rural areas and taxation, impelled Africans to work on colonial European farms. Ochieng (1988: 29) posits that by 1928 more than half of the able-bodied men in the two largest African nationalities (the Kikuyu and Luo) were working for Europeans.

By 1920, the African communities had lost effective access to about two-thirds of the land they had formerly controlled including their most fertile lands and half of all their pasture. Munro (1975), Spencer (1983), and Wisner (1977) assert that along with some of their best grazing land, African agriculturalists and herders lost the freedom to migrate seasonally and periodically in search of water, pasture, and cropland. For the Akamba, Kikuyu, Luo, Luyia and Maasai, the crisis of the era was one of land alienation, as settlers disrupted their tenure system and took away their land. Spencer (1983) argues that these policies contributed to a continuing crisis of cattle disease; agro-pastoralists were left with few options other than to preserve underfed and sickly cattle, their major assets, in

91

overcrowded reserves where diseases spread easily. These colonial land tenure policies also forced the African societies into sedentary settlements and continuous cultivation on relatively small areas of poor quality land. This process of sedentarisation and concentration, in turn, sowed the seeds of future crises, including those of land degradation, overpopulation, and urban migration. Despite some innovations in African agriculture during the colonial period, including the acquisition of ploughs, water-power flour mills, harrows and maize hulling machines by certain wealth *Kulaks* (Mosley, 1983), African agriculture in Kenya remained marginalised. Africans found it on balance more lucrative, or congenial, to work for hire than to exert themselves in cultivation of unfamiliar and inedible crops such as cotton. They, therefore, became more vulnerable to droughts and famines as was the case in 1928-1929. Harlow *et al.* (1965: 147) show how Africans were vulnerable to a disastrous drought in Kenya from 1931 to 1934; they were reduced to starvation due to the famine that ensued from 1933.

Munro (1975) submits that land alienation, land scarcity, and official policy resulted, by the early 1930s, in continuous cultivation of land and enclosure of permanent farms with fences or sisal hedges. Indeed, this entailed decreased fallow and more continuous cropping, which, combined with the concurrent replacement of sorghum and millet with maize. It also resulted in soil exhaustion and reduced yields. The remaining commonage was under severe pressure as a source of forage and wood, particularly because many farmers were growing cash crops, ploughing up their grazing land and putting increased pressure on the commons. As put forward by Silberfein (1989), land sales, tenancy and landlessness, became features of African life. Munro (1975) and Mutiso (1975) argue that social stratification based on land holdings emerged and land disputes became common. Conversely, as land tenure and land use systems underwent transformation, so did dominant economic activities within African societies. Scarcity of pastureland, along with other financial and administrative pressures, resulted in an overall decrease in Akamba and Maasai cattle wealth and a drastic decline, for most households, in livestock holdings. By the beginning of the Second World War, significant numbers of herders had turned to crop cultivation (Munro, 1975).

Much as colonial officials and settlers were increasingly aware of land degradation on the Native Reserves (Dregne, 1990), they unfortunately politicised it. Rather than linking this phenomenon with the successive forces of land theft, population concentration, and disruption of African land tenure and land use systems, colonial officials instead attributed droughts and soil erosion crisis to supposedly poor African cattle-rearing and agricultural practices. While the colonial government continued with the official policies to repress African livestock production and quarantine their cattle (Spencer, 1983), White settlers waged a successful campaign to portray African agriculture as a kind of contagion, spreading insidiously across the landscape and infecting productive European lands. According to Myrick (1975) and Spencer (1983) the 1929 Hall Commission report raised erosion in Machakos to the status of a major hazard in Kenya. Jacks and Whyte (1939: 270) assert that a witness before the Kenya Land Commission opined, "The African people have never established a symbiotic relationship with the land. They are, in the strict scientific sense, parasites on the land, all of them." The poor condition of the reserves and settler political fears coalesced in 1935 with both the global anti-erosion movement and the reaction to the 'Dust Bowl' in the United States. McCracken (1982) argues that the concern over a soil erosion crisis was exacerbated by the new professionalism of colonial agricultural officers, many of whom were trained in Trinidad by a soil conservationist whose zeal was honed in the Dust Bowl. Having adopted the *alibi* of African agricultural and pastoral practices as responsible for droughts and soil erosion crises, colonial authorities responded with an interventionist program based upon destocking and 'reconditioning' of farms and rangelands. Arguably, the politicisation of droughts was tailor-made to justify colonialism and colonial control of African resources in the rural areas.

Even when Africans foiled major destocking campaigns (Tignor, 1971), colonial agricultural officials continued with their propensity to control African resources by focusing on reconditioning, actively encouraging the enclosure and seeding of grazing lands as well as the enclosure of homestead lands. By the end of 1939, over 400,000 acres had been enclosed. Beinart (1984) and Blaikie (1985) posit that for most African farmers during the colonial period, any merit intrinsic to conservation paled before its use as an instrument of colonial control and, thus, a focus of anti-colonial resistance. Conservation officers also treated conservation as a 'special project' separate from everyday farming and herding. While this attitude was in keeping with the administrators' tendency to identify a one-dimensional crisis emerging from a discrete set of African social practices, it was foreign to the daily experience of farmers and was therefore doomed to fail (Wamalwa, 1989). By 1940, the reconditioning program had all but halted, due to both African resistance and to the call-up of agricultural officers to aid the war effort. What is clear is that colonialism made Africans more vulnerable to droughts and famines in Kenya. Not surprisingly, limited rains in 1942 led to severe food shortages in 1943-44 that led to the death of many people (Ochieng, 1988: 31). The famine and its effects lingered on until 1946. Spencer (1980) notes that large-scale maize plantings, in order to meet the colonial war effort, encouraged further soil depletion, while manipulation of the maize market during the war aggravated famine.

After the Second World War, Africans still living on White designated areas were pushed into African reserves in order to create space for settlement of demobilised British officers on land in Kenya. This worsened the plight of Africans in overcrowded reserves and made them more vulnerable to droughts and famines as was the case in 1951-52 and 1961. Dianne *et al.* (1995) assert that the promotion of maize in place of drought resistant sorghum and millet had, by 1960, created an increased vulnerability to droughts, which some farmers partially offset by improved water storage in terraced croplands. By the time Kenya got independence in 1963, the African people had become extremely vulnerable to droughts, land degradation and soil erosion as a result of colonial policies and integration into the colonial economy. Frequent crop loss due to droughts, like sedentary life and land registration, had become facts of life for most residents of the region.

Colonial assertions that poor African agricultural and pastoral practices caused droughts and climatic changes in Kenya were an *alibi* to legitimise colonial rule and justify control of natural resources in rural areas of Kenya. Colonialism, through its economic and labour policies, created a crisis in peasant agriculture. It created an acute labour shortage in African communities, which wiped out the indigenous surplus (*mondo*) storage system thereby making the communities more susceptible to droughts and famines. Land appropriation and rise of African population due to improved medical facilities, put pressure on the remaining land and made it difficult for Africans to continue with their indigenous land rotation agriculture which had allowed land to lie fallow to regain its fertility. By its constant expropriation of land from Africans, colonialism generated overgrazing, soil erosion and land degradation and as such created conditions which aggravated periodic droughts and famines. It caused chronic undernourishment and mal-nutrition of the African people of Kenya. By and large, the official mind of the colonial administration linked the alleged 'environmental misuse', by agriculturalists and pastoralists, to the scourge of droughts and famines.

Politicisation of Droughts in Zimbabwe

The case study of Zimbabwe is not different from the Sahel region and Kenya case studies analysed above in terms of the politicisation of droughts and environmental changes and increased vulnerability of African agriculturalists and pastoralists as a result of colonialism. From the advent of colonialism in 1890, the worst droughts were the 1895-96 drought that was accompanied by rinderpest and locusts, consecutive dry spells from 1911 to 1914, the 1946–47 drought, the 1960 drought, and the 1972–73 rainy season, which was the driest period of colonial Zimbabwe. The country also experienced serious food shortages in 1896-97, 1903, 1916, 1922, 1933, and 1942.

Iliffe (1990: 111) argues that the people of pre-colonial Zimbabwe experienced recurrent droughts, they generally had well-developed coping mechanisms that prevented high death tolls. Famines that killed only occurred when violence intensified scarcity. Zimbabwe's rainfall pattern has always been one of greater precipitation in the northern parts of the country, with gradually diminishing rains from north to south. This has meant that in any given year there is never a total rainfall failure and therefore a total crop failure. Scarcity in most cases has been localised, and local food shortages in pre-colonial Zimbabwe therefore rarely degenerated into famines that killed. As already reflected in the section analysing pre-colonial indigenous knowledge systems, the tradition of sharing among the peoples of pre-colonial Zimbabwe was one of the pillars of famine prevention strategies that had its roots in the ethics of the peoples' culture. Social ties ensued that no one could starve when someone else had a surplus of food. There was a well-established barter trade system, in the form of either in-kind or exchange of food for labour. Only those who were unable to exchange either of the two resorted to begging. Chigodora (1997) submits that even in begging, the beggar provided some form of service, such as entertainment, in exchange for food.

Major settlements in pre-colonial Zimbabwe were centred on the watershed (high rain-fall belt) in the Highveld at the centre of modern Zimbabwe. This region is known for its agriculturally rich soils and abundant natural resources, including game and other wild sources of food. The people had relatively well-developed agricultural skills. They grew drought-resistant crops, mainly sorghum, finger millet and bulrush millet. During times of plenty, the surplus was stored in secluded natural silos (often caves), as a strategic reserve during wartime. These reserves could also be used during a famine. According to Zhou (2012) traditional leaders always kept strategic reserves for their people in case of famine. Above all, the greatest asset that the people had was the over-abundance of wild foods. As put forward by Scudder (1971), early European explorers who came to Zimbabwe noted that starvation was impossible in the Zimbabwean plateau. Arguably, the agro-pastoralists of pre-colonial Zimbabwe had achieved control of famine mortality because of ecological reasons and (more importantly) by a remarkable variety of technical and socio-economic means and strategies thereby preventing famine from causing numerous deaths.

The advent of colonial rule in 1890 was followed by drought, locusts and rinderpest that together with other grievances caused the Shona-Ndebele rising of 1896-97. In an attempt to force the Shona and Ndebele into submission the White settler regime destroyed the means to resist (crops and food). The plunder and destruction of grain by European troops, and the invasion of locusts and rinderpest disease all hurt food security with British South African Company reporting widespread starvation throughout the country in 1897. This section presents an analysis of ten major colonial famines between 1896 and 1973. Within the period 1896-1960, Iliffe (1990) identifies a historical process of change in the character of famines effecting the African population of colonial Zimbabwe. Prior to 1922 the pre-colonial, 'traditional' type of famine prevailed. Iliffe (1990: 31) argues that the famines of 1896/7, 1903, 1912 and 1916 were traditional with 'the leading actors from an older world' in terms of causation, extent and effects and also crisis management. With the exception of the post-Chimurenga famine of 1896-7, these famines were caused by drought and the regions least exposed to early colonialism were the main sufferers from the failure of the rains. These famines threatened but did not cause deaths from starvation in great numbers owing to the continued operation of pre-colonial famine-survival strategies and, to a small but increasing degree, to famine relief by the colonial state. It was these strategies of coping with famines which were firstly affected by colonial changes. Already the great drought of 1912 - although it was met mainly by traditional famine management techniques - carried transitional characteristics. Here government drought-relief operations, as well as what Sen (1981) calls indirect 'entitlements to food' through the colonial economy (wage labour, cattle sales) became important elements in coping with the environmental stress.

The famine of 1922 incorporated most elements of transition from pre-colonial to capitalist famines. This famine was the last one which killed a significant number of people directly. However, in contrast to the previous famines, it was neither confined to peripheral areas or to Southern Mashonaland; nor was it caused by a succession of bad harvests but by one single catastrophic season. Although colonial land apportionment was still not a major causative factor, the severity of the famine was linked to developments in the colonial capitalist economy. As a result of the Depression following the First World War, cattle prices dropped drastically and Africans were unable to secure exchange entitlements to food by cattle sales (Iliffe, 1990). In terms of crisis management there was also an important shift. In the 1922 famine, government drought relief became as important (if not more important) as traditional techniques as the main check on famine mortality. Also in terms of famine-induced labour migration, the 1922 famine marked a turning point in a longer historical process. For the first time a famine caused a marked upsurge in labour migration.

Palmer (1977) asserts that by the Land Apportionment Act of 1930, White colonisers got the lion's share in both quantity and quality of land in colonial Zimbabwe. The Land Apportionment Act also heightened the push of Africans into the reserves. Once settled in the increasingly overcrowded reserves, the Shona and Ndebele in colonial Zimbabwe could aspire to become little more than subsistence cultivators and migrant labourers. Successful agriculture in pre-colonial Africa was based on land rotation cultivation, which became difficult once Africans were brought under rigid European control. By the end of the 1930s the whole agricultural economy of the Shona and the Ndebele, like that of the Kikuyu and Luo in Kenya, had been greatly shattered by land appropriation thereby making them more vulnerable to droughts and famines. Colonial capitalism was dominant by the early 1930s and had profoundly changed the character of famines in Southern Rhodesia. Fatal famine gave way to non-fatal food scarcity which was now geographically concentrated in the areas of most intense White settlement such as Matabeleland (Iliffe, 1990). Malnutrition now affected predominantly the poor and socially weak members of African society. The causes of the food scarcities of 1933, 1942 and 1947 are closely linked to the impact of land theft, evictions, the overcrowding of the Reserves and declining agricultural per capita productivity. Their repercussions were also reflected in the growing social differentiation in African society. Iliffe (1990: 79) argues that "whereas [prior to the 1930s] both rich and poor had fasted and feasted, now food was regularly available to those who could afford it and regularly scarce for those who could not." Until the late 1950s mature colonial capitalism replaced traditional famine control. Also, government famine relief was replaced with exchange-related indirect entitlements to food. For a limited historical period, most African families earned sufficient income from cattle sales and migrant labour to buy enough food to avoid starvation. However, this was not always the case since the poor could not afford to do so.

It is important to note that as the effects of land appropriation became more visible in the late 1930s, politicisation of droughts and environmental change also increased. Supposedly poor African farming was blamed. Yet in reality, Africans were natural conservationists and their environmental knowledge fared better than White colonialists particularly on farming practices. As the enlightened White settler, A. Ward (1938:237) remarked:

> Their [African] methods are simply to go on and on cultivating one piece of land until it gets exhausted and then they take a little bit more…but they do not stamp their land. In wooded country, I do not think the Native cultivation is a menace than the European cultivation on account of the Natives do not clean stumping their land [sic]. It is abandoned fairly soon before the trees are dead, they come up in coppice growth…we had to stump the land to put tea in. With the native method of not stumping, the trees very soon recover. I think European cultivation is a bigger menace.

Unfortunately, such words of wisdom were few and far between, and were generally dismissed or brushed aside. In spite of such highly developed environmental knowledge and technology, the majority of Whites regarded African land rotation cultivation as a senseless form of land use. According to Hailey (1957:819) the European colonisers deplored this system of land rotation cultivation, which they dubbed 'slash and burn', and quite failed to perceive that it was less 'a relic of barbarism' than 'a concession to the nature of the soil.' In their report in 1939 the Commission of Inquiry into the Natural Resources of the Land cited shifting cultivation as the main cause of erosion in the reserves and claimed that Africans were "rarely alive to the importance of conserving the soil." The Commission of Inquiry into the Development and Regeneration of the Reserves wrote in 1943:

> The cause for this rapid and even increasing deterioration is well known to us. The blame for it may be laid at the feet of the Native

people themselves because of their appalling misuse of the land by misguided bad farming…

The Report of the Native Production and Trade Commission in 1944 stated:

> As is to be expected, the Native is rarely alive to the importance of the soil; his concern is to get crops, with the consequence that the disease of erosion is spreading at an alarming pace where the primitive methods of agriculture have given place to the plough…In some districts, the Natives' quest for more and more land has transformed once beautifully clad hills into gaunt spectres of ruin. One trustworthy witness instanced a hill, formerly covered with grass and trees, losing every atom of soil after having been attacked by Native cultivation.

Such assertions were coloured by White colonisers' conception of the superiority of Western civilisation, and of course, its agricultural techniques. They were also tailor-made to justify colonial interventionist regulations of natural resource use. It was within this framework that a minority of state officials who were impressed by indigenous land management system were silenced by the majority of colonisers.

In 1948, the Chief Pasture Research Officer at Matopos (West, 1948), reported in apocalyptic tones, the bad state of reserves. He bemoaned the amount of bare ground and erosion and their consequent disastrous results. This was tailor-made to justify destocking. Not surprisingly, the Land Husbandry Act was enacted in 1951 and fostered the destocking of African livestock. Moyana (1984) calls it a prescription for a wrong disease. The real challenge was not overpopulation of both people and livestock, that consequently caused soil erosion and land degradation, but shortage of land. Arguably, by the 1950s the agricultural and pastoral economies of Africans in Zimbabwe had been destroyed not so much by African bad methods of farming as colonisers would like us

---

to believe, but mostly by land seizures, evictions of Africans from their traditional land, labour demands and taxation. Consequently, the history of food scarcity in Zimbabwe entered a new phase. Increased social differentiation and the marginalisation of the rural poor during the period of economic prosperity that followed the Second World War led to a renewed dependence on colonial government famine relief in the disastrous drought of 1960 which was paralleled by the onset of a long-term structural crisis of colonialism. African agriculture was now clearly undermined by the effects of Land Apportionment Act. Above all, 1960 saw the onset of stagnation of the colonial economy which excluded sections of the African population from acquiring sufficient indirect entitlements to food. Endemic malnutrition of the rural poor and socially vulnerable and a dependence on government famine relief in times of drought replaced earlier patterns of famine mortality and famine crisis management. Even the Land Tenure Act of 1969 had no reprieve on land shortage for Africans and the consequent erosion and degradation in the rural areas. Africans remained vulnerable to drought and famine as was evident in the period 1972-73.

Conclusion

This chapter has traced and explained the historiography and politicisation of droughts in colonial Africa using the Sahel region in West Africa, Kenya in East Africa and Zimbabwe in Southern Africa as case studies. Rather than recognising the efficacy of African indigenous knowledge systems in combating droughts in the pre-colonial period, colonialists tended to write-off droughts as purely natural disasters, or to lay blame for catastrophes at the feet of African agriculturalists and pastoralists. African agriculturalists and pastoralists were accused of systematically over-cultivating and overgrazing the land or otherwise engaging in 'inappropriate land use' practices that caused droughts and climatic change. This was merely a *casus-belli* that justified colonial rule, central planning, and colonial control of natural resources. The advent of colonialism did not only lead to clearing of much land for cash crop production but also cultivation into marginal land, and cumulatively to deforestation, land degradation and neglect of traditional crops such as millet and sorghum thereby making agriculturalists more vulnerable to droughts. Pushed into more marginal areas, and with their access to pasture regulated and restricted by the colonial government, pastoral communities also became more vulnerable to droughts during the colonial period. Therefore, droughts and change of climate seem more attributable to integration of African economies into the colonial economy and global climatic processes than to African agriculturalists and pastoralists' poor methods of land use. African agriculturalists and pastoralists were victims of a changing environment, rather than perpetrators of climate change and related catastrophes.

References

Ahn, P.M. (1970) *West African Soils*. Oxford: Oxford University Press.

Allan, W. (1965) *The African Husbandman*. London: Oxford University Press.

Baier, S. (1976) 'Economic history and development: drought and the Sahelien economies of Niger', *African Economic History*, 1: 1-16.

Ball, N. (1978) 'Drought and dependence in the Sahel', *International Journal of Health Services*, 8, 2: 271-298.

Beinart. W. (1984) 'Soil erosion, conservationism and ideas about development: A Southern African exploration, 1900-1960', *Journal of Southern African Studies*, 11, 1: 52-83.

Berman, B. J. and Lonsdale, J. (1992) *Unhappy Valley: Conflict in Kenya and Africa*. Oxford: James Currey.

Bernard, E.F. and Thorn, D. J. (1981) 'Population pressure and human carrying capacity in selected locations of Machakos and Kitui Districts', *Journal of Developing Areas,* 15: 381-406.

Brett, E.A. (1973) *Colonialism and Underdevelopment in East Africa*. London: Longman.

Bryson, R. and Paddock, C. (2016) 'On the climate of history', in Rotberg, R. and Rabb, T. (eds), *Climate and History: An Interdisciplinary History*. Princeton: Princeton University Press, 1-14.

Caldwell, J.C. (1975) *The Sahelian Drought and its Demographic Implications*. Washington D. C.: American Council of Education.

Charney, J. *et al.* (1975) 'Drought in the Sahara: a bio-geographical feedback mechanism', *Science*, 187: 434-435.

Charney, J. *et al.* (1977) 'A comparative study of the effects of albedo change on drought in semi-arid regions', *Journal of the Atmospheric Sciences*, 9: 1414-1420.

Cheater, A. (1990) 'The ideology of communal land tenure in Zimbabwe: Mythogenesis enacted?' *Africa*, 52, 2: 188-205.

Chigodora, J. (1997) 'Famine and drought: the question of food security in Zimbabwe' *Drought Network News*, 9, 1: 1-13.

Danjuma, M.N. and Mohammed, S. (2015), 'Zai Pits System: A Catalyst for Restoration in the Dry Lands', *Journal of Agriculture and Veterinary Science,* 8, 2: 1-4.

Dianne, E. *et al.* (1995) 'Environment, development, crisis, and crusade: Ukambani, Kenya, 1890-1 990' *World Development,* 23, 6: 1037-1051.

Dregne. H.E. (1990) 'Erosion and soil productivity in Africa', *Journal of Soil and Water Conservation*, 45, 4: 431-436.

DuBois, V.D. (1973) *The Drought in West Africa – Part 1: Evolution, Causes and Physical Consequences.* New York: American Universities Field Staff.

Dunsmore, J.R *et al.* (1976) *The Agricultural Development of the Gambia: An Agricultural, Environmental and Socio-Economic Analysis,* Land Resource Development Centre: Ministry of Overseas.

Fairhead, J. and Leach, M. (1996) *Misreading the African Landscape.* Cambridge: Cambridge University Press.

Glantz, G.M. (1987) 'Drought, famine, and the seasons in Sub-Saharan Africa', in Huss-Ashmore, R. and Katz, S. (eds), *Anthropological Perspectives on the African Famine*, New York, 10-30.

Goldsworthy, D. (1982) *Tom Mboya: The Man Kenya Wanted to Forget.* Nairobi: Heinemann.

Grove, A.T. (1973) 'Desertification in the African environment', in Dalby, D. and Church, R.J.H. (eds) *Drought in Africa.* London: School of Oriental and African Studies.

Hailey, W.M. (1957) *An African Survey.* London: Longman.

Hardinge, A. (1899) 'Report on the British East Africa Protectorate for the year 1897-98', *Reports and Correspondence on British Protectorates in East and Central Africa, 1890-1899.* Shannon: Irish University Press: 397-427.

Harlow, V. *et al.* (1965) *History of East Africa*, 2. Oxford: Oxford University Press.

Hopkins, B. (1974) *Forest and Savanna*, London: Heinemann.

Huntington, N.G. (1834) *A System of Modern Geography*. New York: E. Huntington & Co.

Iliffe, J. (1990) *Famine in Zimbabwe, 1890–1960*. Gweru: Mambo Press.

Iliffe, J. (2007) *Africans: The History of the Continent (African Studies)*, 2nd Ed, Cambridge: Cambridge University Press.

Jacks, G.V. and Whyte, R.O. (1939) *Vanishing Land: A World Survey of Soil Erosion*. New York: Doubleday.

Kennedy, D. (1987) *Islands of White: Settler Society and Culture in Kenya and Southern Rhodesia, 1890–1939*. Durham, NC: Duke University Press.

Ladurie, E.L. (1988) *Times of Feasts, Times of Famine: A History of Climate since the Year 1000*. Garden City: Farrar Straus & Giroux.

Lambert, H. E. (1947) 'Land tenure among the Akamba, Parts I and II' *African Studies (Johannesburg)*, 6, 3: 131-147; 6, 4: 157-175.

Lamprey, H.F. (1975) *Report on the Desert Encroachment Reconnaissance in Northern Sudan*, UNESCO/UNEP.

Lane, C.R. (1997) *Custodians of the Commons: Pastoral Land Tenure in East and West Africa*. London: Earthscan publications.

Laya, D. (1975) 'Interviews with farmers and livestock-owners in the Sahel', *African Environment*, 1, 2: 49-93.

Leach, M. and Mearns, R. (eds) *African Issues: The Lie of the Land: Challenging Received Wisdom on the African Environment*. Oxford: James Currey.

McCann, J.C. (1999) 'Climate and causation in African History', *The International Journal of African Historical Studies*, 32, 2/3: 261-279.

McCracken, J. (1982) 'Experts and expertise in colonial Malawi', *African Affairs*, 81: 110-114.

Miller, J. (1982) 'The significance of drought, disease, and famine in the agricultural marginal zones of West Central Africa', *Journal of African History*, 23, 1: 17-61.

Moore, H. and Vaughan, M. (1994) *Cutting Down Trees: Gender, Nutrition and Agriculture in Northern Rhodesia*. Portsmouth: Heinemann.

Mortimore, M. (1998) *Roots in the African Dust*. Cambridge: Cambridge University Press.

Mortimore, M. and Adams, W.M. (2001) 'Farmers adaptation, change and 'crisis' in the Sahel', *Global Environmental Change*, 11: 49-57.

Mosley, P. (1983) *The Settler Economies: Studies in the Economic History of Kenya and Southern Rhodesia, 1900–1963*. Cambridge: Cambridge University Press.

Moyana, H.V. (1984) *The Political Economy of Land in Zimbabwe*. Gweru: Mambo Press.

Munro, J. F. (1975) *Colonial Rule and the Kamba: Social Change in the Kenya Highlands*. Oxford: Clarendon.

Murray, J. (1989) *The Oxford Dictionary*. Oxford: Oxford University Press.

Mutiso, G.C.M. (1975) *Kenya: Politics. Policy, and Society*. Kampala: EALB.

Myrick, B. (1975) 'Colonial initiatives and Kamba reaction in Machakos District: The destocking issue, 1930-1938', In Myrick, B. *et al.* (eds.), *Three Aspects of Crisis in Colonial Kenya*, Syracuse: Syracuse University, 1975: 1-26.

Neocosmos, M. (1987) *Social Relations in Rural Swaziland: A Critical Analysis*. Manzini: University of Swaziland.

Nicholson, S. (1979) 'The methodology of historical climate reconstruction and its application in Africa', *Journal of African History*, 20: 31-49.

Nyambara, P.S. (2001) ''Traditional' leaders and the Rhodesian State: The power of communal land tenure and the politics of land acquisition in Gokwe, Zimbabwe, 1963-1979', *Journal of Southern African Studies*, 27, 4: 771-791.

Nye, P.H. and Greenland, B.J. (1960) *The Soils under Shifting Cultivation*. Farm Royal: Common Agricultural Bureau.

Ochieng, W.R. 'Colonial Famines in Luoland, Kenya, 1905-1945', *Transafrican Journal of History*, 17: 21-33.

Ogot, B.A. (1967) *A History of the Sothern Luo*. Nairobi: Heinemann.

Palmer, R. (1977) *Land and Racial Domination in Rhodesia*. London: Heinemann.

Phimister, I. R. (1988) *An Economic and Social History of Zimbabwe, 1890–1948*. Harlow: Longman.

Rasmussan, E. (1987) 'Global climate change and variability effects of drought and desertification', In Glantz M. (ed), *Drought and*

Hunger in Africa: Denying Famine a Future. Cambridge: Cambridge University Press, 3-22.

Report of the Anglo-French Commission 1936-37. Lagos: Government Printer.

Richards, P. (1985) *Indigenous Agricultural Revolution*. London: Unwin Hyman.

Rocheleau, D.E. *et al.* (1989) 'Ethnoecological methods to complement local knowledge and farmer innovations in agroforestry', In Pacey, A. *et al.* (eds.), *Farmer First: Farmer Innovation and Agricultural Research*. London: Intermediate Technology: 14-24.

Rodney, W. (1972) *How Europe Underdeveloped Africa*. Harare: Zimbabwe Publishing House.

Scudder, T. (1971) *Gathering among African Woodland Savannah Cultivators: A Case Study - The Gwembe Tonga*. Manchester: Manchester University Press.

Sen, A. (1981) *Poverty and Famines: An Essay on Entitlement and Deprivation*. Oxford: Clarendon.

Silberfein, M. (1989) *Rural Change in Machakos, Kenya: A Historical Geography Perspective*. Lanham, MD: University Press of America.

Southern Rhodesia (1939), *Report of the Commission to enquire into the Preservation, etc., of the Natural Resources of the Colony*. Salisbury: Government Printers.

Southern Rhodesia (1943) *Development and Regeneration of the Colony's Reserves*, Annexure No. 4.

Southern Rhodesia (1944) *Report of the Native production and Trade Commission, 1944*, Salisbury: Government Printers.

Spencer, I.R.G. (1980) 'Settler dominance, agricultural production, and the Second World War in Kenya', *Journal of African History*. 21, 4: 497-514.

Spencer, I.R.G. (1983) 'Pastoralism and colonial policy in Kenya, 1895-1929' In Rotberg, R.I. (ed.), *Imperialism, Colonialism, and Hunger: East and Central Africa*. Australia: Lexington Books: 113-140.

Stamp, L.D. (1940) 'The southern margin of the Sahara: comments on some recent studies on the question of desiccation in West Africa', *Geographical Review*, 30: 297-300.

Stebbing, E.P. (1935) 'The encroaching Sahara: the threat to the West African colonies', *Geographical Journal*, 85: 506-524.

Stebbing, E.P. (1937a) 'The threat of the Sahara', *Journal of the Royal African Society*, Extra Supplement, May: 3-35.

Stebbing, E.P. (1937b) *The Forests of West Africa and the Sahara: A Study of Modern Conditions*. London: Chambers.

Stebbing, E.P. (1938) 'The man-made desert in Africa: erosion and drought', *Journal of the Royal African Society*, Supplement, January: 3-40.

Swift, J. (1996) 'Desertification narratives, winners & losers', in Leach, M. and Mearns, R. (eds) *African Issues: The Lie of the Land: Challenging Received Wisdom on the African Environment*. Oxford: James Currey: 73-90.

Tignor, R.L. (1971) 'Kamba political protest: the destocking controversy of 1938', *International Journal of African Historical Studies*, 2, 2: 237-251.

Timmer, L.A. *et al.* (1996) 'Pruning the neme trees (Parkia biglobosa) on the farmlands of Burkina Faso, West Africa', *Agroforestry Systems*, 33: 87-98.

Wailer, R. D. (1985) 'Ecology, migration, and expansion in East Africa', *African Affairs*, 84: 347-370.

Wamalwa, B. N. (1989) "Indigenous knowledge and natural resources," In Kitiro and Juma (eds.), *Gaining Ground: Institutional Innovations in Land-Use Management in Kenya*, Nairobi: ACTS: 45-65.

Ward, A. (1938) Natural Resources Commission, Oral Evidence.

Watts, M. (1983) 'Hazards and crisis: A political economy of drought and famine in Northern Nigeria', *Antipode*, 15, 1: 24-34

Chapter Three

Climate Change and the Future of Africa: Impacts on Water Resources in Eastern and Southern Africa

Wisdom Sibanda & Fortune Sibanda

Introduction

Climate change presents one of the greatest threats to African water resource systems which are vulnerable to such changes due to their limited adaptive capacity. Climate variability is amongst an array of threats facing agricultural livelihoods, with its effects unevenly distributed. Climate change results in resource conflicts and so it is important to understand the underlying drivers that shape differential vulnerabilities in areas that are double-exposed to climate change conflicts (Swain, Swain, Themner and Krampe, 2011; Powell Powell, Larsen, de Bruin, Powell, Elrick-Barr, 2017). Exposure to climate change and conflict stressors presents a critical challenge for locations where natural resources are declining and livelihood losses are driving people into conflict-structured practices. Climate change has negatively affected the livelihoods of pastoralists and other farmers such that there have been territorial disputes, overgrazing, and water stress. Particularly vulnerable to these climatic changes are the rain-fed agricultural systems on which the livelihoods of a large proportion of the regions' population currently depend. Pastoralists are more vulnerable in terms of climate-structured aggressive behaviour within a water-based livelihoods context where all resource user groups show similar levels of exposure to climate variability.

This chapter focuses on the Eastern and Southern African regions as typical case studies of areas that have been vulnerable to climate change because of their poverty, spatial and temporal diversity and because of the limited resources possessed by their population. Few studies have looked at impacts of climate change on water resources conflicts at local and regional scales. The chapter posits that the primary drivers of many aspects to climate change and related conflicts are largely anchored on anthropogenic factors whose remedy should emanate from responsible human actions. The chapter also draws insights from the Indigenous Knowledge Systems (IKS) to suggest possible solutions to the challenge of climate change. A case study approach of selected countries in Eastern and Southern African regions has been adopted. A desk review on the environmental effects of climate change on water, conflict, climate change patterns and severe droughts was done in order to ascertain the potential impact of climate variability. In a bid to give an analysis of the impact of climate change on water resources in Eastern and Southern Africa, this chapter will start by defining some of the basic terms on climate change.

Understanding Climate Change

This section seeks to examine climate change through explanations of key concepts such as climate, climate change, climate variability and vulnerability. Climate is defined as long-term averages and variations in weather measured over a period of several decades (IPCC, 2007; Swain, 2011). It refers to a statistically-significant trend in climate over many decades. This can be observed in terms of increased temperatures and dryness. This influences the activity and productivity trends, which in turn lead to environmental effects.

The United Nations Framework Convention on Climate Change (UNFCCC) in Article 2 states that "Climate change" means a change of climate which is attributed directly or indirectly to human activity that alters the composition of the global atmosphere and which is in addition to natural climate variability observed over comparable time periods (UNFCCC, 1994; Swain *et al.*, 2011; IPCC, 2007; Bronkhorst, 2011). Climate variability describes the way climatic elements such as temperature and rainfall depart from the average value in given months, seasons, years, decades or centuries (NOAA, 2014). It is the natural variations in climate from year to year due to natural causes like El Nino and La Nina, cyclical solar output variations. In other words, climate variability refers to the climatic parameter of a region varying from its long-term mean. Variability may result from natural internal processes within the climate system (internal variability) or from variations in natural or anthropogenic external forces (external variability). Variation in climate parameters is generally attributed to natural causes.

Vulnerability is the degree to which a system is susceptible to, or unable to cope with, adverse effects of climate change, including climate variability and extremes (Powell *et al.*, 2017; Swain, 2011). The impact of climate variability and change on specific regions depends on their vulnerability, that is, how sensitive they are to even small changes, how exposed they are, and whether they can adapt (Taylor *et al.*, 2011; Kenney, 2017). For farming communities, changes in the frequency and intensity of severe weather events such as dry spells, droughts, wet spells and heat are more important than changes in average conditions.

Climate Change from a Global Perspective

There is strong evidence that global warming is likely to have a range of negative and positive spatially specific impacts on biological systems, precipitation and drought, and give rise to natural phenomena such as cyclones, floods and high sea levels (Taylor *et al.*, 2011; Bronkhorst, 2011). Livelihoods will be affected in various ways – through sea-level rise, changes in weather and rainfall patterns, and human health (Bronkhorst, 2011; Nordas and Gleditsch, 2007). The picture painted for Africa, where the majority of people depend on the environment for a living, is bleak. The IPCC argues that Africa is "one of the most vulnerable continents to climate variability and change because of multiple stresses and low adaptive capacity" (IPCC, 2007: no page), and that although "some adaptation to current climate variability is taking place…this may be insufficient for future changes in climate" (IPCC, 2007: no page).

Climate Change and its variability impacts have both favourable and unfavourable implications in different parts of the world (Kenney, 2017; Akiyode, 2011). It is causing increases in temperature, changes in precipitation and extreme weather events, sea-level rise, and other environmental impacts. Evidence indicates that climate change is associated with collective violence, generally in combination with other causal factors (Akiyode, 2011). Increased temperatures and extremes of precipitation with their associated consequences, including resultant scarcity of cropland and other key environmental resources, are major pathways by which climate change leads to collective violence (Taylor *et al.*, 2011).

The climate system has changed at both global and regional scales since the pre-industrial era, with some of these changes attributable to human activities which have increased the atmospheric concentrations of greenhouse gases and aerosols (Dong-Gill, Thomas, Pelster, Rosenstock and Sanz-Cobena, 2016). Some studies show that shared river basins and variables such as rainfall and temperature variability are positively linked to conflicts (Ross and McConnell, 2016; Bronkhorst, 2011). Other researchers seem to agree that it is unlikely that climate and environmental factors alone will lead to conflicts (Gleditsch *et al.*, 2011), but will rather feed into or exacerbate existing social, political or economic drivers of conflict (Bronkhorst, 2011).

Climate Change from an African Regional Perspective

Africa has been identified as one of the parts of the world most vulnerable to the impacts of climate change (IPCC, 2007; Niang *et al.*, 2014; Serdeczny *et al.*, 2015). Recent studies suggest that agricultural crop productivity in Africa will be adversely affected by any warming above current levels (Otieno, 2013; Ross and McConnell, 2016) as the continent will be experiencing a change in its water resources. Across Africa, many national governments are initiating adaptation programmes which focus on mechanisms such as disaster risk management, public awareness, adjustment to relevant technologies and scientific-based approaches to farming (Bronkhorst, 2011; Touadi, 2018). The continent is described as the most at risk to the negative effects of climate change, both because of the expected change itself and because of the perceived lack of capacity of Africans and their governments to adapt (Taylor *et al.*, 2013).

Most of the rural poor in Africa South of the Sahara rely for their livelihood and food security on highly climate-sensitive rain-fed subsistence or small-scale farming, pastoral herding and direct harvesting of natural services of ecosystems such as forests and wetlands (Almer *et al.*, 2017). The productivity of this livelihood base is highly vulnerable to climate-related stresses, such as changes in temperature, precipitation, and increased frequency of droughts and floods. In Africa, about 40% of land mass is dedicated to pastoralism. Dry lands occupy 70% of the Horn of Africa - ranging from 95% of Somalia, more than 80% in Kenya, 60% of Uganda and approximately half of Tanzania. Pastoralism is practiced in all arid and semi-arid lands (ASALs) of Africa (Goulden and Few, 2011, Akiyode, 2011; Bronkhorst, 2011).

According to Carleton (2017), climate change will lower crop yields on the continent by approximately 20% by 2050. To this end, the then United Nations Secretary General, Ban Ki-moon, once described the war in Darfur, Sudan as the world's first climate change conflict, caused in part by the fighting over scarce water resources (Carleton, 2017). Though water scarcity is the result of varied factors, at the forefront is climate change leading to desertification and the degree to which human industries influence climate (Powell *et al.*, 2017).

Climate change has also taken its toll on livestock production in the region thereby rendering them vulnerable (Lobell *et al.*, 2011). Traditionally for Africa, livestock is an important source of food (such as meat and milk and other dairy products), animal products (such as leather), income, or insurance against crop failure (Swain, 2011). The pastoral systems of the region, for example, are highly dependent on natural resources, including pasture, fodder, forest products and water, all of which are directly affected by climate variability (Goulden and Few, 2011). It is noted that livestock is vulnerable to droughts, particularly where it depends on local biomass production, with a strong correlation between drought and animal death due to water shortage (World Bank, 2013).

Agricultural production in Sub-Saharan Africa is particularly vulnerable to the effects of climate change, with rain-fed agriculture accounting for approximately 96% of overall crop production (World Bank, 2013). Climate change has negatively affected the livelihoods of farmers and led to territorial disputes, overgrazing, and water stress. Particularly vulnerable to these climatic changes are the rain-fed agricultural systems on which the livelihoods of a large proportion of the regions' population currently depend. Agricultural farmers are more vulnerable in terms of climate-structured aggressive behaviour within a water-based livelihoods context where all resource user groups show similar levels of exposure to climate variability (Carleton, 2017).

Climate Change from a Southern African Regional Perspective

Research has shown that climate change-associated extreme weather events, such as droughts and flooding, have emerged as the biggest challenges faced by the fast growing and emerging economies in Southern Africa (Swain, 2011). Temperature is expected to continue warming and rainfall patterns are projected to continue changing, thereby increasing risks and uncertainty in a region with low adaptive capacity (Niang *et al.*, 2014; Mpandeli, 2018; Benhin, 2006). As carbon emissions continue un-abated worldwide, the effects of global warming could be expected. The world's poorest communities are the hardest hit, and those in Southern Africa are frequently experiencing extreme weather outside the natural variability of African climate (Kenney, 2017).

On the basis of the existing literature, it can be argued that climate change encompassing changes in temperature and rainfall will be felt differently across the region, with some areas becoming warmer and wetter, while others will become warmer and drier (Nhamo *et al.*, 2018; Mpandeli, 2018). These changes in climate have differential impacts on agricultural productivity, water resources, food security and other sectors, across spatial and temporal scales (Nhamo *et al.*, 2018; Jury and Funk, 2013). The climate situation is already worse in Southern Africa than in most other regions. While the global average air temperature has risen by nearly 1°C since accurate weather records began a little over a century ago, in Southern Africa, temperatures have risen on average by twice this amount. This means that Southern Africa crossed the 1.5°C warming level some years ago (Kusangaya *et al.*, 2013; Thomson *et al.*, 2010). These trends do not auger well for the future as the water shortages hit the region. Southern African nations must encourage the global community to radically reduce climate change to lower the risks to particularly vulnerable social and ecological systems.

Climate Induced Conflicts in Southern Africa

Climate change is a reality and Southern Africa is going to be one of the hardest hit regions of the world. Studies have shown that current approaches to climate change adaptation are sectoral, which has led to mal-adaptation as trade-offs are not accounted for (Swain *et al.*, 2011; Kenney, 2017; Mpandeli, 2018). The region experiences huge mean variations in rainfall from season to season, periodic droughts and water shortages are a feature of everyday life. It is also argued that dependence on climate sensitive resources in Southern Africa worsens vulnerabilities. Consequently, the region is classified as a climate change hot spot (Deryng, Conway, Ramankutty and Warren, 2014; Mpandeli, 2018). This is particularly so in the Southern African Development Community (SADC) region due to the recurrence of climate change associated extreme weather events and high climatic variability, particularly droughts and floods. Thus, climate change impacts on water, energy, and food resources have negatively affected human wellbeing, poverty reduction, and sustainable development to the extent that their management is vital to achieving the Sustainable Development Goals (SDGs) (Mpandeli, 2018).

Twelve SADC states share 21 river basins, with most of these crossing more than two countries (Ashton, 2000; Maluleke and Mokwena, 2017). It can be illustrated that future water related disputes at local scale are amenable to institutional and government intervention that ensure the protection of individual rights and responsibilities. Being an arid to semi-arid region where the basins of most of the larger perennial rivers are shared by between three and eight countries (Ashton, 2000, Swain, 2011), the region is prone to severe climate change. This has seen downstream countries, that may be economically "poorer" or politically and militarily "weaker" than their upstream neighbours (Joshua, Jalloh and Hachgonta, 2014; Mpandeli, 2018), being exploited over the use of water. To turn around this political impasse, Southern African Development Community member states have agreed to work together to develop and implement joint strategies and protocols for the protection and management of regional water resources (Ashton, 2000).

Most conflicts in Southern Africa occur over freshwater and the discharge of effluent between and within nations (Okpara *et al.*, 2017). The decrease in fresh water is mainly due to climate change. Drought, pollution, desertification and the effects of climate change are making water increasingly scarce and therefore precious just like gold (World Bank, 2013). It was estimated that by 2015, the Gauteng region of South Africa would have exhausted all its available water sources, including the Highlands Water Scheme in Lesotho and its traditional river systems. This huge metropolis is rationing water and the South Africans are studying the possibilities of extracting water from the Zambezi River at Chobe (Swain *et al.*, 2011).

Implications for the Changes in Weather for Southern Africa

Speculative conflicts in the major river basins such as the Okavango, Zambezi, Limpopo, Orange and Lake Malawi have been on the increase thereby calling for a regional water management system to avoid conflict. For example the Zambezi has seen Zambia and Zimbabwe at each other's throat over the use of water from the Zambezi; each of the two countries needs the water for power generation (Swain *et al.*, 2011). At one point in time, Zambia used far more water than it was entitled to in generating power for their country, this nearly resulted in Kariba power stations being closed (Swain *et al.*, 2011). According to Zimbabwe Power Company, the water levels in Lake Kariba once dropped to below 30%, and this seriously affected power generation in the country. Episodes of drought in the past few years coupled with changing rainfall patterns within the country have led to the decrease in Kariba's water levels. The rains have become so erratic in some countries of the region that the United Nations Development Programme predicts agricultural production – the main livelihood source for nearly three quarters of the population – could decrease by up to 30%, which could lead to an increase in hunger and poverty (Joshua *et al.*, 2014).

From another perspective, the low water levels in Lake Kariba have resulted in traditional leaders on both sides of the lake to conduct "rain-making"/rain-inducing ceremonies in line with their Tonga traditions in order to curb the further decline of water levels. The Tonga believed that the low rainfall patterns in the Zambezi catchment area were due to the failure to conduct traditional rites necessary to appease Nyaminyami, the Zambezi River spirit, to which they attribute protection and sustenance (Nyamukondiwa, 2015). In this way, Chief Nebire of Kariba on the Zimbabwean side conducted a public "bira" on 17 October 2015 whilst Chief Chipepo of the Valley Tonga people in Zambia had conducted similar traditional rites earlier and invited their Zimbabwean counterparts. What one can read from these traditional efforts to induce rainfall is that they are already grappling with the effects of climate change and have resorted to their own indigenous ways of resolving the crises for human survival. In addition, the traditional leaders in both countries have had to find common ground in trying to alleviate the effects of climate change, since water sources are communally owned. The Zambezi Water Authority admitted that the declining water levels in Lake Kariba called for controlled water usage (Nyamukondiwa, 2015). It is in this context that Humbe (2017:217) finds the rationale for integrating African indigenous religious strategies of water resource conservation and management into the modern management practices, policies and planning processes. In other words, indigenous knowledge systems related to water, which are often misunderstood and ignored, can be evoked in climate change debates.

South Africa and Botswana's plan to draw water from the Zambezi system at Chobe for irrigation was rejected by Zimbabwe on the grounds that the water in the Chobe was Zambezi water and therefore was subject to regional riparian rights. Thus, conflict was averted by bringing the countries to a round table while negotiating best options for water utilisation that would suit all parties. There is also another water conflict in Southern Africa involving Botswana, Namibia and Angola over the River Cuito. The situation in the Okavango where discussions are centred on plans to construct a pipe to divert water from the Okavango River to the Namibian capital, Windhoek, to promote development and give that country greater water security, has generated intense debate. But a river basin commission saved the day for the state parties whose cooperation in this regard is highly commended (Powell *et al.*, 2017). Drought conditions have had a negative impact on communities and regional economies. These conditions also emphasise the point that water is now one of the region's most finite natural resources. The IPCC has predicted that droughts may lower food production in Africa South of the Sahara by as much as 20 percent (Powell *et al.*, 2017). The impact of climate change on water resources could also be seen when disputes over water in Southern Africa have driven a shift in the water politics of the region (Maluleke and Mokwena, 2017; Kusangaya, 2013). With a crippling drought wiping out crops and threatening its capital, Windhoek with shortages, Namibia has tried to get alternative sources of water but has failed (Swain *et al.*, 2011).

There is need for technological advancement in water uses that are environmentally friendly and adapted to climate change. A case in point is the Mozambique and Zimbabwe dispute over the dispatch of effluent from Mutare City into Muene River polluting Chicamba dam (Mail & Guardian, 5 December 2016). Waste from industries, clinics and homes in Mutare are dumped at the site. Authorities in Mozambique's Manica province, which contains the Chicamba dam, set up a task force to redress the issue. However, Mutare City Council said it did not have the money to find another way to resolve the problem (Kings, 2016). This implies that effectively they ignored the complaint.

Implications for Agriculture

Due to weather changes, Southern African agricultural systems are changing in the sense of discarding peasant or subsistence agriculture in the hope that "modern" farming will be better adapted to climate change. It has been noted that the peasant farmers cannot adapt fast enough, they do not have the resources for adaptation and mitigation and are already net food deficit systems throughout the region (Joshua *et al.*, 2014). The other problem is that communal land ownership systems that prevail in most Southern African states have little or no management of the land and other resources such that some of these areas are experiencing desertification, a process that is almost impossible to reverse (Almer *et al.*, 2017). In Botswana, for example, pastoral agriculture represents the chief source of livelihood for over 40 % of the nation's residents, with cattle representing an important source of status and well-being for the vast majority of Kalahari residents (Dougill *et al.*, 2010; World Bank, 2013). Thus, historical temperature increases have had substantial negative effects on agricultural value added in developing countries.

Notably, the Southern African region is not just a victim of the climate change brought about largely by the major industrialised states of the northern hemisphere but are also contributors to the crisis (Kenney, 2017). Although *chitemene* systems of farming, involving burning some vegetation, have always been practised in Africa, it is alleged that veld or wild fires in the SADC region are a major polluter. Every year people burn millions of hectares of grassland and forest. For instance in Zimbabwe, the Environmental Management Agency (EMA) recorded 27 392 fire incidences between 2009-2013 alone, notwithstanding the cases that went unreported, whilst over 800 000 hectares of land cover was destroyed (Mlambo, 2015). This calls for everyone to be responsible and avoid being negligent. Winter sunsets are legendary but they also point to the vast quantities of carbon dioxide and smoke that is emitted into the atmosphere over Africa. There is damage to the environment as people destroy forests and expand deserts. The Kalahari Desert in Botswana is growing at 5 kilometres a year (Powell *et al.*, 2017). This calls for concerted effort that has traditionally kept the region together in curbing these environmental phenomena as expanding deserts, air pollution and poverty know no boundaries (Loki, 2014). However, as a regional grouping, SADC has proven to be one of the most ineffective organisations in the world. The body is being blamed for failing to take stern measures on regional states that fail to comply with steps that curb climate change challenges. Thus, SADC needs to evolve into a regional cooperation and collaboration group with less reliance on international donors and staff to tackle regional problems is essential (Mpandeli, 2018).

In Southern Africa, 'land grabbing' or 'the farms race' has been registered as one of the ways under which neo-colonial forces in the form of foreign companies and governments tried to annex key natural resources. There is an increased global interest in farmland with statistics revealing that 45 million ha were subjects of negotiations in 2009 alone and 70% of this land under focus was in Africa. Thus, "rich" countries have been accused of buying poor countries' "soil fertility, water and sun to ship food and fuel back home, in a kind of neo-colonial dynamic" (Hall, 2011:194). The

119

Chinese sought 2.8 million ha in the DRC for biofuels and 2.8 million ha in Zambia. This has given rise to conflicts around "food and fuel" in the region. For instance, the failed Daewoo Logistics deal for 1.3 million ha in Madagascar was meant for palm oil for biofuel and maize for food led to the overthrow of the government in 2009. There were biofuel projects focusing on jatropha and sugarcane at the expense of food to eat across the region in Tanzania, Zimbabwe, Zambia, Mozambique, Angola, Madagascar and South Africa (Hall, 2011). In Zimbabwe, Billy Rautenbach, a former South African businessman, was allocated 40 000 ha of land in Chisumbanje for sugarcane (for ethanol) which is benefiting the elite from the government at the expense of the peasants who lost their land to pave way for this grand project. Attention can be drawn to the injustice and the capture of the resources by the elite and (trans)national organisations. In Mozambique, the forestry deals with the Chinese in the Zambezia province provide another dimension of exploitation of resources to the detriment of the locals as the tropical hardwoods were being extracted at an alarming rate (Hall, 2011). All these activities have a bearing on climate change and conflicts over resources. Notably, what is grabbed is not just land, but also water, minerals and cheap labour to extract them.

Perspectives from the Eastern African Region

In the Eastern African region, violent conflicts involving pastoralists are associated with resource competition which is induced by climate change. Research has shown that nomadic herdsmen have been roaming the semi-arid lowlands that stretch across 80 percent of Kenya and 60 percent of Ethiopia for thousands of years (Toudi, 2018). They are descendants of the oldest indigenous societies in the world who survive on the animals they raise and the crops they grow. Their travels are determined by the search for water and grazing lands. These herdsmen have long been accustomed to adapting to a changing environment. But in recent years, they have faced challenges unlike any in living memory. As temperatures in the region have risen and water supplies have dwindled, the pastoralists have had to range more widely in search of suitable water and land (Akiyode, 2011). That search has brought indigenous groups in

Ethiopia and Kenya in increasing conflict, as pastoral communities kill each other over water and pastures.

In Kenya, pastoralism constitutes about 80% of the country's total surface area, and supports 25% of the total human population and 50% of the entire livestock population (Touadi, 2018; Popovski, 2017). Livestock accounts for 95 % of the family income and provides employment to 95% of the population. Pastoral communities solely rely on access to water and pasture for the survival of their livestock. In the recent past, Kenya has been experiencing a prolonged drought due to climate change and this has affected pastoralists' traditional way of life (Taylor *et al.*, 2011). In East Africa, a significant proportion of the population depends on rain-fed agriculture and pastoralism. Hence, the degradation of the natural environment has detrimental effects on people's livelihoods. When these environmental changes – such as the decreased freshwater, degraded grazing lands, or damaged cropland – interact with other pressures on livelihoods, like political marginalisation or unfair land distribution, competing groups may become more likely to solve conflicts through violence or to secure resources by force (Touadi, 2018; Popovski, 2017; Benjaminsen, 2016).

Climate change is seen as the driving force towards resource competition and consequently resource-based conflict. Traditionally pastoralists followed a seasonal migration pattern to find suitable land for their cattle to graze. Due to climate change and persistent droughts in the arid and semi-arid lands (ASALS), the pastoral communities have been forced to migrate. Their movements are no longer seasonal unlike in the past, thereby causing conflict with the farming community (Benjaminsen, 2016).

Effects on Agricultural Production

Climate variability is amongst an array of threats facing agricultural livelihoods, with its effects unevenly distributed (IPCC, 2007; Okpara, 2016). Exposure to climate and conflict stresses presents a critical challenge for locations where natural resources are declining and livelihood losses are driving people into conflict-structured practices (Gleik and Heberger, 2014). It is worth noting that environmental impacts such as climate change patterns and severe droughts are a major source of conflict, as they negatively affect the livelihoods of farmers leading to territorial disputes, overgrazing, and water stress in East Africa (Sikaiga, 2009; Goulden and Few, 2011). Thus, water scarcity due to climate change might lead to desertification. In addition to hampering agricultural yield, desertification leads to dramatic reductions in clean water (Powell *et al.*, 2017; Kenney, 2017).

Seasonal water shortages along river basins are expected mostly in the southern parts of Eastern Africa (Niang *et al.*, 2014). Key challenges for assessing climatic risks to water availability relate to their responses to heat waves, seasonal rainfall variability as well as the relationship between land use changes, evapo-transpiration and soil moisture at different levels of global warming (Akiyode, 2011; Niang *et al.*, 2014; Benson, 2018). Recent droughts have been particularly devastating for agriculturalists (Kimwanja, 2016) and have contributed to a drop in the water level of Lake Victoria where it is claimed that the decrease has been brought about by the prolonged period of drought in the region and over notion of water for power generation (World Bank, 2013; Kimwanja, 2016). This development impacts negatively on the farming community who have been providing for the Great Lakes Region, thereby hindering development in the region.

Effects of Climate Change on Pastoralists

This section looks closely at how climate change has led to resource-based conflicts among the pastoral communities of Eastern Africa as the region is not spared from climate change. Climate change is a challenge and is noted to be responsible for causing conflicts in the Eastern Region of Africa among the pastoralists. As temperatures rise and water supplies dry up, semi-nomadic indigenous groups along the Kenyan-Ethiopian border are coming into conflict with each other as the worsening drought pit groups and nations against one another (Kimwanja, 2016). The herdsmen have long been accustomed to adapting to a changing environment that has seen them facing challenges. The rising temperatures in the region and the dwindling water, have led the pastoralists to range more widely in search of suitable water for their livestock. The search has brought indigenous groups in Ethiopia and Kenya in increasing conflict, as pastoral communities kill each other over water (Goulden and Few, 2011; Akiyode, 2011; Robertson, 2008). The worsening droughts in Eastern Africa, due to climate variability, continues to cause clashes between Kenyan and Ethiopian pastoralists. Although the conflicts are portrayed in terms of ethnic stereotypes, herders and other farmers, locals and immigrants, but in reality, livestock owners – who are misconceived, perceived as Maasai, and therefore as immigrants – have been long in the area but they have less representation in land conflicts (Ross and McConnell, 2017; Al-Labbad, 2013). Thus, the impact of climate change on the Maasai herders has led them to lose their traditional pastures to the growing population and the encroaching farmers.

Research has shown that Lake Turkana has shrunk because of evaporation from higher temperatures and a reduction in the flow of the Omo due to less rainfall, increased diversion of water for irrigation, and upstream dam projects (Serderczny et al., 2015). The lake is disappearing from the Ethiopian territory, retreating south into Kenya leaving farmers vulnerable and forcing them deep into poverty. The Dassanech from Ethiopia have no option but to follow the water, and in doing so have come into direct conflict with the Turkana of Kenya. This resulted in cross-border raids in which members of both groups kill each other, raid livestock, and torch huts. Many people in both indigenous groups have been left without their traditional livelihoods due to climate variability and change. Hence, the future for the indigenous groups of the Omo-Turkana basin looks bleak as the region experiences frequent droughts (Kamwanja, 2017; Kenney, 2017; Powell et al., 2017).

Due to climate change, new weather patterns and prolonged droughts have emerged and pastoralists are now struggling with frequent water shortages, which are threatening their impoverished livelihoods (World Bank, 2013; Gleik and Heberger, 2014). This has led to mass migration of the pastoral communities in search of pastures and water for their animals and for their own use. Many livestock have died and the ones that are left can no longer resist the drought which is causing widespread hunger and thirst. According to Getachaw, Tilahun and Teshager (2014), in pastoral areas of Ethiopia, climate change increased the burden of those who are already poor and vulnerable by affecting their livelihood pattern and strategies and triggering food, feed, water and social insecurity. In the pastoral systems which are reliant on rainfall as the source of pasture growth, seasonal rainfall variability is inevitably mirrored in both highly variable production levels as well as risk averse livelihood and coping strategies that have emerged overtime amongst the rural population (Getachaw *et al.*, 2014). In general, the pastoralists have experienced devastating droughts and their strategies based on centuries of exposure to the droughts are not working due, partly, to an inability to implement them. It is likely that the nature of the climate variability that pastoralists are used to dealing with will itself change adding new momentum to the system (IPCC, 2007; Getachaw *et al.*, 2014).

Effects of Climate Change on Resources

Resource-based conflicts

In the north of Kenya where the drought remains severe, conflicts over access to grazing land and water has erupted among pastoralists from different indigenous groups. In many cases pastoralists have ended up in unfamiliar territory in search of pasture and water for their livestock for example in the bordering nations (Jury and Funk, 2013; Goulden and Few, 2011). Resource-based competition, escalated by prolonged drought, is leading to diminishing access to water and land leading to violent conflict. In Kenya these conflicts have increased with adversity of drought. Dozens of people have died in clashes over water.

A meta-analysis of the situation suggests that deviation from normal precipitation and mild temperatures increases the risk of conflict. The depletion of a dwindling supply of resources has the potential to lead to competition between different groups and heighten the threat of conflict. Conflict is also alleged to lead to environmental degradation and increasing the vulnerability of populations to a range of climate-generated stressors (IPCC, 2007), chief among them being water.

A Shared Future under the Shadow of Climate Change: Towards Harnessing IKS

The reality of climate change and its adverse effects on the depletion of resources and a threat to livelihoods of people calls for urgent action from different stakeholders. The adequate supply of water and food remains critical in Eastern and Southern African communities. It is unfortunate that the anthropogenic impacts of climate change tend to be very drastic in the global south as compared to the global north despite the fact that some of the causative factors emanate from the activities of the industrialised countries. For instance, The New York Times cited by Toudi (2018) published an article whose very title says it all: "How global warming punishes the world's poorest". However, it is under this context that one can ask: How plausible is it to talk of a shared future under the shadow of climate change in Africa? Can the effects of climate change give way to negotiation? Is consensus on climate change issue not an illusion? It is these and many other questions that one grapples with in the era of globalisation.

Like any other region, the Eastern and Southern African communities are equally faced with two different choices: conflict or cooperation pertaining to the issue of water security (Loki, 2014). It is from that perspective of the two choices that one can think outside the box by harnessing the strategies that are local to the communities in question in order to compliment the conventional strategies. What comes to mind is the use of the Indigenous Knowledge Systems (IKS) to avert the threat of conflicts over major water supplies at the backdrop of climate change effects. IKS is quite a broad and all-encompassing concept. IKS refers "to the understandings, skills, and philosophies developed by societies with long histories of interaction with their natural surroundings" (The Herald, 2015). This is important for societies to develop. Today, IKS is the missing link because colonialism debased it. The local forms of knowledge were crucial but the Westerners viewed them as 'unscientific, illogical, anti-development, and or ungodly" (Mawere cited by Dzenga, 2017, no page). This means that in its use, IKS was a forgotten, under-utilised and marginalised asset. In both Eastern and Southern Africa, IKS can be of use to resolve the water conflicts. In Eastern Africa, Sikaiga

(2009) refers to the use of local customs and practices such as *Judiyya* or mediation, indigenous festivals, intermarriage between different indigenous groups as well as the exchange of gifts as some of the indigenous strategies that were once utilised in traditional societies, but which could be useful to revive in the modern set up. In Southern Africa, similar techniques have been in use. Some traditional leaders are reviving the trans-boundary relations, which are part of the social capital from IKS that communities can hinge upon to avert conflict over water scarcity. For instance, as noted earlier on, the Tonga traditional leaders on both sides of the Zambezi River have embarked on holding rain-inducing rites for the Kariba Dam, where they work together. The Gacaca Court system of Rwanda, a system of community justice inspired by Rwandan tradition, could be an essential IKS tool to resolve waters conflicts in Africa.

Recommendations and Conclusion

• There is need to tap from IKS and to adopt crops that are resilient to harsh conditions as well as the promotion of land conservation and reclamation practices.
• Cooperation and working together within countries and across boundaries is essential for shared water resources.
• There is need for dialogue and negotiation on the use of water resources especially in those areas where basin states and riparian states share the vital resource.

Besides cutting emissions, there needs to be a focus on how African states can adapt to the impacts of climate change as a cause of instability. There is evidence to suggest that climate change is a problem for farmers in the Eastern and Southern African region. This calls for climate change risks to be tackled from an Afrocentric perspective whereby the spirit of brotherhood and oneness would prevail after evoking IKS. In fact, IKS is the missing link for a shared future under the shadow of climate change. The agency and active participation of the local communities is an important cog-wheel for local and regional transformation. It is also possible to explore ways in which water resources can be used sustainably and equitably among nations and communities to attain that spirit of togetherness and international cooperation, particularly when local strategies are factored in to complement the conventional ones. The climate change challenge requires everyone to act responsibly, lest humanity would perish under the spell of selfish motives.

References

Adams, C., Ide, T., Barnett, J. and Detges, A. (2018) 'Sampling bias in climate-conflict research,' *Nature Climate Change*, Vol. 8, pp. 200-203.

Akiyode, O.O. (2011) 'Conflict, climate change, and water security in sub-Saharan Africa, Available at: https://www.researchgate.net/publication/215636849_Conflict _Climate_Change_ and_Water_Security_in_Sub-Saharan_Africa, Accessed: 20 March 2019.

Al-Labbad, M. (2013) 'Egypt, Ethiopia headed for war over water', Available at: http://www.al-monitor.com/pulse/politics/2013/03/egypt-ethiopia-water-war, Accessed: 10 March 2019.

Almer, C., Laurent-Lucchetti, J., and Oechslin, M. (2017) 'Water Scarcity and Rioting: Disaggregated Evidence from Sub-Saharan Africa,' *Journal of Environmental Economics and Management,* Vol. 86, Issue C, pp. 193-209.

Ashton, P. (2007) 'Disputes and conflicts over water in Africa', in Mlambo, N. (Ed) *Violent Conflicts, Fragile Peace: Perspectives on Africa's Security.* London: Adonis and Abbey.

Benhin, J.K.A. (2006) 'Climate change and South African agriculture: Impacts and adaptation options' Discussion Paper No. 21, Centre for Environmental Economics and Policy in Africa (CEEPA). Pretoria: University of Pretoria, South Africa.

Benjaminsen, T. A. (2016) 'Does Climate Change Lead to Conflicts in the Sahel?' in Behnke, R. H. and Mortimore, M. (Eds.) *The End of Desertification? Disputing Environmental Change in the Drylands.* New York: Springer Heidelberg, pp.99-116.

Bronkhorst, S. (2011), *Climate Change and Conflict: Lessons for Conflict Resolution from the Southern Sahel of Sudan*, Durban: African Centre for the Constructive Resolution of Disputes (ACCORD).

Carleton, T.A. (2017) 'Crop-damaging temperatures increase suicide rates in India', PNAS, August 15, 114 (33) 8746-8751, https://doi.org/10.1073/pnas.1701354114.

Deryng, D., Conway, D., Ramankutty, N., Price, J., and Warren, R. (2014) 'Global crop yield response to extreme heat stress under multiple climate change futures,' *Environmental Research Letters,* Volume 9, Number 3.

Dong-Gill, K., Thomas, A. D., Pelster, D., Rosenstock, T. S., and Sanz-Cobena, A. (2016) 'Greenhouse gas emissions from natural ecosystems and agricultural lands in sub-Saharan Africa: synthesis of available data and suggestions for further research' *Biogeosciences*, 13, 4789–4809.

Dougill, A. J., Fraser, E. D. G. and Reed, M. S. (2010) 'Anticipating vulnerability to climate change in dryland pastoral systems: Using dynamic systems models for the Kalahari,' *Ecology and Society*, 15(2).

Dzenga, L. (2017) 'Indigenous Knowledge Systems: The Missing Link', *The Herald*, 14 June.

Getachew, S., Tilahun, T. and Teshager, M. (2014) 'Determinants of Agro-pastoralist Climate Change Adaptation Strategies: Case of Rayitu Woredas, Oromiya Region, Ethiopia,' *Research Journal of Environmental Sciences,* Volume 8(6), pp. 300-317.

Gleditsch, N.P., Buhaug, H. and Theisen, O.M. (2011) 'Climate change and armed conflict,' Paper presented to the Sixth General Conference, European Consortium for Political Research, University of Iceland, 26–27 August.

Gleik, P. and Heberger, M. (2014) 'Water Conflict: Events, Trends, and Analysis', Available at: http://worldwater.org/wp-content/uploads/2013/07/www8-water-conflict-events-trends-analysis.pdf, Accessed: 20 March 2019.

Goulden, M. and Few, R. (2011) *Climate change, water and conflict in the Niger River Basin.* London: International Alert.

Hall, R. (2011) 'Land Grabbing in Southern Africa: The Many Faces of the Investor Rush,' *Review of the African Political Economy*, Vol.38 (128), pp. 193-214.

Humbe, B.P. (2017) "African Traditional Religion in Postcolonial Zimbabwe: A Sustainable Heritage for Water Resources Management", in Green, M C., Hackett, R. I. J., Hansen, L. and

Venter, F. (eds.) *Religious Pluralism, Heritage and Social Development in Africa*. Stellenbosch: SUN Media, pp. 205-219.

IPCC (2007) 'Climate Change 2007: Impacts, Adaptation and Vulnerability. Contribution of Working Group II to the Fourth Assessment Report of the Intergovernmental Panel on Climate Change', In Parry, M. L., Canziani, O. F., Palutikof, J. P., van der Linden, P. J., and Hanson, C. E. (Eds.). Cambridge: Cambridge University Press.

Joshua, M., Jalloh, A. A., and Hachigonta, S. (2014) 'Review of Research and Policies for Climate Change Adaptation in the Agriculture Sector in Southern Africa,' Working Paper 101, Africa Interact, International Development Research Centre (IDRC).

Jury, M. and Funk, C. (2013) 'Climatic trends over Ethiopia: regional signals and drivers,' *International Journal of Climatology*, Vol. 33, pp. 1924-1935.

Kagwanja, P. (2007) "Calming the Waters: The East African Community and Conflict over the Nile Resources", *Journal of Eastern African Studies,* Vol. 1(3), pp. 321-337.

Kenney, C. (2017) 'How climate change and water and food insecurity drive instability,' The Center for American Progress, Washington, D.C. Available at: https://www.americanprogress.org/issues/security/reports/20 17/11/30/443465/climate-change-water-food-insecurity-drive-instability/, Accessed: 1 March 2019.

Kings, S. (2016) 'Climate change is testing Southern Africa water agreements' *Mail and Guardian,* 2 December.

Kusangaya, S., Warburton, M.L., Van Garderen, E.A., and Jewitt, G.P.W. (2013) 'Impacts of climate change on water resources in southern Africa: A review,' Phys. Chem. Earth A/B/C, doi:10.1016/j.pce.2013.09.014.

Lobell, D. B., Schlenker, W., and Costa-Roberts, J. (2011) 'Climate trends and global crop production since 1980,' *Science*, Vol. 333 (6042), pp.616-620.

Loki, R. (2014) 'Water wars: Fighting over Earth's most precious fluid,' Blog Entry in *Environment and Climate Change*, Available at: http://www.justmeans.com/blogs/water-wars-fighting-over-earths-most-precious-fluid, Accessed: 10 March 2019.

Mail & Guardian, (5 December 2016) Southern Africa Can Avoid Climate Strife with Water Agreements https://mg.co.za/article/2016-12-05-00-southern-africa-can-avoid-climate-strife-with-water-agreements.

Maluleke, W. and Mokwena, R. J. (2017) 'The Effect of Climate Change On Rural Livestock Farming: Case Study Of Giyani Policing Area, Republic Of South Africa,' *S. Afr. J. Agric. Ext.* Vol. 45 (1), pp. 26-40.

Mlambo, M. (2015) "Curbing Veld Fires is Everyone's Responsibility", *The Standard*, 7 December.

Mpandeli, S. (2018) 'Climate Change Adaptation through the Water-Energy-Food Nexus in Southern Africa', *Int. J. Environ. Res. Public Health*, 15(10).

Nhamo, L., Ndlela, B., Nhemachena, C., Mabhaudhi, T., Mpandeli, S and Matchaya, G. (2018) 'The water-energy-food nexus; Climate risks and opportunities in Southern Africa,' *Water*, Vol. 10, April.

Niang, I., Ruppel, O.C. and Abdrabo, M. (2014) 'Africa', in Barros, V.R., Field, C.B., Dokken, D.J., Mastrandrea, M.D., Mach, K.J., Bilir, T.E., Chatterjee, M., Ebi, K.L., Estrada, Y.O., Genova, R.C., Girma, B., Kissel, E.S., Levy, A.N., MacCracken, S., Mastrandrea, P.R., and White, L.L. (Eds.) *Impacts, Adaptation, and Vulnerability: Part B: Regional Aspects. Contribution of Working Group II to the Fifth Assessment Report of the Intergovernmental Panel on Climate Change*, Cambridge: Cambridge University Press, pp.199-1265.

NOAA (2014) 'The State of the Climate', 25th edition, *Bulletin of the American Meteorological Society*, Available at: https://www.ncdc.noaa.gov/news/state-of-the-climate-2014, Accessed: 20 February 2019.

Nordås, R., and Gleditsch, N. P. (2007) 'Climate Change and Conflict,' *Political Geography*, Vol. 26(6), pp. 627-638.

Nyamukondiwa, W. (2015) "Rain-Making for Lake Kariba", *The Herald*, 28 October.

Okpara, U. T., Stringer, L. C. and Dougill, A. J. (2017) 'Using a novel climate-water conflict vulnerability index to capture double exposures in Lake Chad,' *Regional Environmental Change*, Vol. 17 (2), pp. 351-366.

Otieno, J. (2013) 'Understanding Africa's Water Wars', *Africa Review*, 6 November, Available at: http://www.africareview.com/Special-Reports/Understanding-the-water-wars-in-Africa/-/979182/2062968/-/13c54d5z/-/index.html, Accessed: 10 March 2019.

Popovski, V. (2017) 'Foresight Africa viewpoint: Does climate change cause conflict?' *Brookings: Africa Growth Initiative*, Available at: https://www.brookings.edu/blog/africa-in-focus/2017/01/20/does-climate-change-cause-conflict/, Accessed: 20 March 2019.

Powell, N., Larsen, K. R.; de Bruin, A., Powell, S., Elrick-Barr, C. (2017) 'Water Security in times of climate change and intractability: Reconciling conflict by transforming security concerns into equity concerns,' *Water*, Vol. 9(12).

Robertson, C. (2008) 'Beyond 'Tribes': Violence and conflict in Kenya,' in *Origins: Current Events in Historical Perspective*, Vol. 1 (7)

Ross, M. and McConnell S. J. (2016) "Forget star wars; Get ready for water wars", Huffington Post, 20 January, Available at: https://www.huffingtonpost.com/marc-ross/forget-star-wars-get-ready-for-water-wars_b_9020188.html, Accessed: 10 March 2019.

Serdeczny, O., Adams, S., Baarsch, F., Coumou, D., Robinson, A., Hare, W., Schaeffer, M., Perrette, M., and Reinhardt, J. (2015) 'Climate change impacts in Sub-Saharan Africa: From physical changes to their social repercussions,' *Regional Environmental Change*, Vol. 15 (8). DOI: 10.1007/s10113-015-0910-2.

Sikaiga, S. J.A. (2009) 'The World's Worst Humanitarian Crisis: Understanding the Darfur Crisis,' in: *Origins: Current Events in Historical Perspective*, Vol. 2(5)

Swain, A., Swain, R.B., Themner, A., and Krampe, F. (2011) *Climate Change and the Risk of Violent Conflicts in Southern Africa*. Pretoria: Global Crisis Solutions.

Swain, A.K. (2011) 'Challenges for water sharing in the Nile basin: changing geo-politics and changing climate', *Hydrological Sciences Journal*, Vol. 56 (4), pp. 687–702.

Taylor, R.G., Bridget Scanlon, B., Döll, P., Rodell, M., van Beek, R., Wada, Y., Longuevergne, L., Leblanc, M., Famiglietti, J.S., Edmunds, M., Konikow, L., Green, T.R., Chen, J., Taniguchi, M.,

Bierkens, M.F. P., MacDonald, A., Fan, Y., Maxwell, R.M., Yechieli, Y., Gurdak, J.J., Allen, D. M., Shamsudduha, M., Hiscock, K., Yeh, P. J.-F., Holman, I., and Treidel, H. (2013) 'Ground water and climate change', *Nature Climate Change,* Vol. 3, April.

The Herald, (2015) 'Indigenous Knowledge System explained', *The Herald*, 17 February.

Thomson, A.M., Calvin, K.V., Chini, L.P., Hurtt, G., Edmonds, J.A., Bond-Lamberty, B., Frolking, S., Wise, M.A., and Janetos, A.C., (2010) 'Climate mitigation and the future of tropical landscapes' Proceedings of the National Academy of Sciences of the United States of America, November 16, 107 (46) 19633-19638; https://doi.org/10.1073/pnas.0910467107.

Toudi, J.L. (2018) 'Climate change, conflicts and permanent instability in Kenya,' Available at: https://www.ispionline.it/en/pubblicazione/climate-change-conflicts-and-permanent-instability-kenya-19961, Accessed: 10 March 2019.

UNFCCC (1994) 'United Nations Framework Convention on Climate Change' Available at: https://unfccc.int/resource/docs/convkp/conveng.pdf, Accessed: 10 March 2109.

World Bank (2013) 'Climate Extremes, Regional Impacts, and the Case for Resilience,' Available at: http://www.worldbank.org/en/topic/climatechange/publicatio n/turn-down-the-heat-climate-extremes-regional-impacts-resilience, Accessed: 10 March 2019.

Chapter Four

Chipping and Refashioning the Soapstone? A Symbolic Re-appraisal of the Colonial Wresting of Climate and Weather Control from African Spirit Mediums

Dube Edmore

Introduction

The discussion takes a symbolic approach to the emasculation of indigenous spirit mediums and their territorial chiefs with regards weather control. The visual image of the craftsman chipping at soapstone to refashion it into something else drives the message home, especially that the finished product is no longer called soapstone. The refashioned soapstone is called by the name of the object the craftsman sought to depict visually - an eagle, the Zimbabwe bird, a lion, a horse and so on. It is argued that in addition to sheer political force, the coloniser employed Christianity and education as chisels for reshaping the African's weather world view. Christianity and western education as symbols of the western concept of "modernity" gradually refashioned the African mindset to reject the indigenous worldview as backward and superstitious. This was despite the fact that western "modernity" was in itself a plunder of the African tangible and intangible heritage (Taiwo, 2010:51).

Deterrence was used as a mode of breaking African unity both in the secular political and Christian arenas. Zimbabwean spirit mediums such as Mbuya Nehanda and Sekuru Kaguvi were captured, hanged, and demonised to deter Africans from relying on spirit mediums (Lan, 1987:264). Likewise, Makewana of Chisumphi in Malawi was converted from national medium to chief, with influence over weather limited to the boundaries of the new miniature chiefdom. It was difficult to control the weather without authority over the taboos that reinforced the macrocosm, which the Whites disregarded with impunity. The missionaries particularly sought to supplant African Indigenous Religion (AIR) with Christianity. To do that they dangled 'education for employment' without which one could not take up good jobs in the new colonial economic system. Missionaries gradually brainwashed their African graduates, who were also converted and renamed on entry, into anti-AIR stalwarts. Attending traditional ceremonies cost one's job in missionary schools. By gradually 'chiselling away indigenous knowledge systems' the new system eventually produced an 'African [soapstone] Christian' oblivious of weather patterns as understood in African worldviews.

The Chipping of Soapstone Analogy

Indigenous Africans had agency - were lively actors and not lifeless- and the soapstone analogy is used here just as a metaphor. Soapstone is a ubiquitous indigenous rock used by local craftsmen and women in their endeavours to earn a living out of art. Many Zimbabweans would be aware of soapstone crafts displayed on the main highways and in places frequented by tourists. Only the transformed rock can be sold, but not the pure rock, here representing the pure indigenes. The soapstone remains pure and natural until the artist arrives to refashion it as s/he chooses, fully aware of what it takes to transform the natural rock into commercial form. The first step is to dislocate it from its usual habitation, before applying various defacing technologies which alter its outward appearance attracting new nomenclature - Zimbabwe bird, praying mantis, Jesus Christ – as the likeness or tradition may dictate. The process of translocation and chipping off is both arduous and protracted, as the artist struggles with the application of mattocks, picks and metal pivots to move the soapstone, before carefully applying the chisels – some of which are powered by hammers. Eventually the artist applies the rasp and sand paper to smoothen the object before finally polishing it with selected oil. Despite the change of name, however, the objects basically remain soapstone.

The analogy is that it was not an easy task to move the African out of his natural environment encompassing the epistemic, cultural, social, political, material and religious worldviews. There was use of military force (digging and pivoting) as well as aesthetic packages including Christianity, education and employment (chipping). Even then it took decades before the refashioned Africans started 'owning' new name tags, which in principle seemed diametrically opposed to African culture. Such names included 'Christians, elite, progressives or rationalists' which derogated Africans as 'pagan, illiterate, backward, superstitious,' despite the fact that pre-colonial Africans were literate modernists who built such universities as Timbuktu, Tedmakkat and Walata in West Africa and devised Hieroglyphics and the *shaduff* in Egypt (Adu Boahen *et al,* 1986; Haron, 2016). In that regard, like refashioned soapstone, Africans continued to eulogise their pre-colonial values resulting in periodic open resorts to indigenous rituals in times of crises (Daneel, 1970:59). As will become apparent subsequently, some got possessed by territorial spirits in the midst of Christian worship and returned home to be spirit mediums (Matsuhira, 2013:169). These are technically called "soapstone Christians" as the refashioning has failed to take the indigenous African spirits out of them. The next section locates this analogy within the context of the current discussion.

Context of the Discussion

The current discussion is located within the topical discourse on climate change; seized with a positive search for its mitigation from within the African indigenous knowledge systems (AIKS). Of particular concern have been the observations that the reactions of African indigenes to climate change have been gradually getting "lethargic," resigning to fate and leaving western methods to dominate the weather discourse (Daneel, 1970:66-67). The interpretation of this situation has been to project that something (in the image of a craftsman) has been gradually gnawing away the African worldview, polishing the remnants and renaming them in western terms. Conversely, on the scholarly arena there has been a gradual growth of discourses centring on the African Renaissance. This body of scholarship has unearthed credible evidence of the African having been master of his/her own destiny, with a complete philosophy about modernising his worldview (Taiwo, 2010; Asante, 2007; Hudson-Weems, 1993).

The African philosophy of life gave prominence to *mhondoro* (territorial spirit mediums) who acted as the axis mundi in relation to Mwari who was the source of life-giving rain (Nhemachena, 2014:65). The *mhondoro* spirit independently chose a medium for the purposes of denoting an intercessor for the community. Once someone claimed possession, the elders visited diviners to verify the authenticity of the spirit, before brewing beer to receive and confirm the spirit on the chosen medium (Matsuhira, 2013). Regalia were bought for the medium in accordance with the specifications of the spirit and bore a "spiritual quest… and are to be worn with pride and responsibility" (Belcourt, 2010:19). Of particular importance is the fact that traditional regalia of "societies ruled by kings and chiefs are an indispensable part of these societies" (Osei-Bonsu, 2010:iv). The regalia are tangible heritage which can only be passed on to successors for the uninterrupted continuation of the ritual functions of the office of the chief or medium. Such regalia are endowed with sacral powers to the extent that it is sacrilegious *kupunjira* (to desecrate) them. *Kupunjira* includes being handled or kept in custody by forbidden people (such as prostitutes, homosexuals, incestuous people or those accused of infanticide (see Nhemachena, 2014:105), which is why a specific *mukaranga* (medium assistant) is attached to each medium to ensure the purity and sanctity of the regalia. Desecrated regalia lose powers to master the weather patterns and harness them for purposes of enhancing ecological flourishing. To disempower famous mediums, the White colonisers took away their regalia and made them objects of internal and external museums (Matenga, 2011:52-53). A case in point is that of the sacred Remba Ngomalungundu which was wrestled away by Whites from the Remba's Dumbwi (Mberengwa) stronghold in the 1940s. The Ngomalungundu was the repository of the Remba efficacious sacred objects which they used to master the weather and to deter enemies, which earned them the famous name Mposi, meaning one who inflicts pain remotely from afar off. Today the Ngomalungundu has been reduced to 'one of those visual objects' in the Harare Museum of Human Sciences (Le Roux, 2003:169), leaving the Remba at the mercy of harsh weather and climate patterns. This was an effective emasculation strategy which was exacted on several communities in

Africa to feed European and American museums, at the expense of African fertility cults.

Afrocentric scholars and historians of Africa are clear that the *mhondoro* (and their equivalents in the various African communities) wielded power to install chiefs, who were the political heads of the communities. They ensured that justice flowed in the communities under the chiefs' control. Injustice, prostitution, homosexuality, incest and the spilling of blood in any circumstances, political or private, were causes for withholding rains by the world of the spirits (Lan, 1987:265; Murimbika, 2006:174; Amanze *et al.,* 2015:8). This could only be corrected by confession and cleansing by the relevant priestly mediums (Haruna, 1993:232). Our observation is that the spilling of blood has become rampant both on the political and social scales. Many people have perished in political and economic violence right from the beginning of the colonial era, through to Zimbabwe's liberation struggle, known as Chimurenga II (1965-1979), and the postcolonial era (Goronga, 2014).

On the social level road accidents have become a daily feed with the increase of unqualified drivers and unroadworthy vehicles on our roads. The salient accompaniment of all these has been lack of relevant cleansing ceremonies, which are generally becoming moribund (Haruna, 1993:236). Might this not be a serious breach of African weather protocols? In an interview with one Pentecostal pastor, the author was told that "the dead know nothing" which makes the cleansing ceremonies irrelevant. The pastor was adamant to the extent of viewing the AIR doctrine of the "living dead" as misplaced innovation; and yet he acknowledged the existence of *ngozi* (avenging spirit) in his own backyard. Avenging spirits come from people murdered in cold blood, who return to demand compensation to be given to their close kin: after compensation is paid, cleansing ceremonies have to be performed (Goronga, 2014). This is proof enough that the spirit lives on and has power over the living. The next section explores the African worldviews as reflected by their responses to weather and climate patterns.

African Responses to Weather Patterns

Ceremonies for harnessing the weather to the advantage of the ritual participants were rampant throughout the gigantic African continent. According to Haruna (1993:227), who presents the *Rituals and Ceremonies Accompanying Rainmaking among the Guruntum and Bubbure People* of Nigeria, such rituals were invaluable among agriculturalists. Agriculturalists sought to enhance human, animal and plant fertility for a smart ecological flourishing. The same assertion has been echoed by Gelfand (1959:5) and Daneel (1970:15) in their writings on Zimbabwe, and Babane and Chauke (2015:108-114) in their presentation of the same rituals among the Vatsonga of South Africa. These sedentary African societies viewed rainfall as a blessing from God who was understood to sit at the head of the spiritual realm dominated by "spirit elders [who] continued looking after the territories they once ruled when they were still alive …by providing rain and ensuring soil fertility" (Chirozva *et al.,* 2007:14). To receive this gift of rain which emanated from the spiritual realm, humanity acted its part by supplicating the spiritual world. Communal petitioners observed rain soliciting processes whose leadership was confined to particular clans or groups of people who wielded both political and religious powers (Haruna, 1993:228). Such powers were exercised at the request of the community (Haruna, 1993:229; Lan, 1987); which means that the authority of the medium was exercised in conformity with community procedures of presenting petitions to the spiritual world (Nhemachena, 2014:62). In other words, mediation had to be requested for, and not just a spontaneous whimsical activity of the medium. Africans had faith in their mediums, the *mhondoro* (Ngara *et al.,* 2014) or the *vurlimbo* (the man who does not tell a lie) (Haruna, 1993:229), whose oracles were divine law.

The rain rituals observed the annual water cycle, with the request for 'tillage rains' coming in the months of September-October in southern Africa, and the thanksgiving ceremonies coming in April-May as the authorisation ceremonies for the consumption of the new harvest. This petition-thanksgiving axis was sustained as a way of cultivating a positive relationship with the spiritual realm. Though the Africans did not distinguish space as strictly sacred and profane

138

(Eliade, 1959; Mbiti, 1990), the seasonal fertility ceremonies were held in places considered sacred because they were shrines to fertility spirits. These spaces could be natural places such as tree shades, rocky places or man-made shrines. The Nsolo, the Baobab, the Mukamba and the Muhacha trees are considered some of the most conducive shrines of the fertility spirits (Haruna, 1993; Dube, 1995:65; Chemhuru and Masaka, 2010:129). Depending on the traditions of the community and the availability of such trees, one of them is designated a clan or territorial shrine. The Chewa and the Yao of Malawi make use of the Nsolo tree, which is decked in black during the ritual act to symbolise dark clouds (Dube, 1995:65). The Korekore of northern Zimbabwe use Mukamba or Baobab trees – there is no Muhacha in their territory (Murimbika, 2006:179) – and during droughts they petition the chief to consult *mhondoro* in their hierarchy including Nehanda, Hwatira, Karembera, Dzivaguru and finally Chaminuka (Bourdillon, 1976:311). To bring the discussion closer home the next section discusses the *mhondoro* and Mwari cults in Zimbabwe.

The *Mhondoro* and Mwari Cults in Zimbabwe

The *mhondoro* spirits dominated all rain cults throughout the pre-historic Zimbabwe, though the Mwari cult was visibly at the apex of the *mhondoro* rain requests in the southern half of the country. It follows that while all territorial cults were controlled by mediums possessed by the spirits of the deceased kings, paramount chiefs or founding fathers, the mediums of the southern region ceded the ultimate authority to Mwari/God whose voice was heard at the Matopos/Matonjeni, from whom they sought further guidance annually. According to Daneel (1970: 14):

> Of all the southern and eastern African tribes the Southern Shona have the most elaborate cult for worshipping and consulting the Supreme Being. For centuries they have believed in Mwari as the final authority behind their ancestors, a High God who was perhaps less directly involved in the affairs of individual lives than the ancestors, but one who could be consulted on matters of communal import. Far from being a remote deity, Mwari was believed to control the fertility of

Shona occupied country, to give rain in times of drought and advice on the course of action in times of national crisis.

Manyusa (rain emissaries) left Chipinge, Masvingo and parts of the Midlands from the end of August to early October depending on their distance from Matopos; for the foot journey was intended to be concluded just about the same time. These messengers carried with them gifts collected from all members of their communities as sacred accompaniments of their petitions; a forgone commitment that they would accept the verdict of Mwari whatever it was (Daneel, 1970:15, 55). They sought prescriptions from the voice of Mwari manifesting from the shrine rocks. The oracles of God coming from the rocks in Matopos/Matonjeni gave them specifications necessary for carrying out successful annual *mukwerera/mutoro* (rain-petitioning ceremony), which was "understood and appreciated as an equivalence of life itself" (Amanze *et al.,* 2015:7). If any crimes were committed against God or ancestors, the messengers were directed on how to cleanse the land of such abominations in order to unlock a good rain season. Good rains would not fall unless proper cleansing ceremonies had been conducted, with the chief and the medium overseeing the process. If rains came before the propitiation ceremonies were done, it tended to be very destructive, as in having hailstones or causing serious flooding. The fact that Mwari controlled taboos or crimes against himself and ancestors, meant that he was the owner of the land often dominated by supplications directed towards the territorial ancestors.

Mwari controlled the land that he owned in order to ensure its cleanliness, for purity was the basis of human flourishing. To ensure this life-guaranteeing purity, each territorial spirit ensured that the king or paramount chief followed the purification procedures in order to make the land clean. One way of ensuring purity was to prevent foreigners oblivious of/intransigent towards/ local traditions from assuming control of the territory because their activities would defile the land (Daneel, 1970:31). This is exactly what happened when the Pioneer Column took over the land of Zimbabwe on the pretext of a hunting license; they ended up partitioning the land among the Column fortune seekers (Chinamasa, 2001:13). Control over the land was wrestled from Mwari and the *mhondoro* and placed in the hands of a force that missionaries termed the 'Christian God', though it is doubtful that this amounts to the authentic Christian God, the originator of the Decalogue which forbids crimes against humanity as done by colonists with impunity. As though by cue, a marauding drought ensued and *rinderpest* wiped out a lot of cattle, the bastion of indigenous wealth. Worse still, the colonisers insisted that carcasses of cattle (proven source of protein) from infected cattle be burnt or thrown away. This was too much for the locals who petitioned their mediums for direction.

The spirit mediums rose to the occasion with Mbuya Nehanda, Sekuru Kaguvi and Chaminuka leading the Korekore and the Zezuru in the north and Mukwati, the priest of Mwari, leading the southerners in a concerted effort to drive out the White colonisers in order to resuscitate control over purity rituals. The Mwari cult was a unifying force behind this cleansing effort affectionately known as the First Chimurenga (1896-7), with its spirit mediums acting as intelligent superimos. The oracle of Mwari against the sacrilegious acts of the Whites has been succinctly captured by Daneel, 1970: 31):

> These whites are your enemies. They killed your fathers, sent the locusts, caused this disease among the cattle and bewitched the clouds so that we have no rain. Now you will go and kill these white people and drive them out of our father's land and I Mwari will take away the cattle disease and the locusts and send you rain.

It is clear from the quotation that the colonisers affected the weather patterns and as long as they remained in control, Mwari would refrain from giving good rains, which disempowers *manyusa* (rain mediums). Mwari distances himself for as long as the defilement lasts. Worse still, their "indirect rule and land grabs led to the contestation for power between colonial authorities, chiefs, and spirit mediums" (Kaoma, 2016:57). Kaoma (2016:58) observes that the most iconic names in Zimbabwean history to date have remained those of the spirit mediums associated with the first Chimurenga: Mukwati, Nehanda, Chaminuka and Kaguvi, whose names now adorn coveted streets as well as important administrative buildings as memorial names. This all emanates from the mediums' place in the indigenous purity code, responsible for sustained rainfall and fertility.

The Zimbabwe situation dictated the sacrosanctity of land because "where land symbolises the continuity of the social group (the clan) from mythical times to the present, the land could not be sold for money without destroying the identity of the group itself" (Rosman, 1985:153). For that reason, instead of demanding compensation from the White usurpers, the people demanded their land heritage back for it was the shrine of their God and their ancestors, and a definition of their very being. The land was therefore a common heritage, a source of interrelationships which could neither be mortgaged nor individualised (Eyerman and Jamison, 1991:70). This is why invaluable tribute is directed toward the mediums as heroes of the First Chimurenga, a war which was essentially a concerted effort for the restitution and cleansing of the desecrated land (Kamudzandu, 2013:14). Before turning to the sustained 'refashioning' of the indigenes which followed the pacification of the local belligerents of the First Chimurenga, we need to consider *chisi* (territorial holy day) regarded as inviolable by AIR adherents (Fontein, 2006:173).

Chisi (Holy Day)

Each territorial chieftaincy has a holiday during which inhabitants abstain from working on the land, in addition to a host of other taboos including fetching firewood and cleaning the yard. Underlining the importance of *chisi* chief Mposi of the Remba community of Mberengwa noted:

> The *svikiro,* a local medium of the *Mwari* cult, who is invariably of our clan, ensures that the day is accorded its rightful honour. We enforce the oracles of *Mwari* accessed through her by levying cattle or goat fines on offenders, depending on the extent of the crime. Expulsion is the stiffest punishment the land can ever impose on a persistent holy day breaker (Dube, 2013:33-4).

The penalties for breaking the taboos associated with *chisi* outlined above clearly set it apart as a highly coveted tradition, associated with the rain cult of Matonjeni. The stiff penalties were meant to deter wrong doers, cleanse the land of the abomination and

142

assuage Mwari against imposing reprisals, which included natural disasters and targeted blights. And yet Lugard, the philosophical think tank behind the British Empire categorically states that "the impact of European civilization on tropical races has indeed a tendency to undermine that respect for authority which is the basis of social order. The authority of the head, whether of the tribe, the village, or the family, is decreased, and parental discipline is weakened" (Lugard, 1965:426). Taiwo (2010:91) is critical of the imposition of this "African individuality on individual Africans," which disregarded African rules of respect, and tended to be sacrilegious to say the least. What is worse is that some "Africans bought into the new civilization with aplomb. They fancied themselves as inheritors of a new civilization and sought to rearrange their mental and physical spaces to reflect their embrace of the new" (Taiwo, 2010:91).

Western enterprises tended to operate on *chisi* days with impunity, because European colonialism was presented contra-AIR which was seen as infantile (Taiwo, 2010:92; Ray, 1976). For example, schools could work on their plots on territorial holy days which tended to fall within the school week, since they ranged from Tuesday to Friday. On the commercial and church farms the "holy days" were Saturday if the owners were Seventh Day Adventists and Sunday for the rest of the farmers. Industries tended to knock off midday, Saturday. Reconciling this western working week with the territorial week was a mammoth task, leading to irreconcilable differences with the rain cult. How could people working in the same territory observe three different holy days – territorial, Seventh Day and Sunday? Could these sardonic dealings in contravention of the law of the land not bring wrath upon the population? The chief and the medium are wont to answer this question in the affirmative. What is worse is that the loosening of authority alluded to by Lugard (1965:144) no longer allow the chief and the medium the authority to summon everyone to the shrine for the cleansing of the land, which therefore perpetually remains unclean to the great chagrin of Mwari. In furtherance of this view the next section discusses the general 'refashioning' of the indigenes by the westerners.

The Chipping and Refashioning of 'Soapstone'

When the Christian missionaries came to Matabeleland in the nineteenth century, they found the Ndebele kingdom fortified against foreign cultures, with king Lobengula fully behind the rituals of Nkulunkulu and the Mwari rain cult. The missionaries failed to scull through the indigenous fertility traditions in their efforts to subvert local traditions in favour of Christianity. Fr Prestage, a Jesuit Catholic cleric, was forced to lead his mission back to South Africa after a dismal sojourn at Lobengula's Bulawayo. Failure to penetrate the local traditions was the key reason why Fr Prestage allowed members of his mission to join the invading Pioneer Column as chaplains and nurses (Zvobgo, 1996), which gave the invading forces the much needed moral justification.

The process of 'chipping and refashioning' the indigenous worldview started earnestly with the hoisting of the Union Jack in Salisbury on 12 September 1890. Such hoisting of a foreign flag contravened the local oral codes of governance, because it was a symbolic appropriation of territory. This amounted to the defilement of the land, since its occupation by strangers without duly informing its spiritual owners was a sacrilegious act which invoked spiritual reprisal in the form of natural disasters not excluding droughts. The first step in the emasculation of the indigenes with respect to weather control, therefore, involved unilateral occupation of the land in defiance of the local political authorities jointly in charge of implementing environmental taboos with the territorial mediums. The foregoing has demonstrated that the spirit mediums worked with chiefs and kings to master the rain rituals. Now with the imposition of a new over-arching authority that symbiotic relationship between the political (king/chief) and the religious (medium) was adversely affected. It is therefore important to understand that the current framing of the 'chipping and refashioning' of the local traditions is a description of the outcome of AIR's encounter with European culture as a result of this colonialism (Babane and Chauke, 2015:108).

No sooner had the settlers encamped and re-named Harava, Salisbury in honour of the then British Prime Minister, than they set out to prospect for gold and other minerals without due respect to the "guardians of the land," the *mhondoro* (Schoffeleers, 1979). Worse

144

still, with the failure to discover enough mineral deposits, the members of the White community started parcelling out the land, the sacred abode of the ancestors. This was followed by droughts, locusts and *rinderpest*, which shook the land leading to the ill-fated First Chimurenga. The pacification of both the Shona and the Ndebele in this first united effort to rid the land of the "new abomination" put the indigenes at the mercy of the new system.

The *mhondoroship* was 'banned' with the decapitation of Kaguvi and Nehanda among others. The severed heads of some of the mediums and key chiefs were taken as trophies to England, which further angered Mwari, the fertility God (Mangwana, 2015). According to Kaoma (2016:59), "colonial authorities pacified chiefs (whose authority was assumed to be political), but outlawed spirit mediums—leading to the contestation of power between colonial authorities, chiefs and mediums." Clergymen like von Sicard took to ethnography aimed at understanding what held the Africans together as a united entity (Beach, 1980). It was discovered that they had a Bantu philosophy of forces which was pro-life (Tempels, 1953), and was often communicated in symbols. Such symbols had to be retrieved from the people to disempower them, which would compel them to seek protection in the new western philosophy, strange to Mwari the fertility God. This is how the Ngomalungundu found its way into the hands of the colonisers at the recommendation of von Sicard, the anthropologist credited with studying the Mberengwa communities at length (Beach, 1980). To that end the colonisers and their missionary allies employed both political force and research to empower themselves at the expense of the locals who suffered recurrent punishments at the hands of their fertility deity.

The chiefs having lost authoritative control over the lands to which they had been confirmed by the *mhondoro* were left only with virtual authority allowed them by the Lugard system of indirect rule. The Whites now controlled the country through the chiefs whom they appointed. The *mhondoro* lost control over the selection and appointment of chiefs. Chiefs who disobeyed colonial orders by listening to the *mhondoro* were deposed and new ones appointed, sometimes from subordinate headmen or even outright new genealogies at variance with territorial spirits. This left the *mhondoro* at loggerheads with the new non-royal government appointees oblivious of the *mukwerera* procedures. Family squabbles that ensued have survived the test of time and still exist to this day, though a few have been reversed by the current government which returned some chieftainships to the original genealogies. The continuous assault on the chief-*mhondoro* partnerships left many ordinary citizens gravitating towards Christianity, whose major goal was to supplant AIR by creating conditions that painted it in bad light. Mapara (2011:16) contends that missionaries misconstrued AIR as promoting witchcraft and the worship of ancestors in place of God. This depiction by missionaries was in bad faith because missionaries also honoured their own saints whom they believed to be intercessors between human beings and God.

Upon safe arrival in Zimbabwe, which the Whites named Rhodesia in honour of Cecil John Rhodes who was a British homosexual colonial magnate behind the Pioneer Column (Brown 2015), the missionary organisations which had given moral support to the invading force were rewarded with large tracts of land. Mwari withheld rains and sent pests to ravage the land in opposition to the dedication of the land to the homosexual foreigners. Worse still, the missionaries sardonically 'eradicated' the rituals directed towards Mwari, the fertility God, and his subordinate *mhondoro* from the designated lands. This was the inauguration of the bitter AIR-Christianity acrimony which still rages on to date. To begin with, missionaries introduced 'deportation and importation' of local population from the designated mission lands, some of which were re-named Christian villages including the Catholic missions of Chishawasha and Gokomere and the Anglican Daramombe (Chipeneti, 2015). Those who failed to live by the strict Christian dogmas were 'deported' from the Christian villages, while those from without who promised to comply with the letter were 'imported' onto the farms. Fear of deportation from one's people and graves of elders forced many to comply, though internally they retained their religion for long periods, practising it secretly (Daneel, 1970:19). The final segment will show us how the Second and Third Chimurenga tried to reignite the fire of AIR.

Missionaries also introduced mission schools, which ushered the locals into the colonial job market (Bone, 2000), but Olufemi Taiwo (2010:49) accuses missionaries of acting in cohort with colonial administrators and traders to plunder and distort African modernity. This view is pertinent here because the missionaries abused their capacity to provide education for employment knowing fully well that it was directly or indirectly compulsory to work for Whites in order to earn the non-negotiable hut and head tax imposed on the indigenes by the colonisers (Mandivenga, 1983; Moore, 2005). Missionary education was one of the most lethal weapons in the refashioning of 'soapstone' to suit the new Western order, as it touched on security needs since one who absconded from tax-payment faced imprisonment with no recourse. One clear sign of western missionary educational influence was the foisting of 'Christian names', onto many indigenes, including Simon, Jonas and Adam (Daneel, 1970:62). Many of the graduates of mission schools were converted and re-named on entry into mission schools, which was done without any government sanctions. The government, complicity in missionary machinations, put the Africans at a disadvantage. Africans were forced to abandon their pristine rain rituals, on the pretext that they were "evil and uncivilized": this amounted to a breach of indigenous covenant with Mwari who decided to withhold good rains (Amanze *et al.*, 2015:8).

Despite all the concerted pressure on AIR, it is gradually becoming apparent that refashioning amounted more to reorientation than to eradication or total recreation. As described above, officials at Matonjeni were named Simon, Jonas and Adam – they had been christened in their short stint at school and they still maintained their posts at the rain shrine. According to Haruna (1993:237), "through modern education or values many of the traditional beliefs of the people are distorted, changed or partially abandoned." Noko (2017:v) concurs that the tension created by the new system led to the deterioration of indigenous culture as reflected by the Basutho culture around Gwanda area.

Mwari's covenant with the indigenes was further disregarded by the African Initiated Churches, such as the Zion Christian Church of Bishop Samuel Mutendi. Bishop Mutendi went further to try and supplant the *mhondoro* rain cult by banning his followers from taking part in it and instead introducing his own *mbeu vungano* (seed conference) held every October (Daneel, 1970:66). He took upon himself the role of blessing the seeds traditionally done by the *mhondoro* or the priests of the Mwari cult in Matopos. Mutendi's popularity as a rain petitioner earned him the allegiance of fourteen paramount chiefs from Gutu, Masvingo, Mwenezi, Bikita, Zaka and Buhera (Daneel, 1970:67). The gifts traditionally meant for Matonjeni were diverted to Mutendi as the new rain official, with no respect for the traditional water spirits including Mwari of Mabweadziva in Matopos. Unfortunately this "disdain for and rejection of water spirits contributed to the environmental failure" (Machoko, 2013:285). This is because "in a mechanistic model of the natural environment, the power and authority of water spirits in Zimbabwe have been usurped by western modernity" (*Ibid*). The following section shows us that despite sardonic refashioning, 'soapstone' remains materially 'soapstone.'

The Reality of Refashioned 'Soapstone'

Haruna (1993:237) argues that although AIR rituals and ceremonies have been distorted or abandoned due to western education, "but they are by no means extinct." Indeed, like the carved soapstone which remains soapstone, the tempered rituals remain AIR rain rituals. Matsuhira (2013) credits AIR with untamed efficacy capable of bringing Christian converts back to the AIR fold through spirit possession. An example is given of how a female *mhondoro* spirit named Biri possessed Chipo Mushambadope while in the Methodist church in 1982 forcing her to throw away the church uniform to embrace mediumship of the rain cult of Biri and Ganire (Matsuhira, 2013:169). The Nyandoro elders of Masasa in Chikomba held a ceremony to ascertain the authenticity of the claims to the Biri spirit, and the result was positive. The medium went on to exercise pristine authority of selecting the chief, though the government decided to appoint his rival resulting in the ritual chief who leads worshippers during *mukwerera* and the administrative chief who never sets foot at the shrine. Biri remained adamant that her choice was the legitimate one throughout all vicissitudes of binary chieftainship: "thus, one of the main characteristics of the spirit mediums was their absolute independence from the political leadership, and they were free to support or to criticise the political incumbents" (Chung, 2006:198).

The Biri and Ganire shrine itself is a large circular hut made of burnt brick and cement motor, with a grass thatch. Use of cement has not desecrated the shrine despite its association with western economy. For that reason the Nyandoro people hold their week long *mukwerera* in the shrine every September with no qualms. Afterwards they observe a thanksgiving ceremony at the onset of harvest, which is followed by the last ceremony to welcome winter (Matsuhira, 2013). Noko (2017:3) also observed the resilience of the Gwanda Basutho rain ceremonies despite an acute sandwiching by both western and Ndebele cultures. These cultural pressures on the indigenous rain rituals broaden to include Islam, Bahai and Hinduism (Bourdillon, 1995) as well as Rastafarianism and Buddhism (Sibanda, 2016).

In addition to religious faiths, secular urbanisation has played its part, but *mukwerera* has stood the test of all these influences to retain its relevance albeit in a hugely fragmented society (Chirozva *et al.,* 2007:45), marked by continual loosening of the patriarchal hold (Beattie, 1964). As a matter of fact:

> Mwari vaMatonjeni has remained the God of the rural people. To those who live on a subsistence level and are therefore dependent on a rain-giving God for their crops, and to those who are involved in the intrigues of tribal politics, the God of Matonjeni still matters a great deal. In the bustle of town life this need is less felt, and although townsmen generally know about this deity one can often hear them remark, "Mwari vaMatonjeni is the God of the 'old men' *(vakuru)* in the tribal lands." It now seldom happens that a woman travels from the African township at Fort Victoria to Matonjeni in search of *'chibereko'* (lit: fruit; i.e. the power of bearing children), as townsmen recollect to have often happened in the past. An organized *munyai* system does not exist for this urban community (Daneel, 1979:60).

Chung (2006:197) concurs that the verdict of the spirit mediums was law to the peasantry who formed 70% of the population, even with regard to the freedom fighters of the Second Chimurenga War. Chung (2006) notes the revival of AIR during the liberation struggle, which had a *mhondoro* quarter in every camp. The major focus of the *mhondoro* was restitution of the ancestral land and provision of rains, which brought them into a symbiotic working relationship with the liberation fighters (Kazembe, 2011:94). After independence there was an attempt to inculcate a spirit of national *bira* for the placating of the spirits of the dead war combatants (Fontein, 2006:194; Cox, 2005). The war veterans in particular have continued to "invoked a shared war legacy of co-operation with spirit mediums and the ancestors… recognising the ancestral ownership of the land… and the provision of rain" (Fontein, 2006:17). There continues to be traditional chiefs who value the rain spirits greatly. A case in point is that of the thirteen Binga chiefs who foot to visit the Nevana rain spirit in Gokwe annually despite their area being more prone to better rains than the Shangwe area hosting the spirit (Ngara *et al.*, 2014:83). Further to that, a national constitution guaranteeing freedom of worship was promulgated in 2013.

Conclusion

The sustained sandwiching of AIR by western forces has only managed to 'chip' away absolute dependence on AIR by some indigenous Africans, but has neither invalidated it nor effectively eliminated it from the hearts of indigenous Africans. Education, including research, has been the most lethal weapon upon which western culture relied to emasculate Africans with regards weather control. On the political level, British theorist Lugard advised on indirect rule which left chiefs with nominal powers, insufficient to guide communities through cleansing rituals necessary for mastering the weather. In terms of sustained empirical research, clerical anthropologists like Tempels and von Sicard publicised the sources of indigenous power, exposing them to abuse by the colonial authorities and missionaries. All this went into 'chipping and refashioning' of indigenous cultures, loosening control over weather, and creating clone control in the hands of ineffective Christian pretenders who failed to completely wean Africans from *mukwerera*. The end result has been the development of a marauding climate change eluding controls possibly due to continuous defilement of the covenant of Mwari.

References

Adu Boahen, J. F., Ade Ajayi and Tidy, M. (1986) *Topics in West African History*. Singapore: Longman.

Amanze, P. O., Sibanda, L., Madembo, C. D. and Mhlanga, J. (2015)'Comparative study of marriage, rain making and livelihood rituals in Christianity and African Traditional Religion', Paper presented at the 3rd international conference on *The Future of Higher Education in Africa,* August 24 – 26, 2015 (Seventh Day Adventist).

Asante, K. M. (2007) *An Afrocentric Manifesto: Toward an African Renaissance*, Cambridge: Polity Press.

Babane, M.T. and Chauke, M. T. (2015) 'The preservation of Xitsonga culture through rainmaking ritual: An interpretative approach', *Stud. Tribes Tribals, 13,2*, pp. 108-114.

Beach, D. N. (1980) *The Shona and Zimbabwe 900-1850.* Gweru: Mambo Press.

Beattie, J. (1964) *Other Cultures: Aims, Methods and Achievements in Social Anthropology.* London: Routledge and Kegan Paul.

Belcourt, C. (2010) *Beadwork: First Peoples' Beading History and Techniques.* Owen Sound: Ningwakwe Learning Press.

Bone, D. S. (2000) 'The Development of Islam in Malawi and the response of the Christian churches c.1860-1986', in D. S. Bone (ed) *Malawi's Muslims: Historical Perspectives.* Blantyre: Christian Literature Association in Malawi, pp.113-153.

Bourdillon, M. F. C. (1976) *The Shona Peoples.* Gwelo: Mambo Press.

Bourdillon, M. F. C. (1995) *The Shona Peoples: An Ethnography of the Contemporary Shona with Special Reference to their Religion.* Gweru: Mambo Press.

Brown, R. (2015) *The Secret Society: Cecil John Rhodes' Plan for a New World Order.* Johannesburg: Penguin random house.

Chipeneti, J. (2015) 'Analysis of the church's social response to the community it serves: A case study of mission and evangelism in the Anglican diocese of Masvingo', BA Honours dissertation, Zimbabwe Open University.

Chirozva, C., Mubaya, C. P. and Mukamuri, B. (2007) *The Traditional African Family in the age of Globalization:* Literature Review Report for Centre for Rural Development a Barefoot Education for Afrika Trust (BEAT) partner.

Chemhuru, M. and Masaka, D. (2010) 'Taboos as sources of Shona people's environmental ethics', *Journal of Sustainable Development in Africa* 12, 7, pp.129-133.

Chinamasa, M. G. (2001) 'The human right to land in Zimbabwe: The legal and extra-legal Resettlement Processes', unpublished LLM thesis, Makerere University.

Chung, F. (2006) *Re-living the Second Chimurenga: Memories from the Liberation Struggle in Zimbabwe.* Stockholm: The Nordic Africa Institute.

Cox, J. L. (2005) 'The Land Crisis in Zimbabwe: A Case of Religious Intolerance?' *Fieldwork in Religion* 1, 1, pp.35-48.

Daneel, M. L. (1970) *The God of the Matopo Hills: An Essay on the Mwari Cult in Rhodesia.* Paris: Mouton.

Dube, E. (1995) 'The impact of proselytising religions on traditional beliefs and practices: A study of the interaction between Islam and the Chewa and Yao Traditional Religions in the Inter-Lakes Region in Malawi', unpublished MA thesis, University of Zimbabwe.

Dube, E. (2013) *A Tradition of Abstinence and Ritual Identity: The Ruling Sadiki Remba of Mposi in Mberengwa.* Lambert Academic Publishing.

Eyerman, R. and Jamison, A. (1991). *Social Movements: A Cognitive Approach.* University Park: Pennsylvania State University Press.

Eliade, M. (1959) *The Sacred and the Profane: The Significance of Religious Myth, Symbolism and Rituals within Life and Culture.* New York: Harcourt.

Gelfand, M. (1959) *Shona Rituals: with special reference to the Chaminuka Cult.* Cape Town: Juta.

Goronga, P. (2014) 'Ngozi as post-election restitution: A case study of Masvingo District, Zimbabwe', unpublished BA Honours dissertation, Zimbabwe Open University.

Haruna, A. (1993) *Rituals and Ceremonies Accompanying Rainmaking among the Guruntum and Bubbure People.* Frankfurt: German Research Foundation.

Hudson-Weems, C. (1993) *Africana Womanism: Reclaiming Ourselves.* Michigan: Bedford Publishers.

Fontein. J. (2006) 'Shared legacies of the war: Spirit mediums and war veterans in southern Zimbabwe", *Journal of Religion in Africa*, 36, 2, pp.167-199.

Haron, M. (2016) 'Africa's Islamic Civilization: and its Continental Challenges', *Journal of Education and Social Sciences*, 4, pp. 262-273

Kamudzandu, I. (2013) *Abraham our Father: Paul and the Ancestors in Postcolonial Africa*. Minnesota: Fortress Press.

Kaoma, K. J. (2016) 'African religion and colonial rebellion: The contestation of power in colonial Zimbabwe's Chimurenga of 1896-1897', *Journal for the Study of Religion* 29, 1, pp. 57 – 84.

Kazembe, T. (2011) 'Divine angels and vadzimu in Shona Religion, Zimbabwe', *The Rose Croix Journal* 8, pp.89-98.

Lan, D. (1987) *Guns and Rain: Guerrillas & Spirit Mediums in Zimbabwe*. London: University of California Press.

Le Roux, M. (2003) *The Lemba: A Lost Tribe of Israel in Southern Africa?* Pretoria: University of South Africa.

Lugard, F. D. (1965) *The Dual Mandate in Tropical Africa*. London: Frank Cass.

Machoko, C. G. (2013) 'Water spirits and the conservation of the natural environment: A case study from Zimbabwe', *International Journal of Sociology and Anthropology* 5, 8, pp.285-296.

Mandivenga, E. C. (1983) *Islam in Zimbabwe*. Gweru: Mambo Press.

Mangwana, N. N. (2015) 'The role of culture in Zimbabwe', *The Herald* 23 June.

Mapara, J. (2011) 'Avoiding potential knowledge death: Protecting indigenous knowledge in a global world', *Southern African Journal for Folklore Studies*, 21, 2, pp.12-24.

Matenga, E. (2011) 'The soapstone birds of Great Zimbabwe: Archaeological heritage, religion and politics in postcolonial Zimbabwe and the return of cultural property", *Studies in Global Archaeology* 16, pp1-262.

Matsuhira, Y. (2013) 'Rain making ceremony in the Nyandoro region, Zimbabwe', *African Religious Dynamics*, 1, pp.165-182.

Mbiti, J. (1990) *African Religion and Philosophy*. London: SPCK.

Moore, D. S. (2005) *Suffering for territory: Race, place, and power in Zimbabwe*. Harare: Weaver Press.

Murimbika, M. (2006) 'Sacred powers and rituals of transformation: An ethno-archaeological study of rainmaking rituals and agricultural productivity during the evolution of the Mapungubwe state, AD 1000 TO AD 1300', unpublished PhD Thesis, University of Johannesburg.

Ngara, R., Rutsate, J. and Mangizvo R. V. (2014) 'Shangwe indigenous knowledge systems: An ethnometrological and ethnomusicological explication', *International Journal of Asian Social Science* 4, 1, pp.81-88.

Nhemachena, A. (2014) 'Knowledge, *Chivanhu* and struggles for survival in conflict-torn Manicaland, Zimbabwe', unpublished PhD thesis, University of Cape Town.

Noko, V. (2017) 'An Ethnography of *setapa* music of the Basotho in the context of *holoba pula* rain making ceremony', unpublished BA Honours Dissertation, Midlands State University.

Osei-Bonsu, M. (2010) 'Stool regalia of the Dwaben state of Asante (Ghana): Relevance to art education, unpublished PhD Thesis, Kwame Nkrumah University of Science and Technology.

Ray, B. C. (1976) *African Religions: Symbol, Ritual and Myth*. Amazon: Prentice Hall.

Rosman, A. and Rubel, P. G. (1985) *The Tapestry of Culture: An Introduction to Cultural Anthropology*. New York: Random House.

Schoffeleers, J. M. (ed) (1979) *Guardians of the Land*. Gwelo: Mambo Press.

Sibanda, F. (2016) 'Rastafari perspectives on land use and management in postcolonial Zimbabwe', in Green, M. C., Hackett, R. I. J., Hansen, L. and Venter, F. (eds) *Religious Pluralism, Heritage and Social Development in Africa*. Stellenbosch: African Sun Media, pp. 189-204.

Taiwo, O. (2010) *How Colonialism Preempted Modernity in Africa*. Indianapolis: Indiana University Press.

Tempels, P. (1953) *Bantu Philosophy*. London: Presence Africaine Collection.

Zvobgo, C. J. M. (1996) *A History of Christian Missions in Zimbabwe 1890-1939*. Gweru: Mambo Press.

Primary Source

Runesu Mahembe, Interviewed Mberengwa Turn Off, 10/02/2019, ZAOGA FIF Pastor.

Chapter Five

Rain Petitioning in African Indigenous Knowledge Systems: Insights from *Ifá* among the Yorùbá People of Nigeria

Olúwọ́lé Tẹ́wọ́gboyè Òkéwándé

Introduction

Ifá, the foundation on which the culture of the Yorùbá people rests, basically encapsulates the scientific and religious knowledge. Therefore, this study investigates the Yorùbá worldview through the *Ifá's* prescriptions about climate change, which is the latitude condition in the determination of heat or cold in regards to rain petitioning. Rain petitioning occurs when the hot climate seems unbearable to the extent that, the negative effects result in a lot of hazards such as famine, drought, sicknesses and diseases. Semiotic approach is adopted because; symbolism is basic to *Ifá.* The study is divided into introduction, what *Ifá* is, *Ifá* mythical code, *ẹbọ Ifá* (Ifá sacrifice) and the rain petitioning, *Ifá* prescriptions and discussion on the rain petitioning and conclusion. Relevant *Ifá* corpus that evinces on the rain petitioning are explored to establish the Yorùbá indigenous system of rain petitioning. The *Ifá's* corpuses suggest that the implementation order of rain petitioning is sanctioned by the spiritual forces mediated by *Ifá.* This is because, to the Africans generally and, the Yorùbá people in particular, the control of the physical and invisible aspects of the peoples' lives, including climate, depend on the ancestors, divinities, supernatural agents and spirits and human beings. It is found out from the study that, on one hand, among the Yorùbá, climate change in relation to rain petitioning is impossible without *Ifá* and on the other hand, rain petitioning is one of the means by which the Yorùbá people overcome or reduce the effects of climate change for their favourable and peaceful system of living.

One of the global challenges facing different nations of the world is that of climate change. As a result of this, different nations especially, the continent of Africa are developing 'coping strategies' to deal with unusual changes in the weather resulting in very hot, dry, cold, wet, raining, flooding, wind or tornadoes among others and the associated social, economic and health effects of climate change in human society. One of the ways by which Africans address the effects of climate change is rain petitioning. In a typical Yorùbá society, when there is a problem, *Ifá* is consulted on the causes and the solution to it. Rain petitioning is one of the ways by which the Yorùbá people adapt to weather and climatic changes. For example, Maciver and Page (1950: 76-8) identified three forms of adaptation to environmental changes: physical, biological and social. However, social adaptation is more relevant to this study because it is concerned with:

> The process of adjustment or of accommodation…But *if* we are to live in ways we desire we must find or make an appropriate environment. Man does what every living creature does in proportion to its intelligence: he modifies his environment in such a way that the inevitable adaptation shall admit the greater fulfilment of his wants…In terms of our desires we criticize the adaptation which, considered only as a "natural" or physical phenomenon, is always perfect. What we are really criticizing is the environment to which our lives are adapted or ourselves because of our failure to control it – to change the condition of the equilibrium.

Taking a cue from the opinions of these scholars, I will argue that the Yorùbá apply their indigenous knowledge through *Ifá* in time of excessive dry and hot weather by resorting to rain petitioning- the central goal of this essay.

Methodology: Semiotic Approach

Semiotics, which is the scientific study of signs is adopted because, symbolism is basic to *Ifá* divination. The use of symbols in communication forms a stage of human development generally and Africans in particular. It was through the use of symbols as a medium of communication that Africans developed oral forms of communication, before the use of letters or written words. For example, Richard reports that, Faik Nzuji "undertakes a semiological analysis of the code of representation in different groups… Dogon graphic symbolism has been the study of several studies. It is indeed of the utmost importance because these symbols are in close relation to speech: they are produced within speech communities and demand interpretation by these communities (2009: 9). *Ifá* symbols are media of communication that are read and interpreted as Yorùbá ancient speech forms, including coding the voices of the divinities, ancestors and the spirit beings.

Semiotics can be traced to the pioneering works of Charles Sanders Peirce (1931), the American philosopher and Ferdinand de Saussure, the Swiss Linguist. According to Saussure, semiology is the study of signs as part of social life. He focuses on the functions of social and cultural phenomena within semiotic systems. Saussure (1974: 60) classifies signs into two entities: 'signified and or sign-vehicle or meaning.' He refers to the signified as forms of materials (objects, images, sounds and so on). Saussure is credited with structuralism approach. To him, language is formed by signs which are related in multiple ways. A sign or a word consists of two parts: one part is its form; the other part is its meaning. The association between form and meaning of a sign is fixed by conventions of language use. The link between the form and meaning are inseparable.

According to Peirce, Semiotics is an abstract entity. Sign is something which stands for somebody or something in some respects or capacity. This relation of 'standing for' is mediated by an interpretant. According to Peirce (1931: 35), 'a sign is anything which determines something else (its interpretant) to refer to an object to which itself refers (its object) in the same way the interpretant becoming in turn a sign.' This means anything can be adopted as a sign.

Three modes of significations are regarded to be sufficient to describe any form of sign. These are icon, symbol and index. In an iconic mode, the signifier is perceived as resembling or imitating the signified in one way or the other. According to Peirce, one can perceive a direct resemblance between the signifier and the signified.

For instance, a picture of an individual is an iconic symbol. This may be in the form of an animal. This belief is associated with some Yorùbá traditions that forbid some families to eat, kill or harm some animals. It is forbidden for the *Alápa's* family to eat, kill or harm snakes, just as for the twins or the family of twins to eat any species of monkey. In the symbol mode, there is no resemblance or connection between the signifier and the signified, that is, the object and what it stands for. A symbol's connection with its object is a matter of convention, rule or agreement between the users. In Yorùbá tradition, it can be realised in form of *Àrokò*, as such an object or something stands for something or somebody in real life. The link rule of signs and their meanings are made known by code.

Code is the semiotic element employed for this study. A code is 'a means of conveying messages, a vehicle of communication…The coding takes place simultaneously on different levels, and many other factors, such as memory span and general extralinguistic knowledge, play a part' (Geoffery and Short, 1981: 122-124). The linkage of signs and their meanings are made known by code. This may be realised in a multi-level coding as in this study, where there is simultaneous or concurrent use of moral code to establish the relationship of *Ifá* philosophy and rain petitioning. Code helps to simplify phenomena in order to make it easier to communicate experience.

Despite the fact that the *Ifá* text is a culture bound genre, our data is translated into English for the benefit of a wider audience. Some cultural terms or names are not translated to preserve the local or cultural flavour, colour and values of African oral arts; this is to avoid misinterpretation and low comprehension 'since the indigenous language is more conducive to the interpretation of an indigenous genre' (Ilésanmi, 2004: 111). However, such are explained as may be necessary to ensure their understanding.

Ifá and the Yorùbá People

Ifá has been defined by scholars in different ways that establish the inexplicable and unlimited scope of its knowledge, wisdom and values. Indeed, it is regarded as the bedrock of other aspects of Yorùbá life. Therefore, to simply define *Ifá* as a religion, without exploring its social and cultural links will be inadequate. However, the religious knowledge of *Ifá* is explored in this chapter.

Akíntọ́lá (1999: 36) sees *Ifá* as the philosophy of or wisdom divinely revealed to the Yorùbá deity of *Ifá, Ọ̀rúnmìlà*. Farrow describes *Ifá* to be the greatest oracle of the Yorùbá that is 'consulted on all important occasions.' *Ifá* is regarded as the spokesperson, not only for the gods, but also for the living. It is regarded as the living foundation of Yorùbá culture (Abímbọ́lá, 1976: 14). Munoz (2003: 179) sees *Ifá's* scope beyond the Yorùbá cultural society when he says, '*Ifá* is the most universal divinity among the Yorùbá and other West African people.' Because of the widespread nature of *Ifá* that cuts across the nations of the globe, *Ifá* is known to different people by different names. For example, *Ifá* is known as *Fá* among the Fon of Republic of Benin, *Eva* to Nupes, *Ifá* in Cuba, USA, Brazil, Trinidad and Tobago, Jamaica, Surinam and Togo. *Ifá* is referred to by the Ewe as *Afa, Ephod* by Jews, *Geomancy* by Europeans and Margays (Ọdẹyẹmí, 2012: 5). In fact, *Ifá* has over 70 million followers in Africa and the America. In 2005, the United Nations Educational, Scientific and Cultural Organization (UNESCO) proclaimed *Ifá* as one of the 86 traditions of the world to be recognised as masterpieces of oral and intangible heritage of humanity (Robinson, 2012: 1). *Ifá*, as a religion, science or literary text, has over time been of great interest to scholars in different areas of human endeavours, like medicine, philosophy, religion, art and culture. *Ifá* religion has been a means by which Yorùbá culture (including language) is propagated at home and in the diaspora. As a result of the different roles of *Ifá* in various aspects of the Yorùbá life, *Ifá*:

> …is perhaps the most accomplished product of Yorùbá traditional culture…. No one who has studied *Ifá* in detail will fail to see the fact that the people of traditional Africa societies were not ignorant as we have often been told. The peoples of traditional Africa were largely illiterates to be sure. But they were no fools. Among them were elite classes such as the *babaláwo* who have preserved all the ingredients of their own culture in an almost completely oral form but in such a way that knowledge is codified and transmitted orally with care, patience and perseverance. *Ifá* is the Yorùbá traditional thought system *per excellence* (Abímbọ́lá, 1976: vi).

159

The above opinion shows that, art works and objects are means by which the beliefs of the people, especially the Yorùbá, are keenly associated with the supernatural or the divine.

All the cultural contents of *Ifá* have been 'codified.' The codifications are realised as *Ifá* symbols in forms of *Odù* (major and minor). *Ifá* poetry is a sacred Yorùbá genre that nobody may add or subtract from. Like Holy books of Quran and Bible to the Muslims and Christians, the same is *Ifá* epistles to the Yorùbá indigenous worshippers, because, the *Ifá* epistle is, 'preserved and disseminated from ancient times. It is believed that in this way the text in the *Ifá* literary corpus have been kept free from errors. The corpus, therefore, remains till today, one of the reliable genres of the Yorùbá oral literature' (Abímbọlá, 1976: 20). In the opinions of other authors, like as Yémitàn and Ògúndélé (1970: ix), *Ifá* 'jẹ́ imọ̀ ijìnlẹ̀ lọ́tọ̀ ara rẹ̀, ohun tí a lè pè ní ẹ̀ka imọ̀ sáyẹ́nsì. Èkejì, ó jẹ́ oríṣìí ẹ̀sìn ibílẹ̀ ilẹ̀ Yorùbá kan.' Meaning that *Ifá* is knowledge of science on its own. Secondly, it is a separate Yorùbá religion. The implication of this statement is that *Ifá's* knowledge can be properly and better understood by scientific analysis or theory. In short *Ifá* is basic to the understanding of all aspects of Yorùbá life. This observation makes Ọbáyọmí to succinctly say that *Ifá* 'is fundamental in the explanation of the components of the Yorùbá culture' (1983:76). As a result of *Ifá's* connections with various aspects of Yorùbá life, investigating *Ifá's* relationship with climate change is necessary.

Ẹsẹ-Ifá is historical, containing the past histories as well as its links with the present and the future. 'Ifá literary corpus can therefore be regarded as a set of historical and mythical poems offering to us through the use of analogy images and symbols what to do in order to be at peace with God, the supernatural powers, or neighbours and indeed, ourselves' (Abímbọlá, 1975: 446 -44 7). All *ẹsẹ-Ifá* are events, stories that have happened in the past, coded in *Odù* (sixteen principal and two hundred and forty minor Odu). This means, Ọrúnmìlà, who is the *Ifá* progenitor is linked with some of the Yorùbá folktales as examined by this work. 'What has emerged so far is that *ẹsẹ-Ifá* is a type of "historical" poetry. Every poem of *Ifá* is an attempt to narrate, through the particular structure of *Ifá* divination poetry, things which the Ifá priest has been taught to believe actually happened in the past by narrating these stories of the past' (Abímbọlá, 1977a: 20).

The involvement of supernatural forces is mediated by *Ifá*. Sometimes the consultation results in knowledge of indigenous medicine which is made possible by *Ifá*. There is no divinity that is more associated with medicine than *Ifá*,

> ...*Ọwọ́ Ifá ni gbogbo oògùn ti wà.*
> *Ọwọ́ Ifá nìkan ni gbogbo oògùn ti wà pátápátá poro-n-godo.*
> *Oòṣà ni Ifá, nnkan àalò ni*
> *Oògùn tún ló jẹ́ fún aráyé* (Ilesanmi 1998: 10-11).

> ...They all came from *Ifá*.
> All the medicine related things came from *Ifá* in its entirety.
> *Ifá* is a divinity; it is equally an instrument being used
> It is equally medicine for the world.

Medicine is an important *Ifá* scope of knowledge and specialisations. This aspect of *Ifá* specialisation is so important that 'no *Ifá* priest can have a successful practice if he does not know anything about medicine. This means, medicine is a general knowledge in *Ifá* profession; even though it is a specialised scope for some *Ifá* practitioners. The scientific knowledge of *Ifá* plays a vital role in the good living of the Yorùbá people. The knowledge of *Ifá* in coping with the climate change cannot also be overemphasised among the Yorùbá.

Ẹbọ (Sacrifice) Symbolism in *Ifá* Divination

The role of *Ifá* in the preparation ẹbọ cannot be overemphasised. *Ifá* is the starting point of consultation (finding the cause(s) of an action or problem) and solution or the way out of the problem. Rain petitioning, as a way out of the challenges of climate change, is mediated by *Ifá*. As earlier explained, *Ifá* is the spokesperson, an intermediary among and between the Yorùbá divinities. *Ifá* bridge the gap between the visible and invisible beings. To Yorùbá people, the society is comprised of the forces that operate in the universe - divinities, ancestors, supernatural agents and human beings (Abimbọlá, 1976). Therefore, to side-line any of these powers is regarded as a rape of Yorùbá belief system and tradition.

In Africa, the society is comprised and controlled by two worlds-
the visible and invisible:

> For traditional Africans, community is much more than simply a
> social grouping of people bound together by reasons of natural origin
> and/or deep common interests' values. It is both a society as well as
> unity of visible and invisible worlds; the world of the physically living
> on one hand, and the world of the ancestors, divinities and souls of
> children yet to be born to individual kin-groups in a wider sense…The
> invisible members, especially ancestors and spiritual beings are
> powerful and by far superior to human beings. Their reality and
> presence in the community are duly acknowledged and honoured
> among various traditional groups. Neglect could spell disaster for
> human beings and the community (Ejizu, 2007: 9).

The opinions of the invisible beings must be sought and approval
or consent obtained on important issues, including climate that
bothers on the community at large. This is buttressed by the fact that
without the past, there can't be present, just as today is an input on
tomorrow.

Ẹbọ serves as a means of interaction and peaceful co-existence
between the human (visible or physical) and the supernatural beings,
divinities and ancestors (invisible or spiritual) world. 'From religious
perspective, the world can be said to be divided into the physical
(visible), and the metaphysical (or the spiritual) levels. Both realms
have binding and interactive forces exchanging between them to
function harmoniously' (Salami, 2002: xiv). *Ẹbọ* serves as Holy
Communion- an interactive forum or gathering between the human
and the spirit (other world), 'without which the glimpse into the
hallowed and holy becomes an illusion' (Ahiaba, 2016: 107). One of
the contents of *ẹsẹ Ifá* is *ẹbọ*. There is no one exempted from
performing sacrifice:

> It is compulsory for every individual to perform sacrifice no matter
> whether the *ori* he chose in heaven is good or bad. The divinities will
> not support anyone who refuses to offer sacrifice since this is their only
> reward for their ceaseless watch over human life…Thus, sacrifice is
> presented in *ẹsẹ Ifá* as the means whereby a man makes his peace with

162

the divinities and improves upon the defects inherent in his own life. (Abimbọlá, 1977a: 33).

No human being can live a peaceful and meaningful life or exist without *ẹbọ*. *Ẹbọ*, must be carried out within the specified period of time. In other words, sacrifice offered outside the specified time by *Ifá* is as sacrifice not offered at all. Therefore, 'Timing is very crucial under any prevalent circumstances in the Yorùbá custom, religion, deity, and tradition. Spiritual resonance and intonation changes with time' (Salami, 2002: xv). Timing, in the *ẹbọ* performance is important. For instance, rain petitioning arises in very dry and hot seasons. In other words, it will be out of place to resort to rain petitioning when it is already raining.

Likewise, the river goddess known as *olódò*- the owner of the rivers, is consulted and appeased to give way for bridge construction across the rivers. So, some forms of sacrifices are offered to the river goddess- spirit of the river.

In Yorùbá religion, the prescription of the sacrificial order is exclusively given by *Ifá*. The prescription in regard to the time the sacrifice must be offered, how the sacrifice must be conducted, who is charged with the sacrifice obligation and where the sacrifice is to be carried out, are prescribed or ordered by the *Ifá* priest to the *Ifá* client. In addition, the order of the sacrifice must be given or directed by an initiated *Ifá* priest- *Ifá* priest through *Ifá* divination. Therefore, the consultation to the *Ifá* priest must be the first step towards the implementation of the sacrificial order.

Sacrifice serves as a unifying force between the human and the supernatural.

The psychological function of sacrifice in the community is rated very high by *Ifá* priests. They maintain that sacrifice helps to unite all the forces both natural and supernatural that operate in the Yorùbá society. Broadly speaking, these forces are four in number namely the gods, the ancestors, witches and other supernatural powers, and human beings. The function of sacrifice is to enlist the support of these four forces for whatever one may want to do so that none of them may work against one's purpose (Abimbọla, 1976: 37).

The unification, co-operation and integration roles or functions of ẹbọ between the human and the supernatural beings and in the ultimate, to God, the Olódùmarè is negotiated by ẹbọ. Ẹbọ, is inevitable to the Ifá clients or supplicants. It is a means of exchange of material things for his or her life.

The Yorùbá believe that the invisible agents (earlier identified above), will be appeased when certain material things are offered to the ajogun (a group of Yorùbá supernatural agents) in form of sacrifice, they would take or receive those things and leave the supplicant untouched. Therefore, ẹbọ is a material means of exchange between the human, supernatural and God:

> Sacrifice, in its ritual or ceremonial use, means "a making sacred, an offering that becomes divinized." Whatever is sacrificed crosses from humans to the divine, and objects are empowered to facilitate the process. Indigenous Africans speak and think of sacrifice essentially as a religious act, which takes the form of rendering something to the supernatural being or beings, and with various purposes (Adogame, 2009: 75).

Therefore, 'Sacrifice is a means whereby man can influence the supernatural power so that the "good" powers may co-operate with him and the evil powers will leave him alone in the execution of his plans on the earth' (Abimbọlá, 1977a: 33). Ẹbọ is a means that opens channel or network of communication or interaction between man and the ancestors, divinities, supernatural agents and with God, the Olódùmarè.

Sacrifice is so important in Ifá divination to the extent that the Ifá divination process is incomplete without sacrifice:

> Sacrifice is therefore central to Ifá divination and to Yorùbá religion as a whole. Sacrifice keeps the belief system going and links the client, the diviner, the divinities and the ancestors together through a system of service and reward. When the client refuses to perform sacrifice, he makes it impossible for this system of action and reaction be completed. Such a client therefore commits a rape of the belief system since he has exploited the divinities by inviting them to identify

164

and solve his problem for him without providing them with their stipulated reward (Abímbọlá, 1977a: 11).

To this effect, *Ifá* divination sacrifice is a prescribed portion for divinities and supernatural beings who have been invited by the *Ifá* client to solve his problem for them. Therefore, the sacrifice is sacred.

Mythical Code of *Ifá* in Relation to Rain Petitioning

Preamble

Myth, in Greek language means muthos that is 'narrative.' Eco (1976: 69) opined that 'myths, legends, and popular or folk literature, in general, are of the greatest interest for semiology' Myths are sourced from stories in forms of folk-literature, legend, historical, traditional or oral poems that constitutes *Ifá* corpus. Myth is a means by which we resolve some ancient problems. Myths 'implicitly symbolize some profound truth about human or natural existence' (Kennedy and Gioia, 2007: 254). Every culture recognises myths and its impact and influence are equally felt in human life. 'One of the characteristics, signs and symbols of a specific cultural society is the fact that it makes no difference whether the myth in question is that of a story that actually took place. Whether it is the product of the imagination, or whether it was merely a work of literature or the lyrics of a poem' (Cohen, 2003: 53). Myths in a given culture serve as historical and cultural semiotics, since those myths relate to the activities of past events in the remote time. The extent to which we can accept or reject myths is sometimes minimal, since the time is located to the 'remote' period in a society. However, some events of today are influenced by the past, and myths explain the origin of human existence and experience.

Ọ̀ṣúndáre (Ọ̀ṣúndáre, 2008: 20-2) asserts that myth and literature are inseparable and their meaning does different things to different writers and critics. Myth is associated with symbols and therefore relates to semiotics. Both language and myths enjoy an intricate relationship. 'Apart from the fact that both belong to the larger semiotic construct we call culture, myth is the silent, enigmatic submarine in communal depths ... Myth has also always been a constant genre in literature. Nearly all literature is woven from myth.'

It is noted that, myths proffer solutions to some current mysteries. The notion of myths further informs us that there is evolution relationship between human and animal world. Ilésanmí (2004: 40-2) also asserts that myths solve problems from the root or source and that 'mythical statements are fundamental principles which should be accepted by faith.'

Data Presentation and Discussion

Myths form a vital aspect of the basis of *Ifá* corpus. *Ẹsẹ-Ifá* remains the main source of information about Yorùbá mythology (Abímbọ́lá, 1977b). It is by these mythological documents in *Ifá* that we are able to solve some cultural problems. *Ifá* mythology is important in resolving some cultural and religious issues. That is 'Myth and religion serve as forms of its reflections in ideas' (Ogundọwọle, 2003: 46). In this case, *Ifá's* mythological events in this study are 'reflections in ideas' of the Yorùbá belief. 'Ifá literary corpus can therefore be regarded as a set of historical and mythical poems offering to us through the use of analogy images and symbols what to do in order to be at peace with God, the supernatural powers, or neighbours and indeed, ourselves' (Abímbọ́lá, 1975: 446-447).

Generally, natural or environmental challenges are not new to Ọ̀rúnmìlà, the *Ifá* oracle as he had faced such challenges in the past. Ọ̀rúnmìlà assured his disciples that:

> When danger threatens my devotee
> I will respond like the cry of Blue-Touraco
> Reverberating across oceans;
> I will hiss with the fury of Aluko-Bird
> Reaching to the end of seas;
> I will respond with the twitter of innumerable birds
> Echoing to the furthest shores (Lijadu, 1908: 33).

It is believed that *Ifá's* knowledge covers the past, present and future events. This is why *Ifá's* guidance and directives are prerequisites in all the undertakings of the Yorùbá people. 'There is hardly anything people of a traditional Yorùbá society would do without seeking support and approval from Ifá, the god of wisdom' (Àjàyí, 2009: 8). This is because; *Ifá* provides instruction and guidance about the future and/or the cause of an action. This is done, to seek the endorsement and sanctions of the ancestors, divinities and supernatural agents of which *Ifá* serves as spokesperson. The Yorùbá equally applies the knowledge of *Ifá* in times of climate change generally and, in particular to rain petitioning.

The ancestors, divinities and the spirits are regarded as man's best confidants in trying periods, including unfavourable climate. The invisible agents are the last hope of human community especially when there is change of climate, season or weather as underscored by Abímbọ́lá (1976: 156-157) (with author's translation):

> *Ọ̀sán ni ò sán pẹ́*/ Daylight does not keep longer than usual;
>
> *Òru ni ò ru pẹ́*/Night does not keep longer than usual;
>
> *Òkùnkùn ò kùnpẹ́*/Darkness does not keep longer than it usually keeps.
>
> *Ọ̀ pa bàtà m'ọmọ lẹ́sẹ̀ pẹ̀ẹ́ pẹ̀ẹ́ pẹ̀ẹ́*/He who provides a pair of sandals for a child's feet.
>
> *A díá fún Báalẹ̀jọ́*/Ifá divination was performed for Báalẹ̀jọ́
>
> *Tí nt'Ìkọ̀lé ọ̀run bọ̀ wáyé*/Who was coming from heaven to earth.
>
> *Bá a bá lẹ̀jọ́ o,*/If one has a problem,
>
> *Ṣe b'ọ̀run ẹni là á báá sọ*/One should take it to ones ancestors.
>
> *Yóò gbè ọ́ o,*/He shall protect you;
>
> *Baba ẹni kì í gbe'ni tì.*/One's dead farther never fails to protect one.
>
> *Yóò gbè ọ́ o,*/He shall protect you;
>
> *Iye ẹni kì í gbe'ni tì* /One's dead mother never fail to protect one.
>
> *Yóò gbè ọ́ o,*/It shall protect you;
>
> *Ikin ẹni kì í gbe'ni tì* /One's sacred Ifá divination palm-nuts never fail to protect one.
>
> *Yóò gbè ọ́ o* /It shall protect you.

The roles of ancestors as well as *Ifá* divination in times of troubles are evinced from the above *Ifá* corpus. It is equally evident from the *Ifá* excerpts above that, there is normal state of seasons- daylight, night and darkness, that is, climate change.

One of the major ways out of climate change, especially in severe dry season that have side effect on the condition of living and health of the Yorùbá people is rain petitioning. *Ifá* epistle contains in Abímbọ́lá (1968: 75-83), *Ọ̀sá Méjì* says:

> *Òkè-ṣe-ríbìtì-ṣorí-ṣónṣó*/A big mountain with pointed sharp head;
> *A díá fún oba Àjàláyé*/Performed divination for the Chief of the Earth.
> *Òkè-ṣe-ríbìtì-ṣorí-ṣónṣó*/A big mountain with pointed sharp head;
> *A díá fún oba Àjàlọ́run*/Performed divination for the Chief of the Heaven.
> *Àwọn méjèè ńjìjà àgbà rele Olódùmarè.../*The two were fighting on the seniority among themselves, presenting their case to the *Olódùmarè...*

The above *Ifá* introductory part shows that there are two forces contesting the seniority- the Earthly force (Àjàláyé) and the Heavenly force (Àjàlọ́run). As earlier explained, the forces in control of African environment generally and in Yorùbá society in particular comprises of the visible and invisible forces. The visible, represented by the Earth and the invisible represented by the Heaven.

The consultation and sanction of the authorities of the invisible forces are peculiar to the Yorùbá method of rain petitioning. In the present time of the globalisation, the invisible transnational corporations and Euro-American states and institutions generally influence or control the African environments. The two forces, the African forces, enforced through the spirit beings and the Euro-American states and institutions work together to sometimes influence the weather.

In the quoted *Ifá* corpus, not quite long after the misunderstanding among them the *Àjàlọ́run* went back in annoyance to Heaven. The Earth then witnessed chaos- there was no rain. This type of situation of closure of rain is rendered by *Ọ̀wọ́nrín Méjì,* that:

> *Ọ̀wọ́n omi, ọ̀wọ́n omi*/Scarcity of water, scarcity of water
> *Ọ̀wọ́n ni orúkọ tí à á pe ọ̀wọ̀nrín*/Scarcity is refers to as Ọ̀wọ̀nrín
> (Abímbọ́lá, 1977a: 32).

The climatic effects were felt on farm produce, such as maize, beans and yams were at zero level. Not only this, there were outbreaks of diseases and sicknesses. The *Ọ̀sá Méjì* corpus unveil on the persistence climate change that:

> *Ló bá di wí pé ojò ò rọ̀ mọ́*/Then, there was no rainfall any longer.
> *Ìrì ò sẹ̀*/ There was no dew.
> *Àgbàdo tápẹ́ ò gbó…*/maize cannot produce…
> *Aboyún ò bí mọ́…*/Pregnant woman can no longer give to birth…

It is observed that climate change causes some diseases and sicknesses among the Yorùbá people. For example, Clarke reports about the climatic effects of the Yorùbáland that:

> My observation goes to prove that the principal cause of sickness is mainly attributed to imprudence and the want of such comforts and conveniences as are necessary to protect the system amid those changes of season that are generally attendant with more or less danger to the physical constitution, and not to certain conditions of the country as to its locality…From all the facts and a four years' observation of the climate and its effects in my own case and in those of others, I feel I should do injustice to the country not to say that it is one highly favoured of providence with many of the elements of health (1972: 212-213).

Some of the sicknesses and diseases are as a result of climate. According to Clarke:

> intermittent and remittent fever, diarrhea and dysentery, ophthalmic diseases in some places, whitlows, carbuncles, and some cutaneous diseases, among which we find smallpox in a very light form, may be mentioned as embracing the catalogue (1972: 214).

The descriptions of the situation in the *Ifá* corpus above show that there must be an agreement between the visible and invisible forces for peace to be experienced by human-beings. This equally concerns the rain petitioning. The petition order must be sanctioned by the invisible agents mentioned earlier in this study. In order to lessen the effects of the diseases and sicknesses mentioned above, the Yorùbá people resort to rain petitioning.

African climate generally, and in the Yorùbá society in particular, comprises very hot weather especially, during the dry season. There are perceived inconsistences in the weather of the Yorùbá climate. That is:

> There are extreme of heat and cold, wet and dry, in the torrid and frigid zones, and of temperature and moisture in the mean of latitude. Independent of these generally laws there are modifying circumstances that vary very much a climate and seem at times to come into conflict with these fixed principles. I make these observations because we find such peculiarities in the climate of Yorubaland. To say we have a hot and dry climate or a cold and wet climate would be equally untrue. Notwithstanding our preconceived notions, based as is supposed on facts, there is neither of these climates in the proper understanding of these terms (Clarke, 1972: 205).

The disorderliness and discomfort caused by the severe droughts, hot weather as a result of climate change brought about attempts to consult *Ifá* oracle, to find out about the cause and the way out of the predicaments. The *Òsá Méjì* corpus unveil on the effects of climate change that:

> *Nígbà tí gbogbo ayé ò gbádùn mọ́*/When everyone was fed up,
> *Ni wọ́n bá gbára jọ*/They then came together in agreement;
> *Wọ́n méèjì kẹẹta,*/They took along with them divination fees- two and three cowries
> *Wọ́n looko aláwo*/They went to Ifá Priest.
> *Wọ́n lọ kẹ sí*/They invited,
> *Àwọn Òkè-ṣe-ribìtì-ṣorí-ṣónṣó*/ The big Chiefs.
> *Awo ni wọ́n*/They are cult.

In the above *Ifá* excerpts, the *Ifá* divination revealed that disagreement between the Earthly and Heavenly forces, who are cult, the forces that must be in agreement for peace to be. The opinion above shows that *Ifá* consultation guides the activities of the Yorùbá people, especially, in times of problems and troubles. It is the belief of the Yorùbá people and *Ifá* worshippers generally that whatever *Ifá* says shall undoubtedly come to pass and his guidance can never be regretted.

> It shall come to pass,
> It shall come to be,
> Whatever word is uttered by Ifá,
> Shall surely come to pass (Lijadu 1908: 49).

One of the instruments prescribed by *Ifá* to avoid unforeseen challenges is to carry out sacrifice by the *Ifá* supplicant(s). As earlier mentioned, *ẹbọ Ifá* (Ifa sacrifice) is prerequisite to solution in *Ifá* divination. There is no *Ifá* consultation or inquiry that will not involve sacrifice. The sacrifice is not only to be reluctantly or haphazardly performed but, must be faithfully and strictly obeyed. This is in regards to the time, manner and how the sacrifice should be performed. Without compliance, there will be no desired result or output. This is because; sacrifice paves way for reconciliation between the two (visible and invisible) opposing forces (as earlier explained). This is rendered in the *Ifá* corpus on rain petitioning in *Ọ̀sá Méjì* corpus reveals that:

Wọ́n ní kí wọn ó rú eku méjì olúwéré/They were to sacrifice with two rats.
  Kí wọn ó reja méjì abìwẹ̀gbàdà/ They were to sacrifice with two fishes.
  Kí wọn ó rú obìdiẹ méjì abẹ̀dọ lùkẹlùkẹ́/ They were to sacrifice with two hens.
  Ewúrẹ́ méjì abàmú rẹderẹdẹ/Two big goats.
  Ẹ̀nlá méjì tó fìwo sọ̀sùkà/Two big donkeys.
  Wọ́n ní kí wọn ó fẹmọ́ tó dìjà náà kẹbọ rú/ And to add the rat that caused the disagreement between them.

In order to make the journey to Heaven easier and possible, the birds were invited to carry the sacrificial material to heaven to appease the Heavenly Chief and *Olódùmarè* (the God). However, we should be reminded that the invisible agent in Yorùbá society comprises of the ancestors, divinities and the spirit beings. For instance, in *Ọ̀sá Méjì*, Abímbọ́lá (1969), because of the severe famine

171

in the animals' kingdom, they prepared sacrifice to be taken to heaven; to *Olódùmarè. Àsá,* (Hawks) was first invited forward to carry the sacrifice, as the other animals began to sing songs of motivation and encouragement. *Àṣádì,* (a bird), also came forward to try the assignment of carrying the sacrifice to *Olódùmarè* in heaven. Shortly, it came back with unaccomplished assignment, as *Àkàlà,* (a bird) took the turn. *Igún,* (Vulture) could not be initially saddled with the assignment; as everyone knew that its mother was severely sick. But, it was like a joke when Vulture summons courage and came forward to carry the sacrifice. It should be noted that *Igún* (vulture) is personified in the above *Ifá* corpus as a stylistic feature of *ẹsẹ Ifá.* That is:

> When subject-matter of an *ẹsẹ Ifá* pertains to an object or creature of nature, the stylistic devise of personification is employed apparently because of the need to cast the material in the distinctive Ifá style. The object or creature concerned is therefore given human attributes it is made to perform sacrifice, and to express various feelings characteristics of human beings.
>
> This approach to the appreciation of nature not only emphasizes the importance the Yorùbá attached to the created things of nature. It also shows the high capacity of the Yorùbá for the appreciation of nature in all its aspects. It also leads to a more critical and less emotional vision of human problems. It must be emphasized however that this is a feature common to Negro African literature in general. In many African folktales, narrative upon narrative brings this on clearly. Animals, nature, God, they have all been thoroughly humanized and, as man is assessed. Perhaps this is why there is no special genre devoted to satire in African literature neither in prose nor poetry. Man is depicted as he is. That is a sufficient satire (Abímbọ́lá, 1976: 195).

Ifá divination will be incomplete without the involvement of animals, including birds. For instance, Abímbọ́lá (1977a) notes that, the role of animals in the accomplishment of sacrifice cannot be underrated, as most of the animals and birds are agents of implementation of sacrifice orders. In fact, the *ajoguns* (a type of supernatural beings) exists in form of birds. For instance, according to *Ìrẹ̀tẹ̀ Méjì*, verse eight contained in Abímbọ́lá (1968: 138):

> ..*Igún wáà jẹbọ*
> *Kẹbọ ó le baà fín; ...*
> *À ṣé bá ò rí gúnnugún*
> *A kì yóò le ṣẹbọ...*

> ...Vulture then eat the sacrifice
> So that sacrifice can be acceptable
> So, without the Vulture
> We will be unable to perform sacrifice.

The role of Vulture in the above *Ifá* corpus attests to the complementary role played by animals (including birds) in the implementation of *Ifá* divination. Some Yorùbá beliefs revealed that *Igún,* must have played some roles in the *Ifá* divination system.

> *Ìgbà tí Igún dé ibodè isálọ̀run*/When the Vulture got to the gate of Heaven,
> *Ó kànkùn gbọ̀n gbọ̀ọ̀n gbọ̀n*/It knocks on the door vehemently.

Vulture presented the sacrificial materials and says there was no peace since the time of the disagreement between the two Chiefs. No rain and, as a result of which the weather is unbearable for both the plants and humans to produce. The Earthly Chief was ordered to apologise to the heavenly Chief. The implication of this action demonstrates that the invisible forces are more powerful than the visible forces as explained earlier.

It was after the mediation and reconciliation through the means of *Ifá* sacrifice in the *Ọ̀sá Méjì* corpus that normalcy was restored.

> *Ni Olódùmarè bá mú Igún bọ̀ sí àgbàlá*/Then God took Vulture to the open palace.
> *Ó ni kí ó ká àdó mẹ́ta lágbàlá òun.../* It was instructed to pluck three *àdó* in the yard...
> *Olódùmarè ni bí ó bá tí kúrò ní bodè*/God says immediately it left the gate
> *Kí ó la ọ̀kan mọ́lẹ̀*/It should break one on the ground.

173

Bi ó bá dé idaji isálayé àti ìsálọ̀run/On the mid-way of Earth and Heaven.

Kí ó la ọ̀kan mọ́lẹ̀/It should break one on the ground.

Bí ó bá kù dẹ̀dẹ̀ kí ó dé òde ìsálayé/If it remains a little distance to get to the Earth

Kí ó la ọ̀kan yóókù mọ́lẹ̀/It should break the remaining one on the ground.

The Vulture complied with the order and before it reached the surface of the Earth, rain began to fall heavily, even, on an attempt to break the second *adó*. The *Ọ̀sá Méjì* corpus further evinces,

Ni ojò bá bẹ̀rẹ̀ sú rọ̀/Then, rain begins to fall

Kí Igún ó tó fẹsẹ̀ tẹlẹ̀/Before vulture steps on the ground,

Òjo ti rọ̀, odòó ti kún/Rain has fallen to the extent that rivers have been flowing.

The torrential rainfall type is like the one reported as:

Ọ̀wàawa, ọwọ sìṣìṣì/ Ọ̀wàawa, ọwọ sìṣìṣì

Bí wọ́n bá ń rọ̀/If the types of the rain fall,

Wọn kì í dá mọ́/don't normally stops early.

Eji a ya sílé/Rain will fall at home

Eji a ya soko/rain will fall on the farms

Àbàta rẹ̀gẹ̀dẹ̀ a sì dodo/muddy place turns into a river…

(Abímbọ́lá 1977a: 32).

The rain fell as a result of the rain petitioning through the cooperation of the visible and invisible being mediated through *Ifá* and *ẹbọ Ifá*. The *ọ̀wàawà* rain type is a heavy rain that lasts for several hours. It cools the heat and hot weather. The plants, animals and human beings are refreshed. Likewise, the rivers are full to their banks. The torrential force of rain petitioning can equally be regulated by *Ifá*.

174

Conclusion

This study concludes that, African indigenous knowledge, especially, *Ifá* is employed to control or regulate climate to favour the Yorùbá people. One of the ways that this objective is achieved is through rain petition. On one hand, *Ifá* knowledge on rain petitioning can be applied during very hot or dry weather, when, the weather is causing additional economic, social and health havoc to their state of living. On the other hand, African indigenous knowledge of rain petitioning can be applied to reduce the excessiveness of rainfall which can also cause havoc or hazard for the good living of the Yorùbá people. In Africa and particularly among the Yorùbá, rain petitioning is only possible with the involvement of the ancestors, divinities and the supernatural spirits. The residual power of both the physical and invisible control of weather or climate is centralised in them. Before the advent of Euro-American beings, the Yorùbá had indigenous means of rain petitioning. The Yorùbá, till today, consult the invisible beings through *Ifá*, the mediator between the human and supernatural beings to control their weather, especially in rain petitioning. This is done through the mediation of *ẹbọ Ifá- Ifá* sacrifice order.

References

Abímbọ́lá, W. (1969) *Ìjìnlẹ̀ ohùn ẹnu Ifá Apá kejì.* Ìbàdàn: Oxford University.

Abímbọ́lá, W. (1975) ʾÌWÀPẸ̀LẸ̀: The concept of good character in Ifá literary corpus' *Yorùbá oral tradition.* Ifẹ̀: Department of African Languages and Literature, University of Ifẹ̀. Vol.; 1, No.; 1. Pp. 389-420).

Abímbọ́lá, W. (1977b) *Àwọn ojú odù mẹ́rẹ̀ẹ̀rìndínlógún.* Ìbàdàn: Oxford University Press.

Abímbọ́lá, W. (1968) *Ìjìnlẹ̀ ohùn ẹnu Ifá* Apá Kíìní. Ọ̀yọ́: Aims Press & Publishers.

Abímbọ́lá, W. (1976) *IFÁ: An Exposition of Ifá Literary Corpus.* Ìbàdàn: Oxford University Press.

Abímbọ́lá, W. (1977a) *Ifá Divination Poetry*. New York: Nok Publishers.

Adogame, A. (2009) 'Practitioners of Indigenous Religious of Africa and the Diaspora' Graham Harvey (ed.) *Religions in Focus: New Approaches to Tradition and Contemporary Practices*. New York: Routledge Tylor and Francis Group Limited. Pp 75-96. https://books.google.com.ng/books?id=DrxsCwAAQBAJ&pg =PA93&1pg=PA93gdq=cosmas+and+damian+and+yoruba+i beji&soui...

Ahiaba, M. (2016) 'Reading *Ẹbọ* as Spirit: The Foundation of Authentic Christian Pneumatology among the Igala in Nigeria' *International Journal of African Catholicism*, Winter (7)2. www.saintleo.edu/academics/schools/school-of-arts-sciences/international journal.of-africa-catholicism/past-issues.aspx

Àjàyí, B. Y. (2009) Yorùbá Cosmology and Aesthetics: The Cultural Confluence of Divination, Incantation and Drum-Talking. The Ninetieth Inaugural Lecture Delivered on March 19, University of Ilorin, Ilorin. Nigeria. Ilọrin: Library and Publications Committee.

Akíntọ́lá, A. (1999) *Yorùbá Ethics and Metaphysics*. Ògbómọ̀sọ̀: YALOYN Publishing Ventures.

Clarke, W. (1972) *Travels & Explorations in Yorùbáland, in* Atanda, J. A. (ed.) Ibadan: University Press.

Cohen, Y. (2003) *Why religion?* Jerusalem: Priest Publishing.

Eco, U. (1976) *A theory of semiotics*. London: Indiana University.

Ejizu, C. (2007) African Traditional Religions and the Promotion of Community Living in Africa. http:/www.afrikaworld.ne/afre/community. htm.

Geoffery, L. and Short, M. (1981) *Style in fiction: Linguistic introduction to English fiction prose*. New York: Longman.

Ilésanmí, T. M. (1998) *Aroko létí Ọpọ́n-Ifá*. Ilé-Ifẹ̀: Amat Printing and Publishing Ltd.

Ilésanmí, T. M. (2004) *Yorùbá Orature and Literature: A cultural Analysis*. Ilé-Ifẹ̀: University Press.

Kennedy, X. J. and Gioia, D. (2007) *An Introduction to poetry* (Twelfth Edition). New York: Pearson and Longman.

Lijadu, E. M. (1908a) Translated into English by Emmanuel, A. (2010). *A Prophet Called Òrúnmìlà*. Lagos: West African Book.

Maciver, R. M. and Page, C. (1950) *Society: An Introductory Analysis*. India: Trinity Publishers.

Mákindé, M. (2007) *African philosophy: the demise of a controversy*, (Second Edition). Ilé-Ifẹ̀: Ọbáfẹ́mi Awólọ́wọ̀ University Press.

Munoz, L. (2003) *A Living Tradition: Studies in Yorùbá Civilization*. Ìbàdàn: Bookcraft.

Ọbáyọmí, A. (1983) 'History, Culture, Yorùbá and Northern Factors' G. O. Olusanya (eds.) *Studies in Yorùbá History and Culture*, Ibadan: University Press Limited, 72-87.

Ọdẹ́yẹmí, J. (2013) 'Ifá and Orìṣà Temple' 13 July 2012. <oyekuofun.com/what-is- ifa/>.

Ògúndọwọle, K. (2003) *Nature of Man: History and Philosophy in 10 Modules*. Lagos: Correct counsels Publishers.

Ọ̀ṣúndáre, N. (2008) *Style and literary communication in African prose fiction in English*. Ìbàdàn: Hope publications Nig. Ltd.,

Peirce, S. (1931) *Semiotics*. http://www.singnosemio.can/peirce/semiotics.asp.

Richard, A. (2009) 'Africa and Writing', in Ọláníyan, T. and Ato, Q. (eds.) *African Literature: An anthology of criticism and theory*, Malden: USA, 7-15.

Robinson, B. A. (2008) 'Ifá: The Religion of the Yorùbá People' 26 July 2012. http://www.religioustolerance. org/Ifá.htm.

Salámì, A. (2002) *Ifá: A Complete Divination*. Lagos: NIDD Publishers.

Sassure de, F. (1974) *Course in general linguistics*. London: Collins.

Yémíítàn, Ọ. and Ògúndélé, Ọ. (1970) *Oju Ọ̀ṣùpá Apá kìnní*. Ìbàdàn: Oxford University Press.

Chapter Six

Perceptions and Experiences of Climate Change in Rural Zimbabwe: The Case of Elderly Women in Goromonzi District

Ignatius Gutsa

Introduction

This chapter, which draws from close to nineteen months of ethnographic field research, addresses the epistemological and ontological premises which structure the ways in which people perceive, understand, attribute and experience climate change at the local level in rural Zimbabwe. This is achieved by specifically examining ten elderly women's narratives regarding *kushanduka kwemwaka* (seasonal change) in Gutsa village, Domboshava in Goromonzi District, Zimbabwe. These narratives by the elderly women demonstrate how climate change, as evidenced in seasons, derives its meaning from everyday life experiences. The key questions addressed in this chapter are: how is indigenous knowledge about the weather and climate change shaped in this village. What factors do elderly women attribute to climate change? How do indigenous people perceive climate change? What is the nature of contestations within indigenous knowledge around the explanations of climate change? This chapter explores a central vernacular meteorological belief widely shared in the village; it shows how villagers account for the changes in weather and climate, the seasonal variations and the nature of extreme environmental events. This central indigenous meteorological philosophy does not fit neatly with the supposed detached universalism of the Western scientific perspective and theory of weather and climate change (Rosengren, 2018) which mainly emphasises quantification and measurement of weather and climatic phenomena divorced from indigenous settings (Orlove *et al.*, 2002).

The chapter further explores the indigenous meteorological philosophy shared in the village, to explain ongoing climate change. This central vernacular meteorological philosophy is explored focusing on '*kushanduka kwemwaka*' (seasonal change) and '*kushanduka kwemamiriro ekunze*' (change in the state of the environment/surroundings) in Gutsa village. Also explored are contestations regarding causality of the weather and climate changes. Climate change as presented in this chapter is *kushanduka kwemwaka* (change in seasons) and not *kushanduka kwemamiriro ekunze* (change in the state of the environment/surroundings) which could refer to the hourly, daily, weekly and monthly weather and not to seasonal changes. In exploring *kushanduka kwemwaka,* emphasis is on the changes in the seasons per se as well as changes in the characteristics which are found in the specific season. These are wind patterns, temperature and rainfall patterns together with their timing (commencement, length, cessation and frequency). Consequently *kushanduka kwemamiriro ekunze* is found in *kushanduka kwemwaka.* Mabika and Salawu (2014: 2397) point out the challenge of translating everyday Shona words into English. Shona, the language used in the study setting is an indigenous language spoken in Zimbabwe; it also refers to people who speak the Shona language. The language is referred to by linguists as 'ChiShona'; in this chapter the more common 'Shona' without the prefix is used.

In line with Roncoli, Ingram and Kirshen's (2002: 413) observations, that environmental indicators are based on experience, the theoretical framework for this chapter is hence inspired by a phenomenological approach. Phenomenology is crucial since it places emphasis on lived experience and the methods of inquiring into such experiences (Desjarlais and Jason, 2011: 89). This is important as our present existence as humans is temporally structured in ways which draw from our past experience and anticipation of future horizons of experience *(Ibid)*. Therefore as a theoretical framework phenomenology is important as it allows for drawing on the wealth of knowledge about indigenous environmental indicators related to changes in the climate,

Gutsa village is situated in Domboshava communal lands in Goromonzi District, Mashonaland Province, some thirty-five kilometres north-east of Zimbabwe's capital city, Harare. There are three chieftainships in Goromonzi District, namely Chinamhora, Rusike and Chikwaka. Domboshava communal lands fall under Chief Chinamhora's jurisdiction. Goromonzi District has twelve wards with Gutsa village, the specific study location, falling under Murape Ward in Domboshava. Murape Ward is named after headman Murape who has close to fifty villages under his jurisdiction. Each village is headed by a *Sabhuku* (village head) who administers the households under his jurisdiction. Gutsa village was also named after its *Sabhuku,* Gutsa.

Methodological Issues, Sampling and Contextualisation of Climate Change Discourse

I conducted my field research from the end of April 2014 to November 2015 in Gutsa village of Murape ward, Domboshava in Zimbabwe. My strategy of extended fieldwork was influenced by Schumaker (1996: 238) who pointed to the need to adopt extended fieldwork as a data collection strategy since this strategy provides an opportunity to understand the worldview of the local people as well as collect various kinds of data through observation of daily activities. Observation was complemented by two focus group discussions (FGDs) with the elderly women as well as life-history interviews. In selecting life histories as an approach, the research was influenced by Anderson and Jack (1991) and Kakuru and Paradza (2007: 288) who noted that using life history research methods is extremely valuable for generating new insights into women's experiences which are not easily generated through other research techniques.

In this respect, ethnographic research in the context of climate change can serve as a form and activity of knowledge production as it can highlight salient aspects of climate change and common indicators used to predict it (Roncoli, 2006). Furthermore, an ethnographic approach allows for the inclusion of people's understanding and interpretation of their experiences over time (Wilson and Chadda, 2010: 549).

In climate change research, there are also a number of factors which make anthropology important for the study of climate change. The most significant one is that the discipline draws attention to the cultural values and political relations which shape climate-related knowledge creation and interpretation which form the basis of responses to continuing environmental changes (Einarsson, 2011; Barnes *et al.,* 2013: 541). My research experience therefore, mirrors anthropology's in-depth fieldwork methodology, long engagement in questions of society-environment interactions and a broad, holistic view of society which can yield valuable insights in climate change scholarship.

The importance of my approach is grounded on anthropology's insistence on the importance of context, history, and particularity (Low and Merry, 2010: 204). Ultimately, my methodological approach truly privileged a contextually rich and nuanced type of qualitative social research, in which fine grained daily interactions form the lifeblood of the data produced (Falzon, 2009: 1).

This was made possible by the agency of an ethnographic approach which made it possible to decipher and uncover the cognitive and cultural landscape in which elderly women's understanding of climate change is grounded (see Vedwan, 2006; Artur and Hilhorst, 2012; Crate 2011: 175). Such an approach is important as it helps in advancing our understanding of indigenous perceptions of the weather and climate; explanations of environmental changes should be seen as a function of human-environment interactions (Vedwan, 2006). By focusing on the indigenous understanding of climate change, the chapter highlights the cosmologies and epistemologies which help in unravelling the existing vernacular conceptions of the environment which are not necessarily captured in western supposedly scientific knowledge (Orlove *et al.,* 2002).

Sampling for this study was purposive; participants had to be elderly women above sixty years of age. Observations by Knodel and Ofstedal (2003) show that the sixty year old benchmark has been used in most developing countries to define elderly people, hence Zimbabwe is not an exception. Resultantly, in line with Antwi-Agyei *et al's* (2012: 6) further observations, it is important to note that inasmuch as the study focuses on these elderly women's narratives they cannot be divorced from the wider community. Thus, perceptions and experiences about climate change were situated within the context of the wider community. Participation in this study was centred on the notion of informed consent with interlocutors' anonymity and confidentiality protected through the use of pseudonyms so as not to divulge their real identities.

Putting Climate Change into Perspective in Gutsa Village

During fieldwork, I soon noticed that day to day banter and at gatherings of different types and sizes, conversations generally drifted towards '*mamiriro ekunze*' (state of the environment/surroundings). For example by focusing on *mamiriro ekunze* during the rainy season, villagers at this time are simply referring to the rain, its onset, frequency, duration, amount and cessation. It appears villagers pay a lot of attention to the weather and its fluctuations as it is tied to crop production and the availability of water for domestic, livestock and other livelihood activities. During the rainy season, depending on what was desired at a point in time, it was common to hear villagers saying: 'Hey the sun is now so hot. But the rains are not coming down. We leave it up to God'; 'Rain has fallen too much now'; 'Rain does not want to fall'.

This was reflective of the seasons of the year. For example at the onset of the rainy season and also during the course of the rainy season, conversations easily and swiftly shifted to concerns about the rain and also projections of the coming winter season based on rainfall intensity. During the dry summer period, conversations shifted towards heat and the prediction of the coming rainy season. During the winter period after general banter conversations and concerns, interest would shift towards the severity of the winter period and the likelihood of rains again. Concerns in conversations on weather, all year round, in Gutsa village mostly had a bearing on forecasting rains. This is also similar to Sander's (2000) observations among the Ihanzu in northernmost Iramba District in semi-arid North Central Tanzania as here questions on rain were an all year long topic of discussion. In Gutsa village, this is because livelihoods depend very much on rainfall. Furthermore, in Gutsa village, conversations about the weather act as icebreaker topics, just like in other cultures as observed by Barayazarra and Puri (2011: 22).

In Gutsa village, seasons are differentiated into three main ones, '*zhizha*' (rainy season- October to April), '*chando*' (winter- May to August and) '*chirimo*' (dry season- July to October). Most elderly

183

women acknowledged that Gutsa village is experiencing climate change, as the normally hot days are getting cold with the winter conditions extending well into summer. The central vernacular meteorological philosophy in the village shows that there is evidence of climate change which has seen a number of changes in the daily, weekly, monthly and annual weather patterns. This is consistent with observations, by other scholars, that during different seasons, local people expect natural phenomena such as temperature changes, wind, clouds, and rain to conform to a certain pattern that is defined as the norm (Muguti and Maphosa, 2012; Mararike, 1996; Roncoli, Ingram and Kirshen, 2002).

Reflecting on August of 2014 to 2015 and September of 2014 to 2015, I would say the famous winds which are characteristic of August *Nyamavhuvhu* (windy month) were not experienced. Instead, calm conditions prevailed in the village. In August it is expected that the wind will blow from different directions with the village occasionally experiencing *chamupupuri* (whirlwind). During 2014, the expected winds only started to blow way into the middle of September. During fieldwork I never witnessed any *chamupupuri*. Elderly women highlighted that *chamupupuri* winds are necessary and if they come on time it was assurance that the weather was not changing. On the other hand, if *chamupupuri* came too late, it would chase the rains away and hence reduce the number of rainy days in the village. With temperatures still low in August and September 2014, some villagers noted that 'the cold is refusing to go away'. For most of September 2015 it was still cold, windy and overcast, forcing people to spend time outdoors basking in the sun wearing warm clothing. This was unexpected as normally from late August onwards temperatures are generally expected to start rising marking the transition from winter into the hot dry *chirimo* period. *Mbuya* Ku (*Mbuya* is a Shona word for grandmother) pointed out that in the olden days it was normal for villagers to sleep outdoors during these months as it would become too hot to sleep comfortably indoors. In 2015, the weather anomalies continued with ground frost being observed in September along Nyaure River which coursed near the village. Although in the village it was acknowledged that the winter period had extended over the past years, experiencing ground frost in September was a first experience in the village for these elderly women. As a result of these changes, a number of elderly women pointed out that the lack of *chamupupuri* in August and the uncharacteristically low temperatures in September were significant markers that the weather had really changed. For *Mai* Njere:

> *Uku kushanduka kwemwaka nokuti ukaona chamupupuri chava kushaikwa muna Nyamavhuvhu wozochiwana kupera kwaGumiguru zvinongoratidza zvega kuti mwaka yashanduka.*

This points to climate change because if we see the whirlwinds no longer being experienced in August and only to be seen towards end of September then it shows that the climate has changed.

In 2014, the dry season continued to stretch beyond its 'normal' period (up to mid-October) with no sign of rains. By the beginning of November 2014, there were still no rains in the village as well as in other nearby villages and districts. In everyday conversations in the village, there was agreement that the rains should have fallen down to signify the end of the dry season and the commencement of the farming season. Though in a majority of villages in Domboshava, rains were received on the 8th of November there was still no rain in the village. Thereafter in the village for the greater part of November, it became a common sight to see clouds forming and just disappear without precipitating. In 2014, the clouds would look promising as if they would bring rain; unfortunately they would later disappear paving way for a totally clear blue sky leaving people with unanswered questions regarding the rains. Worby (1992) found out that, in Gokwe, such scenarios in which rain bearing clouds come and disappear were attributed to the power of rival *svikiros* (spirit medium) or claimants to recognition as *svikiros*, who were trying to demonstrate their powers to influence weather conditions to show their role and legitimacy. Still, with no *svikiro* or rival *svikiros* in the village, elderly women attributed the lack of rain to the ancestors who were punishing their children for disrespecting the laws of the land. *Mbuya* No specifically pointed out that: *"Vadzimu vakatsamwa nekuti vanhu havachatevedzera tsika dzechivanhu"* (The ancestors are angry and are therefore punishing the people because they are no longer following the traditions.)

Even though the rains later on fell on the evening of 16th of November 2014, they were light and not sufficient for planting. Other villages in Domboshava appeared to have received fairly good rains which allowed them to plant their maize. I remember the sound of the rain on the asbestos roof as I lay awake on the night of the 16th of November 2014 relishing the arrival of rains; it felt as if it was a very heavy downpour. Nevertheless, with the coming of dawn on 17th of November, it was a huge disappointment stepping outside and noticing that the rain had not watered the ground deeply and not even sufficiently for the planting season to commence, let alone to replenish the water table for the benefit of the wells or even for the rivers to start flowing. The same thing happened on the night of 18th of November and even those who had dug up holes in their fields in preparation to plant did not risk their seed by planting. On the other hand, some villages appeared to have received fairly good rains which allowed planting of maize to begin. Planting in the village only began at the end of November 2014 when the rains that fell had made the ground wet enough to plant maize.

As the 2015-2016 rain season was about to begin, the first thunder in the village was heard in late afternoon of Thursday 28th of October 2015 when it became windy and appeared to be building up for a heavy downpour. Somehow, it did not rain that day. On the 3rd of November 2015, it had been very hot like most days before it, with clear blue skies and in the late afternoon the weather took a dramatic turn becoming windy with thick clouds covering the village. This was regarded as a sure sign that rain was about to fall; as in other villages, one could see signs of rainfall thereby giving hope to the villagers. In spite of this, it did not rain even though there were still thick promising clouds in the skies, with temperatures dropping and becoming very cold and windy. By morning, there was no rain and villagers complained that the wind was chasing the rain away.

On the 15th of November 2015, after a number of days with clear blue skies and extremely uncomfortable high temperatures, clouds appeared by midday and by late afternoon the sky was overcast with signs of rains in villages to the south-east. With the wind blowing from that direction, one could smell the scent of soil which had been soaked in rain. On Monday 16th of November 2015, the same pattern was repeated, but still there were no rains in the village; only a noticeable drop in temperatures, and another overcast sky. It was only around mid-day on 22 November 2015 that it started raining and went on raining well into the morning of 23 November. Those rains appeared to mark the beginning of the farming season as some people got into their fields to plough and to a limited extent to plant, adopting a wait and see approach. *Mai* Reni acknowledged that such a cautious approach to planting was important as one needed to spread the planting of their crops due to the increasing uncertainty of the rains: *"Sezvo mvura yacho haichavimbika saka haungaise mbeu dzese muvhu nguva imwe chete. Unotofanira kusiyanisa mizera kuti ukohwe."* (Since the rains are no longer reliable so you cannot put all your crops in the soil at once. You need to spread the crops if you are to harvest.)

Understanding the Early Drying up of Water Sources in Gutsa Village

In one of the FGDs, a number of elderly women did acknowledge that the various water sources in the village were drying up faster than in previous years. *Mbuya* Tarai pointed out that: *"Mvura haichagara mese mumatsime nemunzizi. Tava kungoziva kuti tinoiwana kwenguva shoma. Zvotopera. Nhamo yototanga."* (Water is no longer available for long in all the wells and rivers. We now know that we get it for a short time. That's it. Thereafter life becomes difficult.)

The main factors attributed to the early drying up of these water sources are mainly that the rains are starting late and ending early, the village is receiving increasingly less and less rainfall, there is a lack of observance of customs regarding use of these water sources (especially communal wells). By early June 2015, the level of water in one of the three communal wells was already getting lower and lower and by November it was dry. Early in November of 2014, the second of the three communal wells from which people in Gutsa village draw their water, had completely dried up and people were now queuing for between ten minutes to close to an hour at the well on the border with Mashonganyika village. This same pattern was repeated again in 2015 with some villagers going to the well near Mashonganyika as late as at midnight to collect water. Villagers exchanged nasty words and relations got strained day by day at the well due to intense jostling for water. Villagers would manually draw water from the well and

187

carry the twenty litre water containers either on their heads or using wheelbarrows as motor powered water pumps are not allowed near the wells. It was believed that bringing motor pumps to the wells would cause them to dry up as the noise from these motor pumps would disturb the sacred *nyoka dzemvura* (snakes for water) forcing them to move away. The wells would subsequently dry up. One of the elderly women, *Mai* Cha, pointed out that at the well close to her garden; the snake was often seen hanging from one of the trees beside the rock looking into the well from where people scooped water for domestic use. Though I never saw the snake myself, it is said it never harmed anyone. *Mai* Cha said that: *"Dziripo nyoka dzemvura mumusha muno. Vaenzi muno zvinovanetsa kuti vachere mvura mutsime iyo nyoka yakarembera."* (There are snakes for water in this village. Visitors and newcomers in the village always have a hard time summoning the courage to fetch water from the well while a snake is hanging from a tree branch.)

With communal wells increasingly drying up early and causing serious water challenges and conflict in the village, a number of wells located at people's homes have been drying up early in the village too. The walls of some of these wells have over the years collapsed in the wake of torrents of rains over a few days. *Mbuya* No's well collapsed in 2011 and she rebuilt it and in 2013 it collapsed again. She said either this could have been caused by evil spirits or probably it was not built well. As she said: *"Kudonha kwakaita mugodhi wangu mabasa emweya yestvina isingade kuonawo ndichiita zvakanaka."* (The collapse of my well was a result of evil spirits that do not want to see me doing well.)

It appears the major contributor, singled out for the early drying up of water sources in the village, was the breaking of customs related to the use and preservation of wells. When these customs were observed, the wells did not dry up even in the harshest climatic conditions. *Mbuya* Gone held that: *"Vagari vemunzvimbo ino havachachengetedza tsika saka matsime, zvitubu nenzizi zviri kukurumudza kupwa."* (Residents of this village are no longer observing the customs so the wells, springs and rivers are drying up early now.)

In the second FGD, the elderly women pointed out a number of taboos which are no longer being respected. These taboos are that no black containers were to be used to fetch water at the wells and springs; no soap products were to be allowed near a well, no laundry was to be done at the well. In very extreme circumstances, one should fetch water and do their laundry some distance from the well. *Kukupa tsime* (cleaning of the well) should only be done either by young girls who are not yet menstruating or elderly women who have reached menopause. Villagers who are menstruating, prostitutes, incestuous people, homosexuals, as well as those who are breastfeeding are not supposed to *kukupa tsime* as they are considered unclean. No one should drink water directly from a well or spring, ideally one should use *mukombe* (gourd) or a cup or they should use leaves from *mikute (Ilex mitis)* trees to scoop water to drink. Because women in the village have been going to the wells to do their laundry near the wells, rather than having to engage in the laborious task of carrying water to their homes and doing laundry there, the wells are drying up. *Mai* Njere was very much concerned as these behaviours simply meant that residents were causing the changes resulting in water shortages: *"Kuita kwedu vagari vemuno ikoku ndokuri kugadzira matambudziko ekushanduka kwemwaka kwese uku."* (It is our behaviour as residents here that is creating troubles for us causing all the changes in the climate.)

As I will explain below, the early drying up of these various water sources was also said to be a consequence of changes in morality as seen in *makunakuna* (incest), lack of respect for *chisi* (rain season day of rest designated by the recognised *svikiro* (spirit medium) who has authority over the area) and prostitution, adultery, homosexuality and casual sex. Other contributory factors are the desecration of places such as mountains and caves which are sacred; the places are now being trampled on by white garment apostolic churches. The low rainfall is also explained in terms of failure to hold *chipwa* (rain petitioning ceremony). In a study in Mwenezi, Zimbabwe, Gandure (2011, 165) also observed that climate variability in the district was attributed to failure to conduct rain petitioning ceremonies and disrespect for elderly people. Blame has also been pointed to the settling of people in the *water chans* (water channels). The rampant cutting down of trees, the use of black/prohibited materials near springs or wells and the use of the ubiquitous motor water pump to extract water from these sources are also regarded as contributory factors.

Putting into Perspective the Changes in the Rainfall Patterns in the Village

The final arrival of the rains in late November 2014 and the unrelenting rains received in January 2015 made a lot of people to heave sighs of relief that at least the ancestors had heard their prayers. Somehow, this excitement was mixed with the fear that as the rainy season was yet to reach the half way mark, it appeared the downpours had made the village to receive the maximum rains for the season in just a few days. As the rains continued to fall through January and into early February 2015, villagers began to express their fears about the distribution of the rains. Most elderly women were now worried about the patterns for the onset of the rains, distribution over the course of the season and quantity. The fear was that instead of the rains being spread over a number of months in a normal agricultural season, they were spread over two months, mid-December to early January.

For the elderly women, it was important that a sufficient quantity of rains fall in and beyond the village in order to replenish the various water sources to guarantee that the next rain season could be reached without experiencing water problems. Timing of the rains was also important as it allowed people to plant on time to increase the chances of a good harvest. The spread of the rains over the rain season was also important for the elderly women as rainfall, evenly distributed over the farming season in the village, would allow crops to reach full maturity, increase the likelihood of a good harvest and enhance food security. So, even if the right quantity of rainfall was received in a year and was enough to replenish water sources, that was not sufficient on its own if there were episodes of severe moisture stress or severe water logging. These factors would destroy the prospects of a good harvest. It pointed to the need to have a balance in rainfall onset, distribution, quantity and its cessation.

By the 5th of January 2015 all the rivers and small streams in the village were now flowing while the seasonal wetlands had also become saturated with water. This is not usually the case under 'normal' conditions when the wetlands are usually thriving in mid-February when *'mubvumbi'* (drizzle) occurs. This new development was attributed to the prevalence of drizzle which was received from late December to early January.

Although in one of the FGDs one of the elderly women, *Mbuya* Gone, could not point to a specific year when rainfall had changed, she indicated that there were significant changes in onset, distribution, cessation and quantity of rainfall. In conversations with the elderly women, it appeared they could not really point to the exact years from which there was a turn in the general weather patterns. *Mai* Chota indicated that this change appeared to have been gradual over time and hence it was difficult to pinpoint the exact year with certainty: *"Kuti unyatsonongedza kuti iri ndiro gore rakashanduka mwaka zvinonetsa. Asi unongoona kuti mwaka iri kushanduka nekufamba kwemazuva."* (For one to point to an exact year in which the climate changed it is difficult. However you can see that the climate is changing with the passage of time.)

One of the elderly women *Mai* Reni indicated that she was concerned about the year which ended with a '2' as that year had a problem in terms of the likelihood of a drought/a poor rainfall year. She said her conclusions were based on the fact that the years 1982, 1992, 2002 and 2012 were drought years. Observations of rainfall data in Zimbabwe have also confirmed these years as drought years (Nangombe, nd; Kinsey, Burger and Gunning, 1998).

Having been born in the village, *Mbuya* Gone appeared to have a long history of the village and the rainfall changes it had experienced. She pointed to 1980, the year of Zimbabwe's independence from British rule, when she was thirty two years old, as the year that she recalled had much rains in her living memory. Talking to other elderly women, it appeared there was also consensus that just after the war of liberation in 1980 the country received good rains like never before. The elderly women pointed out that spirit mediums explained these rains in terms of washing the blood which had been spilt during the war of liberation. *Mbuya* No said that: *"Kubva kwatakaita muhondo kwainaya mvura inonzi iri kupara ropa. Yakanaya zvakatyisa mvura iyoyo vanhu vakafunga kuti haichanaya futi. Yaive yekugeza ropa iri."* (When we were coming from the war it rained rainfall which was described as scouring the blood. It rained so terrifyingly that people thought the rains would never come again. It was cleaning this blood.)

Proceeding with fieldwork into the 2014-2015 farming season, I soon noticed that most conversations in the village during the rainy season revolved around production and performance of *zvirimwa* (crops which generally refers to maize) in the fields. In the village, among both the young and the elderly, it is known that the rain for the village mainly comes from the 'traditional directions', Eastern and Southern sides. In spite of this belief, there is now confirmation that the rains appear to have changed the direction they were known to come from (previously east and south). Nevertheless there were increasingly a number of days when the rains were not coming from the 'normal' direction. It is therefore the winds that blow from these directions that usually drive rain bearing clouds towards the village and ultimately rain to the village. Among the Bonam in Burkina Faso, the direction of the wind also points to where favourable rains should be coming from and during the rainy season, farmers expect rain after a sultry day and if winds blow toward the east (Roncoli, Ingram and Kirshen, 2002: 414). *Mbuya* Ku, one of the elderly women in the village, indicated that when the wind comes from these directions, then the village will receive rain; on occasions when the wind blows nonstop from East or South then the wind can also send the rain bearing clouds much higher up into the sky and the rain would not fall in the village: *"Mvura yemumusha muno inowanzobva nekumabvazuva nekuti ndiko kunonyanyobva mhepo inouya munzvimbo muno. Asi mhepo yacho ikawanda inodzinga futi mvura."* (Rain for this village mostly comes from the east because that is where the wind which comes to this village also comes from. However if the wind is also too much it can chase rain away.)

Cessation of *Chipwa* Impacting on Rainfall Patterns in the Village

In the general history of Zimbabwe *chipwa* (rain petitioning ceremonies) were annual events (Mandaza, 1970) just as they were supposed to be in Gutsa village. *Chipwa* is held to plead for good rains from the ancestors to ensure that the rains fell on time, in the right quantities and spread adequately over the rainy season. *Chipwa* is traditionally held before rainfall and before people planted their crops. The failure to conduct *chipwa* was singled out as the leading cause of the changes in the rainfall being received in the village. *Mbuya* Tawira indicated that: *"Zvimwe zvese hazvo zvinganzi zviri kutadzisa mvura kunaya asi ndoona kuti kusaitwa kwechipwa ndiko kwanyanyokonzeresa kusanaya kwemvura."* (We can point to all these other things as causing rain not to fall but I see that not conducting *chipwa* is the mainly contributor for rain not falling.)

The main factor attributed to the cessation of *chipwa* in the village is the war of liberation as at the height of the war of liberation in 1978, people from Gutsa village fled and settled in nearby Mashonganyika village with others going further afield. On returning to the village at Independence in 1980 people's interest in *chipwa* had significantly diminished as the rains had continued to fall in the village despite nonperformance of *chipwa* ceremonies. After the death of the village *Gombwe,* in 1974, who had *'mudzimu wemvura'* (rain petitioning spirit), no one was subsequently possessed by the *mhondoro*. With the passing away of the village rain petitioner, there was just no one to continue with the rain petitioning ceremonies. Due to the increasing demand for wood, the entire forest where *chipwa* was carried out disappeared. Thus, the *muhacha (Parinari curatellifolia)* tree where *chipwa* was held was cut down as people needed firewood. Finally the specific site at which *chipwa* was held has now been parcelled out and sold to some immigrants who have since settled on the specific *chipwa* site.

What made the rain petitioning ceremony in Gutsa village unique is that this was carried out not because the rains had failed to come but rather it was just an annual practice which had to be done towards the start of the rainy season. Among the Ihanzu of Iramba District in semi-arid North Central Tanzania, villagers would hold their rain petitioning rituals to request for rain after it had failed to come. After the rain petitioning ritual the rains would come down to signify acceptance of the request (Sanders, 2000). This situation appears different from Gutsa village where the rain petitioning ritual was an annual event which had to be held before the start of every season. On the other hand despite *chipwa* being held every year there still were years that had very poor rains such as 1982, 1992 and 2012. *Mbuya* Ku said that if this was the case people would just comfort themselves and say: *"Aaah, inguva yacho: igore racho rino nekuti rainzi igore renzara."* (Aaah, it is time; it is this year because it would be referred to as a year of hunger.)

She recalled that even as she was growing up and for a long time after her marriage, there were a number of years which had been considered *makore enzara* (years of hunger). During those years they had survived on eating '*kenya*' (imported yellow maize). Nonetheless, *Mbuya* Ku recalled that even in Gutsa village sometimes *makore enzara* were not caused by poor rains but were caused by the scourge of the locusts. These locusts would appear and devour all the maize in the fields especially at the time that the maize was tasselling. For Ndiweni and Ndlovu (2013), the appearance of locusts in large numbers has also been used to predict a drought year in Southern Zimbabwe. Crop failure leading to famine has also been caused by pests (bush crickets) among the *Kenyah Badeng* farmers of Sarawak, Malaysia (Barayazarra and Puri, 2011) and by locusts among the Linga in Southern Africa (Angara, 1996).

The uncertainty of the rains, despite resuming the *chipwa* ceremony, revealed that the villagers did not have total control of the weather or the rains. Even when they made pleas for rain from the ancestors they still might not get the rain. The belief among the elderly women was that the most severe famine in the village was in the 1990s when villagers had stopped conducting *chipwa*. Consequently rain petitioning ceremonies are no longer being performed due to changes in people's belief systems (During, 1995: 88-89). In the Mutema chieftaincy in Chipinge, Zimbabwean men and women believe that ancestors keep away rain if chiefs have conflicts among themselves and if they fail to collectively honour their ancestors (Vijfhuizen, 1997: 31). In Mozambique this belief in the power of ancestors to control nature is also seen as a way which reinforces and strengthens ancestors' hold on people (Artur and Hilhorst, 2012).

Blaming the Advent of Christianity on Poor Rains

As more and more people in the village turn away from traditional religion and profess to be Christians, Christianity is increasingly also being blamed for the change in weather patterns in the village as people disregard traditional rites. As pointed out by

Mbuya Tarai, in Gutsa village due to Christianity, traditional observances such as *chipwa* and *chisi* are now being shunned and denigrated. *Chipwa* and *chisi* were supposed to be observed and respected as they were in a way responsible for favourable rains as well as giving deference to and acknowledging the power of the ancestors/owners of the village over people's lives. So for *Mai* Chai villagers now say: *"Kunyeba hakuna zvakadaro zvekuti mvura inonaiswa nevadzimu. Ngatinamatei chete, kuna Mwari, ehe zvinogumawo ka zvinonzi chiinaisai tione. Nekuti munoti vadzimu hakuna, vadzimu muri kushora ka, ko ari kunaisa mvura munomuziva kuti ndiyani?"* (You are lying, there is nothing such as rain comes from the ancestors. Let's just pray to God, yes that will also come to an end, they (the ancestors) will say now let the rains come down then. Because you say *vadzimu* are not there, spirit mediums you disrespect, the one who is making the rains come do you know them?)

Nevertheless, considering Christianity to have played a significant part in the demise of *chipwa* in the village is problematic. Even some elderly women who attributed the demise of *chipwa* to Christianity, such as *Mbuya* Tarai, were affirmed beer brewers for *chipwa* even though they were also members of the Salvation Army church. During (1995: 88-89) also noted that, in Biriwiri, drought was associated with the changing culture and the impact of Christianity as people no longer honour their ancestors. In Mozambique Artur and Hilhorst (2012) found that increased flooding, drought and other natural hazards were seen as connected to the end of the world and the urgent need for people to follow the church's guidance.

Lack of Observance of *Chisi* Resulting in Poor Rains

Changes in rainfall patterns in the village are also being attributed to the lack of observance of *chisi* in Gutsa village. *Chisi* as noted by *Mbuya* Tarai and *Mai* Cha was proclaimed many years ago in the village by the *svikiro* on the day that the elder of the area had passed away. In the village *chisi* is on Thursday and this day is announced by the village head when maize plants have reached knee level, usually in January in a 'normal' rainy season. By mid-January 2015 in the 2014-2015 rainy season I observed that the majority of the maize plants in the fields was way below knee level. This was unusual as people had planted late, since the village had received rainfall late. If people had planted early in mid-November/late November or early December, by January most of the maize in the fields would at least have reached waist level or above and *chisi* would have been proclaimed early or in the middle of January. Subsequently the announcement of *chisi* was delayed until the start of February showing that the date for proclamation of *chisi* is not fixed but is rather dependent on when the rains have fallen and an 'assessment' of people's maize crop.

Regarding concern about respect and observance of *chisi*, the elderly women observed that people in the village are disregarding *chisi*, mocking it as backward and unproductive. This was compounded by the fact that there appeared to be no punishment befalling those who broke the *chisi* taboo when they worked in their fields on that specific day. Previously punishment for those breaking *chisi* could come in the form of ravens chasing the errant villager from the field, crops being destroyed by *udyi* (pests which destroy crops) or harmless lightning strikes which would strike objects like trees at the person's homestead. For *Mbuya* Ku the lightning bolts which struck or killed people were not the *chisi* caution but these were brought by; *".....vanhu vari kushandisa midzi kutsvaga mari."* (.....people using harmful medicine to look for money.)

Mbuya Gone said that on *chisi* day villagers were not allowed to weed maize but they could work the field very early in the morning to weed ground nuts and round nuts and then leave the field when dew has disappeared. Therefore c*hisi* as part of local knowledge systems is supposed to provide members of the community in Gutsa village to act within rules of thumb to maintain security and assurance, or risk isolation from their community (also see Nyong, Adesina and Osman Elasha, 2007). Somehow this is not happening in the village as villagers (especially the original inhabitants) are losing respect for *chisi*. Just as in Gutsa village, lack of respect for *chisi* has also been cited by Risiro *et al* (2012) as a leading cause of change in rainfall patterns in Chimanimani District in Zimbabwe.

Speaking to elderly women who had migrated into the village from other places namely *Mai* Chota, *Mai* Njere, *Mbuya* Tawira and *Mai* Mizhu) their concern was that it is mainly the new comers to the village who are observing *chisi* more strictly than the original inhabitants. Having migrated into the village *Mai* Mizhu said she never broke *chisi* in the manner she had seen others around her doing as she did not want to break the laws of her new found home. As a result of their religious practices (especially the apostolic sect churches) with their *Sabata* 'Sabbath day' (Friday, Saturday or Sunday) these villagers do not work their fields on this day. Consequently, they are left with only five days to work in their fields after observing *chisi* and their respective *Sabata* during the rainy season.

Attributing Poor Rains to Prevalence of Loose Morals

Loose morals in the village are also believed to be the reason the village is receiving poor rains as well as leading to the early drying up of water sources as the ancestors are said to be angry and are therefore withholding rains, as punishment. *Mbuya* Tarai pointed out that previously water in the rivers and wells never used to dry up like what is currently happening in the village. However she said this was changing because of immoral things some people are doing like having prostitution, adultery, incest, homosexuality and other forms of casual sex. This was supported by *Mbuya* No who lamented the incidences of people who were taking photos of their naked friends and partners in the sacred Domboshava Mountains. The mountains are a popular tourist attraction and weekend outing place due to the attraction of the caves and the bushman rock art and paintings there. *Mbuya* No also confirmed that in the early 1990s a number of young women in Domboshava who were forced to have sex with White people's dogs: *"Vanasikana vemunzvimbo ino vaienda kuBorrowdale uko kunorara nembwa kuti vapiwe mari. Saka zvakadai hazvifadze varidzi venzvimbo avo vanotipa mvura."* (Young girls from here would go to Borrowdale there to have sex with dogs so that they could be given money. So these things do not please the owners of the place who give us rain.)

The ancestors were withholding rainfall as punishment because they were believed to be very angry with such abominable behaviour. As late as December 2014, with no meaningful rains having been received in the village, I was making my way into town (Harare) from the village in an eighteen seater *kombi*. On that day the animated conversation in the *kombi* was centred on the poor rains that had been

197

received up to December 2014. The consensus in the *kombi* was also that the lack of rains in the village was related to the defilement of the land as evidenced by the lack of morals among people (especially women). Some elderly women in the *kombi* said it was surprising that women or young girls would take a bath in an enclosed area and dress in the privacy of their bedrooms. Surprisingly they would then emerge half naked into the public sphere. They pointed out that it was better that these same women who preferred going around semi-naked would just bath and dress where everyone would see them. Despite these elderly women showing concern about dressing, covering up and morality, in my conversations with elderly women in the village they had indicated that they had grown up swimming naked with young boys in their villages. No one seemed to have been bothered about that at all. *Mbuya* Tawira said nowadays that would be impossible due to the sex crazed young generation fed on a diet of pornographic material available everywhere. In any case, in the precolonial and early colonial era, there were virginity tests conducted to ensure that sex was not performed wantonly and indiscriminately. In the contemporary era, Euro-America human rights activists demonise those that conduct virginity tests for allegedly violating the rights of young women and girls – Euro-American human rights have come to legitimise inhuman, nonhuman and immoral behaviour patterns among the villagers.

Makunakuna has also been singled out as one of the major contributor behind the changes in rainfall in the village. *Mai* Cha pointed out that *makunakuna* is a sign of the breakdown of the moral fabric. An example would be very close relatives in the village going to the extent of having sex with each other, impregnating each other and even becoming as bold as to marry each other. She went on to point out six examples of close relatives in the village that had married each other and were either continuing to live together or had married each other and had later divorced. She observed that it was traditionally known that: *"Kukaitwa makunakuna mvura hayizonayi. Paifanirwa kubviswa kana cheka hukama."* (If there was incest the rains would not come. The remedy was to pay *mombe yechekaukama* or Cow paid to dissolve an existing relationship).

Even if the *mombe yechekaukama* was paid the incestuous couples were not allowed to live together. Most of the elderly women opined that nowadays things had changed as once *mombe yechekaukama* is paid the incestuous couple insist on living together as they will be arguing that a sort of part payment for *roora* (bride wealth) has already been made. Furthermore, previously the offspring from the incestuous relationship would not survive but nowadays the same offspring grew up healthy. Due to this *Mai* Cha believed that the change in the weather and climate was a direct punishment from the ancestors and God. She stressed that the punishment from the deities should really strike people so hard by denying them rain so that they could repent from their evil ways as villagers had succeeded in making the sacred profane. Defilement of previously sacred places in the village and surrounding areas is also being blamed on the white garment apostolic churches whose members frequent sacred mountains for prayer retreats thereby making these areas profane.

Justification of this Study in Climate Change Discourse

Mugandani *et al.* (2013: 13), Makarau (1999) and Low (2005) have all acknowledged the existence of climate change in Zimbabwe. Climate change in Zimbabwe has led to increased variability of rainfall, reduction in the number of rain days, changes in wind direction and temperature changes. Subsequently climate change has seen some parts of Zimbabwe getting drier and warmer (Low, 2005) resulting in most meteorological stations recording a decline in rainfall over the past 100 years (Mugandani *et al.*, 2013).

In the face of this acknowledgement of climate change in Zimbabwe this chapter contributes to the growing body of knowledge which focuses on how climate change derives meaning, is translated in everyday practices, understood and experienced (Artur and Hilhorst, 2012; Lavrillier and Gabyshevd, 2018; Pyhälä *et al.*, 2006) especially at the local setting (Pettenger, 2007: 3). This is important as contemporary global climate change has cultural implications. Culture frames the way people perceive, understand and experience climate change (Barnes *et al.*, 2013; Crate, 2008; Crate, 2011: 176). As with Fiske (2014, 16); Crate (2011); Pyhälä *et al.* (2006), the chapter therefore demonstrates the insight into alternative systems of thought which do not fit neatly with the western supposedly scientific perspective and theory of climate change. The western "scientific" theory of climate change mainly focuses on quantification and measurement of weather and climatic phenomenon supposedly divorced from particular local settings (Orlove *et al.,* 2002). Furthermore, the monopoly of natural scientists in the climate change field has made climate change issues incomprehensible to the lay person (Terry, 2009: 6). Resultantly most studies on climate change mainly adopted a quantitative approach in both data gathering and analysis (Nguyen *et al.,* 2015; Crate, 2011) largely focusing on the impact of climate change on the macro level without zeroing in on the micro-level (Vedwan and Rhoades, 2001) an approach that this study moved away from.

As this chapter demonstrates for local level explanations of climate change, emphasis is on understanding local perceptions of environmental change as part of larger local systems of knowledge which have developed in the course of interacting with the environment (Berkes, 2009; Orlove *et al.,* 2002). In this study, it was important to focus on elderly women as generally women experience climate change differently from men (UN Women Watch, 2009; Nelson *et al.,* 2002: 51; Dankelman, 2002: 24; Skinner, 2011: 2). Women constitute the majority of the world's population living in poverty and they are also more dependent for their livelihood on natural resources which are threatened by climate change (UN Women Watch, 2009). Furthermore, in a gendered division of rural labour, elderly women appear to have intimate knowledge of environmental change and adaptation over time than men (Gorman, 2013). This derives from their expertise as guardians of seeds, plant varieties and soils (Mukoni, 2015). Women are also responsible for pumping, carrying, conserving and utilising household water (Mahlangu and Garutsa, 2014).

Following Boillat and Berkes (2013), I argue that the current experience of climate change in Gutsa village can be explained via a historical contextualisation of the issues. This is important when the term local knowledge is seen as referring to knowledge rooted in local cultures and associated with long-settled communities with strong ties to their natural environments (Orlove *et al.,* 2010). This is significant as local knowledge based climate information systems are very useful to the indigenous people. As such, the stocks of knowledge can help indigenous people to manage their production activities and hence minimise risks during unfavourable seasons as well as helping in maximising opportunities during favourable conditions (Ziervogel and Opere, 2010: 1).

Conclusion

In this chapter, I have examined the socio-cultural relations that structure the way in which climate change is perceived, understood, explained, attributed and experienced at the local level in rural Zimbabwe. This was achieved by focusing on elderly women's narratives regarding *kushanduka kwemwaka*. Elderly women as situated individuals in the village have an experience of their environment spanning a number of years and this has afforded them an opportunity to accumulate knowledge and an understanding of their local environment. As shown in this chapter, to understand climate change, it is important to focus on the local level perception of social reality and the contestation, the contradictions and attributions of explanations of causality regarding climate change as experienced at the micro level. This is important as the chapter demonstrates how within the particular social and historical context of Gutsa village, weather and climate phenomena are understood and interpreted in the wider cosmology (Also see Rosengren, 2018).

The chapter also demonstrated the existence of a central vernacular meteorological philosophy in the village which is shared by both the young and the old. This demonstrates the need to understand the relationship of people in their environment and how other actions such as breaking of taboos are also attributed as causes of the change in the climate of the village. As has been shown in this chapter, it is those subjective explanations of the changes in the climate that are important in understanding issues of causality and attribution at the micro level. Effectively, this demonstrates the challenges of reconciling local knowledge systems and "scientific" knowledge in climate change knowledge construction at the local level as such knowledge needs to be understood in its specific historical and spatial context and the associated patterns of power (see Kaijser and Kronsell, 2014). Furthermore, the chapter contributes to the larger methodological and epistemological challenges faced by scholars to presume consensus in 'traditional beliefs and customs' regarding the causes of weather patterns or climate change, the complexity and variety of understandings. This becomes equally problematic in the face of individuals' struggles to reconcile competing propositions about the weather and climate change.

References

Anderson, K., & Jack, D. C. (1991). Learning to Listen: Interview Techniques and Analyses, In Gluck, S. S. & Patai, D. (eds.), *Women's Words: The Feminist Practice of Oral History* (pp. 11-26). New York: Routledge Press.

Angara, T. O. (1996). Grassroots indicators among the Langi and their importance to district and national planning, In Hambly, H. & Angara, T. O. (eds) *Grassroots indicators for desertification experience and perspectives from Eastern and Southern Africa* (pp. 105-109). Ottawa: IDRC.

Antwi-Agyei, P., Andrew, J., Dougill, E., Fraser, D, G., & Stringer, L. C. (2012). Characterising the nature of vulnerability to climate variability: empirical evidence from two regions of Ghana. *Centre for Climate Change Economics and Policy Working Paper*(105).

Artur, L., & Hilhorst, D. (2012). Everyday realities of climate change adaptation in Mozambique. *Global Environmental Change, 22*(2), 529-536.

Barayazarra, G. G., & Puri, R. K. (2011). Smelling the monsoon: Senses and traditional weather forecasting knowledge among the Kenyah Badeng farmers of Sarawak, Malaysia. *Indian Journal of Traditional Knowledge, 10*(1), 21-30.

Barnes, J., Dove, M. R., Lahsen, M., Mathews, A., McElwee, P., McIntosh, R., *et al.* (2013). Contribution of Anthropology to the study of climate chang. *Nature Climate Change*(3), 541-544.

Berkes, F. (2009). Indigenous ways of knowing and the study of environmental change. *Journal of the Royal Society of New Zealand, 39*(4), 151-156.

Boillat, S., & Berkes, F. (2013). Perception and interpretation of climate change among Quechua farmers of Bolivia: Indigenous knowledge as a resource for adaptive capacity, ecology and society. *Ecology and Society, 18*(4).

Crate, S. A. (2008). Gone the Bull of Winter? Grappling with the Cultural Implications of and Anthropology's Role(s) in Global Climate Change. *Current Anthropology, 49*(4), 569-594.

Crate, S. A. (2011). Anthropology in the era of contemporary climate change. *Annual Review of Anthropology, 40*, 175-94.

Dankelman, I. (2002). Climate change: Learning from gender analysis and women's experiences of organising for sustainable development. *Gender & Development, 10*(2), 21-29.

Desjarlais, R., & Jason, C. J. (2011). Phenomenological approaches in anthropology. *Annual Review of Anthropology, 40*, 87-102.

During, A. (1995). *Playing the rains: Natural resources use and degradation in the Biriwiri sub catchment, Zimbabwe and the perceptions of these by the local population.* MSc. thesis, Agricultural University of Wageningen, Department of Irrigation and Nature Conservation.

Einarsson, N. (2011). Culture, conflict and crises in the Icelandic fisheries: An anthropological study of people, policy and marine resources in the North Atlantic Arctic. *48.*

Falzon, M. A. (2009). Introduction-Multi-sited Ethnography: Theory, Praxis and locality in contemporary research, in Falzon, M. A. (ed) *Multi-sited Ethnography: Theory, praxis and locality in contemporary research* (pp. 1-24). Surrey: Ashgate.

Fiske, S. J., Crate, S. A., Crumley, C. L., Galvin, K., Lazrus , H., Lucero, L. *et al.* (2014). *Changing the atmosphere. Anthropology and climate change.* Arlington, VA: American Anthropological Association.

Gandure, S. (2011). Reducing climate change risks "living with drought": Investigating local institutional design in Zimbabwe. In Kondlo, K. & Ejiogu, C. *Africa in focus: Governance in the 20th century* (pp. 163-175). Cape Town: HSRC Press.

Gorman, M. (2013). *Older women, Older farmers-the hidden face of agriculture.* London: HelpAge.

Kaijser, A., & Kronsell, A. (2013). Climate change through the lens of intersectionality. *Environmental Politics, 23*(3), 417-433.

Kakuru, D. M., & Paradza, G. P. (2007). Reflections on the use of the life history method in researching rural African women: Field experiences from Uganda and Zimbabwe. *Gender and Development, 15*(2), 287-297.

Kenyatta, J. (1938). *Facing Mount Kenya: The Tribal life of the Gikuyu.* London: Martin Secker & Warbug.

Kinsey, B., Burger, K., & Gunning, J. W. (1998). World Development. *Coping with drought in Zimbabwe: Survey evidence on responses of rural households to risk, 26*(1), 89-110.

Knodel, J., & Ofstedal, M. B. (2003). Gender and aging in the developing world: Where are the men. *Population and Development Review, 29*(4), 677-698.

Lavrillier , A., & Gabyshev, S. (2018). An emic science of climate. Reindeer Evenki environmental knowledge and the notion of an "extreme process". *Études mongoles et sibériennes,, 49*, 1-34.

Low, S. M. (2005). *Climate change and Africa.* New York: Cambridge University.

Low, S. M., & Merry, S. E. (2010). Engaged Anthropology: Diversity and dilemmas: An introduction to supplement 2. *Current Anthropology, 51*(S2), S203-S226.

Mabika, M., & Salawu, A. (2014). A tale of failure: Indigenous language radio broadcasting in Zimbabwe. *Mediterranean Journal of Social Sciences, 5*(20), 2391-2401.

Mahlangu , M. P., & Garutsa, T. C. (2014). Application of indigenous knowledge systems in water conservation and management: The case of Khambashe , Eastern Cape South Africa. *Academic Journal of Interdisciplinary Studies, 3*(4), 151-160.

Makarau, A. (1999). Water for agriculture: Policy and management options for the smallholder sector, in Manzungu, E. van de Zaag, P. & Senzanje, A. (eds) *Zimbabwe climate: Past present and future* (pp. 3-17). Harare: University of Zimbabwe Publications.

Mandaza, D. M. (1970). Shona customs: essays by African writers, in Kileff, C. & Kileff, P. (eds) *Traditional ceremonies which persist* (pp. 54-60). Gweru: Mambo Press.

Mararike, C. G. (1996). The use of trees, birds and animal behavior as measures of environmental change by the Shona people of Zimbabwe, in Hambly, H. & Angura, T. O. (eds) *Grassroots indicators for desertification experience and perspectives from.* http://hdl.handle.net/10625/15868

Mugandani, R., Wuta, M., Makarau, A., & Chipindu, B. (2013). A Revisit to the agro-ecological regions of Zimbabwe-Evidence of climate variability and change? *OSSREA Bulletin, X*(2).

Muguti, T., & Maposa, R. S. (2011). Indigenous weather forecasting: A phenomenological study engaging the Shona of Zimbabwe. *The Journal of Pan African Studies, 4*(9), 102-112.

Mukoni, M. (2015). Traditional gender roles of men and women in natural resource conservation among the Vhavenda people in Zimbabwe: Implications for sustainable development. *International Journal of Humanities and Social Science, 5*(4), 76-84.

Nangombe, S. S. (nd). Drought conditions and management strategies in Zimbabwe. www.droughtmanagement.info/wp-content/uploads/2016/01/Zimbabwe.pdf

Ndiweni, J. A., & Ndlovu, C. (2013). An exploration of the value of indigenous knowledge adaptation strategies in ensuring food security and livelihoods in Southern Zimbabwe. *Global Journal of Human Social Science, Geography, Geosciences, Environmental Disaster Management, 13*(7).

Nelson, V., Meadows, K., Cannon, T., & Morton, J. M. (2002). Gender & Development. *Uncertain predictions, invisible impacts, and the need to mainstream gender in climate change adaptations, 10*(2), 51-59.

Nguyen, A. L., Truong, M. H., Verreth, A. J., Leemans, R., Bosma, R. H., & De Silva, S. S. (2015). Exploring the climate change concerns of striped catfish producers in the Mekong Delta, Vietnam. *SpringerPlus, 4*(46).

Nyong, A., Adesina, F., & Osman Elasha, B. (2007). The value of indigenous knowledge in climate change mitigation and adaptation strategies in the African Sahel, Mitigation Adaptation Strategy. *Global Change, 12*, 787-797.

Orlove, B. J., & Cane, M. (2002). Ethnoclimatology in the Andes: a cross-disciplinary study uncovers a scientific basis for the scheme Andean potato farmers traditionally use to predict the coming rains. *American Scientist, 90*(5), 428–435.

Orlove, B., Roncoli, C., Kabugo, M., & Majugu, A. (2010). Indigenous climate knowledge in southern Uganda: the multiple components of a dynamic regional system. *Climatic Change, 100*, 243-265.

Pettenger, M. E. (2007). Introduction: Power, knowledge and the social construction of climate change, in Pettenger, M. E. (ed) *The social construction of climate change: power, knowledge, norms, discourses* (pp. 1-18). Hampshire: Ashgate.

Pyhala, A., Fernandez-Llamazares, A., Lehvavirta, H., Byg, A., Ruiz-Mallen, I., Salpeteur, M., *et al.* (2016). Global environmental change: local perceptions, understandings, and explanations. *Ecology and Society, 21*(3).

Risiro, J., Mashoko, D., Tshuma, D. T., & Rurinda, E. (2012). Weather forecasting and indigenous knowledge systems in Chimanimani district of Manicaland, Zimbabwe. *Journal of Emerging Trends in Educational Research and Policy Studies, 3*(4), 561-566.

Roncoli, C. (2006). Ethnographic and participatory approaches to research on farmers' responses to climate predictions. *Climate Research, 33*, 81-99.

Roncoli, C., Ingram, K., & Kirshen, P. (2002). Reading the rains: Local knowledge and rainfall forecasting in Burkina Faso. *Society & Natural Resources, 15*(5), 409-427.

Rosengren, D. (2018). Science, Knowledge and Belief. On Local. *Ethnos, 83*(4), 607-623.

Sanders, T. (2000). Rains gone bad, women gone mad: Rethinking gender rituals of rebellion and patriarchy. *Journal of Royal Anthropological Institute, 6*, 469-486.

Schumaker, L. (1996). A tent with a view: Colonial officers, Anthropologists, and the making of the field in Northern Rhodesia, 1937-1960. *The History of Science Society, 11*, 237-258.

Skinner, E. (2011). *Gender and climate change.* BRIDGE: Development And Gender.

Terry, G. (2009). No climate justice without gender justice: an overview of the issues. *Gender & Development, 17*(1), 5-18.

UN WomenWatch. (2009). *The UN Internet Gateway on Gender Equality and Empowerment of Women.* https://www.business-humanrights.org/en/womenwatch-the-un-internet-gateway-on-the-advancement-and-empowerment-of-women-0

Vedwan, N. (2006). Culture, Climate and the Environment: Local Knowledge and Perception of Climate Change among Apple Growers in Northwestern India. *10*(1), 4-18.

Vedwan, N., & Rhoades, R. E. (2001). Climate change in the Western Himalayas of India: a study of local perception and response. *Climate Research, 19*, 109-117.

Vijfhuizen, C. (1997). Rain-making, political conflicts and gender images: A case from Mutema chieftaincy in Zimbabwe. *Zambezia, XXIV*(i), 39-41.

Wilson, W. J., & Chaddha, A. (2010). The role of theory in ethnographic research. *Ethnography, 10*(4).

Worby, E. (1992). *Remaking labour, reshaping identity: cotton, commoditization and the culture of modernity in northwestern Zimbabwe.* PhD Thesis, McGill University.

Ziervogel, G., & Opere, A. (2010). Integrating meteorological and indigenous knowledge-based seasonal climate forecasts in the agricultural sector. Ottawa: International Development Research Centre.

Ziervogel, G., Nyong, A., Osman, B., Conde, C., Cortés, S., & Downing, T. (2006). *Climate variability and change: Implications for household food security.* AIACC Working Paper20.

Chapter Seven

Neoimperial Engineering of Droughts and Famine on Post-Colonial Zimbabwe? Knowledge Systems and the Politics of Land Repossession in Africa

Beatrice Lantern

Introduction

In pre-colonial Africa, droughts and famines, that killed were a rare occurrence. It was only from the beginning of colonialism that Zimbabweans experienced droughts and famines that killed (Iliffe, 1990; Chigodora, 1997) and colonialists also destroyed African granaries to ensure that Africans succumbed to colonisation. Droughts and famines have become common in postcolonial Zimbabwe wherein Euro-America is also anxious to prevent land repossession by indigenous Africans. In this vein, scholars have noted the increasing incidences and intensity of droughts, cyclones and famines particularly since the inception of the land redistribution programme in Zimbabwe (Richardson, 2007; BBC News, 3 March 2017; Mutasa, 2010; Nangombe, 2014). While Eurocentric thinkers and scholars blamed Robert Mugabe for bad governance and for doctoring election results, Robet Mugabe blamed the United States of America and Britain for covertly doctoring the weather in southern Africa, as a gimmick to arm-twist the African governments to capitulate to the neoimperial agenda (Nhemachena, 2015; 2017). In essence, while Euro-America accused Mugabe of stealing elections, Mugabe accused Euro-Americans of stealing good weather and climate from southern Africans. Euro-America has engaged in weather and climate warfare in history and in various parts of the world. An example of weather warfare is that of the Vietnam war where the U.S. Military used cloud seeding from March 1967 until July 1972. Novak (2015) and Winston (2015) share the same sentiments on this Vietnam incident. They state that the goal was to extend the monsoon season and flood the Ho Chi Minh Trail, the system of supply routes used by enemy fighters in Vietnam. The Americans hoped to cause landslides, wash out river crossings, and generally disrupt the movement of North Vietnam troops. This program went by many names like Operation Popeye, Operation Motorpool, and Operation Intermediary-Compatriot according to Novak (2015). The former Zimbabwean President Robert Mugabe often chided the West on issues of climate change (Nkomo 2009; News24) partly because the west is also responsible for underdevelopment and impoverishment on the continent of Africa (Thornton, 1980: 557). These, often surreptitious, practices of engineering or manipulating the weather and climate should be factored in the contemporary discourses about anthropogenic causes of climate change.

The dispossession and exploitation of Africans since the enslavement and colonial era is also responsible for the death and suffering of many Africans on the continent. In terms of African religion, because God and ancestors do not want to see their children and adherents suffering landlessness, they would also visit droughts and famine as ways to ensure that action is taken to repossess land and other resources that were stolen and are still in the hands of descendants of colonialists. In this sense, climate change including droughts, famine and floods can be explained in terms of the displeasure of God and ancestors who expect justice in a world where Africans and other colonised peoples were/are robbed, dispossessed and exploited since the enslavement and colonial eras (Nhemachena & Mawere, this volume).

Given the history of weather and climate engineering, and the history of the cruelty of imperial dispossession and exploitation on Africans, it is arguable that climate and weather changes during the recent Zimbabwean land redistribution/repossession exercise were also caused by the west. The west has strenuously resisted the repossession of the land by the indigenous rightful owners. Whereas in indigenous knowledge systems, some sorcerers and witches are known to bewitch the weather and climate so as to caused droughts and famine on their opponents or enemies (Nhemachena, 2016), in the contemporary era the west uses weather and climate engineering to cause droughts and famine on their enemies or opponents. Manipulating electromagnetic waves in the atmosphere, the west is able to remotely control the weather and climate over other regions of the world (Nhemachena & Mawere, this volume). The chapter argues that drought and famine can be "curses" from the neoimperial centres wherein some human beings consider themselves as owners and controllers of the weather and climate in the whole world. Whereas Eurocentric scholars have derided African spirit mediums and indigenous knowledge systems dealing with control of the weather and climate, ironically, Euro-America has over time, been strengthening its own control of the global weather and climate. Euro-American control of weather and climate is often surreptitiously used for nefarious purposes on countries and states that refuse to follow neoimperial edicts and commandments. Euro-American imperialists have battled and belittled African indigenous knowledge systems (IKSs) by disregarding and caricaturing African religion. Owing to the grudge between Zimbabwe and Euro-American imperialists, a grudge which was magnified by the so-called fast-track land "invasions" in Zimbabwe, the chapter submits that [Western] Europe and North America are determined to change Zimbabwe's role in SADC from being a bread basket to a begging basket by distorting weather patterns on which Zimbabwean agriculture depends. Because the genetically modified organisms that are being produced by American companies like Monsanto and Syngenta need markets, empire is prone to subject the world to weather and climate engineering to force the world to succumb to GMOs. Deemed to be climate smart crops, these GMOs are fashioned out in the name of alleviating the effects of climate change and under the cover of improving global food security, even as the GMOs compromise the health of African citizens (Mawere & Nhemachena, 2017). Thus, now there is availability of many varieties of Syngenta maize seed like Syngenta MR1624, Syngenta MR 1514 in Farm and City Centres in Zimbabwe. On this understanding, the chapter advocates for the revitalisation of IKSs and directly engaging Europe and America to avert the consequences of external weather engineering.

African religion and African humanity were once inseparable in the traditional past. The philosophical worldview of an African was religiously embedded. In other words, Africans saw their religion as a fabric that held the cosmos together. In a penetrating analysis, Mbiti

211

(1969:1) observes that "Africans are notoriously religious... Religion permeates into all the departments of life so fully that it is not easy or possible always to isolate it." This means that African religion was the spine of the African traditions and knowledge systems that anchored indigenous practices of weather and climate control.

Rain is a central element in African religion and also central to peoples' lives. Mbiti (1969:180) observes that the physical life of the people, as well as their prosperity and wellbeing, depend on rain. Therefore, rain is a deeply religious rhythm, and those who 'deal' in it, transact business of the highest religious calibre (Mbiti, 1969:181). In African religion, rain was petitioned for in territorial cults that have served African people well before the neocolonial disruptions. Considering the importance of rain, Africans viewed it as a duty to carry out rain petitioning ceremonies to avoid disasters like droughts and famines. Through rain-petitioning ceremonies, African religion could be used to control climate and weather.

However, with the inception of colonialism in Zimbabwe, things changed. The African religion, indigenous to Africa and rooted in the African cosmology was confronted by a colonial religion - western religion –or Christianity, rooted in the western cosmos. Euro-Americans in the name of Christians caricatured African religion as primitive, underdeveloped, devilish, superstitious and hellish to the extent that Africans who followed precepts of traditional religion were despised and mocked until they lost confidence in their religion. As a result, in the years that followed, many Africans were converted to and immersed in Christianity and increasingly assumed 'Christocentric identities' as they gradually lost touch with their ancestors. Although African religion was heavily weakened by Christianity, it never became extinct as in times of grave crisis people still revert to it, sometimes secretly.

African religion was heavily relied upon during the liberation war. Euro-American imperialists had dispossessed Africans, robbing them of their land, minerals and livestock which were looted during the colonial era. In response, Africans launched the liberation struggle against colonialists and imperialists. The liberation struggle became the only viable means by which Africans could set themselves free. The liberation struggle saw the victory of Africans and ensured political sovereignty but land was not restored to Blacks until the year 2000 when the Robert Mugabe government embarked on land repossession. The land repossession programme, famously known as Fast Track, attracted the attention of many people, both at country and international levels. This land repossession was meant to restore land to original Black owners. The Fast Track Land Reform Programme (FTLRP) became a thorn in the flesh of Euro-American imperialists who were determined to turn this programme into a farce. In an effort to settle their scores on grudges with Africa, they engineered weather and climate patterns on which Zimbabwean agriculture depends.

It is worth mentioning that Zimbabwe is one of the SADC member states, and had been allocated, in 1980, the responsibility of coordinating crop production, food, agriculture and natural resources. With this responsibility in mind and considering the current Zimbabwean situation mirred in droughts and famines, it is indeed worrying. The imperialists are determined to change Zimbabwe's role in SADC, from being a bread basket to a begging basket, by engineering the weather on which Zimbabwean agriculture depends. Commenting on this state of affairs Mitchinson (2016) says Zimbabwe has gone from being the breadbasket of Southern Africa to its basket case. More than 75% of Zimbabwe's working population is employed in the agriculture sector, meaning that by destroying the agricultural sector, this significant figure will be rendered jobless. This relegated the majority to hunger, poverty, and to beggars for food. Africans need to revert to African religion.

In light of the above argument, the chapter discusses the history of droughts and famines in Zimbabwe, the contested land question, rain petitioning and geoengineering of rain and also examines the engineering of droughts and famine on Zimbabwe. The chapter concludes by urging Africans to revitalise their traditional religion for the good of their lives.

History of Droughts and Famines in Zimbabwe

Droughts and famines should be understood as induced by unfavourable weather and political conditions. Drought refers to a prolonged period of abnormally low rainfall leading to a shortage of water while famine is extreme scarcity of food over a large area. In most cases, extreme scarcity of food is caused by rainfall failure. The State of the Environment in Southern Africa, SADC (1994) states that drought is associated with suffering and loss of valued crops, livestock and wildlife. This condition of dry weather leading to famine is not new in Africa and Zimbabwe, to be specific. What might be new and shocking is the frequency of occurrence of both in post–colonial Zimbabwe compared to its pre-colonial past.

Drought and Famine in Pre-colonial and Colonial Zimbabwe

In the pre-colonial epoch, droughts and famines in Zimbabwe (the then Rhodesia) were a rare occurrence. The onset of the rains, in agrarian countries like Zimbabwe, is often viewed as a single most important event of the year. As such, Africans were always alert to petition for the rains whenever the season was due. African Indigenous Knowledge Systems (henceforth IKSs) of rain petitioning were always handy in controlling the weather. In traditional African societies rain petitioning practices were regarded as a crucial and strong element in their religion. They were responsible for effectively controlling rainfall patterns throughout the season. It is interesting to note that rain petitioners were prestigious in societies they belonged to. With this background, the occurrence of droughts or famines became a sad experience. The strategies of coping with famines included practising pastoral-nomadism and trading corn in areas of plenty. Iliffe (1990) in Dopcke (1990:101) posits that pre-colonial famines did not normally cause mass starvation.

During colonialism, droughts and famines occurred frequently because the bonds between Africans and their religion were loosened and African land was looted by colonialists. The inception of colonialism and Christianity in Africa saw the caricaturing of African religion as primitive, underdeveloped, devilish, superstitious and hellish to the extent that Africans associated with traditional religion were despised and mocked until they finally lost confidence in their religion. As a result, in the years that followed, many Africans were converted to and immersed in Christianity and assumed 'Christocentric identities' as a result of loss of connections with their ancestors. The condition of losing touch with their ancestors meant

214

that their links with their religion were also weakened. And this meant that rain petitioning practices in territorial cults became moribund, hence the frequent occurrence of droughts and famines.

Dopcke (1990:102) states that Iliffe (1990) presents nine major colonial famines between 1896 and 1960 and these occurred in years; 1896/7, 1903, 1912, 1916, 1922, 1933, 1942, 1947 and 1960. The major cause of the first four famines enlisted above is failure of the rains. The State of the Environment in Southern Africa, SADC (1994) concurs with Iliffe (1990) by stating that the period from 1875 to 1910 was marked by a decrease in rainfall in southern Africa, and 1910 experienced a severe drought. These famines, according to Dopcke (1990) threatened but did not cause deaths from starvation in great numbers owing to the continued operation of pre-colonial famine-survival strategies and (to a small but increasing degree) to famine relief by the colonial state. The colonial officials did many injustices to Africans which include destroying African livelihoods as a way to force them to yield to neoimperial rule. The 1922 famine is said to have incorporated most elements of transition from pre-colonial to capitalist famines. The severity of this famine was linked to developments in the capitalist economy; as a result of the depression following the First World War cattle prices dropped drastically and Africans were unable to secure exchange entitlements to food by cattle sales (Dopcke, 1990). As a result government drought relief became an important check on famine and labour migrations were witnessed in this period.

The famines that occurred in the years; 1933, 1942 and 1947 were largely characterised by dominant colonial capitalism, that is, famines were geographically concentrated in areas of most intense White settlement like Matabeleland in Zimbabwe. Iliffe (1990) in Dopcke (1990:103) asserts that "the causes of food scarcities of 1933, 1942 and 1947 are closely linked to the impact of looting of African land, evictions, the overcrowding of the reserves and declining agricultural per capita productivity." Lastly, the disastrous famine of 1960 resulted from the undermining of African agriculture by the effects of colonial land apportionment.

The dispossession and exploitation of Africans by the colonialists could not have pleased God who valued peace and tranquillity such as existed in precolonial Zimbabwe. The point here is that climate and weather changes can be explained in terms of God's anger with the colonialists who wantonly committed crimes of murder, theft, robbery, looting, plunder, dispossession and exploitation on African people. Transnational corporations continue to dispossess Africans of their land and other resources and in addition Euro-America continues to force Africans to become homosexuals and to behave in immoral and unethical ways that would escalate the anger of God who is the guardian of life, morals and ethics. African people from as far apart as present day Mozambique, Zambia, Zimbabwe, Botswana and South Africa used to consult the shrine of God at the Matopo Hills and thus they were quite peaceful among themselves, contrary to colonial falsehoods that there were barbaric "intertribal" wars and raids (see Nhemachena, 2017; Palmer, 1977; McGonagle, 2007).

Overview of Droughts and Famines in Post – colonial Zimbabwe

Post-colonial Zimbabwe is a droughts and famines hard-hit period. Drought and famine conditions in post–colonial Zimbabwe may be divided into 2 phases; that is, the first phase stretching from 1981 to 1992 and the second phase from 2001 to 2016. The State of the Environment in Southern Africa, SADC (1994) lists the drought years that occurred in the first phase as follows: 1981/2, 1983, 1986/7 and 1991/2. The major cause was identified as low rainfall amounts received in Zimbabwe. It should be noted that the 1980s was a period of independence euphoria and it was also a period when the South African apartheid government destabilised the newly independent Zimbabwean state. The 1990s were also a period when the International Monetary Fund and the World Bank economically destabilised the newly independent Zimbabwe, through neoliberal reforms.

The second phase of famine conditions were experienced after the year 2000. Mitchinson (2016) states that Zimbabwe has had famine conditions in 2001 (the year farm seizures began), 2002, 2003, 2004, 2005, 2008, 2014, 2015 and 2016. This period was characterised by the Fast-Track Land Reform Programme which started around year 2001. This period of land reform programme became the focus of heated and intellectually stimulating debate in Zimbabwe and beyond. A plethora of written literature commenting on drought and famine in this period is presented in a threatening, scaring language and overall in a sarcastic manner. This is evidenced in headlines like, "Zimbabwe's Man-made Famine (by David Coltart, 2002); "Famine becomes Mugabe Weapon" (by Beaumont, 2002); "Zimbabwe Begs White Farmers to Return as Country Plunges into Famine" in (NewsPunch, 2017) and "Zimbabwe's Socialist Famine" (by Mitchinson, 2016). The insinuation in all these identified headlines is that, famine in Zimbabwe was primarily caused by bad governance of the then President Mugabe and his supposedly ruinous policies. During this critical phase, some people of Zimbabwe survived on food donations. The general erroneous feeling in Eurocentric scholarship and thinking in this era was that the land issue was the major contributing factor towards famine in Zimbabwe. Hardly anything about the west's remote electromagnetic manipulation of weather and climate, such as through the High-Frequency Active Aural Research Program (HAARP) (See Nhemachena and Mawere, this volume) has been said in relation to the recurrent droughts and famines on Zimbabwe and Africa more broadly.

The Land Question in Zimbabwe

The land question in both colonial Zimbabwe (the then Rhodesia) and post–colonial Zimbabwe remains a hot debate that has refused to be exhausted in the Zimbabwean socio-economic and political discourses. African land is closely connected with African traditional religion, agrarian economy, general life and dignity. Colonial Zimbabwe has seen massive displacement of Blacks from the most productive land to Reserves characterised by poor soils where there is no life (see for instance Nhemachena, Kangira & Mlambo, 2019). Nasty phrases used to describe these Reserves where Blacks were forced to stay include, as various scholars in Moyana (2002:2) declare, "badly watered, peculiar hydrological content or waterless desert; Kalahari sands, sandy or very low natural fertility; and unfit for settlement." Ramose (1999:3) describes vividly the fateful years of African colonial experiences, thus:

Historically, the unjust wars of colonisation resulted in the forcible expropriation of land from its rightful owners from time immemorial: the Africans. At the same time the land expropriation meant loss of sovereignty by Africans. The close connection between land and life meant also that by losing land to the conqueror, the African thereby lost a resource to life.

The citation informs that the genesis of land segregation in Rhodesia took place long ago, it possibly dates back to around 1894 where the British South African Company (BSAC) allocated two Reserves, that is, Gwayi and Shangani, to the Matabele (Moyana, 2002:1). On the other hand, to Fanon (1961:34), land to an African is of essential value as it gives Africans bread and, above all, dignity. Besides being alienated from their land, Africans also witnessed forced detachment from their religion, drastic reduction of their livestock numbers; they were also compelled to enter into, as Ramose (1999:5) puts it, a new law of economics, that is, money economy. This sad scenario violated Africans' right to life, and Africans were plunged into poverty.

The impoverishment of Africans through violence instigated by Euro-American imperialists made Africans to unite, reason together and seek out strategies as well as suitable weaponry to overthrow the imperial order. The liberation struggle was started. Africans, with the help of other countries, fought and won the struggle. Political independence was attained but with no realisation of economic independence. Since the African economy was agrarian in nature, it meant that the outstanding issue of land had to be resolved if total independence was to be achieved. Commenting on such a state of affairs, Ramose (1999:4) says:

For this [land] reason even decolonisation has failed to restore full sovereignty to the African. What we have is a rather defective and limping sovereignty, that is to say, political sovereignty bereft of economic sovereignty.

Ramose's sentiments imply that Zimbabwe's independence was not a complete independence as long as the land issue was still outstanding. Despite the attainment of independence in 1980, the land issue was not resolved until the year 2000 through a programme famously known as Fast Track Land Reform Programme (FTLRP). Matondi (2012:1) states that:

> The Fast Track Land Reform Programme (FTLRP) has been inscribed on Zimbabwe's political and socio-economic map since 2000.... in Zimbabwe itself it radically altered people's lives and livelihoods, and at the same time reawakened people's memories of the past. The programme radically transformed society, with former landowners being pushed aside.... and new beneficiaries walking into new commercial land...

The above citation underlines the fact that the year 2000 was the beginning of a radical repossession of land by Blacks from White farmers, and to the majority of Zimbabweans this repossession was a realisation of empowerment. It should be noted that prior to land redistribution Euro-Americans had been all along fooling Africans that neoliberalism was empowering, however, Zimbabweans refused the empty promises of participatory development without ownership of land and other resources. They therefore, resolved that they could only be empowered by assuming ownership and control over their resources. Therefore, upon land restoration, Africans or Zimbabweans to be specific, were beaming with happiness and determined to transform Zimbabwe to a new agricultural revolution were hunger and poverty would be things of the past. Not many Zimbabweans were aware that some White farmers had transformed Zimbabwean soils through genetically modified organisms. More so, these imperialists modified the weather and climate as a way of detracting the new African farmers. As such climatic disturbances became a new contesting ground. All these factors contributed to the low agricultural production which almost led to the collapse of Zimbabwe. Although it seems that the FTLRP represents the demise of the colonial land question in Zimbabwe, it should be stated that the significance of land repossession is not fully realised as Zimbabwe is still being subjected to climatic disturbances resulting from neo-imperial climate engineering. Climatic disturbances are engineered by the Euro-American imperialists who are keen to punish Zimbabweans for repossessing their land, as well as to prevent other

African countries from repossessing their land (BBC News 28 June 2005; Nhemachena, 2015).

Rain Petitioning vis-a-vis Rain Making in Zimbabwe

In pre-colonial and colonial epochs, rain petitioning practices [erroneously referred to as rain-making by many scholars] were a common ritual occurrence amongst the people across the African landscape. A rain petitioning ceremony might refer to a sacred ritual process carried out at sacred places where rain petitioners or any suitable elderly appeal for rain to fall or stop as per societal requirements using various sacred objects. In Ndebele, rain petitioning is known as *ukuphehla izulu* while in Shona it is called *mukwerera*. Rain petitioning practices are heavily embedded in African religion. However, during the inception of colonialism, Euro-American imperialists preached that only God can make or produce rain. And rendered rain petitioners as playing a role of intermediaries between people and God and later replaced this intermediary role of rainmakers with Jesus. They also introduced new methods of inducing rain that might be termed rain making operations through geoengineering.

Rain petitioning and rain making display levels of sophistication. Writing about rain petitioning, Mbiti (1969:181) underscores that those engaged in the art of "rainmaking" (and rainstopping) are well versed in weather matters, and many spend long periods acquiring their knowledge. This they obtain from other "rainmakers", from observing the sky, from studying the habits of trees, insects and animals, from a study of astronomy and use of common sense. Also "rain making" through geoengineering requires sophistication in the sense that rain-makers have to check on the type of clouds that are likely to be infused to give precipitation. Another feature shared by both practices is the time when these practices are carried out, that is, they are both done when the farming season is due. Regarding this idea, Mbiti (1969:181) reiterates that "none would be foolish enough to attempt to make [petition for] rain during the peak of the dry season". On the other hand Rafferty (2019) informs that geoengineering of rain has proved less fruitful in winter.

Although rain petitioning and rain making share similarities as shown above, they also have differences. Rain petitioning is cheaper as compared to rain making which is expensive, both in terms of obtaining required substances and mechanisms of injecting them into the clouds. From a traditional perspective, a number of scholars including Mbiti (1969:181); Schoffeleers (1999:35) and Bozongwana (1983:49-51) provide insights about the practice of rain petitioning which involves the use of sacred objects like rain-stones, burning of rain-leaves or other combustibles, use of water in various ways, use of magic, use of charms, use of rain spirits to ruffle the sea, relying on the Ngwali (*Mwari*) spirit in the Matopos and also cleaning the bush known as *ukwebula ingxoza* in Ndebele. The usual trend was that soon after such sacred practices, rain would fall accordingly. On the other hand, Rafferty (2019) states that cloud-seeding is a process that attempts to bring rain to parched farmland by dispersing particles of silver iodide or solid carbon dioxide into rain-bearing clouds. Moreso, the first experiments with cloud seeding were conducted in 1946 by an American chemist and meteorologist Vincent J. Schaefer, and since then seeding has been performed from aircraft, rockets, cannons, and ground generators. In addition to the above point, McNaughton (1981) informs that in the randomised experiments of cloud seeding which they carried out, they discovered that on average, silver iodide treatment of cumulus clouds increased and prolonged their rainfall, particularly when cloud-tops were -13°C or colder.

Rain-petitioning ceremonies indicate that African religion had the capability to control climate and weather. Thus, in the halcyon days, rain petitioning practices were held in high esteem as they responded favourably to peoples' rain needs and it is pitiful to say that in this post-colonial era it has been battled and belittled by Christianity and worse, jeered upon by contemporary geoengineering weather and climate-change-merchants.

Engineering of Droughts and Famines in Post – colonial Zimbabwe

As has been observed in the preceding sections, the primary factor that causes droughts and famines in Zimbabwe is rainfall failure. Droughts cannot be reduced to governance issues in Zimbabwe; in any case the problem is that Africa is governed by too many actors some of whom are not African – as it is said too many cooks spoil the broth. The neoimperial practices of engineering weather and climate need to be factored in as an aspect of global (mis)governance that affects Africa. Regarding this view, therefore the engineering of droughts and famines in post-colonial Zimbabwe, centres around the mischief of distorting weather patterns on which African agriculture depends. Droughts and famines have been engineered by Euro-American imperialists over neo-colonial land control struggles in Zimbabwe.

Weather modification in the form of cloud-seeding used by Euro-American imperialists in the then tranquil Zimbabwe; that is, before independence had proved to be very much helpful. However, it should be noted that this same mechanism was less effectively used in post-independent Zimbabwe because of lack of both financial and material resources. Kaerasora (2018) notes that cloud-seeding in Zimbabwe has been performed yearly since 1980 and has helped the country to overcome some dry spells which, in recent years, have been directly linked to climate change, that is, climate and weather engineering. McNaughton (1981) says that seeding might be ineffective if the cloud-seeding aircraft cannot attend to every suitable cloud in the atmosphere of a targeted area. Such a scenario lessens the impact of cloud-seeding which is premised on the intention to increase rain over the country and augment water availability. One may postulate that the reason for all these drought years (see Mitchinson, 2016) is that cloud-seeding operations were not fairly geographically and systematically distributed across the season owing to underfunding since Zimbabwe is an economically struggling country.

Besides being ineffectively distributed across the farming season, cloud-seeding operations are applied late. Chingwere (2018) notes that despite having been informed early in the year, by the Meteorological Services Department (MSD), of the impending drought, cloud-seeding only started late in January of 2019. Farmers were already anxious for cloud-seeding as evidenced in The Herald news headline on the 28th of December 2018 "Farmers call for cloud seeding". The failure of MSD to timeously supplement natural

222

rainfall through cloud-seeding might be attributed to lack of both finances and equipment. Chingwere (2018) observes, referring to the 2018/19 season, that "... no budget has been announced for cloud-seeding this season". This situation alone is enough to reduce the effectiveness of cloud-seeding in Zimbabwe.

Tropical cyclones have been prevalent in post-colonial Zimbabwe. Although tropical cyclones bring the much needed rain, their effects are much dreaded in African societies. Heavy rains that are brought about by tropical cyclones have adverse effects on agriculture, that is, it may result in drowning of crops, sweeping away of crops, massive soil erosion, leaching of plant nutrients, stunted growth of crops leading to drought and famine, and destruction of infrastructure. Regarding these disastrous scenarios caused by tropical cyclones, it is worth indicating that cloud-seeding can also be used to lessen their impacts. As Rafferty (2019) observes, cloud-seeding has also been used in attempts to weaken tropical storms. There is ignorance about ways of weakening impacts of tropical cyclones in Zimbabwe.

History is awash with evidence of Euro-American "aid" to Zimbabwe, be it financially or food handouts. A penetrating analysis informs that this kind of "aid" is aimed on short term relief which falls far short of sustainable livelihood standards. It has become obvious in this chapter that Zimbabwe is struggling to effectively operate cloud-seeding as a means of supplementing natural rainfall, to evade droughts and famines. Therefore, if Euro-Americans are really intending to be helpful to Zimbabweans, we would expect them to inject some funding towards cloud-seeding exercises. This would promote farming so that Zimbabweans will not have to rely on food aid. There is wisdom in a saying by Cheikh Hamidou in Ngugi (1987:9) that 'knowing how to kill with efficiency and to heal with the same art'. Also, the Italian proverb teaches, "Give a man a fish and you feed him for a day. Teach him how to fish and you feed him for his life time". From these wise sayings we learn that, if Zimbabweans had been taught the skills and financially supported, the sustainability of the cloud-seeding operations would have been ensured.

Fighting Climate Change in Africa

Africans need to revert to their African traditional systems of dealing with the climate and weather issues. African traditional systems are affordable to all people as they are cheap. It is interesting to note that some of the agricultural activities promoted by the so-called climate smart agriculture (CSA) like, as Bafana (2018) observes, 'no till farming', conservation agriculture and inter-cropping, are well-known African traditional strategies of farming. Ndlovu (2018) states that CSA is the brainchild of the United Nation's Food and Agriculture Organisation (FAO) which was launched in 2010 and it is worth noting that by May 2018, 9000 farmers in the Midlands Province had taken up CSA. Considering the number of farmers showing interest in this programme, and given that some of its practices are stolen from African tradition, it is prudent for Africans to revert to their traditional systems of farming.

Another avenue that is open for Africans, is directly engaging Europe and America to stop externally engineering weather and climate conditions over Africa. Euro-Americans may not readily stop engineering the weather and climate because they use it to manipulate African states' sovereignty. Thus, the easier way is for Africans to revert to their traditional religion and indigenous science.

The farming season of 2015/2016 was a difficult one. The dry spell had adverse effects on the country's agricultural sector as well as on hydro-electric power. Bulawayo24news (2016) notes that "as the dry spell persisted, government early this month [January] organised traditional and religious rites in a desperate bid to conjure the much–needed rains". This move by the Zimbabwean government is commendable in that it encourages Africans to remember their traditions.

Revitalisation of African Territorial Cults.

Considering the on-going discussion, it is clear that weather patterns that are troubling Zimbabweans remind them to consider reverting to African traditions as was done by the Zimbabwean government in the year 2016. Gluckman (1963) in Schoffeleers (1999:5) notes that locust swarms, blights, famines and epidemics bring communal disaster and threaten the life of the community. It should be stated that African religion dealt effectively and efficiently with these communal threats.

African religion, if properly adhered to, has the capacity to mitigate droughts and famines. Schoffeleers (1999:4) informs of the history of a Mbona cult in Southern Malawi, which inspired a long-drawn but ultimately successful opposition against certain agricultural rules initiated by the colonial government. The Mbona cult scenario informs that African religion has the capability of safeguarding its people. Although African religion was heavily weakened by Christianity, it did not become extinct as in times of grave crisis people revert to it (Mbiti, 1969:5; Schoffeleers, 1999:4). Apropos to the above view, since African religion can serve in times of crisis, it means that it should be relied on for survival.

Conclusion

The chapter discussed hegemonic tendencies of Euro-American imperialists on African indigenous knowledge systems in post-colonial Zimbabwe. Weather and climate engineering is the means by which Euro-America exercises hegemony over Africa. Droughts and famines are a function of neo-imperial engineering over Africa. The chapter, therefore, discussed the history of droughts and famines in Zimbabwe, the land question, rainpetitioning and rainmaking systems in both African and western traditions. The means and ends of drought and famine engineering in Zimbabwe were also examined. The chapter underscored the strategies that may be considered in fighting climate change and it urged Africans to revitalise territorial cults for the good of their societies.

References

Bafana, B. (2018) 'Policy support gap for "Climate- Smart" Agriculture. Reliefweb Accessed from https://reliefweb.int/report/zimbabwe/policy-support-gap-climate-smart-agriculture on 08/04/2019.

BBC News. (28 June 2005) UK, US 'Cused Zimbabwe Droughts. News.bbc.co.uk/2/hi/Africa/4630443.stm

BBC News. (3 March 2017) Zimbabwe Hit by Deadly Floods after Drought https://www.bbc.com/news/world-african-39152025

Beaumont, P. (2002) 'Famine becomes Mugabe weapon: *The Guardian,* 10 November 2002. Accessed from https://www.theguardian.com/world/2002/nov/10/zimbabwe .famine on 15/03/2019.

Bozongwana, W. (1983) *Ndebele Religion and Customs.* Gweru: Mambo Press.

Bulawayo24news, (21 January 2016). 'Zimbabwe begins cloud-seeding'. Accessed from https://bulawayo24.com/index-id-news-sc-national-byo-81262.html 15/03/2019.

Chigodora, J. (1997) Famine and Drought: The Question of Food Securit in Zimbabwe, in *Drought Networks News* 1994-2001, Paper 40 (1): 1-6.

Chingwere, I. (2018) 'Farmers call for cloud-seeding. *The Herald,* 28 December 2018. Accessed from https://www.zimbabwesituation.com/news/farmers-call-for-cloud-seeding on 15/03/2019.

Coltart, D. (2002) 'Zimbabwe's man-made famine' *The New York Times,* 7 August 2002. Accessed from https://www.nytimes.com/.../07/opinion/zimbabwe-s-man-made-famine.html on 15/03/2019.

Dopcke, W. (1990). Essay Review: 'Famine in Zimbabwe'. *ZAMBEZIA: The Journal of the University of Zimbabwe*, Vol. 17, No. 1, pp101-106.

Fanon, F. (1961) *The Wretched of the Earth.* Middlesex: Penguin Books: Harmondsworth.

Iliffe, J. (1990) *Famine in Zimbabwe, 1890–1960.* Gweru: Mambo Press.

Kaerasora, G. (2018) 'Zim Turns to cloud-seeding'. *Sunday Mail,* 7 January 2018. Accessed from https://www.zimbabwesituation.com/news/zim-turns-to-cloud-seeding on 18/03/2019.

Matondi, B. P. (2012) *Zimbabwe's Fast Track Land Reform.* Sweden: Zed Books Ltd.

Mawere, M. & Nhemachena, A. (2017) *GMOs, Consumerism and the Global Politics of Biotechnology: Rethinking Food, Bodies and Identities in Africa's 21st Century*. Bamenda: Langaa RPCIG.

Mbiti, J.S. (1969) *African Religions and Philosophy*. Nairobi: East African Educational Publishers.

McGonagle, E. (2007) *Crafting Identity in Zimbabwe and Mozambique*. Rochester: University of Rochester Press.

McNaughton, D.L. (1981) *Cloud-seeding in Zimbabwe, and some of its Effects on SR52 Maize Yield*. Harare: University of Zimbabwe.

Mitchinson, R. (2016) 'Zimbabwe's socialist famine'. *The Commentator*, 11 February 2016. Accessed from www.thecommentator.com/article/6222/zimbabwe_s_socialist _famine 15/03/2019.

Moyana, H.V. (2002). *The Political Economy of Land in Zimbabwe*. Gweru: Mambo Press

Nangombe, S. S. (2014) Drought Conditions and Management Strategies in Zimbabwe www.droughtmanagement.info/literature/UNW-DPC_NDMP_Report_Zimbabwe_2014.pdf

Ndlovu, S. (2018) '9000 farmers take up Climate Smart Agriculture', *The Herald*, 10 May 2018. Accessed from https://www.herald.co.zw/9000-farmers-take-up-climate-smart-agric. on 08/04/2019.

NewsPunch, 11 May 2017, 'Zimbabwe begs White farmers to return as country plunges into famine. Baxter Dmitry News, World 273. Accessed on 15/03/2019.

Ngugi wa Thiongo (1987). *Decolonising the Mind: The Politics of Language in African Literature*. Harare: Zimbabwe Publishing House.

Nhemachena, A. (2015) Indigenous Knowledge, Conflation and Postcolonial Translation: Lessons from Fieldwork in Contemporary Rural Zimbabwe, in Mawere, M. & Awuah-Nyamekye, S. (eds) *Between Rhetoric and Reality: the State and Use of Indigenous Knowledge in Post—Colonial Africa*. Bamenda: Langaa RPCIG.

Nhemachena, A. (2017) *Relationality and Resilience in a Not So Relational World? Knowledge, Chivanhu and (De-)Coloniality in 21st Century Conflict-Torn Zimbabwe*. Bamenda: Langaa RPCIG.

227

Nhemachena, A., Kangira, J. & Mlambo, N. (2019) Theorising displacement, elimination & replacement of indigenous people: An introduction to decolonising land issues, in Kangira, J., Nhemachena, A. & Mlambo, N. (eds) *Displacement, elimination and replacement of indigenous people: Putting into perspective land ownership and ancestry in decolonising contemporary Zimbabwe*. Bamenda: Langaa RPCIG.

Nkomo, N. (2009) 'Zimbabwe's Mugabe Accuses West of Double Standard on Climate, Human Rights, *Voice of America (VOA)*, 16 December 2009. Accessed from https://www.voazimbabwe.com/a/mugabe-presence-at-copenhagen-summit-riles-rights-campaigners-16dec09-79427582/1457660.html on 08/04/2019.

Novak, M. (2015). The Secret Weather Manipulation Program of the Vietnam War. Accessed from https://paleofuture.gizmodo.com/the-secret-weather-manipulation-program-of-the-viet... on the 30/04/2019

Palmer, R. (1977) *Land and Racial Domination in Rhodesia*. Berkeley: University of California Press.

Rafferty, J. P. (2019) (ed.) *Encyclopaedia Britannica Articles- Cloud-Seeding*. Accessed from https://www.britannica.com/science/cloud-seeding on the 18/03/2019

Ramose, M. B. (1999) *African Philosophy through Ubuntu*. Harare: Mond Books.

Richardson, C. J. (2007) How Much Did Droughts Matter? Linking Rainfall and GDP Growth in Zimbabwe, in *African Affairs* vol 106 (424): 463-478.

Schoffeleers, J. M (ed.) (1999) *Guardians of the Land: Essays on Central African Territorial Cults*. Gweru: Mambo Press.

State of the Environment in Southern Africa, SADC (1994) 'Zimbabwe: Land Use in Dry Tropical Savannas. GAIA Case Study Zimbabwe (1995-2002)': Drought-ess.co.at. Accessed from www.ess.co.at/GAIA/CASES/ZIM/drought.html on 15/03/2019.The Guardian. (5 February 2016) Zimbabwe Declares 'State of disaster' due to Drought https://www.theguardian.com/world/2016/feb/05/zimbabwe-declares-stte-of-disaster-drought-robert-mugabe

Thornton, J. (1980) Reviewer of Palmer, R. and Parsons, N. (eds.) (1977) *The Roots of Poverty in Central and Southern Africa, Perspectives on Southern Africa,* No.25. Berkeley and Los Angeles: University of California Press. 430p. Source, *Canadian Journal of African Studies,* Vol.14. No.3 (1980) pp557–559. Accessed from https://www.jstor.org/stabe/484270 on 08/04/2019.

What are GMOs?- Purdue Agriculture- Purdue University. Accessed from https://ag.purdue.edu/GMOs/Pages/WhatareGMOs.aspx on 08/04/2019.

Winston, G. (2015). Weather Manipulation during Vietnam War – War History Online. Accessed from https://www.warhistoryonline.com/war.../weather-manipulation-during-vietnam-war.h... on 30/04/2019

Chapter Eight

Climatological Anomalies, Food Politics and the Poor in Africa

Aaron Rwodzi

Introduction

This chapter is premised on climatological anomalies which cause drought and famine to show how these have constantly and persistently been used opportunistically by politicians to bolster political support from the rural poor peasants in a few selected places and countries. These anomalies are deviations from the normal climatic conditions (American Heritage Dictionary, 2016) and are characterised by extreme temperatures which trigger the global phenomena called El Nino and Lan Nina (Concise Dictionary, 2002). In turn, these cause floods, earthquakes, storms, cyclones, hurricanes and typhoons. This chapter has been written in the light of Cyclone *Idai* that recently slowly but surely drifted towards Zimbabwe from the east, after causing heavy destruction of human lives, livestock and property in Mozambique and Malawi, and when there were no official or timely alerts in Zimbabwe from the Civil Protection Unit (CPU) to prepare would-be victims for the calamity. Proactive measures to mitigate its likely negative effects did not exist.

It emerged after the cyclone that the Zimbabwe government had committed only $2.36 million of its budget towards disaster-related matters and this figure fell far too short of what was expected. The Department of Civil Protection (DCP), formerly the Civil Protection Unit (CPU), is the Local Government arm obligated to manage disasters. In the 2019 budget, the DCP was allocated $2.36 million for its work (*The Insider,* 17 March 2019). It was for this reason that the *Insider* editor titled his article on cyclone *Idai* 'Zimbabwe's disaster response is a disaster' (*The Insider,* 17 March 2019).

Cyclone *Idai* affected more than 1.5 million people in the three southern African countries, according to the United Nations and government officials (The Washington Post, 16 March 2019). The statistics of the victims of cyclone *Idai* could have remained quite low if policy-makers listened to the recommendations of weather or climate scientists.

The chapter problematises the connections between weather, food politics and the rural poor in Africa generally and Zimbabwe in particular. More specifically, the chapter teases out the politicisation of food handouts by politicians when elections and periods of drought and famine coincide. It also teases out the politicisation of climatological anomalies, synonymously referred to as political ecology or environmental politics, by Western agents who operate as foreign companies or non-governmental organisations (NGOs). Political parties such as Zimbabwe African National Union Patriotic Front (ZANU- PF) and the Movement for Democratic Change (MDC) among others, often prey on the indigent poor who hardly eke a mere subsistence from their land due to poverty and insufficient rainfall. The political parties provide essential food relief that is conditioned to party support. It is argued in this chapter that in Zimbabwe, as elsewhere in Africa, the vulnerable people are the object of a great deal of political and electoral manipulation and that the politics of the stomach takes precedence over reason in less well-to-do communities. The chapter argues that politicians must not ride roughshod over the poor to advance their "altruistic" ambitions and that more rights education is required to prevent the abuse of food as an instrument of political victimisation.

Climate Change Historiography

Climate is the general or average weather conditions of a certain region including temperature, rainfall and wind. It is influenced by latitude, the tilt on the earth's axis, the movement of the earth's wind belt, differences in temperature of land and sea and topography (The American Heritage Science Dictionary, 2011). Global warming, which is an increase in the average temperature of the earth's atmosphere, causes a sustained increase in heat that is great enough to provoke changes in the global climate (Saud, 2013). Zimbabwe's Initial Communications Commission (ZICC) under the auspices of the Intergovernmental Panel on Climate Change (IPCC) (1988) suggested that by 2050, temperatures and rainfall over Zimbabwe would be 2-4 degrees Celsius higher and 10-20 percent less than the 1961-1990 baseline respectively. The International Food Policy Research Institute (IFPRI) estimated that by 2050 about 50 million more people could be at a risk of undernourishment because of climate change (Mona Nagargade, Vishal Tyagi and Manoj Kumar Singh, 2017).

The history of climate change politics at a global level is important for us to understand the agendas of climate change movements now sponsored by the United States of America. The United Nations Framework Convention on Climate (UNFCC) as it relates to Zimbabwe's adaptation to calamities appears to be lacking and chief among the constituencies that need increased awareness raising are our legislators. These appear to have little knowledge of climate change and the need for an urgent policy framework for response to it. Zimbabwe signed and ratified the UNFCC in 1992 and acceded to the Kyoto Protocol on climate change in 2009 (Chagutah, 2010). In line with the above, the Roundtable Conference on climate change in 2009 noted the absence of a deliberate and focused policy response to climate change and emphasised that by 2009 it was not an issue in the Zimbabwe Parliament and therefore not factored in the country's development plans (Ibid.).

The work by Garrett Hardin (1968) was one of the first to articulate environmental concerns and the impact of politics on the environment (Eugene Thomas *et al,* 2014:21). Food is viewed as an important concept in the politics of the ecosystem or *ecopolitics* because the world is fast moving away from an era of abundance to one of food scarcity (Brown, 2012) due to global warming that is aggravated by the Green House Gases (GHGs). The greenhouse effect is a phenomenon whereby the earth's atmosphere traps solar radiation and is mediated by the presence, in the atmosphere, of gases such as carbon dioxide, water vapour and methane that allow incoming sunlight to pass through, but absorb the heat back from the earth's surface. These GHGs create a blanket effect in the lower strata of the earth's atmosphere and human activities such as industrialisation or the burning of fossil fuels contribute to this blanket covering.

Africa has contributed less than 3% of the world's total emissions of greenhouse gases that cause global warming and climate change (Chagutah, 2010: 1) and yet it suffers the effects of anomalies in climate the worst and more readily than those countries and continents whose industrial emissions into the atmosphere continue to erode the ozone layer. Poverty in Africa is relatively over-romanticised as evidenced by the so many foreign NGOs that are ever-present on the continent to immediately proffer the so-called humanitarian assistance.

This chapter is embedded in the ecological security framework. It seeks to conceptualise the relationship between ecological factors and politics and to find out if changes in ecological factors increase the likelihood of conflicts during election time and in food crisis situations in some parts of Africa. It explores climate adaptation from a broad perspective to show how climate change is influenced by a host of factors such as institutional capacities, political dynamics, interest group mobilisation, bureaucratic politics and donor preferences (Dolsak and Prakash, 2018).

Multilateralism and Africa's Food Security Challenges

Multilateralism refers to international cooperation. From a practical point of view, it is problematic when it comes to implementation on account of the factual inequalities among the nation states. It also relates to globalisation, which concept is very topical and problematic in the 21st century. Creating one big village as implied by globalisation is just but a fantasy, if we take into consideration the history of slavery and the slave trade, colonialism and neocolonial attempts to frustrate the independent growth and development of Third World countries throughout the world. The one 'big village' concept, indeed, inevitably results in the existence of a global chief, in this case the U.S.A., or global queens, headmen and women who are dictatorial in their interactions with the developing world. As Thucydides puts it: "The desire for power is natural within man and gods, and the strong will do what they can and the weak suffer what they must" (Thucydides, 1954:6).

The American Dream of dominating the world is linked to its overseas military bases scattered throughout the world and the chemical or industrial waste that these bases exude (Colgan, 2018). The Europe-American connection urges Africa to desecuritise in a context where Euro- America is deploying its own military to Africa. Euro-America is also grabbing African land, leaving Africans landless and without compensation (Nhemachena, Warikandwa & Mtapuri, 2017). Euro-America is also making efforts to exercise hegemony by using climate change as a lever to manipulate developing countries that are being pulled into the crystallising matrix of a One World Government.

The US President, at the time of writing this chapter, Donald Trump made a decision to withdraw from the Paris Agreement on climate change. This has surprised the rest of the world given the volumes of pollutants that the U.S.A military and other projects emit into the atmosphere. The Paris Agreement involved talks about the necessity of deep cuts in emissions of carbon dioxide and other pollutants, so as to stop the warming of planet Earth. There is need for multinationalism or international cooperation so as to ensure climate diplomacy and security of human kind. The problem in all this is that Africans have never been considered as human beings deserving human security since the enslavement and colonial era. Thus, Africans have, since the enslavement and colonial eras, not been regarded and treated as human beings but as animals and beasts for imperial burdens – this raises the question as to whether human security, in the era of climate change, really includes the security of Africans. Whereas human beings get compensated for wrongs like enslavement, Africans are not compensated. Whereas human beings are accorded restitution and restoration of their land and other resources, Africans are not (Nhemachena, Warikandwa & Amoo, 2018).

Climate change and global warming affect food security and food sovereignty. Food sovereignty and food safety in Africa are contentious issues that are predicated on a long history of dispossession, poverty; and dependence especially on western donor support. Food sovereignty has no universal definition, but it can be described as the newest and most innovative approach to achieving the end goal of long term food security (Food Systems Network n.d,). Indigenous food sovereignty in Africa relates to policy approaches by states to address the underlying issues affecting people (*Ibid.*) so that they can revert back to their healthy and culturally beneficial indigenous foods. Put more simply, food sovereignty is anchored on self-determination which is:

> ...the ability to respond to our own needs [as African] for healthy, culturally adapted indigenous foods. [It refers to] The ability to make decisions over the amount and quality of food we hunt, fish, gather, grow and eat. Freedom from dependence on grocery stores or corporately controlled food production, distribution and consumption in industrialized economies (Ibid.).

The last statement above is an indirect reference to the "Big 6" pesticide and Genetically Modified Organisms (GMOs) corporations headquartered in the United States. These are Baden Aniline and Soda Factory (BASF), Bayer, Dupont, Dow Chemical Company, Monsanto, and Syngenta (Food Rights Network, 2017). They own and control the world's seeds as well as pesticides and related biotechnology. Historically, they have extraordinary power over world agriculture which enables them to control the agricultural research agenda, profoundly influence trade and agricultural agreements and sabotage genuine market competition (*Ibid.*). The mass introduction of pesticides into food and agriculture following World War II and control over the knowledge needed to grow food has tremendously shifted from farmers to the laboratories financed by multinational corporations (*Ibid.*). Kathryn Gilje, Director of Pesticide Action Network of North America, discusses the verdict that was handed down to the aforesaid six largest pesticides for their human rights violations, including internationally recognised rights to life, livelihood and health, (Organizational blog post, December 7, 2011).

The GMOs produced under laboratory conditions by the biochemical industries are being used to distort and destroy the seed's capacity to retain its natural state. For example, these industries manufacture the terminator gene which is a specific genetic sequence inserted into a seed's Deoxyribonucleic Acid (DNA) to render the seed and crop it produces sterile (Machado, 2019). This initiative is patented by the USDA and Delta and Pine Land Company owned by Monsanto (*Ibid.*) which is an agricultural company. This terminator technology has no agricultural and economic benefits for farmers or consumers except to protect intellectual property rights and to extract more money from the dependent farmers (*Ibid.*).

Shiva (2018) in her article 'The Seeds of Suicide: How Monsanto Destroys Farming' argues that Monsanto and Bayer have merged into a powerful cartel which controls not only what we eat but also politicians, scientists and journalists. Engdahl (2007) focuses on how a small socio-political American elite seeks to establish control over the very basis of human survival. Its trade mantra is: 'Control the food and you control the people' (*Ibid.*). Engdahl cogently reveals a world of profit-driven political intrigue, government corruption and coercion, where genetic manipulation and the patenting of life forms are used to gain worldwide control over food production (*Ibid.*). Stopping farmers from saving seeds and exercising their seed sovereignty (*Ibid.*) is the main objective of this socio-political American elite as represented by the six companies. This is also key to their survival.

Keen to ensure food sovereignty, the government of Zimbabwe introduced Command Agriculture during the 2016-17 farming season. It was an initiative planned by government and implemented through the private and public partnership ahead of the 2018 harmonised elections. These were elections in which the electorate would, on the same day, vote to make their parliamentary, presidential and councillor preferences. The rural vote constitutes 67 percent of the voting population (*Shout Africa*, 21 June 2017).

Analysts maintain that the government's scheme is an aid for it to retain political expedience. The distribution of tractors and other inputs was being abused by those who were in positions of authority like chiefs and headmen. Agriculture transformed from being an economic asset into a political asset. According to Magaisa, former advisor to the opposition leader, Morgan Tsvangirai, Command Agriculture could be regarded as a flagship that forms populist political campaigns (*Ibid.*) for ZANU-PF particularly in its rural strongholds.

The politicisation of food production by Monsanto, Syngenta and other American corporations that are producing GMOs and encouraging Africa to do what they call 'climate smart agriculture' is a serious developmental issue for Africa. Lipper *et al.* (2014) define climate smart agriculture (CSA) as an approach for transforming and reorienting agricultural development under the new realities of climate change. Food and Agricultural Organisation (FAO) (2013), the specialised agency of the United Nations, defines CSA as "agriculture that sustainably increases productivity, enhances resilience (adaptation), reduces/removes GHGs (mitigation) where possible, and enhances national food security and development goals. CSA aims to tackle three main objectives: sustainably increasing agricultural productivity and incomes; adapting and building resilience to climate change; and reducing and/or removing greenhouse gas emissions, where possible (*Ibid.*).

Syngenta sells seeds in more than 90 countries and is the world's largest crop chemicals company, generating a whopping $15 billion a year (Julie Wilson, 2015). Another area of great concern for African agriculture and food self-sufficiency relates to the use of drones to bypass African states in the distribution of food "aid". These drones are unmanned aerial vehicles and they have raised understandable concerns for lawmakers. The use of drones, indeed, violates states' sovereignty and privacy. It becomes very imperative for African governments, through their legislators, to mandate that all uses of drones be prohibited unless the government has first provided a warrant (*Ibid.*)

Mkandawire (2010) notes that policy-making has been usurped from African states by NGOs and western states since the neoliberal Economic Structural Adjustment Programme (ESAP) era and this could be used to explain the failure by African states and governments to deliver or their adoption of confused policies. Some poor African countries have vehemently rejected GMO technologies as an instrument of neo-colonial exploitation and subordination fostered by western multinational corporations and their governments. Zimbabwe's President Robert Mugabe refused to accept food "aid" from the United States in the form of GMO corn despite threats of starvation for many of his desperate people (Stewart, 2009: 11). In early colonial Zimbabwe, Iliffe (1990) notes that colonialists destroyed African granaries so as to force Africans to succumb to the colonial authorities. This is an instance of food politics linked to colonisation of Africa. Mawere and Nhemachena (2017 argue that whilst democracy can be demonstrated in electoral politics in Africa this democracy is limited in contexts where people cannot decide what gets into their stomachs. Some recipients of food aid in Zimbabwe and other countries that face unrelenting hunger and starvation have complained that the food they are given is actually animal feeds in the countries of origin (*Ibid.*). They also argue that consumption without producing renders powerlessness to Africans that are reduced to consumers or beneficiaries, including of some toxic waste that is often presented as food (*Ibid.*).

The contemporary ideologies about sharing economies, solidarity economies and resurgence of discourses of social protection (Satgar, 2014; Widlok, 2017), all effectively serve to manufacture global consent to govern Africa. For this reason, global transnational corporations continue to govern the global south that is being increasingly turned more into consumers than competing producers (*Ibid.*). Aid manufactures consent to be governed. The ActionAid report accused rich countries of "political grandstanding" and highlighted the ways in which they were disguising real aid flows (The Guardian, 2005). The report further noted the existence of phantom aid which involves:

> Failure to target aid at the poorest countries, runaway spending on overpriced technical assistance from international consultants, tying aid to purchases from donor countries' own firms, cumbersome and ill-coordinated planning, implementation, monitoring and reporting requirements, excessive administrative costs, late and partial disbursements, double counting of debt relief, and aid spending on immigration services all deflate the value of aid (Ibid.).

The effect of phantom aid is to create an illusion that everybody is benefiting from the so-called global economy and the logical inference would be that everyone is responsible for global warming in so far as it emanates from the global economy from which everyone is benefitting. Whilst there are cries for the deep cut in carbonisation by international NGOs, there are, in this politics of decarbonisation, difficulties in managing the world's energy system because most industrialised countries have their decisions originating from the private sector (Jones and Victor, 2018:5) over which governments have no direct control. What is worse is that detailed researches on state-owned firms indicate that they are 'states within a state' to show that they are organised politically and economically to maintain the status quo (*Ibid*, 2018:6). The Donald Trump case explains in brief the lack of political will and support to sustain worldwide effort at decarbonisation by those countries in the world that are industrialised such as America, Britain and many others from the western world. It also demonstrates unilateralism that is antithetical to multilateralism. The commitment to address climate change is weak, erratic, circumstantial and dodgy as the developed world, in particular, seems fully committed to the protection of its economic and state-security interests at the expense of rehabilitating the environment.

During the Mugabe era in Zimbabwe, it was erroneously thought that increasing humanitarian food aid to Zimbabwe would help neutralise Mugabe's demonisation of the U.S.A. and the West. Mugabe had threatened to block western assistance (*Ibid*, 2018:6). It means that the longer the humanitarian crisis in Zimbabwe would take, the more the pressure the U.S.A. would exert on Mugabe to have economic policies and a political playfield that were well disposed towards America.

With regard to countries in the Horn of Africa, there is need for a climate change mitigation model that speaks to issues of vulnerability, conflict and the environment. For example, the Darfur crisis was not simply due to change in climate, or lack of abundance, but also the result of politics (Young, 2005). Debates are being framed about this Darfur war in order to establish a nexus between climate change and conflict (Ban, 2007; Sachs, 2011).

It is important to note that the global system is skewed to provide instrumental incentives for the adoption of global policy templates as evidenced by the EU's role in popularising the so-called EU Effort by regulating the access of overseas exporters to its markets (Dolšak *et al*, 2018). The 2009 Copenhagen Accords, the 2016 Paris Agreement and multilateral development banks all reiterated the commitment by developed countries to fund climate adaptation in developing countries. The irony is that development is measured in terms of a country's level of industrialisation, and therefore its great capacity to destroy the environmental equilibrium. This support in whatever form ought to be granted unconditionally given that the

Third World, and Africa in particular, suffers the consequences of environmental damage caused by the industrialised and criminocratic world (Nhemachena & Warikandwa, 2019).

According to Rwodzi and Mubonderi (2015), if democracy is to be relevant to Africa, it must also mean that there are equal opportunities for all states in the world to spoil the environment so that they perish together 'as equals'. Climate politics, therefore, is all about who gets what, when and where in the global context. In the U.S.A., climate change in the 2000 elections took centre stage and got biased when the polls that were conducted signposted that the greater percentage of Republican survey respondents thought that media overplayed the seriousness of climate change (Hakeem, 2017) for political and electoral reasons.

Most of the NGOs with particular focus on climate change are UN agencies which coincidentally are controlled and easily manipulated for economic, political, humanitarian and religious reasons by the same powers in the UN Security Council (UNSC). These provide normative templates for the organisations whenever they undertake humanitarian work throughout the world. However, Blair (2010) states that Britain and America actually pursued regime change agendas in selected countries in the Global South, including Iraq and Libya. This is supported by Boyle's (2010) critique of the repeated series of military conflicts and crises between the United States and Libya over the Gulf of Sidra and the fraudulent US claims of Libyan instigation of international terrorism during the eight years of the neoconservative Reagan administration. Britain and U.S.A, in pursuit of an illegal agenda, drew a list of countries targeted for regime change, amongst which were Libya, Afghanistan and Iraq (*Ibid.*).

The regime change narrative, with specific reference to Zimbabwe, was arguably not a ZANU PF figment of imagination as such, as portrayed by the broader front of opposition political parties in the country. Blair (2010), in his book, intimated that leaving Saddam in power was a bigger risk to the British security than removing him. However, Blair does not really grapple with arguments raised by critics of the war on Iraq, namely that the Iraq invasion diverted essential resources from Afghanistan, allowing a Taliban resurgence there; that Saddam's fall ended up making Iran a bigger player in the region; and that, as a former MI5 chief contended, the war radicalised more Islamic youths, arguably giving "Osama bin Laden his Iraqi jihad" (*Ibid.,* 2010). As the first major head of government to bring climate change to the top of the international political agenda at the 2005 G8 summit, Tony Blair worked with world leaders to build consensus on an international climate policy framework.

The Amani Trust in Zimbabwe, together with many other like-minded organisations, are argued to have sponsored the MDC to oust Mugabe and such allegations were corroborated by the behaviours of Britain, U.S.A. and the European Union (EU), all of which did not hide from the world their disdain for Mugabe's land redistribution (Chigodo, 2002). It is argued that Britain and its allies precipitated temporary economic disarticulations to compel the Zimbabwean government to abandon land reform.

The New Dispensation that came into existence after the resignation of former President Mugabe in 2017 has made strides in trying to circumscribe the operations of NGOs from outside the country and those from within. The demonstrations in the early months of 2019 in Zimbabwe enabled the government to reconfigure itself against what it assumed to be a regime change agenda to topple the new political establishment under Emmerson Mnangagwa. The Minister for Information, Media and Broadcasting Services, Monica Mutsvangwa, claimed that Non-Governmental Organisations (NGOs) worked in cahoots with the opposition MDC to organise riots that ground activities in the country's major cities such as Harare, Bulawayo, Mutare and Kadoma (Pindula News, 2019) to a halt for close to a week. On the other hand, attempts were also made to regulate and regularise local organisations whose mandates were to assist the poor and the underprivileged especially on account of vicissitudes in climate.

The Acting Information, Publicity and Broadcasting Services Minister Sekai Nzenza, pointed out that Cabinet received a presentation from the Minister of Public Service, Labour and Social Welfare to amend the Private Voluntary Organisations (PVOs) Act (Chapter 17: 05) in order to render it compliant with the requirements of the Financial Task Force on combating money laundering and financing of terrorism by individuals and organisations (ZimEye, 15

March 2019). Specifically, the amendment sought to ensure that PVOs in Zimbabwe are not used as conduits for money laundering and funding of terrorist activities (ZimEye, 15 March 2019). In a way, this amendment has the potential to circumscribe the organisational capacity of opposition party formations whose activities can be viewed as promoting terrorism in the country.

NGOs that are foreign also find themselves hamstrung by the same policy statement above. The NGOs statute was amended amid speculations and fears that NGOs in the country, especially after the hotly contested presidential elections wherein Mnangagwa and Nelson Chamisa of the MDC Alliance contested, were driving a regime change agenda (ZimEye, 15 March 2019).

Honourable Trevor Saruwaka, the MDC Manicaland spokesman, made appeals to the government of Zimbabwe, NGOs, citizens and all other well-wishers to mobilise resources and come to the rescue of those affected by this climate change disaster, Cyclone *Idai* (The Zimbabwean voice of the voiceless, 17 March 2019). Hughes and Coote (2019) intimate that Beira bore the brunt of the cyclone, where the International Federation of the Red Cross and Red Crescent aid workers described the damage as 'massive and horrifying' (World News, 18 March 2019).

The Role of Non-Governmental Organisations in Climate Change Politics

The Food and Agricultural Organisation (FAO), itself a specialised agency of the United Nations Organisation, regards the right to food in times of scarcity as one of the most important international human rights, yet it is the one most frequently violated (FAO, 1999:32). FAO defines food security as a situation in which all people at all times have physical and economic access to sufficient, safe and nutritious food to meet their dietary needs and food preferences for an active healthy life (World Food Summit, 1996; Cohen, 2005:32). Monbat (2003:130) explores the possibility of involving NGOs at the level of international democracy and considers possible selection criteria where he proposes to appoint to the forum those NGOs with the biggest global membership. It is, however, difficult to entrust that responsibility to NGOs that are affiliated to, or are originally from, Western countries.

Inasmuch as global warming and its consequences are matters requiring collective effort of all world governments, Monbat's views become questionable given the fact that international democracy connotes the unilateral will of those countries from which the NGOs originate. Caldwell (1996:333) highlights the importance of having NGOs that are independent of government agendas and unconstrained by diplomatic protocol and procedure in international, environmental policy-making issues. His argument is that these NGOs have been influential in instigating numerous treaties and international cooperative arrangements. In most cases, these agreements have served, and continue to serve, the political, economic and ideological interests of donor countries. Many governments have cracked down on civil society by, for example, imposing restrictions on the inflow of foreign funds.

Dolšak and Prakash (2018) refer to the role of international forces in motivating local communities to invest in climate change adaptation through a normative logic and an instrumental logic. In the international normative discourses, policy templates that are prescriptive to the recipients of food aid and other donor resources, are outlined for the receiving governments to follow and this is usually done through coercion and pressures such as threats of sanctions should the African governments fail or refuse to comply. It means governments must abide by these prescriptions as long as they are embedded in the international networks of NGOs and Intergovernmental Organisations (IGOs).

In Zimbabwe, the government instructed NGOs in the country to suspend operations on grounds that some of these NGOs were intentionally violating their original terms of reference (Mutasa, 2010). Allegations were that some NGOs were overstepping their terms of reference by using their operations to campaign for the Movement for Democratic Change (MDC). In the case of Chikomba District, humanitarian aid came through organisations such as Goal Zimbabwe, Christian Care and Catholic Relief Services (CRS) under the auspices of the World Food Programme (WFP). Dananai Project, together with Goal and Christian Care, targeted people with HIV and Aids and the 1992 drought saw NGOs as well as government undertaking food for work programmes that led to road rehabilitation and reconstruction throughout the country (Mutasa, 2010:58). Some critics point out that engaging NGOs is a temporary, not a permanent solution to the food crisis. They also argue that people should not invest their hope in foreigners and that most of the time these NGOs did not benefit them in planning for a future of hope and purpose without them.

An assessment of the food situation that was conducted in Zimbabwe by the Civil Monitoring Programme in conjunction with FOSENET for the period 2003 to 2004 established ethical principles for relief and food security. It was agreed that it should be the obligation of the state and other parties to agree on the provision of humanitarian and impartial assistance whenever civil society was lacking in essential supplies that could have been induced by drought or by other calamities; the relief was not expected to bring about unintended advantages to parties or to further partisan positions (Community Assessment Report, 2003-2004). In 2009, former President Robert Mugabe threatened to stop foreign NGO operations and advised his party's Women's League to be wary of the NGOs in the country (Chimhete, 2009). Only local NGOs (The National NGO Food Security Network) (FOSENET) chipped in to financially back those women with access to land as well as those people with the capacity to utilise that land. This could have, nonetheless, opened the floodgates for a partisan support system.

The Sunday Mail (12-24 October 2009) reported that about 14 000 households in 11 wards in Chikomba were set to benefit from support administered through an NGO called Single Parents, Widows and Orphans Support Network (SPWSNET) and the name was nebulous on who they actually wanted to support. In some instances, NGOs and government could work side by side. Under a facility bankrolled by Food and Agricultural Organisation (FAO), seed packs were provided at Sadza Growth Point in 2009 and the government came up with US $210 million agricultural input facility to support the 2009/10 agricultural year, whereas some NGOs organised US$70 million to support the scheme (Sunday Mail, 18-24 October 2009). This shows that relations between government and NGOs oscillated depending on need and circumstance.

Use of Food in Ecopolitics

In Zimbabwe in 2009, the government ordered that all aid related funds to support people who were affected by climate change related conditions would be channelled through it and that meant that the government now had the prerogative powers to determine where to allocate the given resources (Chagutah, 2010:20). NGOs were sceptical of this proposal and argued that interference in the manner they intended to distribute resources would present them with operational and administrative challenges (*Ibid,* 21). The umbrella body for all NGOs in Zimbabwe, the National Association of Non-Governmental Organisations, also argued that there was need for radical institutional change in government soon after the expiry of the Government of National Unity (GNU) wherein ZANU-PF and the MDC contested.

The GNU came in the wake of unprecedented hunger and food scarcity throughout the country in 2007/2008 season and when the then opposition leader Tsvangirai publicly announced that he would rather partner his long-time rival in a GNU than continue witnessing politically motivated civilian deaths and starvation related to MDC's power struggle with ZANU-PF. Quite clearly, NGOs did not trust the government led by ZANU-PF with handling funds earmarked for the poor. Fears were that the government would divert the funds: NGOs therefore, wanted no state control over the disbursement process which they feared, would be compromised. This was a contradiction because NGOs themselves were imperially controlled.

Some of the reasons for NGOs scepticism were based on past allegations that the ruling ZANU-PF used food and other resources to buy votes. Internationally, food aid is used to advance the interests of Euro-America ahead of the One World Government and the New World Order. On the basis of this observation, NGOs are neither apolitical nor neutral because they pursue their 'home' agendas.

Because in Zimbabwe traditional leaders were part of the civil service, in that they receive monthly stipends of US$300, NGOs invoked some sections of the country's Constitution particularly Section 281 (2) which obliges chiefs not to act in a partisan way, not to be members of political parties nor to participate in partisan politics, not to further the interests of any party, not to violate the fundamental rights and freedoms of people, not to mobilise communities to attend party rallies and not to carry out partisan distribution of inputs and food aid (Zimbabwe Constitution, 2013). The concern of the NGOs was that food and resource distribution ought to be free of any politicisation because in food crisis situations, a party in power with complete monopoly over the use of force and resources would always canvass political support from the vulnerable voters based on the apparent availability of patronage resources. There is always a significant political dimension that relates to the politicisation of ethnicity wherein preferential treatment is accorded to some ethnically connected categories that marginalises others.

In Africa, policy makers invest in reactive, as opposed to proactive policies (Healy and Malhotra, 2018). For example, it was found out that the electorate rewards political parties for their reactive policies like delivering disaster relief, unlike in disaster preparedness which is proactive (*Ibid,* 2018). Disasters open the policy window for politicians to introduce new policy initiatives by invoking the inadequacies of the existing policies (*Ibid,* 2018*).* They further argue that disasters permit politicians to demonstrate that they are in charge and that they are responsive to the needs of their communities or political constituencies. That also explains why, according to the broader policy research, political leaders want to invest in the provision of public goods. Relief assistance, in light of Cyclone *Idai* that left a trail of destruction in eastern and southern Zimbabwe, Mozambique and Malawi in March 2019, could be viewed as more important than disaster preparedness mechanisms which would have averted the disaster. By and large, politicians are ready to take advantage of the hardships, created by climate change, which people directly experience by providing the necessary incentives that support visible infrastructure such as reconstruction of destroyed bridges. This allows them to garner political support.

The Lutheran World Federation, among many other organisations, lamented the manner in which food aid, in Zimbabwe, was being politicised (Chigodo, 2002) by westerners. The westerners were bidding to demonise the government of Robert Mugabe for the Fast Track Land Reform Programme (FTLRP) which started in 2000. The government of Zimbabwe ordered the United Nations (UN) and other relief agencies to surrender their food aid to ruling party officials. The WFP insisted that it would distribute its own food aid.

Mugabe had denied food aid to supporters of the MDC (The Independent, 20 August 2003).

The same has happened in many other African countries. For instance, NGOs were attacked so many times in the Central African Republic in 2013 when Seleka's rebels successfully organised a coup against the authoritarian leadership of President Francois Bozize. Sekela's rebels gained mileage by distributing the booty that they seized from NGOs to starving civilian populations. Anderson (1999) in 'Do no harm: How aid can support peace' argues that humanitarian organisations rarely remain neutral when engaged in humanitarian work on the ground, despite the fact that neutrality is constantly emphasised in organisations' mandates. She further intimates that the simple presence of a humanitarian organisation in a war zone makes it partisan to the conflict.

Accessing relief food in Chikomba, Wedza, Ruwa and Marondera in 2003-2004 was problematic. The exercise of food distribution smacked of many irregularities. It was noted that the registration process of deserving cases was unfair and consequently, the process was stopped. Those in the political opposition were left out from the list of people who would benefit from the scheme as queues were being regulated by ZANU-PF youths and war veterans of the liberation struggle (Community Assessment Report, 2003-4). In any case, beneficiaries of food aid were drawn from ward, village and neighbourhood committees and registers whose structures were controlled by members of the ruling party. The Minister of Public Service, Labour and Social Welfare, July Moyo, defended his Ministry's or government's interference in NGOs distribution activities arguing that: "No international donor can tell us that the government should not be involved in food distribution when we are the ones who asked for food in the first place". The decision by government to take over the distribution of food from the accredited NGOs in Zimbabwe around 2004 was made shortly after the European Union (EU) had donated £17 million to help in the relief effort in Zimbabwe (The Independent, 20 August 2003). Such a move was calculated to give a competitive advantage to the ruling ZANU-PF party ahead of the 2005 elections by using the money for patronage purposes.

The Zimbabwean government effectively banned NGOs field activities from June to August 2008 after the disputed presidential elections (Chagutah, 2010:20). ZANU-PF, which constituted the government before the GNU was formed in 2009, insisted that NGOs were being neoimperially used as political tools to frustrate the government or to influence political outcomes. This related so well to the regime change agenda in Zimbabwe which some NGOs were allegedly pursuing in league with their western governments. This also explains why many African leaders who fall out of favour with western governments are quick to conclude that the latter are promoting insurrections from within to topple their popular regimes or their legitimate governments. In Zimbabwe, NGOs have been blamed for decampaigning the agrarian revolution which resulted in the censure of many voluntary movements operating in the country. For example, in 2002, the British government through its High Commissioner Brian Donnelly, was accused of using food aid or handouts to influence election outcomes (Chigodo, 2002). The regime change agenda underscored the fact that the former colonial power, Britain, was at it again, seeking to recolonise Zimbabwe through its support for Morgan Tsvangirai's MDC. The regime change narrative became so strong to the point of acceptability both internally and externally.

Conclusion

This chapter considers mitigation and adaptation as two pillars of climate action governments can plan for because of the reality of global warming. Multilateral agreement on mitigating disasters requires that signatories must, in letter and spirit, commit themselves to this endeavour by increasing their budgets as part of disaster preparedness.

It would appear as if Zimbabwe's approach to natural calamities is haphazard, disjointed, reactionary and weak (Financial Gazette, 21-27 March 2019). In times of disaster, it is imperative for government to timeously and swiftly respond so that many lives are saved. Emphasis should be on prevention and mitigation as opposed to recovery. In the case of Chimanimani district of Zimbabwe where cyclone *Idai* hit the hardest in eastern Zimbabwe, politicians can take advantage by rebuilding the infrastructure destroyed such as roads and bridges. This then gives them the latitude to proclaim their achievements. Zimbabwe needs therefore, to come up with a working model to systematically deal with hazards and disaster management.

Humanitarian assistance comes from both foreign and local NGOs which give assistance in times of droughts, famines and floods. The aid must be available to all the needy and therefore it is improper to politicise it As such, since climate change is a global catastrophe, global efforts which do not except any state will help.

References

Anderson, M. B. (1999) *Do No Harm: How Aid Can Support Peace – Or War*. Boulder, CO: Lynne Rienner Publishers.

Ban, K.M. (2007) 'A Climate Culprit in Darfur', Available at http://www.washingtonpost.com/wp-dyn/content/article/2007/06/15/AR2007061501857.html

Bernstein, S., Hoffmann, M. and Weinthal, E. (eds). (2018) *Global Environmental Politics*, Volume 18, Issue 1, p. 33-51

Blair, T. (2010) Tony Blair: A Journey. Vintage Books.

Boyle, F.A. (2013) 'Destroying Libya and World Order: the three-decade U.S. campaign to reverse the Qaddafi revolution'. Clarity Press.

Chagutah, T. (2010) 'Climate change vulnerability and adaptation preparedness in southern Africa', Zimbabwe country report, Available at www.academia.edu/3063814 (Accessed 18 January 2019).

Chigodo, T. (2002) 'Race and history: Politicisation of food aid resuscitated'. Available at www.raceandhistory.com/cgibin/forum/webbbs_config.pl?md=read;id=1111 (Accessed 14 February 2019).

Community Assessment of food security and the social situation in Zimbabwe, December 2003- January 2004, Civil monitoring programme and FOSENET (Food Security Network). Available at archive.kubatana.net/docs/foodse/cmp040224.doc

David, G. V. and Bruce D. J. (2018) 'Undiplomatic Action - Brookings Institution', Available at www.brookings.edu/wp-content/uploads/2018/02/...

Dean, G. (no date) 'Beyond Kyoto: climate change and political change', New World Politics, World research essay. Available at www.uts.edu.au/sites/default/files/com-student-work-garry-dean.pdf (Accessed 10 February 2019).

Dolsak, N. and Prakash, A. (2018) 'The politics of climate change adaptation', Annual Review of Environment and Resources. Available at www.researchgate.net/publication/325607009_The_Politics_of _Climate_Change_Adaptation

Engdahl, F.W. (2019) 'Genetically Engineered Destruction: The Hidden Agenda of Genetic Manipulation', Global Research, 14 February 2019.

Food and Agricultural Organisation. (2019) FAO workshop to develop guidelines for the implementation of M&E frameworks for Climate-Smart Agriculture (CSA) Available at http://www.fao.org/climatesmartagriculture/news/detail/en/c /1185780/

Food Rights Network. (2017) "Big 6" Pesticide and GMO Corporations', Centre for Media and Democracy. Available at www.sourcewatch.org/index.php/"Big_6"_Pesticide...

Food Systems Network, (n.d) 'Indigenous Food Sovereignty, Working Group on Indigenous Food Sovereignty', Available at indigenousfoodsystems.org/food-sovereignty

Gilje, K, (2011) Pesticide Action Network of North America, 'Guilty as Charged', organizational blog post, 7 December 2011.

Hakeem, K. R. (2017) 'Climate change and the politics', Available at juniperpublishers.com/ijesnr/pdf/IJESNR.MS.ID.555695.pdf 9 (Accessed 2 February 2019).

Hughes, C and Coote, D. (2019) *World News*, 'Cyclone Idai: 1,000 people may be dead, says Mozambique president', 18 March 2019

Levine, S., Peters, K. and Fan, L. (2014) 'Conflict, climate change and politics: Why a techno-centric approach fails the resilience challenge', Overseas Development Institute HPG Working paper. Available at www.eldis.org/document/A67020 (Accessed 20 March 2019).

Lipper, L., Thornton, P. Campbell, B.M. and Torquebiau, E. F. (2014) Climate-smart agriculture for food security, Nature climate change 4:1068-1072.Available at (www.ggwglobal.com/violence-ngos/ published 18 September (Accessed 12 Mar h 2019).

Machado, J. (2019) *The Times of India,* 'What is Terminator Gene Technology?' Available at timesofindia.indiatimes.com/What-is-terminator...

Mawere, M. and Nhemachena, A. (eds.) (2017) 'GMOs, Consumerism and the Global Politics of Biotechnology: rethinking food, bodies and identities in Africa's 21st century'. Bamenda: Langaa Research and Publishing CIG.

McNeal, G. S. (2016) "Domestic Drones and the Future of Aerial Surveillance" available at:
http://papers.ssrn.com/sol3/papers.cfm?abstract_id=2498116

Mkandawire, T. and Soludo, C. C. (1999) *Our Continent, Our Future: African perspectives on structural adjustment.* Trenton: Africa World Press.

Mutasa, M. (2010) 'Zimbabwe's drought conundrum: Vulnerability and coping in Buhera and Chikomba districts', Norwegian University of Life Sciences, Unpublished Masters Thesis.

Nagargade, M., Tyagi, V. and Singh. K. (2017) 'Climate Smart Agriculture: An Option for Changing Climatic Situation' Available at www.intechopen.com/books/plant-engineering/.

Pindula News (21 January 2019) 'NGOs Deny Pushing Regime Change Agenda, Blame Government Policies for causing suffering', Available at news pindula.co.zw/2019/01/21/ngos-deny-pushing-regime-change-agenda-blame-govt-policies-for-causing-suffering. (Accessed 7 March 2019).

Nhemachena, A. and Mawere, M. (2017) *GMOs, consumerism and the global politics of biotechnology: rethinking food, bodies and identities in Africa's 21st century.* Bamenda: Langaa Research & Publishing CIG.

Nhemachena A., Warikandwa, T. V. & Mtapuri, O. (eds) (2017) *Transnational Land Grabs and Restitution in an Age of the (De-)Militarised New Scramble for Africa: A Pan African Socio-Legal Perspective.* Bamenda: Langaa RPCIG.

Nhemachena, Warikandwa, T. V. & Amoo, S. K. (2018) *Social and Legal Theory in the Age of Decoloniality: (Re)Envisioning Pan-African Jurisprudence in the 21ˢᵗ Century*. Bamenda: Langaa RPCIG.

Nhemachena, A. & Warikandwa, T. V. (2019) *From African Peer Review Mechanisms to African Queer Review Mechanisms: Robert Gabriel Mugabe, Empire & the Decolonisation of African Orifices*. Bamenda: Langaa RPCIG.

O'Neal, E. T. (2014) 'Global climate change: The political impact of global warming on developing countries: The case studies of Egypt and Oman', University of Nevada, Las Vegas, Unpublished DPhil Thesis.

Pindula News, (21 January 2019) 'NGOs Deny Pushing Regime Change Agenda, Blame Government Policies for Causing suffering', Available at news.pindula.co.zw/2019/01/21/ngos-deny-pushing-regime-change Accessed 7 March 2019)

Rukuni, C. (17 March 2019) *The Insider,* 'Why Zimbabwe's disaster response is a disaster', 17 March 2019. Available at www.insiderzim.com/why-zimbabwes-disaster-response-is-a-disaster

Rwodzi, A. and Mubonderi, B. (2015) State nations and nation states: The fate of western democracy in Africa, *The International Journal of Humanities & Social Studies*, Vol.3, Issue 9.

Sachs, J. (2011) Case Study of International Conflict: Darfur, Sudan. Available at pmt.physicsandmathstutor.com/download/Geography/A.

Satgar, V. (2014) *The Solidarity Economy Alternative: Emerging Theory and Practice*. University of KwaZulu Natal Press.

Saud, A. S. H. (2013) 'Global warming and its impacts on climate of India', University Malaysia Pahang, Malaysia. Available at greencleanguide.com/global-warming-and-its-impacts-on...

Shout Africa, 21 June 2017, 'Zimbabwe's Command agriculture – a political gimmic', Available at www.shout-africa.com/news/zimbabwes-command-agriculture...

The American Heritage Science Dictionary (2011) Houghton Mifflin Harcourt Publishing Company.

The Guardian, (3 June 2005) 'Donor nations accused of 'phantom' aid flows to poor', Available at www.theguardian.com/world/2005/jun/03/outlook...

The Washington Post. (16 March 2019). 'Cyclone, *Idai* hits Mozambique, Malawi, Zimbabwe, killing 150', www.washingtonpost.com/world/africa/cyclone-idai...

UNDP Programme (2010) 'Zimbabwe: Coping with drought and climate change'.

Vambe, L. (22 September 2016) '*PaZimbabwe*, Broke Zimbabwe Angers Chiefs over Non-Payment of Allowances for 3 Consecutive Months', Available at www.thezimbabwenewslive.com/main-news-27105-broke-zimbabwe-angers-chiefs-non-payment-allowances-3-consecutive-months.html

Victor, D.G. and Jones, B. D. (2018) 'Undiplomatic Action: A practical guide to the new politics and geopolitics of climate change', Paper 1. Available at www.brookings.edu/wp-content/uploads/2018/02/esci_201802_undiplomatic_action.pdf (Accessed 17 March 2019).

Widlok, T. (2016) *Anthropology and the Economy of Sharing*. Routledge.

Wilson, J. (2015) *Natural News*, 'Hundreds of US farmers sue Syngenta over GMO corn' Available at www.naturalnews.com/048927_GMO_corn_Syngenta_US...

World Food Summit. (1996) 'Food and Agriculture Organization', Available at www.fao.org/wfs/index_en.htm (Accessed 10 January 2019).

Zimeye, (15 March 2019) 'Government Amends NGOs Statute amid Fears of so-called Regime Change Agenda by NGO', Available at www.zimeye.net/2019/03/15/govt-amends-ngos-statute-amid-fears-of-so-called-regime-change-agenda-by-ngos

Chapter Nine

Climate Change in Zimbabwe: Challenges and Prospects for Rural Women in Bikita District

Nancy Mazuru

Introduction

Climate change refers to shifts in meteorological conditions lasting a few years or longer (Burroughs *et al*, 2001). These changes may involve a single parameter such as temperature or rainfall, but usually accompany more general shifts in weather patterns which might result in a shift to colder, wetter, cloudier, and windier conditions (*Ibid*). Climate change affects men, women, boys and girls differently. The impacts are never uniform and they also differ according to social class. This chapter examines the impact of climate change on rural women in Bikita, paying particular attention on how these effects exacerbate poverty levels. Since time immemorial, women in rural areas have been playing a pivotal role in harnessing available local resources for livelihoods. Land, water bodies, forests and mountains are key livelihood sources for rural dwellers, particularly women. Rural people engage in agricultural activities where they get both food and income. Forests and mountains also provide fruits, fuel wood, traditional medicines and water for gardening purposes and domestic use. Nevertheless, the availability of these resources in Bikita, just like in many other areas, has been severely affected by low rainfall patterns connected to climate change. It is against this backdrop that this chapter examines how the scarcity of local resources, due to climate change, is negatively affecting women and how this is worsening poverty levels among women. The effects of climate change in this chapter are analysed using a gender lens. This is largely because the roles and responsibilities ascribed to men and women are socially constructed and they result in both men and women facing different vulnerabilities. Women make up 70% of the world's poor (Miller, 2006), hence climate change induced disasters such as droughts and floods exacerbates their susceptibility to poverty.

The study was purely qualitative in nature. It adopted a case study research design where Bikita district was selected. Bikita district is found in Masvingo province of Zimbabwe and it is located about 80km East of Masvingo town (Mushore *et al*, 2013). The district is predominantly occupied by the Karanga people. The term Karanga refers not only to ethnic identity but also to the dialect spoken by part of the Shona people (Mwandayi, 2011). Contemporary chiefdoms in this district are mainly a result of migrations in the 17th, 18th and 19th centuries (*Ibid*). Within this district, all the chiefs belong to the Duma totem and these chiefs include Ziki, Mabika, Mukanganwi, Mazungunye and Budzi (Nyathi, 2008). The district is located at -20[0] 5'45" latitude, 31[0] 36'55" longitude and at an average elevation of 656 altitude (Kassie *et al*, 2012). Around 81% of Bikita district is classified under agro-natural regions 4 and 5 with mean annual rainfall ranging from 400mm to 700mm (Mawere, 2017). Rural areas that fall under region 4 and 5 in Zimbabwe naturally receive low rainfall and are more prone to droughts. Climate change is worsening droughts in region 4 and 5 as rainfall has declined by 15% since 1960 (Chimanikire, 2013). As such, these regions have been a home to famine and water shortages due to climate change (Chirisa *et al*, 2019). Climate change has made rainfall frequency erratic and unreliable in Bikita, making it extremely difficult for peasant farmers to invest in agricultural activities (Mawere, 2017). In Bikita, agriculture is the major livelihood activity, with maize being the major crop grown (Mawere, 2017). In addition to maize, there is also a diversity of crops that are grown in the district which include rapoko, sorghum, finger millet, groundnuts, round nuts, pumpkins and sweet potatoes among others. However, most of these crops are being threatened by low rainfall patterns emanating from climate change. Primary data for this study were gathered through interviews, focus group discussions and observations. Since this chapter focuses on examining the impact of climate change on rural women, key informants in this study were women from different villages across the district because they possess first-hand information about the vagaries that have been brought about by climate change, particularly on their livelihoods.

The Gender Dimension of Climate Change

Gender is an important variable in the relationship between climate change and its human impacts (Verner, 2012). Gender is a concept that captures the social norms for roles and responsibilities of women and men (Roberts and Rodriguez, 2018). The vulnerability to natural disasters and their consequences is gendered and socially constructed, meaning that women and men face different challenges during natural disasters because their roles in societies have been constructed differently (Ramachandran, 2013). Men, women, children and the elderly have different roles, interests, needs and opportunities, hence they are affected by climate change differently (Roberts and Rodriguez, 2018). In Bikita as well as many other rural areas of the developing world, women are responsible for all household chores including cooking, laundry, fetching fuelwood and water. They are also the ones who perform the majority of farming activities. Nevertheless, most of these gendered responsibilities are sensitive to climate change and it is women who are suffering more because of climate variability as compared to men. The sections below examine how climate change is threatening livelihoods as well as reducing the availability of precious resources that matter in the lives of women. They explain how this is increasing poverty levels among women in Bikita.

Decline in Agricultural Productivity

Agricultural production remains the main source of livelihoods for most rural communities in developing countries and Sub-Saharan Africa in particular (Nhemachena and Hassan, 2007). According to World Bank (2008), 75% of the world's poor live in rural areas and most are involved in farming. In Bikita and many other rural areas of Zimbabwe, agriculture plays a pivotal role in providing food security and income to the rural families and communities. As indicated earlier in this chapter, a variety of crops are grown in Bikita such as maize, which is the staple diet in the country; there are also small grain crops like finger millet, sorghum and rapoko. Legumes such as groundnuts, round nuts and cow peas together with root crops such as sweet potatoes are also grown in the area. However, just like in many other societies of the developing world, farming activities in Bikita are largely a female domain because of socially constructed responsibilities that have seen men migrating to urban areas in search of employment, leaving behind agricultural tasks in the hands of women. FAO (2018) states that in countries such as Zimbabwe, Ethiopia, Bangladesh and Indonesia, men constitute about 70% of labour migrants. The migration of men from rural to urban areas leaves women in charge of farming operations (Wong, 2018). Sharing the same view, Ramachandran, (2013) states that the 'feminisation of agriculture' and the resultant 'feminisation of poverty' - terms which are now common in development literature, originate in the exodus of the young male working population to urban areas in search of employment. In Bikita as well as other districts in Masvingo province, recurrent low rainfall patterns due to climate change are threatening livelihoods, thereby forcing young adults to migrate to cities and towns as well as out of the country in search of other means of living. According to Siddiqui and Billah (2014), migration is one of the strategies used by people affected by climate change to diversify their income sources. In the same line of argument, Furlong (2012) states that climate change triggers disasters such as droughts, floods and extreme weather and this leads to new diasporas as people try to make a life for themselves under deteriorating environmental conditions. In Zimbabwe, due to high unemployment rates, migration is no longer predominantly rural-urban, as many people are now crossing borders in search of employment opportunities. Although many Zimbabwean women are becoming migrants, both internally and externally due to economic crisis facing the country, it is important to note that there is not yet parity between the two sexes as male migrants still outnumber female migrants. According to Crush *et al* (2017), in Zimbabwe, males constitute 56% of international migrants while women constitute 44%. In many rural societies in the developing world, women's mobility is constrained by social norms, so migrants tend to be mostly male (FAO, 2018). In the same line of argument Saito *et al* (1994) posit that many rural women are confined to farming activities because of their lesser mobility resulting from child rearing responsibilities. This scenario, results in a gender differentiated economic process which leaves the woman as a de facto head of the household shouldering the burden of the farm and the family (Ramachandran, 2013). In Bikita, most of the agricultural activities including ploughing, weeding and harvesting of crops are done by women. This authenticates the assertion by Sugden, (2014) that in Sub-Saharan Africa, women have been found to be responsible for a significant 75% of household food production.

While agriculture is perceived to be a key livelihood system for rural dwellers, in Bikita, its role in providing food security as well as curtailing poverty is diminishing due to low rainfall patterns that are continuously being received in the area, leading to crop failure and poor harvests. In order for farming activities to be viable, there is need for conducive temperatures and rainfall patterns. Maharjan and Joshi (2013) argue that with climate change, there will be changes in both mean temperature and precipitation that will cause variability between seasons and also increases the frequency of natural disasters and extreme events like droughts. In Bikita district, rainfall is continuously becoming erratic, poorly distributed and it falls predominantly for only a few months each year resulting in livelihood insecurity since water scarcity and food security are interrelated problems (Mushore *et al*, 2013). Roetter *et al* (2007) assert that since most crop production systems are adapted to certain ranges in temperature and water availability, their productive capacity is severely curtailed by ongoing climate change. In areas where temperatures are already warm, such as Zimbabwe and most parts of Africa south of the Sahara, further increases in temperature may slow down rather than stimulate plant growth, culminating in a general decrease in expected yields for most of the current food crops (World Bank, 2007). As noted by Mushore *et al* (2013), in Bikita district, subsistence farmers are producing less on their fields as the years are progressing because effects of droughts are worsening with time resulting in food insecurity. Maize is one of the crops that is being seriously affected by low rainfall patterns being experienced in Bikita. The Zimbabwe Human Development Report, (2017) states that maize, one of Zimbabwe's main agricultural crops, is very sensitive to temperature and precipitation changes, hence production is seriously affected by weather-related stresses and shocks. The reduction in the yields of the maize crop has plunged women in Bikita into hunger and poverty. In an interview conducted by the researcher on the 10th of January 2018, one woman from Magazeni village, Bikita stated that:

> The changing weather patterns have made life difficult for us. This area is no longer receiving good rains and nowadays we hardly make good harvests. In the past decades, food was abundant. I could even sell surplus maize to the Grain Marketing Board and use the money to pay school fees for my children as well as buying groceries and other essentials. However, the maize that I am harvesting nowadays is hardly enough to sustain my family up to the next harvesting season.

Thus, unpredictable rainfall patterns and crop failure have been a common problem experienced in Bikita and this has often diminished crop production in the area, leading to food insecurity. These diminishing harvests are a blow to the wellbeing of women. According to Achamwie (2015), though climate change affects both men and women, in rural communities, women are greatly affected because most of them depend primarily on farming activities which are sensitive to climate change. In the same vein, the World Bank (2007) states that since most developing countries are heavily dependent on agriculture, the effect of climate change on their productive crop lands is likely to threaten economic development and welfare of the population. In this context it is the poor and marginalised that suffer more and rural women are the hardest hit.

What exacerbates the problem of poor harvests in the area is that the majority of these female farmers rely on rain fed agriculture. Roetter *et al*, (2007) states that reduced rainfall negatively affects small scale farmers who sorely rely on rain fed agriculture. In the same line of argument, the Zimbabwe Human Development Report, (2017) states that most livelihood activities in Zimbabwe are primarily centred on rain-fed agriculture and they are highly susceptible to climate-related hazards and shocks, thereby, making rural households vulnerable to shifts and changes in the climate. Relying on rain fed agriculture stems from the fact that most of the female farmers lack funds to purchase irrigation equipment. This is coupled with the fact that irrigation projects in Zimbabwe are governed by the Zimbabwe National Water Authority (ZINWA) which has some regulations that are not friendly to poor communal farmers. For example, Section 41 of ZINWA Act states that use of dam water for commercial purposes is subject to paying water levy (Zimbabwe National Water Authority Act, Chapter 20:25). This is a constraint to rural women who wish to have access to irrigation facilities because most of them do not afford to pay for the water levy. As noted by Nhemachena and Hassan (2007), rural households have few resources to combat the effects of climate change and this exacerbates their susceptibility to hunger and poverty.

Climate change is also affecting gardening activities in Bikita. Many women engage in gardening activities between May and October when farm work will be minimal. Different types of vegetables such as tomatoes, onions, cabbages and carrots are grown during this period for home consumption and for sale. Some of the vegetables are dried and safely stored for future use. Amenu (2013) states that in rural areas of developing countries, water is used for both livelihood productive activities such as gardening and small scale irrigation. However, the low rainfall being received in many parts of Bikita is leading to the desiccation of water bodies such as dams, rivers and pools, thereby affecting the irrigation potential of the area. Sharing the same view, Maharjan and Joshi (2013) state that climate change has an effect on water resource availability, which is a major input in agriculture. Mansell (2003) also shares the same opinion arguing that where temperatures and evapotranspiration rates increase, there will obviously be an increasing demand for irrigation water. In another interview conducted by the researcher on the 13th of January 2019 in Nedombwe village, one woman stated that:

In the past years, we used to have many water sources to support our gardening activities. The small dams that we have in this area together with river pools used to have water that could sustain our gardening activities up to the beginning of another rainy season. This enabled us to have relish for our families as well as getting income from the sale of these vegetables. However, nowadays, our local water sources are quickly drying up because of the low rainfall that we are receiving and we are now struggling to get vegetables for our families.

The effects of climate change on gardening activities are largely felt by women because they are the ones involved in these activities and at the same time, they are the ones responsible for gathering relish as well as preparing food for their families. Thus, water is an important resource for the wellbeing and survival of people specifically in rural areas where it is used for domestic purposes and other livelihood productive activities such as gardening, small scale irrigation and livestock farming, among others (Amenu, 2013). This also validates the assertion by Maharjan and Joshi (2013) that as water resources will become scarce, it will have an impact on the irrigation potential of the area thereby affecting agriculture.

Climate change in Bikita is not only affecting crop production; livestock production is not being spared. Maharjan and Joshi (2013) aver that climate change affects livestock production directly due to physiological stress caused by temperature increase and indirectly through changes in fodder quality and availability. Three women who were interviewed by the researcher in Munyanyiwa village, on the 13th of February 2019, stated that during times of extreme low rainfall, most of their livestock particularly cattle died due to lack of water and pastures. One of these three women stated that:

> Had it not been the continuous low rainfall patterns we are experiencing in this area, I could have plenty of cattle. I lost 5 cattle in 2002 and 3 cattle in 2008 and now I am only left with 3. Owning large herds of livestock is important because whenever there is urgent need of money, you can sell your livestock and have the money. During the past years I was affording to pay school fees for my children even though I am a widow because I had plenty of cattle, so I could not hesitate to sell one or two. However, I can no longer do this because I am only left with 3 cows. My daughter who is doing form three has not been in school for the past two months because I failed to raise her school fees and I am afraid that this will affect her 'O' Level results.

Therefore, climate change affects the socioeconomic wellbeing of female headed households, thereby further worsening poverty levels in these households.

Decline of Agricultural Processed Food for Sale

In many rural communities of Zimbabwe, the processing of agricultural produce for sale is another important income generating activity carried out by many women. In Bikita, women make different foods for sale from their agricultural produce. These include peanut butter, traditional rice, dried vegetables and traditional beer. McCall (1996) states that beer brewing and selling is a significant source of money for rural women to spend on domestic essentials and on their children's needs. However, the decline of agricultural yields due to climate change also entails a reduction in the processing of agricultural foods for sale. One woman stated that:

> Brewing beer for sale is a profitable business. I have been in this business for many years and I have been able to take care of my family. My husband who works in Chiredzi in the sugar plantations hardly gives me money. However during the previous years, I was able to provide for my family through the growing of finger millet, rapoko and sorghum that I would use to brew bear. However, the low rainfall patterns that we are receiving in the area have reduced my crop yields and because of this, I no longer brew beer on regular basis.

Closely related to the above, other women who were interviewed stated that the processing of peanut butter for sale has also declined due to poor harvest of groundnuts. This again increases poverty levels among women.

Decline of Wild Resources

Rural women are more reliant on natural resources for their livelihoods, and these are threatened by natural disasters that stem from climate change. A vast array of edible plant products are collected from forests and these include seeds, nuts, leaves, fruits, roots, tubers and fungi. They are used to supplement agricultural crops as a source of vital nutrition, and they are particularly important during periods of reduced agricultural output (Carr et al, 2013). These products are an important source of rural livelihoods especially for the poorest (Mogaka et al, 2001). Rural communities in Zimbabwe have adopted alternative livelihood activities such as firewood trade, sale of wild fruits to middlemen who resale them in the urban areas, honey production and caterpillar harvesting as income streams (Zimbabwe Human Development Report, 2017). Ecosystem based livelihoods are a critically important source of income for the poor and they help cover critical needs such as school fees as well as deal with unexpected hardships such as illness, unemployment and crop failure (International Union for Conservation of Nature, 2009). However, these alternative livelihoods are dependent on rainfall distribution and quantity (Zimbabwe Human Development Report, 2017). The major wild resources that are threatened by climate change in Bikita are articulated below.

Harurwa (Stink bugs)

In Bikita, the existence of Harurwa (Stink bugs), particularly in the Nerumedzo and Mukanganwi areas has improved the wellbeing not only of the local populace but also of people from distant parts of the district who buy these edible insects for resale. Stink bugs are sold in areas such as Nyika growth point and it is women who dominate the trading of these edible insects. However, just like many natural resources, stink bugs are also being threatened by climate change. Mawere (2013) argues that erratic rainfall being experienced in Mukanganwi area of Bikita is attributable to the indiscriminate cutting down of trees for settlements and extension of farmlands and this in turn has led to diminished harvests of Harurwa. Mawere further states that while natural phenomena is partly blamed for the erratic rainfall in the Mukanganwi area, human causes like deforestation and veld fires seem to be significantly contributing to the climatic changes in these areas. According to Mawere, the drastic decrease of Harurwa which used to be abundant in Mukanganwi area compromises the livelihood of the residents of this area as they used to sustain their families through these resources. This largely affects women because they are the ones who largely engage in the selling of Harurwa.

Mopane Worms (edible caterpillars)

In addition to Harurwa, some women in Bikita also supplement their household diet and income from the gathering of Mopane worms (edible caterpillars). Mopane worms are mainly found in areas such as Zengeya and Devuli resettlement areas, in the South Eastern part of Bikita. The availability of these edible caterpillars in Zengeya and Devuli stems from the fact that the area is endowed with Mopane trees compared to other parts of the district. Mopane worms are seasonal and they are found during the rainy season, hence they are normally dried for sale or for future consumption. According to Cuff and Goudie (2009) rodents, edible caterpillars, insects and other small creatures have long been an important part of the rural diet in virtually all parts of the globe. However, the availability of these edible creatures also depends on the availability of good rainfall. Just like many other areas of Bikita, Zengeya and Devuli resettlement areas have not been spared from receiving erratic rainfall and this has diminished the availability of mopane worms. This has in turn affected household nutrition as these edible caterpillars are perceived to be a delicious relish in the area. Women are greatly affected by the limited existence of mopane worms because they are the ones who are responsible for gathering and cooking of relish and other foods for their families. Sharing the same view, Da Silva (2019) avers that climate change puts at risk indigenous people who depend on the environment and its biodiversity for their food security and nutrition. In an interview conducted by the researcher on the 17th of January, in Village 21, Devuli resettlement area, one woman stated that:

> In the past years, this area was abundantly blessed with mopane worms. We had enough for relish and we could dry and store some for future consumption. We could also sell some to people from neighbouring communities or to traders who came from distant areas, mainly urban areas. Now that we are getting mopane worms in short supply, we are struggling to find alternative relishes for our families and at the same time the amount of income that we used to get from the sale of mopane worms has declined.

Other 3 women from the same village who were interviewed by the researcher stated that before the mopane worms started dwindling, local cross border traders as well as traders from urban areas would come to buy dried mopane worms for resale. The women further indicated that in addition to getting income from the sale of mopane worms, in other incidents they practiced barter trade with the urban and cross-border traders in which they could exchange the edible caterpillars for new or second hand clothes or groceries. Nevertheless, the dwindling supply of the edible caterpillars in the area has also reduced income and other benefits derived from the trading of these delicious worms, thereby plunging women into poverty. This authenticates the assertion by Zimbabwe Human Development Report (2017) that the availability of the seasonal mopane worm and its gathering, preservation and selling are threatened by the frequency of dry spells and drought under a changing climate and consequently, this limits food and income access opportunities for the families, particularly for those that are resource-poor.

Mushrooms

Closely related to the above, climate variability in Devuli resettlement area has also diminished the availability of wild edible mushrooms. Just like mopane worms, mushrooms favour good rainfall. Mushrooms can make a substantial contribution to the diet of poor people in developing countries but they can also be an important source of income (Ferreira *et al*, 2017). Mushrooms are naturally low in fats and are a good source of several vitamins, minerals and proteins (Marley, 2010). As such, the decline in the amount of mushroom has exacerbated relish and income problems in the area and it is women who bear the brunt as they are normally the ones who are involved in the gathering, cooking, drying and selling of mushroom.

Fruits

Climate change can lead to a reduction of production and consumption of some foods that play a critical role in the diets of vulnerable and indigenous populations, such as fruits (Da Silva, 2019). Just like many rural areas, Bikita is blessed with a variety of fruits that can be used to supplement household nutrition. *Mazhanje* (wild loquats) is one of the most delicious wild fruit that is commonly found in the Mukanganwi and Nerumedzo areas of Bikita (Mawere, 2013). Women come from several parts of the district to buy *mazhanje* for resale at busy places such as growth points as well as in towns.

266

Nyii (Birdplum) is another fruit that is found in Bikita. The fruit can be eaten fresh or dried. Just like *Mazhanje*, dried *Nyii* is also sold at growth points and various cities and towns across the country. Other fruits that are usually gathered for home consumption and for sale in Bikita include *Hubvu* **(smelly-berry fingerleaf) and *Matohwe* (snot-aple)**. The selling of these wild fruits helps to improve women's household income. As noted by Cartmell-Thorp (2017), women in developing countries play a critical role in supporting their households and communities in achieving food and nutrition security, generating income and improving rural livelihoods and overall wellbeing. They contribute to household income through the sale of a variety of grown and wild foods (Cartmell-Thorp, 2017). However, wild fruits in Bikita have also become susceptible to climate change and this has reduced the income of women who depend on selling these fruits.

Medicines

Medicines derived from wild species are often the most accessible and affordable health care available to many people (Carr *et al*, 2013). It is estimated that on average, 80% of people in African countries rely on biodiversity for primary health care and wild sourced medicines are also used to treat livestock (*Ibid*). In Bikita, low rainfall is leading to scarcity of precious wild medicines such *Gavakava* (*aloe vera*) which requires moderate to high rainfall. *Aloe vera* is used as a medicine to treat both human beings and livestock. Some of these herbs are used for women's reproductive health. For example, many women in this area as well as in many parts of Zimbabwe use wild herbs during pregnancy to help *open* up the *birth* canal. This is popularly known as *masuwo* in local Shona language and it helps prevent complications while delivering a child. Some herbs are used after giving birth to strengthen the uterus and pelvic muscles as well as tightening the vagina. These herbal medicines also help to flush out remaining childbirth blood and left over placenta in the uterus (Liamputtong, 2017). Closely related to the above, a variety of wild herbal medicines are also used to boost breast milk production soon after giving birth. Others are used to relieve or cure menstrual pain. Hence, the scarcity of local herbs due to climate change entails that women's reproductive and maternal health is at risk as most of them do not afford scientific medicines. This is worsened by the fact that some local clinics in the area do not have medicines, hence local women resort to the use of herbal medicines which are now being threatened by climate change. This buttresses the view by Attia (2010) that herbal medicines are a major source of health care in rural communities of the developing world because modern medicines have not been able to reach the majority of the populace. In an interview conducted by the researcher on the 10th of January 2019 in Magazeni village, one traditional midwife stated that:

> This area used to have diverse wild plants that we use as herbal medicine. However, we are no longer receiving good rains, hence most of these herbs have dried up while others are now in short supply. We are now struggling to get these medicines for pregnant women and some are experiencing complications while giving birth and after giving birth.

Poor health among rural women hinders them from effectively doing their farming activities, household chores and other income generating activities, thereby leading them into poverty. Good health plays a crucial role in reducing poverty.

Firewood

Wood fuels are the largest sources of household energy in Africa south of the Sahara (Saito *et al*, 1994). In Bikita, owing to climate change, the supply of fuelwood is decreasing. According to Saito *et al* (1994), women are the worst affected by fuelwood crisis because as the main gatherers, transporters and users of this resource, they must walk ever further to gather it. In Bikita as in many other rural areas of Zimbabwe, the collection of firewood is largely a female domain. However, climate change has led to a decrease in firewood and this is causing a burden on women and girls as they are now forced to walk for long distances to collect wood fuels. Women who were interviewed by the researcher in Zirabada village stated that they usually walk for about 4 -5km in search of firewood and in certain circumstances, they will be carrying children on their backs. Others stated that they sometimes climb up mountains looking for fuelwood, which is very risky. Thus, gender roles have seen women in Bikita bearing the heavy brunt of climate change. In many rural areas of Africa, there is unequal division of labour that has seen women and girls performing most of the household chores, including fetching firewood and water and Bikita is not an exception. This confirms the assertion by Nombo *et al* (2014) that neither the impacts of climate change on people nor the ways in which people respond to climate change are gender neutral. In the same line of argument, Verner (2012) asserts that gender based inequalities which persist in different societies result in men, women, boys and girls facing different vulnerabilities in the face of climate change impacts. Research has shown that walking long distances in search of firewood negatively affects women's reproductive health as well as making them vulnerable to risks such as rape and kidnapping.

Apart from putting the lives of women and girls in danger, the scarcity of fuelwood due to changing climate increases the already high labour burden for women (Sugden, 2014). When one considers the time already taken for women to collect firewood and water, increased scarcities of these resources means that women and girls have to spend more time on this arduous task (*Ibid*). Chopping and collecting fuelwood is a time-consuming and energy-consuming work which has seen women across the developing world spending up to half of their day engaged in this activity (Brijnath, 2016). This decreases the opportunities for women to invest time and labour in agriculture and other income generating activities (UNESCO, 2013; Sugden, 2014). Most of the women stated that when they walk for long distances in search of firewood, by the time they get home they would be tired. Besides that, fuelwood shortages also limit women's income activities such as food processing and beer brewing which require firewood (Saito *et al*, 1994). All these challenges exacerbate poverty levels among women.

Water for Domestic Use

As mentioned earlier in this chapter, water is another precious resource which is being threatened by climate change. Sultana, (2018) states that drinking water availability, reliability, quality, quantity, and accessibility will be altered with changing weather and climatic patterns and climate-induced ecological change. Such changes exacerbate challenges in daily water fetching tasks. The effects of water shortages on women are similar to those of firewood shortages as in both circumstances, women are forced to walk for long distances in search of these vital resources. In most cases, the risks they face as they search for these resources are similar. As mentioned earlier, they are susceptible to sexual violence and kidnapping. Similarly, the decline of clean water sources and fuelwood strain the reproductive and care giving roles of women. Sultana (2018) states that lack of water that is socially and economically viable can strain gender roles and relations in the household and communities. In addition to that, some of the women who were interviewed by the researcher stated that when they are feeling tired, they resort to unclean water sources such as open wells. This jeopardises their health as well as that of their families.

Conclusion

This chapter has looked at the effects of climate change in Zimbabwe with particular focus on how it affects rural women in Bikita. The chapter focused on Bikita district. It has examined several ways in which climate change is affecting women. The findings of the study revealed that Bikita district is experiencing low rainfall and this is leading to a decline in agricultural produce. The decline in agricultural produce is threatening food security in the district and it is women who largely bear the brunt because they are the ones who dominate farming activities. Agriculture is the major source of livelihood for women in this district. Reduced crop yields affect food security and in this regard, it is women again who shoulder this burden because they are the ones who are responsible for preparing food for their families. At the same time, declining agricultural produce plunges rural women into poverty because they get income through selling surplus yields and home processed foods. The chapter has also found out that the depletion of wild resources such as fruits, mopane worms, stink bugs and mushrooms also affects rural women in terms of the dietary needs of their households as well as reduction of income generated through the sale of these resources. Besides that, climate change is also leading to scarcity of local herbs for both human beings and livestock. Various herbs that are used for women's reproductive and maternal health are at the risk of extinction due to low rainfall patterns being experienced in the area, thereby jeopardising their health. The chapter has also argued that low rainfall in Bikita is leading to scarcity of fuelwood and water sources and this largely affects women.

References

Achamwie, P. K. (2015), 'The Effects of Climate Change on Rural Female Farmers in the Wenchi Municipality' In *International journal of research,* Vol 2 (1).

Amenu, K. (2013) *Assessment of water sources and quality for livestock and farmers in the Rift Valley area of Ethiopia: Implications for health and food safety.* Gottingen: Sierke Verlag.

Attia, A. S. (2010) *Archives of clinical microbiology,* ImedPub.

Balogun, O. L. (2011) 'Sustainable agriculture and food crisis in Sub Saharan Africa' in Behnassi, M. *et al.* (eds) *Global Food Insecurity: Rethinking Agricultural and Rural Development Paradigm and Policy.* New York: Springer Science & Business Media.

Brijnath, B. (2016) 'Death of a *mwana*: Biomas fuels, poverty, gender and climate change' in Butler, C. (ed) *Climate Change and Global Health.* Oxfordshire: CABI.

Burroughs, W. *et al,* (2001) *Climate Change: A Multidisciplinary Approach.* Cambridge: Cambridge University Press.

Carr, J. A. *et al.* (2013) *Vital but vulnerable: climate change vulnerability and human use of wildlife in Africa's Albertine Rift,* Gland: International Union for Conservation of Nature.

Cartmell-Thorp, S. (2017) Big Data and Climate Insurance - Reducing Risk and Maximising Revenues: Spore Magazine 186.

Chimanikire, D. (2013) 'Women and climate change adaptation in Zimbabwe' in International Social Science Council and United Nations Educational, Scientific and Cultural Organization (eds), *World Social Science Report 2013, Changing Global Environments*, Paris: OECD Publishing and UNSECO Publishing.

Chirisa, I. *et al.* (2019) 'Consilience as the basis for community resilience: Lessons for Zimbabwe' in Chirisa, I. and Mabeza, C. (eds) *Community Resilience under the Impact of Urbanisation and Climate*

Change: Cases and Experiences from Zimbabwe. Bamenda, Langaa RPCIG.

Crush, J. *et al.* (2017) Migrants in Countries in Crisis (MICIC), South Africa Case Study: The Double Crisis – Mass Migration from Zimbabwe and Xenophobic Violence in South Africa, International Centre for Migration Policy Development.

Cuff, D, J. and Goudie, A. S. (2009) *The Oxford Companion to Global Change.* Oxford: Oxford University Press.

Da Silva, J. G. (2019) 'Food systems and nutrition in the context of climate change' in Selendy, J. M. H. (ed) *Water and Sanitation-Related Diseases and the Changing Environment: Challenges, Interventions, and Preventive Measures.* Hoboken: John Wiley & Sons.

FAO, (2018) *The State of Food and Agriculture 2018: Migration, Agriculture and Rural Development.* Rome: FAO.

Ferreira I. C. F.R. *et al.* (2017) *Wild Plants, Mushrooms and Nuts: Functional Food Properties and Applications.* West Sussex: John Wiley & Sons.

Furlong, A. (2012) *Youth Studies: An Introduction.* New York: Routledge.

Gukurume, S. (2013) 'Climate change, variability and sustainable agriculture in Zimbabwe's rural communities' in *Russian Journal of Agricultural and Socio-Economic Sciences,* Vol 2(14).

International Union for Conservation of Nature (2009) Ecosystem-based Adaptation: A Natural Response to Climate Change

Kassie, G. T. *et al.* (2012) *Characterization of maize production in Southern Africa: synthesis of CIMMYT/DTMA household level farming system surveys in Angola, Malawi, Mozambique, Zambia and Zimbabwe.* Socio-Economics Programme, Working Paper 4, Mexico: International Maize and Wheat Improvement Centre.

Liamputtong, P (2017*) Childrearing and Infant Care Issues: A Cross-cultural Perspective.* New York: Nova Publishers.

Maharjan, K. L. and Joshi, N. P. (2013) *Climate Change, Agriculture and Rural Livelihoods in Developing Countries. Springer*

Mansell, M.G. (2003) *Rural and Urban Hydrology.* London: Thomas Telford.

Mare, A. (2013) 'Gender and climate change adaptation among agro-pastoral communities: Case study of Chivi district in Southern Zimbabwe' In Getu, M. and Mulinge, M. M. (eds) *Impacts of*

Climate Change and Variability on Pastoralist Women in Sub-Saharan Africa. Addis Ababa: Organisation for Social Science Research.

Mathew, R. A. (2014) 'Climate change and human security' in DiMento, J.F.C. and Doughman, P. (eds) *Climate Change: What It Means for Us, Our Children, and Our Grandchildren.* London: MIT Press.

Marley, G. (2010) *Chanterelle Dreams, Amanita Nightmares: The Love, Lore, and Mystique of Mushrooms.* Vermont: Chelsea Green Publishing.

Mawere, M. (2013) *Environmental Conservation through Ubuntu and Other Emerging Perspectives.* Bamenda: Langaa Research and Publishing Common Initiative Group.

Mawere, M. (2017) *The Political Economy of Poverty, Vulnerability and Disaster Risk Management: Building Bridges of Resilience, Entrepreneurship.* Bamenda: Langaa RPCIG.

McCall, M (1996) 'Rural brewing, exclusion and development policy-making' In Sweetman, C. (ed) *Women, Employment and Exclusion.* Oxford: Oxfam.

Miller, G. T. (2006) *Living in the Environment: Principles, Connections, and Solutions.* Boston: Cengage Learning.

Mogaka, H. *et al,* (2001) *Economic Aspects of Community Involvement in Sustainable Forest Management in Eastern and Southern Africa.* Nairobi: International Union for Conservation of Nature.

Mushore, T. D. *et al.* (2013) 'Effectiveness of drought mitigation strategies in Bikita District, Zimbabwe' in *International Journal of Environmental Protection and Policy*, Vol 1(4).

Mwandayi, C. (2011) *Death and After-life Rituals in the Eyes of the Shona: Dialogue with Shona Customs in the Quest for Authentic Inculturation.* Bamberg: University of Bamberg Press.

Nhemachena, C. and Hassan, R. (2007) *Micro-Level Analysis of Farmers Adaption to climate change in Southern Africa.* Washington D.C: International Food Policy Research Institute.

Nombo, C. I. *et al.* (2014), 'Adaptation to climate change: Changing gender relations in the Meatu and Iramba Districts of Tanzania' in La, R. *et al* (eds) *Sustainable Intensification to Advance Food Security and Enhance Climate Resilience in Africa.* New Yok: Springer.

Nusser, M. (ed) (2019) *Advances in Asian Human-Environmental Research*, New York: Springer Science & Business Media.

Nyathi, P. (2008) *Zimbabwe's cultural Heritage*. Bulawayo: amaBooks.

Ramachandran, N. (2013) 'Gender, climate and household food security: A South Asian perspective' in Behnassi, M. *et al* (eds) *Sustainable Food Security in the Era of Local and Global Environmental Change*. New York: Springer Science & Business Media.

Roberts, T. G. and Rodriguez, M. T. (2018) 'An overview on climate change and impacts on food security on small Island developing countries' in Management Association, Information Resources (ed) *Climate Change and Environmental Concerns: Breakthroughs in Research and Practice*. Hershey, IGI Global.

Roetter, R. *et al.* (2007) *Science for Agriculture and Rural Development in Low-income Countries*. New York: Springer Science & Business Media.

Saito, K. A. *et al.* (1994) *Raising the Productivity of Women Farmers in Sub-Saharan Africa, Parts 63-230*. Washington D.C: World Bank publications.

Sharma, P. *et al.* (2010) *Women in Hill Agriculture*. New Delhi: Concept Publishing Company.

Siddiqui, T. and Billah, M. (2014) 'Adaptation to climate change in Bangaldesh: Migration, the missing link' in Vachani, S. and Usmani, J. *Adaptation to Climate Change in Asia*. Cheltenham: Edward Elgar Publishing.

Sugden, F. (2014) *A framework to Understand Gender and Structural Vulnerability to Climate Change in the Ganges River Basin: Lessons from Bangladesh, India and Nepal*. Colombo: International Water Management Institute.

Sultana, F. (2018) 'Gender and water in a changing climate: Challenges and opportunities' in Fröhlich, C. *et al.* (eds) *Water Security across the Gender Divide*. New York: Springer.

Swaminathan, M. S. (2017) *50 Years of Green Revolution: An Anthology of Research Papers*, Toh Tuck Link: World Scientific Publishing Company.

Tatlonghari, G. T. and Paris, T. R. (2013) 'Gendered adaptations to climate change: A case study from Philippines' In Alston, M. and Whittenburry, K. (eds) *Research, Action and Policy: Addressing the Gendered Impacts of Climate Change*. New York: Springer Science & Business Media.

UNESCO, (2013) World Social Science Report 2013: Changing Global Environments.

Verner, D. (2012) *Adaptation to a Changing Climate in the Arab Countries: A Case for Adaptation Governance and Leadership in Building Climate Resilience.* Washington D.C: World Bank Publications.

Wenden, A. L. (2011) 'Women and Climate change: Vulnerabilities and challenges' in Weissbecker, I. (ed) *Climate Change and Human Well-Being: Global Challenges and Opportunities.* New York: Springer Science & Business Media.

Wong, S. (2018) 'Decentralised off-grid solar pump irrigation systems in developing countries: Are they pro-poor, pro-environment, pro-women?' in Castro, P. *et al* (eds) *Climate change-resilient agriculture and agroforestry: Ecosystem.* New York: Springer.

World Bank, (2008) *Agriculture and rural development: Gender in agriculture source book.* Washington D.C: *World Bank.*

World Bank (2007), *Assessment of the economic impacts of climate change on agriculture in Zimbabwe.* Washington D.C: World Bank.

Yaro, J. A. *et al.* (2016) 'An assessment of determinants of adaptive capacity to climate change/variability in the rural savannah of Ghana' in Yaro, J. A. and Hesselberg, J. (eds) *Adaptation to Climate Change and Variability in Rural West Africa.* New York: Springer.

Zimbabwe Human Development Report, (2017) Climate Change and Human Development: Towards Building a Climate Resilient Nation.

Zimbabwe National Water Authority Act, Chapter 20:25.

Chapter Ten

Towards an Ecotheology? A Postcolonial Analysis of the Ecological Depletion at Kwenda Mission of the Methodist Church in Zimbabwe

Martin Mujinga

Introduction

The Methodist Church in Zimbabwe (MCZ) is one of the denominations with Eurocentric origins that enjoyed the privileges of the colonisers' and missionary land grabbing. The church benefitted eight farms of which seven have mission schools. Kwenda being one of the mission farms is having ecological challenges ranging from deforestation, soil erosion, veld fires and gullies. These environmental challenges are argued to be perpetuated by tenants and squatters making efforts to reclaim their lost heritage. These efforts increased in 2000 when the Zimbabwean government embarked on land redistribution. The movement into Kwenda mission like any other White farms was partly necessitated by President Mugabe's statement that;

> ...the land reform is consistent with biblical mandate to identify with the orphans, the widows and the landless. The land was given to the Blacks by God and that the struggle for land had been at the heart of the 1970s war of liberation. Zimbabweans were only taking back land that was originally stolen from them (Chitando, 2005:182).

Verstraelen (1998: 102) adds that 'the history of the land in Zimbabwe is the history of the alienation and marginalization of the peasantry. The land alienation process favoured the White settlers who occupied the more fertile parts of the country while the peasantry was forced into more marginal land'. Using postcolonial framework, the research seeks to explore the idea of the supremacy of God in an area with an environment that is suffering destruction.

Definition of Ecotheology

Ecotheology has not received much attention in the scholarly discourse in general and Africa in particular (Van Dyk, 2009: 188). This is in spite of the fact that Africa is replete with ecological challenges. Hallman (1994:4) testifies that, the global north has achieved materially rich standards of living environmentally at the expense of the global south which they colonised, dispossessed and exploited. For Pieris (1988:1): 'economically and politically, Africa is categorized in the so called "Third World countries" and Third worldliness is a situation of oppressive poverty, socially underside, politically oppressed, economically marginalized and religiously uninformed.' This statement has to be understood in the context of the enslavement and colonial eras when Africans were treated as nonhumans or as indistinct from nonhumans, including animals.

Ecotheology arose to address the plundering of natural resources by "humanity". In 1997, the Ecumenical Patriarch Bartholomew I emphasised that;

> To commit a crime against the natural world is a sin. For humanity to cause species to become extinct and to destroy the biological diversity of God's creation is sin; for humans to degrade the integrity of earth by causing changes in its climate, by stripping the earth of its natural forests, or destroying its wetlands; for humans to injure other humans with disease; for humans to contaminate the earth's waters, its land, its air, and its life, with poisonous substance; are all serious sins (McLaughlin, 2014).

Instead of being the stewards of God's creation, "humanity" plundered resources with the colonisers being the worst plunders. The major problem here is that while Eurocentric scholars are quick to allege that it is a sin to destroy the environment and biodiversity, they do not want to acknowledge that they committed sins and crimes by dispossessing, robbing and exploiting Africans. The centuries-old sins and crimes of enslavement and colonisation have neither been admitted nor have they been made good by the Euro-Americans many of whom are now ironically quick to allege that humanity, including Africans, is committing sins and crimes against the environment. This point was buttressed by Warikandwa and Nhemachena (2019:6) who stress that Africa is a victim of enslavement and economic robbery, theft, plunder and exploitation. According to Francis Bacon (1561-1626);

> Only in the last few centuries have technologies and attitudes of domination stemming from the Scientific Revolution turned the tables, enabling humans to threaten nature with deforestation and desertification, chemical pollution, destruction of habitats and species, nuclear fallout, and ozone depletion … humanity has gained an increasing ability to destroy nature as we know it today. Some groups of people have gained great power over nature and other human groups using the interlinked forces of science, politics and religion (Merchant, 2008:225).

It is evident that after the west plundered African resources, scholars like Daneel (1999: 57-59) claim that "humanity" used, misused and abused authority and so ecological degradation is prevalent in Africa. Daneel (1999: 57-59) further states that 'tree destroyers must be arrested because trees are brothers and sisters and must not be subject to human mindless destruction. The kingdom of God starts with the Garden of Eden meaning that trees come first and land is the priority'. The sad part of this argument is that colonialists also preferred land over African people – for them land and trees came first; land was the priority for colonialists as well. The irony is also that instead of also arguing for the arrest of those that enslaved, neocolonised and destroyed the lives of Africans, the scholar merely argues for the arrest of those that are alleged to be destroying trees, which the Eurocentric scholars address as brothers and sisters. Thus, Francis Bacon in Merchant (2008:739) opines that, like the human and the cosmos, nature, as a living being, has body, soul, and spirit. He argues that nature, as personified, has breasts, a bosom, and a womb, as well as circulatory, reproductive, and elimination systems. This assertion puts nature at par with humanity; but because no Euro-American leaders, scholars and institutions are advocating for the arrest of those that committed sins and crimes of enslaving and colonising Africans, I argue that Eurocentric scholars are in fact preferring nature over African human beings. The point raised by Daneel (1999) has a problem in as far as ecotheology in Africa is concerned. The two scholars present some animistic tendencies where Africans are viewed as indistinct from or even worse than trees, animals and the rest of nature. To say that those that destroy trees are sinful criminals who must be arrested while ignoring the sins and crimes of enslaving and colonising Africans is hypocritical.

According to the Audiopedia (2016) 'ecotheology is a form of constructive theology that focuses on the interrelationships of religion and nature particularly in light of the environmental concerns'. The discipline explores the interaction between ecological values, such as sustainability, and the human domination of nature (Merchant, 2008). The image of man's dominion over nature and other peoples is deeply rooted in western thought. Since Africa was colonised by the west, western environmental theories are being used to depict Africans as ecological domineers yet Africans are themselves oppressed and dominated by Euro-Americans who consider them to be indistinct from animals. Ecotheology thus seeks to uncover the theological basis for a proper relationship between God, humanity and the cosmos (Deane-Drummond, 2008: xii). Since the research is grounded in African discourse, it is important to note that this proper relationship between God and humanity also calls for the restitution, restoration and compensation to Africans, by the colonisers who stole African natural resources. In its nature, ecotheology raises a number of questions in an attempt to present God as the God of justice only to natural resources but not justice to African human beings. Such questions include;

'How do we understand ourselves and our role as creatures within a bio-diverse ecosystem? ... What do our religious traditions say about how we are to live in our societies, our environment, and our world? What does it mean to confess God as creator under the looming possibility of extinction or annihilation? What gives us hope for our world and how should we effect positive change for all?' (McLaughlin, 2014).

Since Ecotheology is a postcolonial theology, it arose as a force to challenge the widespread claim that God will judge the Africans in particular for using, abusing and misusing the environment. The theology seeks to clarify the fact that, the postcolonial environmental crisis in Africa is emanating from crisis of neoimperial plunder, robbery and theft of other people's natural resources. Because economic, social, cultural and political crises impact on the environment, I argue that the colonial dispossession, robbery and exploitation of Africans is also causing the present environmental crisis. The crisis may not be primarily an environmental crisis but a colonial and economic crisis. Mugambi (2003:35) maintains that Ecotheology is a theology that is not controlled by race, "tribe", social set up or any form of human oppression, but the oppression of creation in general. However, it is important to note that ecological crisis in Africa is first of all a crisis of colonisation and enslavement of Africans, as such, the behaviour of humanity is contrary to the ultimate purpose of creation in God's glory where humanity was made special to rule all creation. Euro-American transnational corporations continue to dispossess, rob and exploit Africans, in the process they destroy the environments belonging to Africans – thus, environmental destruction and ecotheology are racial and neoimperial issues. In fact, Euro-America would want to play God in the world while ironically destroying African environments.

The relationship of theology to the modern ecological crisis became an intense issue of debate in western academia in 1967, following the publication of the article, 'The Historical Roots of Our Ecological Crisis', by Lynn White. White (1967) put forward a theory that the Christian model of human dominion over nature has led to environmental devastation (1967:34). In 1968, The Sixth Resolution of Lambeth Conference of Anglican Bishops (2003:10) urged Christians to ensure human responsibility and stewardship over nature in particular. They wrote that 'the relationship with animals and with regards to the conservation of soil and prevention of the pollution of the air and oceans must be a priority'. Ecotheology thus deals with challenging the human dominion over nature. This challenge is in-spite of the fact that Africans still have unresolved historical wrongs such as enslavement and colonisation. The major problem with arguments that attribute environmental destruction to domination over nature is that they erroneously presuppose that domination is the problem that explains destruction. By extension they presuppose that God Himself is destructive because He dominates over humanity and nature in general. In essence arguments that problematise domination, by extension, vilify God and saints (who are deemed to be also domineering and patriarchal). Thus such arguments, problematising domination, do not seek to serve God but they seek to condemn Him. For this reason, as far as Africans are concerned, problems of environmental destruction do not emanate from domination but they emanate from colonial dispossession, robbery and exploitation. Colonialists did not dominate African nature but they stole African nature, including natural resources, and this is where problems of environmental destruction are coming from.

Postcolonial Theoretical Framework

Postcolonial theory emerged in the 1970s. Young (2009) defines postcolonial to mean resistance to the colonial at any time, literally in the case of decolonised societies, and ideologically for still colonised societies. The use of the word "resistance" by Young in the African set up skirts the essentials of decoloniality like reparations, restitution and restoration of what was stolen during the colonial era. When Africans engage neo-colonialists and neoimperialism, their objective is not necessarily to resist but to get restitution, reparations and restoration of their resources that were stolen. The core issue is not resistance but it has to do with restitution, restoration and reparations for enslavement and colonial crimes. Gandhi (1998:4) nebulously defines postcoloniality as a process of returning to the colonial scene that discloses a relationship of reciprocal antagonism and desire between the colonisers and the colonised. For Gandhi (1998:8):

> The colonial past is not simply a reservoir of raw political experiences and practices to be theorized from the detached and enlightened perspective of the present, but it is also a scene of the intense discursive and conceptual activity characterized by a profusion of thought and writing about the cultural and political identities of the colonized subjects.

282

The history of Kwenda mission is both political and theological. It is political because MCZ benefitted the land from the colonialists who dispossessed Africans. It is theological because the mission was established as one of the ecclesiastical centres during the colonial era (Mujinga, 2017). As such, a discussion on ecotheology of Kwenda mission, entails visiting the colonial past so that it will speak to the postcolonial and decolonial life of the MCZ today.

Brief History of Kwenda Mission

The historical development of MCZ, has been oversubscribed that it is not important to labour much on the already researched area (see Mujinga, 2017). However, for this research, it suffices to state that Kwenda Mission is one of the products of colonisation, partitioning and evangelisation of Africa into accepting Western Christianity. It is one of the eight mission stations of the MCZ namely Epworth, Chemhanza, Waddilove, Moleli, Thekwane, Pakame, and Sandringham. The Mission lies about one hundred and sixty kilometres South-East of Harare in the Sadza area in Chikomba district of Mashonaland East Province (Mujinga, 2011: 40).

Kwenda mission comprises the farm, which is the major area of research, and primary and secondary schools of the MCZ. According to the Title Deeds of the mission signed on 17 December 1911 by the British South African Company; Kwenda mission has 31 747149 Acres. The mission is situated at the centre of three mountains namely Chimedza which demarcated the primary and secondary schools, Mugoroondo which stretches from the high school to the communal lands and Mudege which is behind the primary school and also stretches to the other side of the communal lands (Mujinga, 2011:41). The Mission is surrounded by four chiefs namely, Chief Kwenda who occupies the Northwestern side and whose name was given to the mission, Chief Mtekedza on the Southwest, Mkandatsamba on the Southeast and Mhurushomana on the East (Patsanza, 2011).

Cecil John Rhodes allocated land to the Wesleyan Methodist missionaries who later established a mission station (Zvobgo, 1991). The coming of the missionaries created disputes among the locals. A case in point was Chief Kwenda and chief Neshangwe. The missionaries intervened in the land dispute and gave the land to Kwenda (Njanjari, 2011). The first assumption of the missionary intervention is that they were not interested in solving the land row, but to create a further dispute among the locals so that they would not join forces against the Whites. Second, they were also interested in the land as such they chose the weaker characters like Chief Kwenda who would not resist them when they wanted to possess the land for missionary activities.

Since chief Kwenda was now in charge of the land, he invited his other brothers so that when Neshangwe would think of fighting back, Kwenda would seek defence from his brothers and the missionaries. Chasi; who was Chief Kwenda further invited the missionaries and evangelists from South Africa to come to evangelise his area (Njanjari, 2011). This action made the surrounding chiefs who had squabbles with him to organise the killing of the missionaries and the evangelists. Kwenda gave sanctuary to the missionaries and sent some of his people to escort them to Salisbury (Harare) to report to Rev John White. Rev White appealed for assistance from the colonisers who sent an army to Kwenda to maintain peace and order. It was from this action that Rev John White proposed to give a tribute to Chief Kwenda by naming the school after him (Njanjari, 2011).

The mission was established as a place of education and evangelisation of Africans, in order to strengthen the faith of the converts and to pacify them (Mujinga, 2011). The mission station was a place where those who would have repented would go and stay. Although the missionaries were more corrupt themselves, they regarded the village as the corrupt place because some locals resisted the Europeanisation of their culture in the name of foreign religion. In spite of the fact that the missionaries acted unBiblically by dividing the locals, by taking their land and bribing them, they set the rules, including, 'those people who were found going against the Biblical principles were chased from the farm as renegades' (Zvobgo, 1991:65). Missionaries acted unBiblically by stealing African land and livestock (see Schmidt, 1992) yet they demonised Blacks as unBiblical with respect to polygamy, drunkenness and traditional beliefs. Since the missionaries were part of the colonial masters, their sins of colonisation, disposition, exploitation and plundering were not challenged.

The mission was also a "sanctuary" where the faithful locals would be kept in the environment of worship and receive free education. Rev John White was quoted as saying 'if our work is to be a success as we desire, we must have better educated men' (Zvobgo, 1991:45). All the displaced people lived a poverty stricken life while those in the mission enjoyed good life with fertile land and good vegetation. When the land redistribution was introduced in 2000, Kwenda mission became the target of the locals seeking to reclaim their lost heritage.

The history of the land in Zimbabwe is centred on the dispossession, alienation and marginalisation of the indigenous people. The land theft favoured the White settlers who occupied the more fertile parts of the country while the indigenous people were forced into more marginal land (Bakare, 1993). However, of interest to note is that, when the land redistribution was introduced in 2000, Kwenda mission like most of the mission farms, did not suffer ["the official"] land repossession by the war veterans. However villagers started to "invade" the mission piecemeal. The surrounding fence was stolen and the environment was destroyed for firewood and medicinal plants, among other reasons.

The Land Question in Zimbabwe

The colonisation of the country by the White colonialists in 1890 signalled the systematic subjugation and dispossession of the indigenous Black population. Bakare (1993) cites President Mugabe as saying:

It makes no sense of our liberation struggle that the majority of our peasant families have remained outcast of our Land Tenure system...at independence there was joy of liberation and a great anticipation of regaining stolen land..." (1993: vii). One issue that remains central to the land issue in Zimbabwe is, "land was stolen by the colonizers.

The theft and resultant Land Tenure system benefitted the Whites and oppressed the Blacks. There were wars of plunder and looting, and the Blacks were defeated and were then pushed from the "central watershed" to the peripheries of the national agricultural economy. When land allocations were done after these battles, the displacements of African peasants during the wars were not considered. Thus, 'reserves were demarcated in areas where Africans were living particularly the more densely settled areas, and little account was taken of the population displacements that had occurred during the rebellion'(Masengwe, 2011:22). As a result of series of legislations (Bakare, 1993), the Black population was restricted to (reserved) Tribal Trust Lands (Communal Areas) that, by the 1970s, were to emerge as the overcrowded, degraded, and poverty stricken domicile of the majority of the indigenous population.

The overall effect of the restriction on land ownership and utilisation was that by 1980 42% of the land in Zimbabwe, being marginally productive and drought prone land, was reserved for Blacks; 51% being the more fertile, better watered, more productive and better serviced regions, was technically reserved for Whites (Masengwe, 2011:22). Cattle belonging to Blacks were taken on the pretext that large numbers cattle would lead to overgrazing. Grazing rights were restricted, water for irrigation was reserved for large-scale agriculture, pass laws were introduced and farmers were not allowed to grow some of the most profitable crops, such as coffee (Munro, 1998). Until the land redistribution, some records do indicate that there were farms that were neither utilised for farming nor occupied for any commercial activity because some White settlers were never in commercial agriculture (Munro, 1998). This colonial system of land ownership was unfair and so it attracted African resistance to European settler possession and domination in landownership, which partly increased land fights and the consequent ecological destruction (Bonarjee, 2013).

In the period from 1980 to 1990 the post-independence Zimbabwean Government respected the Lancaster House Agreement and focused its efforts on addressing the land question, on resettlement and projects to modernise African agriculture (Bonarjee, 2013:4). The policy of 'reconciliation' prevented any substantive reform to the legacy of White monopoly over the economic sphere from being undertaken. In Zimbabwe, as elsewhere in southern Africa, disenfranchisement of rural households was part of an active policy pursued by the colonial governments.

Fast Track Land Reform Programme (FTLRP) and its Impact on Ecology

Bakare (1993) takes us through the different theological, historical and legal debates about the land issue in Zimbabwe. The coming of the FTLRP, in 2000 was not a new idea. As early as 1993, Bakare had professed that:

> The land issue is existential and has to be dealt with here in the present where the Kingdom of God has already began. Salvation is now, not tomorrow and justice is to be experienced in the present and not left to the future. The least of Jesus' brothers are the landless, homeless, squatters, unemployed, poor and hungry who need to be cared for now (1993:4).

The FTLRP was triggered by a number of factors including Bakare's theology of land in Zimbabwe. Nationwide, the FTLRP was politically and economically motivated and organised by occupations of largely White owned large scale commercial farms after Zimbabweans rejected a new draft Constitution at a referendum in February 2000 (Fox, Chigumira and Rowntree, 2007). When the constitutional procedure failed, the next step was to repossess land by force.

President Mugabe categorically stated that, land was given to the Blacks by God and they were only taking back land that was originally stolen from them (Chitando, 2005:182; Bakare, 1993). Mugabe further declared that, 'his' FTLRP which had taken eleven million hectares of mainly White-owned commercial farmland and redistributed it to rich and poor Black Zimbabweans, had ensured the success of his revolution (Derman, 2002:2). He further states that, 'gone are the days when Africa produced tragic revolutions. We have to defend our policies and pursue them unhindered - Africa for Africans!' (Derman, 2002:2). The FTLRP was initiated in Zimbabwe, ostensibly to redress the racial imbalance in land ownership.

Although Mugabe was aggressive on land redistribution, his policy on mission farms was clear that they were not supposed to be "invaded". Matondi (2012:9) states that, 'the land that was not legally gazetted for acquisition and remain in the hands of its "original" owners holding their title deeds. Land owned by parastatals, churches, schools, colleges, universities and mines was supposed to be reserved'.

The FTLRP took place under adverse macroeconomic and unstable political conditions (Chigumira, 2010). In the early years of the reforms, the programme captured international attention and imagination, while in Zimbabwe, it radically altered people's lives and livelihoods, and at the same time reawakened people's memories of the past. In this case, the land reform programme was not simply about land, but also about people, especially the farmers and the communities in which they lived, originated from and settled in. The programme radically transformed the society, with former landowners being pushed aside, farmworkers having their livelihoods 'withdrawn', and new beneficiaries walking into new commercial land, without structured or sustained support (Buckle, 2001).

In the FTLRP, land was seen as an economic resource for development, employment creation and livelihoods, the struggle was couched in the *rambai makashinga* (don't lose hope) jingles, song and dance on the national broadcaster both television and radio. The FTLRP also known as the *Third Chimurenga (third struggle)*, sought to redistribute productive land to households and individuals. In 2000 FTLRP policy was enacted to allow Blacks to take land, reversing all previous laws on land. Advancing Black interests was not a process free from quests to control the environment (Masengwe, 2011:35).

In spite of Mugabe's clarion call not to "invade" mission farms, "squatters" from the surrounding of Kwenda continued to move into the mission unlawfully. In definition, squatters are a diverse group of people composed of migrants from other communal areas, as well as long-term residents who did not receive land for farming, and family members of residents not registered (Derman, 2002:11). In a brief comment upon the communal areas by the Presidential Land Review Committee on the implementation of the FTLRP (known as the Utete Report): it states that;

Decongestion had not significantly taken place in the communal lands. This situation had been worsened by some land reform beneficiaries who maintained dual homes i.e. both in the communal areas and in the new resettlement schemes owing to the uncertainty of tenure (Derman, 2002:16).

As Chigumira (2010:1), rightly puts it, 'The clearing of woodland, bushland and grassland for settlement, cultivation and energy consumption has reduced vegetation cover and will initially lead to lowered biological productivity and impacts on soil conditions'. Kwenda mission fell prey to these challenges. Furthermore, household livelihood struggles in response to the resettlement process, climatic variability and macroeconomic environment, have led the sale of firewood, gold mining, gold panning and sand extraction for building purposes. These activities impacted negatively on runoff processes, particularly the transportation of sediments and the triggering of gully erosion as well as land degradation (Fox *et al*, 2007). Rural areas were the most affected by deforestation.

The main cause of deforestation in the so called "tribal" areas has been the extension of croplands under conditions of increasing population pressure: as a result, the collection of firewood and building materials became increasingly more difficult (Masengwe, 2011:33). Animals in most Zimbabwean rural areas overgraze and cause tracks on the ground. Where there is poor plant cover, sloppy, weak soils that can be easily eroded like Kwenda, animals contributed heavily to soil erosion. During the White regime, laws and policies reduced animal overgrazing by enacting that a family needed to have only ten cattle. Cutting down trees and overgrazing affected much of the land in rural areas. The washing away of top soils reduced the productive capacity of the land. Much of these soils were washed into rivers and dams. The increasing volumes of sand on river beds lower the water tables (Masengwe, 2011:34).

Gullies are formed when large amounts of soil are washed away by heavy or continuous rains. If they are not controlled the gullies become large (Masengwe, 2011:36). These features are common in Kwenda mission leading to challenges in vegetation growth. Masengwe (2011) presents the major challenge posed by deforestation in Wedza, which affected Save River. He argues that, "deforestation has led to the silting of the Save River and change in rainfall patterns. Save is one of the biggest rivers in Mashonaland East that stretches through Kwenda area. The river is less than ten kilometres from Kwenda mission.

The Impact of Ecological Destruction at Kwenda Mission

Kwenda mission has two categories of people who stay in the mission namely the tenants and the "squatters". The mission is faced with serious challenges of such "illegal" tenants and "squatters". According to the Project Officer of the Methodist Church in Zimbabwe, Careful Chikomba (2011), legal tenants refer to those tenants who have applied, to the Church, for the land for farming; those who were given offer letters by the Church and the District Administrators and are paying their rentals prescribed annually by MCZ. On the other hand, "illegal" tenants refer to the siblings of these people who are now living in the farm without the consent of the Church. These "illegal" tenants are not abiding by the rules and regulations of MCZ which are stipulated in the Lease Agreement summarized as follows:

Every tenant must be a member of MCZ and is expected to attend Church service. (ii) Not expected to work on Sunday. (iii) Are not allowed to brew or drink beer/alcohol and to engage in traditions ancestral worship. (iv)Tenants are not allowed to cut down trees, cause veld fires or soil erosion because this retards development. It is the responsibility of the tenant to prevent the destruction of the environment. (v) Tenancy in the mission farm is not inherited. (vi)Tenants on mission farm are expected to pay development fees in addition to their annual rent. (vii) Goats are not allowed on mission farm. (viii) Tenants are not allowed to keep more than 12 head of cattle (MCZ Mission Farms Memorandum of Understanding (1996).

Although MCZ got its autonomy from the British Conference in 1977, its Mission Farm Memorandum is a Eurocentric surrogate document. The document makes it clear that anything that causes any problem to the mission is not allowed. It is worth noting that the issues of "illegal" tenants and squatters had always been a problem to the church. On 11 March 1997, Judah Gwatiringa who was the Administrative Officer of MCZ wrote to the then Member of Parliament for Chikomba Constituency expressing the challenges of the church caused by "squatters" (Mujinga, 2011). This letter is a clear testimony of how Kwenda has been vulnerable to tenants.

Squatters "invade" the forbidden land without permission. Squatters at Kwenda mission comprise of the victims of a draconian 2005 clean up exercise *"Murambatsvina"*. Some people were just ferried to rural areas by the government (Njanjari, 2011). Secondly, there are also communal people who are seeking refuge from the poor soils in the communal areas. Some of the settlers are even putting their gardens less than five meters away from the Save river (Mujinga, 2011:51).

The Former Bishop of Kwenda District Rev Aaron Makiwa argues that legal tenants are putting their children on the peripheries of the farm in order to protect the mission from communal "invasions" but to no avail (Mujinga, 2011). The farm offers the only grazing area in the vicinity. The "invasions" frustrate the Church which is also losing the fence to thieves from the surrounding villages. The same villagers cut down trees for firewood for themselves and for their friends in the communal land. They use the trees for their gardens, fencing and making kraals (Mujinga, 2011:54).

MCZ has been grappling with this challenge for some years and this is demonstrated by the Church's 1998 Conference resolution to hand over the big portion of the farm to the government for resettlement. The resolution states that;

> The unregistered tenants and those who have entered into formal agreements have faced the danger of the misuse of the land and the consequent lack of suitable direction and purpose which leads to non-productivity. The church resolved to take a smaller portion for missionary work and leave the remainder to sell to the government to be used in their resettlement programme (MCZ, 1998:23).

Regrettably, the government refused the offer because the land was no-longer arable and the relationship of the church and state would not allow the state to buy the land from it (Mujinga, 2011:56). From the resolution MCZ was going to sell almost ninety one percent

291

and remain with nine percent of the total mission land. Faced with such a predicament, MCZ had to endure environmental degradation from the "squatters" ranging from land degradation which results in soil erosion. Erosion was also caused by grazing of the tenants' herd, grazing of the communal flocks, cutting down of trees and stream bank cultivation (Njanjari, 2011). Other challenges in Kwenda include gullies emanating from roads which are created by communal people as they come to "poach" firewood in the farm for various reasons leading to deforestation.

According to Phiri (1986:161), the rate at which the environment is being destroyed is a great concern. Methodist Annual statistics show that Kwenda Secondary School, had a population of 68 teachers, 795 students, Primary School had 14 teachers, 487 students, which gives a total of 1364 people." (MCZ Handbook, 2010:84-88). This census does not include the families of the teaching staff, non-teaching staff, legal tenants, illegal tenants and squatters. The number might come to more than 2000 people who benefit from the mission's forest where they get firewood (Mujinga, 2011).

The situation is worsened by the high school which is a boarding school that uses firewood as a source of energy. Thus, trees are cut on a daily basis. The school has big cords of firewood. Such a scenario causes serious deforestation on the mission (Mujinga, 2011:57). An interview with the Information and Communication Manager of the Forestry Commission, Marufu (2011), shows that people cut trees for firewood. Villagers surrounding Kwenda mission also use firewood for kilns to bake bricks. Other villagers use firewood in their tobacco barns.

Besides the foregoing, challenges in Kwenda mission include veld fires especially during the winter seasons. Veld fires are common in Zimbabwe and so organisations like Environmental Management Agency (EMA), Forestry Commission, Environmental Management Services and Local Environmental and the Southern African Research and Documentation Centre proscribe the veld fires. In 2011, the then Minister of Environment and Natural Resources Management Honourable Francis Nhema launched a nationwide fire awareness campaign that saw him visiting all the provinces conscientising people on the dangers of veld fires. The objective was to reduce incidences of fire and avert destruction of ecosystems, property and human lives (Kangata, 2010:2).

EMA statistics for 2011 shows 7 409 fire incidences that affected ninety five thousand hectares of land. Nhema (2011) states that uncontrolled fires have wide and far reaching effects that disrupts everyday life. They are a cause of severe environmental degradation in Zimbabwe. More specifically, veld fires reduce land cover thus exposing the land to agents of accelerated soil erosion. In Kwenda Mission veld fires are caused by human activities like clearing the forest for the preparation of agricultural land, improving grazing area and hunting; fires are also used in livelihood activities such as honey harvesting, cooking or to keep warm (Mujinga, 2011:55). Apart from the mentioned causes of fire, research by Southern African Network for the Division of Early Warning and Assessment shows that;

> High temperatures add the conducive climate that renders Zimbabwe prone to fires. The country experiences two distinct season's summer and autumn which facilitates the growth of grasses and other herbaceous vegetation and the dry winter/spring when temperatures are initially cold and then very hot affectively drying the vegetation. The hot and dry season is ideal for fire as there in enough dry fuel loads, low humidity and the temperatures are high enough to sustain ignition (Kangata, 2010:2).

The winter season also tallies with bees collecting nectar for honey. Poachers collect honey by burning the bees and eventually, fire breaks into the mission farm. In addition, there are stipulated days of resting in the communal areas and the best recreational activity will be in the mission farm hunting. To avoid hunting in the "big jungle" which seems to be dangerous and disturbing, people resort to burning grass first. Equally so, both "illegal" tenants and "squatters" extend their farming land by "illegal" means of cutting and burning the trees and grass. Poachers even drop lit cigarettes and in this way, they cause veld fires.

The Ecotheological analysis of this chapter demonstrates that people in Kwenda mission destroyed the environment. Fire destroys grasslands and this has a negative impact on the biological diversity. The reduction in the grass cover and the destruction of the habitats can result in the extinction of some small animals. The impact of veld fire on the fauna is very significant. In Kwenda mission, few species are in existence because of this problem; the breeding patterns of wild animals like hares, impala, and kudu among others have been affected. Cowling (1997:348).) argues that, winter is the breeding period of most birds and animals. When grasses have been burnt, soil remains bare and loses its protective cover. This results in the soil becoming loose and susceptible to agents of erosion. The patterns of environmental destruction are traceable to the colonial dispossession and exploitation of indigenous Africans who apart from losing ownership and control over their resources were also crammed in reserves or dry and poorly endowed communal land.

Ecotheology as Confessional Theology for MCZ at Kwenda Mission

According to Hallman (1994:14) environment and ecology are not merely natural concerns that can be left to physical scientists, business people and politicians, the use, misuse and abuse of the environment affect everyone including the unborn children. Environmental crisis presents the church with an evangelical opportunity. In spite of the fact that MCZ got the land through the coloniser, a postcolonial critique of the MCZ reaction compels the Church to confess the sin of depleting the environment in Kwenda mission. The Book of Joel in the Old Testament is the centre of environmental protection that MCZ should learn from and confess. Joel chapter 1 laments that:

> The animals groan, the herds of cattle wander about because there is no pasture for them, even the flocks of sheep are dazed... for fire has devoured the pastures of the wilderness and flames have burned all the trees of the field. Even the wild animals cry to you because the water houses are dried up... fire devours in front of the land behind them a flame burns. Before them the land is like the Garden of Eden, but after them, a desolate wilderness and nothing escapes them (Joel 1:1ff).

One of the reasons why MCZ should engage in earthkeeping is from the sense of guilt for the ecological damages that some humans have caused in the area where they are the custodians. Christianity bears a huge burden of guilty for the environmental crisis. Christianity has encouraged some members of humanity to think of themselves as nature's absolute looters, in their thought, everything that exists was designed for them (Hallman, 1994) and therefore they do not hesitate to grab even what is not theirs. This is a sin of commission by humanity. Creation is groaning (Romans 8:3-23) because of ecological abuse, and because of dispossession and exploitation since the enslavement and colonial eras. The Theology of Creation is radically attentive to the experience of creation itself and these lamentations must not be oblivious to the groaning of Africans who have endured exploitation, dispossession and robbery since the eras of enslavement and colonisation. Africans are also part of Creation and so their suffering must not be covered up by neocolonial and neoimperial pretences of caring for the environment – or what is called environmental escapism (Hughes, 2010; Nhemachena & Warikandwa, 2019). The Christian God is not separated from creation, including from Africans as part of Creation. What is in pain, suffering and most abused today is the creation, including Africans. It is essential if ecotheology and liberation theology become the proper business of theology today. Ecology and Africans are not mere objects of "human ownership" and unqualified manipulation but they are God's handiwork and should be treated as such with care and respect. The phrase "human ownership" is inclusive because the colonialists and their descendants claim ownership and control over resources belonging to others. In fact colonialists and their descendants are still stealing resources that belong to others and claiming that they own them. It is only Africans that are denied ownership of their resources – and this is reminiscent of enslavement and colonial eras. Ecotheology as constructive theology continues to challenge the colonial tendencies that are being presented in many forms to degrade Africa into a desert and to turn African lives into neocolonial cannibalistic desserts. Evidently, some Churches, including the Church of Euthanasia [headed by Reverend Chris Korda], have already been established in Euro-America to promote suicide, euthanasia, cannibalism, homosexuality and human infertility [by the poor] under the guise of saving the environment from supposed collective human indiscretion (see Nhemachena & Mawere this volume; Forest, n.d; Mukherjee, 2016). Eco-injustice in Kwenda mission is a matter of urgency because many African preachers have become so obsessed to preach heaven and hell which are eschatological at the expense of the current lives of the ecology and Africans that are groaning and bleeding in the hands of neocolonialists and neoimperialists. The church is a centre of many people hence ecotheology and liberation theology have to be part of teaching in the church, community and political arenas.

Conclusion

During the process of writing this chapter, a number of issues came out clear. First, the Methodist Church in Zimbabwe inherited land as the privileges of the colonisers' including missionary land grabbing. Most of these mission farms in general and Kwenda in particular are experiencing ecological challenges perpetuated by tenants and "squatters" seeking to reclaim their lost heritage. Politically, in 2000 the Zimbabwean government embarked on land redistribution this was an opportunity for the Black majority to regain their land that was stolen by the colonisers. Socially, land distribution was a way to emancipate the Black populace since the colonial land alienation process favoured the White colonialists while the African indigenous people were forced into more marginal land. Second, environmental degradation is also a making of the colonisers who plundered African resources. Ecotheology arose to address the plundering of natural resources by "humanity". Third, the kingdom of God starts with the Garden of Eden meaning that trees come first and land is the priority – yet it is noted herein that this logic, that trees come first, was sadly also foundational to colonisation – colonialists preferred land over African people. In this sense, by dispossessing Africans, colonialists are the ones that deprived and took Africans from the Garden of Eden and now they hypocritically blame Africans for the disappearance of the Garden of Eden that was stolen by the same colonialists and imperialists. Fourth, since environment and ecology are not merely natural concerns that can be left to physical scientists, business people and politicians, the use, misuse and abuse of the environment affects everyone including the unborn children. Environmental crisis presents the church with an evangelical opportunity.

References

Bakare, S. (1993) *My right to land- in the Bible and in Zimbabwe: A Theology of Land in Zimbabwe*. Harare: Delsink Publishers.

Bonarjee, M. F.B. (2013) 3 decades of land reform in Zimbabwe. Perspectives of social justice & poverty alleviation. Bergen Ressurssenter for Internasjonal Utvikling.

Buckle, C. (2001) *African tears: The Zimbabwe land invasion*. Tamarisk: Covos Day Books.

Chikomba, C. (2011) MCZ Projects Officer, Interview, Harare, 17 March.

Chigumira, E. (2010) Livelihoods *after Land Reform in Zimbabwe. My land, my resource: assessment of the impact of the fast track land reform programme on the natural environment, Kadoma District, Zimbabwe.* Working Paper 14. Available on programme (www.larl.org.za).

Chitando. E. (2005) "Sacred Remnant? Church Land in Zimbabwe's Fast Track Resettlement Programme," *In. Studies in World Christianity, 11 (2)*, Edinburgh.

Cowling, R.M. (1997) *Vegetation of the Southern Africa*. Cambridge: Cambridge University Press.

Deane-Drummond, C. (2008) Ecotheology. Darton: Todd Ltd.

Daneel. M.L. (1999) *African Earthkeepers: Environmental Mission and Liberation in Christian perspectives, (2),* Pretoria: University of South Africa.

Derman, B. (2006) *After Zimbabwe's Fast Track Land Reform: Preliminary observations on the near future of Zimbabwe's efforts to resist globalization. Colloque international "Les frontières de la question foncière At the frontier of land issues",* Montpellier.

Forest, J. J. F. (n.d) The Final Act: Ideologies of Catastrophic Terror https://www.aclu.org/sites/default/files/field_document/ACL URM002778

Fox, R.C, Chigumira, E and Rowntree, K.M. (2007) 'On the Fast Track to land degradation? A case of the impact of the Fast Track Land Reform Programme in Kadoma District Zimbabwe', Unpublished report.

Hallman. D.G. (1994) Ecotheology, voices from South and North, New York: Orbis Books.

Hughes, D. M. (2010) Whiteness in Zimbabwe: Race, Landscape, and the Problem of Belonging. New York: Palgrave Macmillan.

Gandhi, L. (1998) Postcolonial theory: A critical Introduction, Crow's Nest: Allen & Unwin.

Kangata. S. (2010) Environmental Management Agency Bulletin, 1(1), Harare: EMA Publications.

Masengwe, G. (2011) Land reform and the theology of Development: The Zimbabwean Fast Track Land Reform Program and Environmental Ethics. Pretoria: University of South Africa.

Matondi, P. (2012) Zimbabwe's Fast Track Land Reform, London: Zed Books.

McLaughlin. R. P. (2014) Preservation and protest: theological foundations for an eco-eschatological ethics. Available at http://fortresspress.com/product/environment-economy-and-christian-ethics-alternative-views- Retrieved on. January 30.

Merchant, C. (2008). "The Violence of Impediments: Francis Bacon and the Origins of Experimentation," Isis, 99. 731-760.

Mugabe, R.G. (2005) Address by President Mugabe on the commemoration of Heroes' Day at the National Heroes' Acre. The Herald. August 9.

Mugambi. J.N.K. (2003) Christian theology and environmental responsibility. Nairobi: Acton Publishers.

Mukherjee, S. R. (2016) Para-Religions of Climate Change: Humanity, Eco-Nihilism, Apocalypse, in Bristow, T. et al., (eds) A Cultural History of Climate Change. Taylor & Francis

Mujinga. M. (2011) Towards an Ecotheology: A Case Study for Kwenda Mission of the Methodist Church in Zimbabwe. Unpublished MA. Dissertation, University of Zimbabwe.

Mujinga, M. (2017) The Historical Development of Methodism: A North-South paradigm. Harare: Connexional Bookshop.

Munro W. A. (1998) The Moral Economy of the State: Conservation, Community Development and State Making in Zimbabwe. Athens, Ohio: Ohio University Centre for International Studies.

Nhemachena, A. & Warikandwa, T. V. (2019) *From African Peer Review Mechanisms to African Queer Review Mechanisms? Robert Gabriel Mugabe, Empire & the Decolonisation of African Orifices.* Bamenda: Langaa RPCIG.

Njanjari, P. (2011) *Interview,* Kwenda Primary School, 21 March.

Patsanza. M. (2011) *Interview,* Kwenda Primary School, 21 March.

Pieris, A. (1988) *An Asian theology of liberation,* New York: Orbis Books.

Phiri, I.A. (1986) "The Role of Women in Preserving the Environment." in, *Women Healing the Earth: Third World Women on Ecology, Feminism and Religion,* Mary knoll: Orbis Books.

Schmidt, E. (1992) *Peasants, Traders & Wives: Shona Women in the History of Zimbabwe, 1870-1939.* Harare: Baobab Book.

The Audiopedia. (2016). *Ecotheology: meaning, definition & explanation.* Published on Oct 5, 2016. Available at.https://www.youtube.com/watch?v=04-KyAN03Kg. Retrieved on January 30, 2019.

The Methodist Church in Zimbabwe, Minutes of Conference, (1998) *Rationalization in the use of farms the title of which is registered in the name of the Methodist Church.,* August

The Methodist Church in Zimbabwe. (1996) *Mission Farms Memorandum of Understanding.*

Van Dyk, P. (2009) Challenges for Ecotheology. *OTE* 22. (1), pp. 186-204.

Verstraelen, F.J. (1998) *Zimbabwean Realities and Christian Responses.* Gweru: Mambo Press.

Warikandwa, T. V. & Nhemachena, A (2019) Grid-locked African Economic Sovereignty: Decolonising the Neo-imperial Socio-economic and Legal Force-fields in the 21st Century. Langaa. RPCIA.

White. L. (1967) *"The historical roots of our ecologic crisis:* Science 155, (3667)."Washington Meeting of A.A.A.S Journal.

Young, R.J.C. (2009) What is the Postcolonial? Available at. https://journalhosting.ucalgary.ca/index.php/ariel/article/download/33560/27604, retrieved on Jan 31 2019.

Zvobgo, C.J.M. (1991) *The Wesleyan Methodist Missions in Zimbabwe 1891-1945,* Harare: University of Zimbabwe Publications.

Chapter Eleven

Land (Dis)possession and Environmental Destruction in Zimbabwe: A Critical Reflection of Events since the Beginning of the 21st Century

Alex Munyonga

Introduction

Evidence of environmental degradation is manifest in Zimbabwe, as in many other states. Severe gullying, massive deforestation, uncontrolled fires, siltation of water courses and the like are witnessed. A close assessment shows that the lack of care about the environment is a manifestation of absence of ownership and control of land and its resources. Indigenous Zimbabweans were dispossessed and robbed of their land and other resources and they have had to endure this imperial crime for centuries since the year 1890. Colonialists not only exploited African unpaid labour but they also stole the land, minerals, cattle, sheep, goats and other livestock. Because the British granted Zimbabweans empty independence that was shy of restitution, restoration and compensation for imperial crimes, Zimbabweans embarked on repossession of their land and other resources in the year 2000. This chapter argues that it was paradoxical and hypocritical for colonialists and their descendants to expect Africans to care for African environment that had been stolen from the indigenous people. Africans need to own and control the environment in order for them to take good care of the same. The argument is that, it is hypocritical for those that have stolen African resources to expect the Africans to take care of what has been stolen from them. Much as it is often argued that productivity on White farms is dependent on ownership or tenure over the farms, I argue that similarly good care for the environment is also dependent on ownership and control over such environments. In this vein, Africans who have been imperially dispossessed and robbed of their land and other resources cannot be expected to care for the land and other environmental resources that are stolen from them. For Africans to take good care of the environment on the continent, it is necessary to ensure that they recover ownership and control over their environments – at the present moment even African states do not own and control environments in Africa. It is the West in the form of transnational corporations, descendants of colonialists, western nongovernmental organisations and western "civil" society organisations that own and control the environment in Africa yet they expect the dispossessed Africans to care for the same environment. To expect Africans to care for what they neither own nor control is to replicate the enslavement and colonial exploitation. Put in other words, Africans may have good indigenous knowledge systems to care for the environment but if they do not repossess ownership and control over the environment, including land and minerals, their knowledge systems will not be meaningful – without ownership and control of the land, the knowledge systems may not even be implemented efficiently. The other point that will be made in this chapter is that a return to indigenous knowledge systems necessarily implies a return to African indigenous ownership of land and other resources.

The Traditional African Environmental Ethic

It is the window from which one views the world that determines what he/she sees. A people's worldview is the password to unlock their understanding of life and its processes. African environmental history has a complex conjuncture, adaptation, cultural and environmental flux. It is interesting to note that traditional African society had viable industries, including trade but there was no damage to the environment. Economic activities such as mining of minerals like gold, iron ore, copper and the like were witnessed. Iron smelting, wood carvings, animal rearing, crop production and hunting were other economic activities that were conducted (Nhemachena & Warikandwa, 2017). Despite the vibrant nature of the socio-economic activities in these traditional societies there was a lot of consideration for sustainable utilisation of the environment.

The Relative Sustainability Model (Kwashirai, 2010) provides that Africans as consumers and convertors perceived nature analogically as a granary, pharmacy, butchery, source of construction and building material. The forest was a granary in as far as it provided grain, edible fruits, mushroom and the like. It was considered a pharmacy since herbs to heal various ailments were obtained from these forests. Hunting, that provided meat as well as hides and other medicinal components, also took place in the forests. Thatching grass, roofing and building poles were also provided by the forests. Worth noting is the fact that there was a very close attachment to the environment as they owned it and benefited a lot from it. The idea of a granary implies that there is food stored and reserved for future use. The value of the granary as a source of livelihood for the people is epitomised in the Shona proverb, 'Usaguta ukasunda dura.' (Hamutyinei, 1974). The proverb is translated to mean, 'Never be as satisfied as to push (wreck) the granary.' The proverb cautions against presumptuous lack of foresight to an extent that one abuses his/her benefactor. In the light of this explanation, it can be noted that the forest and the whole environment was considered by the traditional African people as a chief benefactor they owned. In this respect measures were put in place so that no one harmed this communal property serving as a lifeline. Ownership and control of the environment was therefore a motivating factor for environmental respect, care and preservation.

The concept of land ownership in traditional Shona society is strongly connected to the Chiefs and the ancestral spirits. Land, for the Shona people forms a close and enduring bond between the living and the living dead (Bourdillon, 1987). The living dead are described as the departed members of up to five generations for that particular group of people (Mbiti, 1976). Mbiti adds that the living dead have interest in what will be going on in the daily lives of the living. The living dead are said to enquire about family affairs, may warn of impending danger or rebuke those who have failed to follow their special instructions (Mbiti, 1976). Part of the instructions often given by the ancestors are that of keeping the environmental observances like observing sacred places, sacred groves, mountains, pools and rivers. Ancestral spirits are thus guardians of the land (Bourdillon, 1987). The environment in traditional Shona society was a treasure that was supposed to be guarded jealously. Sacred grove tradition for instance forbade societies from cutting vegetation from the sacred places. As a result, both vegetation and game survived. As the places were kept sacrosanct, they become a prototype of contemporary national parks. Such excellent care and conservation of the environment was motivated by existence of ownership and control of the environment.

Chiefs were highly esteemed as the earthly custodians of the land in a traditional Shona society of Zimbabwe. There was a strong connection between the Chiefs and the land in a traditional Shona society. When the Karanga Chief Ziki was installed (Bullock, 1928: 290 as quoted in Bourdillon, 1987), he opened his hands which were filled with two handfuls of earth while he was addressed, 'You are now Ziki, we hand you the country to hold. Look after us all.' The address to Chief Ziki of the Karanga people of Zimbabwe implies that the Chief together with all his people had ownership and control of the land and all that abides. Jurisdiction over the land was thus bestowed to the chief. The territory of the Chiefdom contained all its members, the living and the dead and even the yet to be born. The owners of the soil are therefore the whole group of indigenous people, more especially the deceased ones (Mar, 1962). Interestingly even those who were away from home had rights in the land pending their return. It is this oneness in ownership and control of the environment that instilled a sense of responsibility in the utilisation of the resources. The prolongation of the human race depended on the earth's fecundity, as such the living jealously guarded against the exploitation of the resources in their localities.

Resources in a traditional Shona society were owned and managed on a common property basis by all people though the overall authority was vested in the chief of the area. Similarly, the colonial state owned and managed the land collectively on behalf of colonialists. In precolonial Africa, each of the members of the community had a sense of belonging and ownership of the resources therein. In this regard conservation of wild fauna and flora was steeped in community bases, rules, beliefs and taboos. Several forest phenomena like trees especially large trees, mountains, pools, animals, snakes as well as spiritual figures like mermaids were revered and conserved by cultural and spiritual design. The use of fire in regenerating pastures or driving game was greatly prohibited, hunting during animal breeding season was also proscribed (Kwashirai, 2010).

It is important to note that though some of these rules could be infringed upon by mischievous members of the society, it is the conservation philosophy inculcated that need to be appreciated here. The concerted effort, by the members of the community, to take care of the environment was driven by the fact that the resources were theirs. As such they could not harm what they owned. Ownership and control of the environment is therefore a crucial ingredient towards environmental care and management.

African metaphysics is inclusive in its understanding of the environment. Human beings and the non-human beings sometimes worked together (Murove, 2009). In this vein the minerals, plants, animals, the air, water and the like all form a whole and a well-knit composite net of relationships that is punctuated by interdependence as well as aversions. The relations or connections were not always harmonious such that there were also ruptures. The fragile nature of the relationship between man and the environment has been described by Tempels through the analogy of the spider's web. Temples remarks that, the world of forces in an African setting is like a spider's web of which one single thread cannot be caused to vibrate without shaking the whole net-web' (Temples, 1956). Unlike the Western philosophers who accord moral status to non-human beings on the basis of sentientism, the Africans use the cosmic relations and interdependence as the basis (Mangena, 2012). The Africans understood the environment as their property for which they were custodians. Mountains and forests for instance were owned by the Africans, and they were also the abode of the ancestors. The belief in the existence of mermaid pools protected the purity of water sources. Various taboos were also lined up to protect the environment from being exploited. A good example is the taboo which says, '*Ukauraya datya tsime rinopwa,*' translated to mean (if you kill a frog the well will dry up.) This points to the fact that animals as small as frogs had some spiritual and inherent value to humanity. Human beings will protect the well from drying up by protecting the defenceless frog from human cruelty.

Zimbabwean Loss of Environmental Ownership and Control Since 1890

The colonial period was a period of development for colonial homelands and a wave of socio-economic underdevelopment for the indigenous people of Zimbabwe. In 1890, Cecil John Rhodes entered Zimbabwe from South Africa after missing the gold rush in Witwatersrand (Bond, 2000). The land belonging to native Zimbabweans was named Southern Rhodesia, after the chief imperialist Cecil John Rhodes. The implication here is that Rhodes had personalised the land without considering the fact that the land belonged to indigenous Zimbabweans who were the rightful owners. In this respect the ownership and control of the land bestowed on them by their forefathers was stolen by the imperialists for no compensation whatsoever. Africans became aliens in their own land.

Rhodes's pioneer column had the aim of plundering the African indigenous resources for the benefit of the British economy back home. It is important to note that the colonial economy was extractive in essence. Indigenous peasants were forced off their land into mines, commercial farms and nascent factories. Their land and cattle were stolen. Various taxes were exacted from the Blacks and these included charges for grazing and dipping fees (Palmer, 1977). It is a pity that the indigenous Zimbabweans were paying for their cattle to graze on the indigenous pastures. Such developments signalled the end of Zimbabweans' socio-economic freedom. Ownership and control of the environment and its natural resources was quickly waning away. The changing patterns of ownership and control of the environment had detrimental effects on environmental management by the Blacks as will be indicated later.

Economic hardships are a very fertile seedbed for environmental plundering. The syphoning of African resources laid firm and harsh economic conditions for the indigenous Africans. An increase in exports by the Rhodesian colonialists was not to the advantage of the indigenous people. In 1929 it is said mineral and agricultural export returns from Rhodesia rose to 6.6 million British Pounds (Palmer, 1977). The rise in exports is nothing but a testimony of how Zimbabwean wealth was being syphoned to Britain and other Western economies while the indigenous Zimbabweans sink further into socio-economic impoverishment. Though surrounded by their vast resources Zimbabweans were very far away from them as they were stolen. It is the theft and robbery which are argued in this chapter to be the basis of environmental neglect and destruction.

The brutality of the Europeans against the Africans is summarised by Mbiti (1976) who states that Europeans slaughtered Africans like beasts. Villages for the Africans were burnt. In-fact Africans were detached from the land to which they were and are mystically bound. Colonial rule in Zimbabwe expropriated most of the best land to the colonial robbers while the Africans were packed in 'reserves' which added considerably to the people's burdens (Palmer and Parsons, 1977). They were displaced off their land to become labourers in colonial robbers' farms, mines and the like for very meagre earnings which could not sustain their livelihoods. The little earnings coupled with pressure in the overpopulated reserved areas triggered a lot of environmental plundering as people fought for survival. Forests were cleared for arability, fuel wood, building material and the like. Such an environmental damage cannot solely be blamed on these locals but on the colonial robbers who stole the land and other resources. Without that colonial thuggery the pressure on resources being experienced now could have been absorbed and evened out.

In colonial Zimbabwe gold was dug, diamonds and copper were looted, cattle were stolen while nothing was being done for the human welfare of the indigenous people. Colonialists bullied indigenous people in environmental matters. Absolute impoverishment of the native Zimbabweans was witnessed as the wealth of the country was massively extracted from the rural areas by fraud and fiat.

Rectifying Skewed Resource Ownership: Post Independence Efforts by the Zimbabwean Government

The Land question in Zimbabwe is best described as a classic case of robbery and exploitation (Moyo, 2000). The war of liberation in Zimbabwe was triggered by the need to solve the theft of land and other resources. It is not the task of this chapter to narrate the historical events surrounding the war of liberation. Instead the war of liberation is highlighted only to reinforce the point that struggles over ownership and control of the land date back to the colonial period. It is the intention of this section to explore efforts by the Zimbabwean government to solve resource ownership disputes. The goal being to highlight that as long as the indigenous Zimbabweans do not own and control the environment then care for the environment remains side-lined.

Political independence in Zimbabwe, post 1980, was just political independence; economically the Zimbabweans remained dispossessed and exploited. Skewed ownership and control policies over resources remained. The Blacks remained congested in the reserves. The Zimbabwean government was quite aware that the land question that had triggered the liberation struggles was supposed to be solved with finality. However, efforts to redistribute land were so slow and marginal due to the land policies that existed (Moyo, 1995). Through the Lancaster House stipulation of willing buyer, willing seller policy, the government would only allocate land willingly released by the colonialists for resettlement. Land reforms pursued by the government from the period from 1980 to the 1990s saw transfer of relatively small proportion (15%) of White controlled lands to 6% of the peasantry (Moyo, 1995). The goal of the government was to promote collective and public land ownership and its use. The success of such an initiative would have at least restored some authority over land and its resources to the Black Zimbabweans. Environmental care and management could have been enhanced through ensuring of ownership and control as was the case in pre-colonial Zimbabwe. There would be a sense of belonging, ownership and control of the resources hence responsibility over the preservation of such resources. It is crucial to note that the Whites were not willing to relinquish ownership and control over the land. In a bid to evade the compulsory land acquisition that was planned for the 1990s, the Whites adjusted land use frameworks so as to protect their ownership and control of the vast tracks of land. This way, the Blacks remained politically independent but economically incarcerated. Of interest in this chapter is the fact that economic marginalisation through lack of ownership and control of land and its natural resources triggered environmental challenges that have ravaged Zimbabwe up to today.

The next section presents a summary of policy tactics used by the White colonialists to keep on clinging to ownership and control of land and its resources in Zimbabwe.

Colonialists' Effort to Cling on to Land Ownership and Control in Zimbabwe

From the enslavement era through the colonial and contemporary era, Africans have been denied their human essence (Nhemachena, 2019). It is important to note that Western imperialists employed legal systems and other conventions to suppress the Africans. The main thrust was to continuously rob Africans of their resources. Use of legal force and other conventions can be traced back to the colonial period in Zimbabwe. The Whites pushed for legislation that protected White interests against those of the Blacks. Resultantly pressure on resources as well as Black frustration over being robbed of their resources intensified and manifested in environmental deterioration.

In 1890 Zimbabwe was colonised and the Blacks were dispossessed of their land, livestock and other resources. The Native Reserve Commission of 1915 and the Morris Carter Commission further looted more land from the Blacks for White settlement (Gonese, 2006). Legal statutes for stealing were also instituted. Good examples are, The Land Apportionment Act of 1930, Consolidated Land Apportionment Act (1941), Native Land Husbandry Act (1951), Land Tenure Act (1969), Land Tenure Amendment Act (1977), The Tribal Trust Lands (1979), Economic Structural Adjustment Programme (ESAP) of 1990s (Gonese, 2006). The Zimbabwe Democracy and Economic Recovery Act of 2001 is the most recent form of economic bullying with devastating socio-economic and environmental consequences. It is not the thrust of this chapter to unpack the details of each of the Acts. However, the itemisation of the Acts serves to unveil the incessant effort by the colonialists to cling on to ownership and control of African land and resources through promotion of the sanctity of colonial property rights. The Lancaster House Constitution of 1979 for instance provided that, 'No property of any description was to be acquired compulsorily' (Moyo, 2000).

The Western Economic Bullying Through ESAP in Zimbabwe

The Economic Structural Adjustment Programme (ESAP) was imposed in Zimbabwe in 1990 by the World Bank (Moyo, 2000). Though ESAP was said to have the aim of improving the livelihoods of the rural people through improved agricultural productivity, the real issue was to protect the vast tracks of White owned land through change of land use. Land use changed from food into export-market oriented production. Nature tourism, wildlife production and horticulture for foreign markets were the focus of ESAP. The implication of such a development was to safeguard idle and underutilised White owned tracts of land.

The ESAP programme saw a group of London based commercial banks availing $20 million in 1990 to support horticulture projects in Zimbabwe (Mbiba, 1995). Shockingly no production for the local market was supported by the amount. This proves that ESAP had no interest on the wellbeing of the indigenous Black people. Most of the idle tracks of land were amalgamated and registered under one name of a private company (Moyo, 2000). In this light, these conservances removed the visibility of the human face of land ownership. Land ownership was thus shifted into abstract legal entities. The whole idea here is to shut the African from accessing ownership and control over the land. The landless Black majority were forced to work in the conservancies and horticultural commercial entities, but for meagre salaries. Decline in food production also meant that food production-aligned industries downsized hence massive retrenchments were witnessed. ESAP proved that it was not for poverty alleviation but it deepened poverty amongst the Blacks. The wage employment coupled with lack of ownership and control of the resources raised the levels of rural poverty. Blacks resorted to squatting due to this poverty, massive streambank cultivation for food production led to massive siltation and the like. Such environmental challenges can be blamed on the theft of the Blacks' resources, in this case through ESAP. Economic bullying did not end with ESAP, more bullying was unleashed whenever the White monopoly over ownership and control of the land and its resources was threatened.

The Fast Track Land Reform Programme and the Resultant Zimbabwe Democracy and Economic Recovery Act (ZIDERA): A synopsis

Efforts by the Zimbabwean government to provide a solution to the land question were met with bullying from the White land owners and their local and international accomplices. The willing buyer-willing seller programme had proved to be too slow since willing sellers were not coming forth as expected. The rise of conservancies through ESAP in the 1990s further blocked the Blacks from owning their land and resources. The patience of the freedom fighters together with the Black masses was waning away.

Simon Chimbetu, a war veteran and a renowned musician released an album entitled *Zuva Raenda* in 1997, whose title track, *Zuva Raenda* expressed discontent over the slow pace with which the land repossession programme was taking shape. The lyrics of the song had it that, *'Mukoma zuva raenda, govai minda.'* Translated to mean (brother time has lapsed, redistribute the land.) Music is a powerful tool of communicating grievances or airing opinion. In this case Chimbetu directed the message to the then President, Mugabe, here referred to as brother, to fast track the land redistribution exercise as the people were becoming impatient. Chief Svosve of Wedza district is said to be the pioneer in airing discontent over lack of land ownership and control in 2000. He led a group of villagers to repossess White owned farms. Widespread repossessions then followed. Of interest here is not the political aspect of the fast track land repossession but the hunger for ownership and control of the land and its resources displayed in the whole exercise. All being equal, such ownership and control would have given the Black Zimbabweans a sense of responsibility in the utilisation of their resources. However, the ownership and control efforts through the fast track repossession programme were met with yet another barricading factor in the form of United States of America initiated economic sanctions against Zimbabwe. It is the resource ownership wrangles and associated detrimental effects on the socio-economic and environmental wellbeing of Zimbabweans that are of interest in this section. It is for this reason that the period 2000-2019 has been selected for analysis in this chapter.

ZIDERA as an Ingredient for Environmental Woes in Zimbabwe

It is true that ZIDERA is often interpreted as mainly a direct expression of discontent over political violence, lack of democracy and absence of rule of law in Zimbabwe (Bond and Manyanya, 2001) but this chapter takes a different focus. The chapter looks at ZIDERA, not as chiefly a means to recover democracy and the economy in Zimbabwe, but as an expression of discontent over loss of White ownership and control over the land and its resources due to the fast track land repossession program (FTLRP). In fact, Robert Mugabe sought to democratise the ownership and control of land by extending ownership and control to Black Zimbabweans – he was not acting against democracy and human rights but he was executing an African form of democratisation of land ownership and control (see Nhemachena & Warikandwa, 2019). Just like foreign aid, ZIDERA has hidden goals. Important to note is the fact that this chapter is not meant to defend any political ills that could have been perpetrated prior to and during the FTLRP. Following the FTLRP, international and local financiers pounded the Zimbabwean dollar for reasons including punishing Mugabe for allowing the FTLRP in 2000 (Bond and Manyanya, 2001). There is a sense therefore, in which neo-liberalism catapulted economic chaos in Zimbabwe from the year 2000 onwards. Focus of this section will be on how the economic chaos triggered by ZIDERA negatively impacted on the Zimbabwean economy and subsequently on the environment.

ZIDERA was pioneered by the United States of America in 2000. It is summarised as a tool to support the people of Zimbabwe in their struggle to effect peaceful, democratic change, achieve equitable broad based economic growth and restore the rule of law (Read the Bill: S.494, 2001). In 2000 the International Development Association (IDA) suspended all funds to the Zimbabwean government for ongoing projects. No loan credit was supposed to be extended to Zimbabwe. "Indebtedness" of Zimbabwe was not supposed to be cancelled. The Bill also makes it clear that any organisation that would assist Zimbabwe would also be under sanctions (Read the Bill: S.494, 2001). These economic restrictions were going to be lifted only when Zimbabwe managed to meet specified conditions (Read the Bill: S.494, 2001). Of particular interest, among the conditions is one that states that the sanctions will only be lifted, if 'There is restoration of the rule of law, including respect for ownership and title to property.' There was a command for the Zimbabwean government also to embark on a transparent land reform that is legal, and equitable as guided by agreements reached at the International Donors' Conference on Land Reform and Resettlement in Zimbabwe, held in Harare in September 1998 (Read the Bill: S.494, 2001). A close look on these conditions testifies that the US was much disgruntled by White farmers' loss of ownership and control of the Zimbabwean land and its resources. In retaliation, the U.S and its allies decided to effect economic hardships for Zimbabwe. The legal framework referred to by the US as a guide for the land reform is actually skewed towards Western colonialists' benefit. From such an observation, it can be ascertained that neo-colonialists always assault African identities so as to diminish or erode African claims to their heritage (Nhemachena *et al*, 2018). Without the right and control to their heritage, the Africans won't have any motivation to take care of the environment that is owned and controlled by others such as descendants of colonialists. In fact, no one will follow the flock without drinking some of the milk. There is need for the Africans, in this case Zimbabweans to own and enjoy proceeds from their resources fully if meaningful environmental conservation is to take shape.

Economic Hardships and Environmental Challenges Following the "Smart" Sanctions

A brutal economic situation punctuated the Zimbabwean society for the past two decades following ZIDERA. Struggle for survival for the general populace was the order of the day from the year 2000 onwards. It is accepted that economic challenges in Zimbabwe date back to the colonial era. It is however, the economic impact of the "smart" sanctions that is focused on in this section. This is mainly because, the economic hardships manifest a contemporary array of economic bullying by the Western neocolonialists for their selfish gain. The impact of the harsh economic situation on the environment will be elaborated in the next section. Industrial closure and relocation of companies accompanied the imposition of sanctions on Zimbabwe. Formal employment rates fell while informal employment rates rose. However, most participants in informal employment had no specified line of business. They would pursue any line of business at their disposal. Such an approach to business is popularly referred to as hustling *(kukorokoza)* in Zimbabwe.

Profit for *makorokoza* is now the defining attribute, the climatic or environmental consequences lying ahead are ignored. The general slogan is food first and everything else later. They argue that, care about the environment does not bring food on the table, neither does it pay school fees for the children. However, (Bujo, 2009) makes it clear that humanity should be worried of tomorrow since today has lapsed already. The problem is that the Africans who are constantly in the shadow of death cannot hope for the morrow if they cannot survive decently today. In this respect the soaring economic wars on Zimbabwe have uprooted the poverty stricken citizens from ownership and control of the environment. They can get into mining, agriculture, fishing, hunting and the like. The dilemma with these players however is that, in most cases they have to interact with the natural resources which they neither own nor control. The main objective will be to harvest as much as possible without preserving for future use. Conservation of the environment for future use is only possible where the individual has ownership and control of the resources. Such an ownership motivates one to care because he/she will be sure that there will be access again in future.

Competition and fight for survival, in the absence of ownership and control of the resources pushes one to harvest as much as possible whenever a chance strikes since future access may be denied. It is the position of this chapter that economic deterioration in a country coupled with lack of ownership and control of the resources will definitely lead to the environment falling prey to human struggle for survival. The chapter maintains that ownership and control struggles erode ecological values that cemented society and the environment together especially when the people lack uninterrupted ownership and control of their environment. Western colonisers deliberately disturb the entitlement of the Africans to ownership and control of their resources. Colonialists want to create space for themselves to steal and loot from Africans.

Western colonisers used racial superiority and their barbarity as bases to subdue traditional practices including environmental conservation strategies (Daneel 1998). They try their best to invent and reinvent the order of the African society. Cultural onslaughts on Shona metaphysics has unsettled the ownership and control of the environment that existed in the traditional Shona society. An alien, individualistic, criminalistic and selfish mode of economy has caught the generous and communal Shona philosophy unawares. Weber (1958) says that man is dominated by the making of money as the ultimate purpose of life. From this understanding, business for the imperialists is not a way of life as the case with the traditional Shona's sense of business; it is not a way of earning a living. Their general thrust is to reduce expenditure as much as possible and accrue as much profit as possible by exploitation, acquisition, stealing and looting.

Economic aid and sanctions are very sharp tools that are employed by Western imperialists to gain looting access to Africa's resources. In fact, the so called economic aid is trapping Africans into economic colonialism again (Mbiti, 1976). Interesting to note is the fact that aid always comes with strings attached. The benefits from the aid is so small compared to the magnitude of natural resource loss as well as loss to freedom and control of the resources in a particular locality. Through aid, the richer nations get richer as they get access to looting and stealing while the poor get poorer and lose their freedoms and control over their resources. It is through the so called economic aid that the African environment is plundered by these colonialists through their multinational companies who syphon African resources back to their home countries.

'Developmental projects' by the developed world in the developing countries are described by (Bujo, 2009) as nothing but avenues by the industrialised to syphon the ubiquitous natural resources from the developing countries. The poverty and propertilessness of the developing countries force them to rely more on foreign exchange. As a result, there are times when the third world countries sacrifice their sacred resource reserves for the much needed foreign currency or technology. It was made clear by (Murove, 2009) that radioactive waste is offered to the third world in return for debt reduction. Such a situation is pathetic for the developing world as they are presented as a dumbing site for defunct technology. It is crucial to observe that the corrosive nature of radio-active technology is more monstrous to humanity and ecology than the debt itself. While technology is not bad, it is the lack of respect to native cultures and their ownership and control of their environment that is worrying. It is so disturbing to observe that due to poverty the future generation is ignored in the matrix of environmental ownership, control and management.

European countries have always been at the gaining end of the parasitic and asymmetrical relations between them and the developing world, (Oguejiofor, 2015). The so called modernity and industrial revolution is nothing but a bait for the African and other third world countries. Transnational looting, plunder, theft, robbery and dispossession are perpetuated in the guise of aid for industrial revolutions (Nhemachena *et al*, 2019). The looting machine may come camouflaged under economic and advisory aid. There is in fact no aid without a bait, and few are the men who see the trap, and fewer still are those who can entirely escape it. The smart sanctions for Zimbabwe can thus be described as a trap designed to push Zimbabwe into surrendering ownership rights and control of resources to the West. The economic hardships that accompanied the smart sanctions created confusion in the socio-economic to political well-being of the country. It is in this confusion that local Zimbabweans can be used as agents for looting precious resources like gold to the west.

A report by Mambondiyani (2017) indicated that Tarka Forest in Chimanimani had been destroyed by illegal gold panners. Syndicates of these exploiters have destroyed the forest with ferocity in order to eke a living. Farmlands and forests have been destroyed especially in the Eastern Highlands of Zimbabwe bordering Mozambique. An estimated 600 hectares of prime timber forests in Tarker forest, Chimanimani, have since been destroyed and massive pits and tunnels created in Chimanimani (Mambondiyani, 2017). The panners argue that buyers of their loot from Mozambique are giving better offers compared to the Zimbabwean folk. The implication here is that the local Zimbabweans are being used as agents for looting by western imperialists who provide a ready market for the loot while blacklisting formal marketing channels of the same minerals. Tarker forest referred to above is privately owned so the miners have no attachment to it whatsoever since they do not own it. They therefore resort to looting without care about the environment since they have no motivation to care for what they don't own. Poverty and lack of ownership and control of the resources thus prove to be cancerous to environmental conservation. A slump of the economy in Zimbabwe can thus be blamed for the environmental destruction by the 'hustlers'. They are left with no avenue for survival as they lack ownership and control over the country's natural resources and poverty ravages them. Important to note is the fact that insatiable appetite for monetary riches at the expense of environmental management brands one as an environmental destroyer (Murove, 2009). Lack of control over the countries coupled with the need to survive triggers ignorance about environmental care and management.

The Eastern Highlands of Zimbabwe are known to be host to thick forests. Such forests are instrumental in purifying the air by absorbing excess carbon dioxide in the atmosphere. Massive clearance of the forests automatically leads to an accumulation of greenhouse gases which absorb heat in the atmosphere resulting in the rise of air, land and sea/ ocean temperatures. The risk of violent storms and oceanic currents become highly probable. On 15 March 2019 Mozambique, Malawi and Eastern Zimbabwe ravaged by Cyclone Idai. Bridges were stripped open, homesteads were swept to level plains, trees were uprooted, mountains buckled and landslides flowed.

There is a sense in which the devastating nature of Cyclone Idai and its damage to fauna and flora in Chimanimani could have been heightened by environmental mismanagement though not confined to that. In this sense poverty due to lack of ownership and control of the resources is pushing care for the environment to the shores but at a cost. While Africans in traditional society looked at the environment as their property, the west looks at the trees and the general environment as a Devil given paradise awaiting to be exploited (Daneel, 1998) and stolen from indigenous people.

Members of the developed world are encouraging the underwater forest clearance for timber as well as the illegal mineral mining in the developing world. At times porous developmental deals are signed with the main goal being that of syphoning natural resources from Africa. Some of the pseudo-developmental projects benefit just a few high ranking politicians who receive kickbacks. The Herald (9 September 2013) had an article published by Fungai Lupande with the heading, 'Gold panning destroys Mazowe River. He highlighted that some Chinese companies were harvesting gold along Mazowe River. River diversion was practiced by the Chinese so as to make gold harvesting easy. They brought their excavators, caterpillars and other sophisticated machinery for the purpose. From Lupande's report residents in Uzumba Maramba Pfungwe are now facing acute water shortages, especially those living downstream of the diverted sections of the river. Water levels are shrinking with the holding capacity of most water reservoirs having dropped to ranges of 40-60% for the period 2000-2018 due to siltation (Newsday, December 2018). Mr Joseph Kafura, a resident of Uzumba Maramba Pfungwe, even complained that water in the area was no longer drinkable due to heavy doses of chemicals into the rivers (The Herald, September 2019). Surprisingly, the companies do not offer meaningful employment to the locals. As such the residents continue being sprawled in the mud of poverty. They are alienated from their natural resources. They will be nearer to their natural resources but very far from them in terms of enjoying the proceeds. In misplaced aggression they also do all they can to plunder the environment for their benefit. With regard to the ecological cost, it is the whole nation that bears it. The justification is simply that they cannot care for what they do not own.

Whereas the poverty and colonial plunder stricken citizens would justify plundering of the environment on the need to survive, a closer look shows that they have inherited the imperialist behaviour of looting resources without care about the environment. An element of greedy is evident. A snap survey on both the illegal and legal miners in Zimbabwe shows that they amass more than they need for survival. They are so luxuriant in lifestyle. During the diamond stampede in Marange area in Manicaland province of Zimbabwe it was common to see a fleet of cars belonging to one person parked by the side of a ramshackled hut. The fleets of vehicles proved that the miners and dealers were earning more than they needed for survival. Surprisingly, no one was bothered by the need to reclaim the land from which the gems were harvested. The forests cleared were never replaced. Siltation of water reservoirs became a common phenomenon. The end result is the creation of an uninhabitable environment for both human beings, the animals and vegetation. The precious nature of the gems in Marange area of Manicaland in Zimbabwe therefore, did not translate to the precious care for sustainable utilisation of resources. The hunt for the precious mineral only left traits of environmental degradation with no precious development for the nation. This way, the cycle of poverty and destruction towards the environment becomes endless.

The economic travails in Zimbabwe also pushed a number of families to the urban peripheries like Calidornia farm in Harare, Dema area in Chitungwiza, Epworth and the like where they settled on private properties which they have neither ownership nor control over. Electricity supply became a nightmare during the period of 2000 and after. Those in the urban peripheries had no other alternative source of energy other than firewood. As a result forests in urban peripheries were destroyed. A thriving business of firewood sale surfaced in most urban centres. Forests in Zimbabwe disappeared at a horrendous rate (Daneel M, 1998). The lucrative timber trade, overpopulation, the ever-increasing need for firewood, clearing of land for construction and farming acted as the direct causes of environmental damage. Whereas it is true that the poverty streaking citizens will be fighting for survival it has to be ascertained that in return they get cash and desertification.

Droughts occurred in Zimbabwe, with less rain than the average being received between January and March each years since 2000 (Rakacewicz, 2005). Shorter growing seasons punctuated by mid-season dry spells are common, heat waves are also prevalent (Chanza, 2015). Harvests have dwindled and failed, thus burgeoning poverty levels. Droughts and floods have also increased their frequency with floods usually following drought years (Rakacewicz, 2005). The above narration is testimony of climate change in Zimbabwe. Without revising the African approach to environmental ownership, control and management then the future remains doom and gloom.

Environmental Care through Ownership and Control

The past ecological destruction in Africa is manifesting itself today through natural challenges like heat waves, droughts, food insecurity due to poor harvests, diminishing water levels, both surface and underground, floods and the like. This should be a lesson to humanity and a challenge to safeguard the environment for the sake of the future generation. The future of Africans is brighter and optimistic if the age old questions about ownership and control of their resources is addressed (Nhemachena *et al*, 2019). It follows that there is no motivation for environmental care and management for Africans without them owning and controlling their environment. It is when the economic conditions of the world's poor are improved through ownership and control of their resources that the African environment can be protected (Noyoo, 2017). From this observation it can be argued that there is a direct link between the economic well-being of a people and environmental ownership and management.

There is a sense by most impoverished Africans that the 'West is best': such perceptions are championed by institutions like the IMF and the World Bank. The west talks of modernity as progress that heavily relied upon the spread of western thought system of resource exploitation, plundering, looting and stealing (Sinkala, 2000). The west thus practices rapid extraction of mineral resources in the guise of bilateral trade agreements with limited to no care about environmental impacts. Through the so called developmental projects, massive losses of common resources are witnessed. These include, grazing land, topsoil, woodlots and even ancestral burial grounds (Bond, 2000). What the Africans need to do therefore is to wake up from the economic slumber, and fight for ownership and control of their resources. If colonial paradigms are followed then more and more Africans will be concentrated in small localities without direct control over their resources (Warren, 1992). Such colonial realities lead to large scale economic impoverishment due to lack of economic alternatives. In the end it is the environment that is destroyed. Ownership and control of the natural resources for Africa is thus the best incentive for environmental care.

The colonial mode of education has been described by Datta (1998) as having the sole aim of educating the young Africans to serve in the colonial system as menial workers. This was an 'education for slavery' system. The learners thought of how to convert knowledge into money while they relegate their right to ownership and control of their resources. They also tend to ignore indigenous knowledge values and a sense of belonging to African societies. Such an approach to life is flawed since it can trade resource ownership for money, but with detrimental effects on the environment. A paradigm shift for Africa is therefore called for whereby ownership and control issues of the African environment should be fostered to all generations. Armed with such an empowerment drive, environmental care by the Africans will be improved.

Effective African environmental care is possible if Africans are accorded the right to preserve their own knowledge and heritage as they see it fit. In this vein widespread and continued exploitation of Indigenous Knowledge and heritage by Eurocentric institutions and scholars is in fact a form of contemporary colonialism geared towards exhausting the indigenous people's tangible assets (Batiste and Henderson, 2000). For this reason, the indigenous people's search for belonging and respect for their knowledge and heritage is the password for meaningful environmental care and management in Africa. Such efforts will go a long way in mitigating climate change and its effects on humanity. It is identification and removal of conditions that reinforce powerlessness of the Africans that is called for. Clamouring for the conservation of what people do not own remains theoretical and futile. Meaningful strides towards climate change mitigation in Africa is only possible if Africans fully own, control and manage their environment.

Africans have to win their own dignity, ownership and control of their resources first then care for the environment as their source of livelihood then follows smoothly. Aid that is directed to Africa thus, should remove any strings attached and help to promote self-determination for the Africans. Political liberties without corresponding voice over ownership of resources is thus meaningless. Changing the flag over the court house is therefore nothing but a cosmetic change. An active participatory epistemology of the Africans in economic matters that concern them is crucial. Resolving issues of knowledge like ownership, control, benefits and other contested issues surrounding the natural resources therefore need to be addressed first before environmental conservation issues are brought to the table. In this vein talking of efforts to mitigate climate change and promoting lasting development in Africa without ownership and control of their environment is impossible.

There is need for peaceful African ownership and control (Murove, 2009) of resources. An affront to the environment therefore annihilates humanity. This is witnessed through numerous human triggered environmental calamities. As such care for the environment is crucial in addressing issues of climate change.

It needs to be affirmed that the connection between humanity and the environment is intricately fragile such that it needs to be handled with maximum care. Neither technological advancement nor poverty should undo the human obligation to care for the environment. But rights are jural correlatives of obligations – the problem with colonialists is that they imposed obligations of environmental care without ownership rights to Africans. It has been ascertained by (Mveng, 1985) that the task of humans is not to dominate and enslave nature in total, instead they should be custodians who own the environment guided by a sense of responsibility and ownership. As long as the environment is used in furtherance of profits then climate change and related natural disasters will be ever-present in the lives of the people.

Lack of ownership and control of the African environment by Africans breeds poverty and poverty breeds ignorance for environmental care; greed for wealth have forced people to only think of today without conscience about tomorrow. However, (Gelfand, 1973) makes it clear that, the present is the whole of the past looking into the future. Gelfand is thus stressing that future existence is basically an extension of the past because future environmental calamities are brewed today. Ecological disasters today have been manured through environmental mismanagement in the past. It is due to such an interconnection of time and activities that ownership, control and care about the environment constitutes the most precious inheritance to be enjoyed by the future generation. The therapy for ecological tragedies in Africa therefore, is nothing other than retracing footsteps of humanity back to ownership and control of the environment. Damage from ecological challenges grossly outweigh profits, wealth and luxury accrued through environmental malpractices. As such there is need for pro-activity towards African environmental ownership and control and action should be now and never later.

Murove (2009) proposed valuing the concept of *ukama* as a password for ownership and control of the environment in Africa. *Ukama* is a Shona adjective that implies relationship and an understanding of reality in terms of ownership and interdependence (Murove, 2009). Of interest is the stem *-kama* which can be understood as a verb for milking. Milking among the Shona people of Zimbabwe is an activity that displays ownership, affection and closeness between the farmer, the cow and the calf. The farmer owns, controls and cares for the cow and the calf then enjoys the milk in return. Generally, among the Shona people, a nursing cow is not yoked. Also the farmer does not exhaust all the milk from the adder, instead, he spares some for the calf. Without the calf, the milk source will dry up. According to (Murove, 2009) relationships among the Africans are not determined by blood alone as alleged by Western anthropologists. From the *Ukama* concept, it is evident that care for the environment can be motivated through ownership and control of the environment. With ownership and control of the environment the African mind is oriented towards ecological concern rather than ecological curiosity (Mazrui, 1977). For Mazrui, reasoning based on curiosity elevates humanity to the level of a demon desirous of the resources of others. If such a state of affairs is allowed, then there is a tendency for humanity to view the environment as an object to be stolen from indigenous people. This gives a lee way for environmental destruction. It therefore follows that ecological concern calls for humans to conserve nature. In this vein, ecological concern goes beyond mere fascination. Instead, it implies a commitment to own, control, conserve and enrich the environment. Existence of humanity is thus meaningful when understood as a continuum with all else that exist, except the Devil and his demons. It is this unity of purpose that can help bring value to the way humanity connects with the environment. Ramose (1999) supports connection with the environment by making it clear that, mutual foundedness of the individual and even the community is bolstered by complementariness with other beings. An urge exists to contribute positively to the welfare of not only human beings, but even that of animate and inanimate things. Care for the environment today shapes tomorrow, the ecological sanity of tomorrow is designed today.

Conclusion

Zimbabwe is being haunted by climate change related challenges. Droughts and floods have increased their frequency. More dry days are being recorded during the supposedly rainy season. Rivers, streams, ponds and wetlands are drying up. Debates surrounding the arrest of such environmental challenges have called for more ownership, control, sustainable environmental care and management. This chapter, however, has argued that the long history of lack of ownership and control for natural resources by the indigenous people in Africa in general and Zimbabwe in particular is to blame for improper environmental care and management. The general argument is that as long as the Africans in general and Zimbabweans in particular are alienated from their resources then there will be no incentive to care for the environment. If Western imperialist forces own and control African natural resources then environmental plundering will persist as these forces are geared towards looting, stealing, grabbing and syphoning African resources to build their economies back home. They enforced egocentric and stringent legislation to protect their looting space for African natural resources from the colonial era up to now. It is the position of this chapter that ZIDERA in Zimbabwe has clauses that advocate for the western ownership and control of Zimbabwean land and its natural resources. Such a call trivialises the locals from ownership and control of their resources, thus pushing them far into poverty.

References

Bourdillon, M. (1987). *The Shona Peoples.* Gweru: Mambo Press.

Bujo, B. (2009). Ecology and Ethical Responsibility from an African Perspective. In: *African Ethics: An Anthologyof Comparative and Applied Ethics.* South Africa : University of Kwazulu NAtal Press, pp. 281-287.

Daneel M, L. (1998). *African Earth Keepers Volume 1*. South Africa: Unisa Press.

Daneel, M. (1998). *African Earth keepers. Volume 1: Interfaith Mission in Earthcare*. South Africa: Unisa Press.

Fleshman , M. (2017). *Climate Cahnge: Africa gets ready*. Chicago: McMillan Publishing.

Gelfand, M. (1973). *The Genuine Shona: Survival Values of an African Culture*. Gweru: MAmbo Press.

Gonese, F. T. M. (2006). *Land Reform and Resettlement Implementation in Zimbabwe: An Overview of the Programme Against Selected International Experiences*. Harare: Sappes.

Hamutyinei, M. A. (1974). *Tsumo-Shumo*. Gweru: Mambo Press.

Kwashirai, V. C. (2010). *Environmental History of Africa*. Essen: Alexander von Humboldt.

Mambondiyani, A. (2017). *Gold Rush Fever among poor Zimbaweans leaves a trail of destruction,* Harare: Thomson Reuters.

Mangena, F. (2012). 'Moral Status and the State of Creation Account: Critical Prospects.'. *ZAMBEZIA: Journal of Humanities of The University of Zimbabwe*.

Mazrui, A. (1977). *Africa's International Relations: The Diplomacy of Dependence*. London : Heinnermann.

Mbiti, J. (1976). *African Religions and Philosophy*. London: Heinemann.

Moyo, S. (1995). *The Land Question in Zimbabwe*. Harare: Sappes Trust.

Moyo, S. (2000). *Land Reform Under Structural Adjustment in Zimbabwe: Land Use Changes in the Mashonaland Provinces*. Uppsala: Nordiska Afrikainstitutet.

Murove, M. F. (2009). *African Ethics: An Anthology of comparative and applied ethics*. Kwazulu Natal: University of Kwazulu Natal Press.

Mveng, E. (1985). *L'Afrique dans l'Eglise:Paroles d'un Croyant*. Paris: Presence Africaine.

Nhemachena, A. & Warkandwa, T. V. (2019) *From African Peer Review Mechanisms to African Queer Review Mechanisms? Robert Gabriel Mugabe, Empire & the Decolonisation of African Orifices*. Bamenda: Langaa RPCIG.

Nhemachena, A. *et al*, (2019). *Social and LegalTheory in the Age of Decoloniality: Re-Envisioning Pan African Jurisprudence in the 21st Century*. Bamenda.:Langaa RPCIG.

Nhemachena, A. & Warikandwa, T. V. (2017) *Mining Africa: Law, Environment, Society and Politics in Historical and Multidisciplinary Perspectives.* Bamenda: Langaa RPCIG.

Palmer, R. and. Parsons, A. (1977). *The Roots of Rural Poverty in Central and Southern Africa.* London: Heinemann.

Ramose, M. B. (1999). *African Philosophy Through Ubuntu.* Harare: Mond Books.

Temples, P. (1956). *Bantu Philosophy.* Paris: Presence Africaine.

Timberlake, L. (1958). *Africa in Crisis : The causes,the cures of Environmental bankruptcy.* Chicago: University of Cicago Press.

Weber, M. (1958). *The Protestant Ethic and the Spirit of capitalism.* London: Unwin.

Chapter Twelve

A Benchmarking Framework to Boost Africa's Standards to Reduce Emissions from the Transportation Sector

Semie M. Sama

Introduction

Greenhouse gases (GHGs), including carbon dioxide, methane, nitrous oxide, water vapour, and ozone, acknowledged as the chief driving forces behind climate change, absorb and emit radiation to the atmosphere and alter human and natural systems and make some of them uninhabitable (IPCC, 2018:550). The transport sector is a vital source of GHG emissions, mainly driven by fossil fuels burning for road, air, rail and marine transportation. In 2010, this sector accounted for 27% of final energy use and 6.7 $GtCO_2$ direct emissions with baseline CO_2 emissions projected to double by 2050 (IPCC, 2014:21). A similar study by the World Health Organization shows that transportation contributed nearly 23% of global CO_2 emissions in 2010 and 27% of end-use energy emissions with urban transport responsible for almost 40% of end-use energy consumption (WHO, 2019).

Governments all around the world have pledged to cap national GHG emissions, to avert global average temperatures from rising to 2° C above preindustrial levels and from causing irreversible impacts. Nonetheless, transport emissions continue to grow. While the contribution of transport emissions in some western jurisdictions, including British Columbia and Sweden, have been declining mainly as a result of road pricing, higher fuel taxes, and stricter fuel efficiency standards, the reverse is the case in Africa, a region with about 2% of the world's motor vehicles (Chrisa *et al.*, 2015:317). According to the World Bank, transport CO_2 emissions in sub-Sahara Africa grew from 22.678.120.262.759 in 1971 to 228.503.074.823.255 in 2014 (% of total fuel combustion) (World Bank, 2019). With the world population projected to reach 8 billion people in 2023

(Worldometers, 2019), faster economic growth in Africa means more GHG emissions from burning fossil fuels for transportation.

The problem with this increase is that the released GHGs trap more heat in the atmosphere and cause global warming and climate change, blamed for floods, heatwaves, downpours, global sea level rise, biodiversity depletion, among other impacts that can alter human and natural systems and make some of them unbearable. Many social systems, as well as ecosystems in Africa, including some of the services they provide, have already been lost or altered, profoundly, due to global warming and climate change (IPCC, 2018). Africans have been experiencing the frequent occurrence of extreme heat events, changes in rainfall, increasing aridity, sea-level rise, floods, displacement, biodiversity loss, desertification and decrease in agriculture productivity yields (Awojobi, 2015; Serdeczny *et al.,* 2016). If the trend continues and CO_2 emissions double by 2050 as projected (IPCC, 2014:21), climate-related risks to vulnerable communities will amplify in Africa and making the Sustainable Development Goals to end poverty and hunger, achieve food security and promote sustainable agriculture a reality will be complicated.

Most African countries have issued laws to reduce emissions and vulnerability to climate change and strengthen national adaptive capacity and resilience. Translating these laws into action in a way that will not compromise the prospects for holding global temperature increases to well below 2° C is crucial. This chapter attempts to inform transport policy in Canada's British Columbia and Sweden, two of the 15 jurisdictions that received the 2018 United Nations Momentum for Change Climate action award. The idea is to offer a framework upon which Africa can be benchmarked against so that lessons can be drawn for the sake of interpreting the gap and evaluating alternative pathways for public policy. First, a brief review of the international climate change regime is provided. Second, an appraisal of a range of transportation sector instruments in Canada's British Columbia is offered. Third, an overview of regulatory approaches controlling transportation in Sweden is presented. Finally, recommendations are presented based on the findings in Sweden and British Columbia, to support the development of climate actions in Africa.

However, this research does not evaluate the effectiveness of the implementation/enforcement of these measures. Online international legal databases, government websites, literature, and media reports were very instrumental in locating the laws and regulations for this empirical study. Learning from the experiences of the governments of Sweden and British Columbia could help further momentum to lessen transportation emissions and protect the global climate. The report should enable future research by enhancing the understanding of current legal requirements such as incentives and disincentives, that have been enacted/strengthened to combat climate change and contribute to Paris Agreement goal of limiting global temperature increases to well below 2°C (Decision 1/CP.21 2015: Article 2) while promoting clean growth in Africa.

A Brief History of the Climate Change Regime

The purpose of the 1992 UN Conference on Environment and Development in Rio de Janeiro, Brazil was to craft an emergency response to the harsh realities of, among others, climate change, a problem that has been dubbed 'super wicked' (Levin *et al.,* 2012) and 'one of the greatest challenges of our time' (UNFCCC, 2009). Climate change involves a modification of the composition of the global atmosphere which is attributed directly/indirectly to anthropogenic activities, and to natural climate variability observed over comparable periods. Discussions over climate change, which permeate environmental, economic, social, and human rights forums, dominates law to science, to religion, to economics, to medicine, to politics and development studies, now rank high on global political agendas (Ivanova, 2017:17).

A critical legal instrument that emerged from the Rio conference was the United Nations Framework Convention on Climate Change (UNFCCC). The UNFCCC, adopted on 9 May 1992 and entered into force in 1994, binds state Parties to collaborate in addressing the adverse impacts of climate change and in stabilising the atmospheric concentrations of GHGs at a level that would avert unsafe interference with the climate system. Such a standard should be accomplished within a time frame enough to allow ecosystems to adapt naturally to climate change (United Nations, 1992: Article 2).

Hence, mitigation (a human effort to decrease the emission of GHG to the atmosphere) and adaptation (adjusting to the catastrophic and irreversible harmful effects of climate change) contribute to the Article 2 objective. The promotion of rapid and far-reaching transitions in the energy, built environment, transportation, industry, forestry, agriculture and waste sectors of every economy is crucial to achieving climate change mitigation and adaptation.

Regarding transport emissions, achieving this goal involves adopting regulations and standards for pricing carbon pollution and supporting innovation in rapid transit lines, walking and biking commuting and clean vehicles and fuels that enhance air quality, while generating new jobs in the clean-tech industry and creating. It also includes shifting more public transit to low carbon fuels; supporting new vehicle incentives and infrastructure and guiding the development of safe and dependable transportation infrastructure that is constructed to withstand extreme weather events and reduce congestion. Reducing transportation footprint also involves strengthening enabling factors for system transitions—increased investments, policy instruments, accelerated technological innovation, mobilisation of finance and behaviour changes.

A significant feature of the UNFCCC is its recognition that the highest share of historical and existing global emissions of GHGs has originated in developed countries and that the per capita GHG emissions in developing countries are still relatively low but will grow to meet their social development needs (United Nations, 1992). Ever since this agreement was adopted, the principle of common but differentiated responsibilities and respective capabilities has received increasing recognition in the UNFCCC regime. This principle acknowledges the different capabilities and differing responsibilities of developed and developing countries, economies in transition, least developed countries and small island developing states in addressing climate change (*Ibid*). By this principle, developed countries have a more significant role in mitigating climate change.

To effectively reduce atmospheric concentrations of GHGs to a safe level, another climate change negotiation was launched in 1995, with the outcome being the adoption of the *Protocol to the United Nations Framework Convention on Climate Change* (Kyoto Protocol) in December 1997, which came into effect on 16 February 2005. The

Kyoto Protocol builds upon and enhances many of the existing obligations under the UNFCCC. It binds Annex I countries (developed countries) to emission reduction targets, with its 1st and 2nd commitment periods—2008 to 2012 and 2013 to 2020 respectively, thereby placing a substantial burden on them under the common but differentiated responsibility principle.

Annex I countries are obligated to undertake national policies and actions to reduce emissions and provide additional financial resources and transfer clean technology to promote the implementation of commitments by non-annex I countries such as developing countries, least developed countries, economies in transition, and small island developing states (Protocol to the United Nations, 1998). Even though it is a legally binding instrument committing Annex I countries to reduce their emissions by an average of 5% below their 1990 levels, the Kyoto Protocol was insufficient to stabilise global GHG emissions. It was 'a clear case of institutional failure, with the design itself bearing substantial blame for the outcome' (Rosen, 2015:30).

In the space of 15 years (from 2005 to 2015) the global climate change narrative was adjusted (from 'wicked' to opportunistic (sustainable development)) with the adoption of the Paris Agreement in 2015 by over 195 state Parties to the UNFCCC at the 21st Conference of the Parties. This agreement aims to address the weaknesses with the Kyoto Protocol in enhancing the implementation of the UNFCCC. It reiterates the goal to hold global temperature increases to well below 2° C above pre-industrial levels and pursue efforts to limit the temperature increase even further to 1.5° C. At the heart of this landmark agreement is Article 3 — Nationally Determined Contributions (NDCs) — representing each Party's ambitious efforts to reduce domestic GHG emissions and adapt to climate change impacts, with the view to achieving the purpose of the Paris Agreement.

Parties are required to prepare, communicate and maintain NDCs and to pursue domestic measures aimed at attaining them. Developed countries have a binding obligation (Article 9) to mobilize and provide financial resources to assist vulnerable nations, among other developing countries, regarding climate change mitigation and adaptation. Developing and transferring clean technology to and building the capacity and ability of countries with the least capacity, including those that are most susceptible to the adverse impacts of climate change, to implement mitigation and adaptation actions effectively (Articles 10 and 11) are crucial in turning Parties' political commitments, as signified in Parties NDCs, into action in the ground.

Nearly three decades after the UN 1992 conference in Rio, there was another climate change conference in Katowice, Poland in 2018, to agree on the rulebook for the Paris, a step required to avoid catastrophic climate change. The 'Katowice Climate Package' was adopted on 15 December 2018 and includes rules relating to, among others, the transparency framework (how Parties are to develop and report on their NDCs). It also comprises targets on finance from 2025 onwards; procedures for conducting the first Global Stocktake of climate action in 2023; and on how to evaluate progress on technology development and transfer to vulnerable nations and communities. Unresolved issues include guidelines on the use of cooperative approaches and the sustainable development mechanism, as contained in Article 6 of the Paris Agreement: such guidelines would enable each Parties to cut a part of its national emissions using 'market mechanisms' (Decision 1/CP.21 2015).

With recent efforts in some GHG generating countries such as the United States to subvert international environmental efforts (Clark, 2018:108), the adoption of the implementation guidelines for the Paris Agreement is notable. While some parties to the UNFCCC focus their messaging on the role of nuclear power and fossil fuels in promoting energy security and addressing climate needs, others are concerned about the short-term economic costs of climate action on those least capable of affording them such as increased carbon tax and loss of jobs associated with coal exit. Notwithstanding the oppositions, global climate leaders, including the European Union and Canada, are determined to foster a more meaningful conversation that can ensure a just transition of the labour force, create decent jobs and guarantee a successful and inclusive transition to climate resilient and low GHG emission development, nationally, regionally and globally.

The science is clear that climate change is affecting every fibre of our being together as a community, and Africa tops the list of the most vulnerable hotspots to global warming and climate change. Existing research indicates that among the most disturbing effects of global warming in this region is the impact on agriculture and forestry, infrastructure and building and water supply. Africa has a predominantly agrarian economy, meaning cultivating the land is the primary source of food and wealth in the continent and the agriculture sector. The African economy is most vulnerable as it relies heavily on rain-fed crops. Weather variability and a substantial increase in mean temperature and precipitation within the farming season will have a considerable consequence on agricultural output, and hence livelihoods, according to agronomic research in Africa (IPCC, 2018; Kahsay and Hansen, 2016; Eriksen, 2008). The above state of affairs illustrates the need for a better understanding of how climate change affects African countries, and for the identification of processes, methods, and tools which may help African nations to adapt. There is a perceived need to showcase successful examples of how to cope with the social, economic and political problems posed by climate change in Africa.

Many African countries have issued laws and policies to reduce emissions and vulnerability to climate change and strengthen national adaptive capacity and resilience. A Global Climate Legislation study that focuses on national level legislation of 32 Annex I countries and 67 Annex II countries, which together contribute to roughly 93 % of world emissions (47 of the top 50 global carbon emitters) shows that by 2014 there were 804 climate change laws and policies. These numbers represent a rise from just 54 laws and policies in 1997 and 426 in 2009 following the signing of the Copenhagen Accord (Nachmany *et al.,* 2015:2). Hence, African countries are among the 67 developing countries that have put in place laws and policies that are crucial to combat climate change.

However, despite this significant development we can expect that translating these policies and intentions into action will face formidable challenges. Without domestic transport policies, Africa will not reach the Paris Agreement goal, making policy research in Africa crucial. Africa is at the crossroads due to, among others, 'ineptitude leadership' that has resulted in national insecurity and poverty (Ajulor, 2017:1497). This is the right time to contribute in finding solutions that substantially reduce GHG emissions and promote clean growth in Africa. This policy analysis will play an essential role in supporting African policymakers to develop low-emissions and climate-resilient pathways that take a sector-specific approach, focusing on transportation emissions.

An Overview of Regulatory Approaches Controlling Transportation in Canada

Transportation accounted for 23% of Canada's emissions in 2014, typically from passenger vehicles and freight trucks. Heavy-duty trucking is the swiftest growing sub-sector of transport emissions, with freight accounting for about 60% of the total 55 MT increase in transportation emissions between 1990 and 2014 (Pan Canadian Framework, 2016:17). Remarkably, Canada's GHG emissions from transport dropped from 202 Mt CO_2 equivalent in 2013 to 199 Mt CO_2 equivalent in 2016 despite increased motorization that the world has been witnessing for the past five or more decades (*Ibid* 7). This drop is mainly a result of transport emissions standard that is being implemented nationally, including low-carbon transportation systems that use cleaner fuels, encourage zero-emission vehicles, promote affordable transit and support the swing from higher to lower-emitting categories of transportation.

The government of Canada has taken several giant steps to meet its target under the Paris Agreement. Among the actions, one can mention, it submitted its intended NDC to the UNFCCC (which included an economy-wide target to reduce GHG emissions by 30% below 2005 levels by 2030), adopted the *Vancouver Declaration on Clean Growth and Climate Change* (2016) and signed and ratified the Paris Agreement on Climate Change (2016). The federal governments also adopted the Pan-Canadian Framework on Clean Growth and Climate Change (Pan-Canadian framework) which constitutes the federal government's planned policies to grow the economy, reduce emissions and build resilience to adapt to a changing climate. It includes pricing carbon pollution; complementary actions to reduce emissions; policies to adapt to climate change impacts and build resilience; and measures to fast-track innovation, create jobs and support clean technology.

Actions taken in British Columbia

According to the Climate Leadership Plan of British Columbia (B.C.), a province in Canada, the transportation sector accounts for almost 37% of the province's GHG emissions, with road transportation (mostly from motorcycles, cars, pickups, minivans, SUVs, and other light passenger vehicles) responsible for 63% of these emissions (Climate Leadership Plan 2016:18). To work to achieve Canada's climate action goals, the government of B.C. committed in legislation to lessen GHG emissions by at least 33% below 2007 levels by 2020 and 80% below 2007 levels by 2050 and build a clean economy. This action is expected to reduce B.C.'s emissions by up to 25 million tonnes below current estimates by 2050 and create up to 66,000 jobs by 2026 (Pan Canadian Framework, 2016:18).

Pricing for carbon pollution

B.C.'s *Greenhouse Gas Reduction Targets Amendment Act*, 2018 provides a statutory basis for setting up a direct carbon price on fossil fuels consumption, and a framework for cap-and-trade market-based to reduce emissions. B.C.'s carbon tax on the purchase and use of fossil fuels (such as gasoline, diesel, natural gas, heating fuel, propane and coal, and certain combustibles) is set at $35/tonne of CO_2 equivalent emissions and will rise annually by $5/tonne/year until it gets to $50/tonne in 2021. Tax rates based on $35/tonne of emissions for gasoline, diesel (light fuel oil) and natural gas are set at 7.78 ¢/litre, 8.95 ¢/litre, 6.65 ¢/cubic meters respectively. Revenue generated will be used in providing carbon tax relief, maintain industry competitiveness, and encourage new green initiatives in the province (British Columbia Carbon Tax). Although carbon pricing in the province makes the burning of fossil fuels more expensive for British Columbians, it can reduce GHG emissions and encourage a shift from carbon-intensive energy sources to carbon-free alternatives.

Moreover, B.C. has created a market for carbon emissions by putting a fixed ceiling on the amount of carbon emissions allowed (cap-and-trade) according to the *Greenhouse Gas Reduction (Cap and*

Trade) Act which provides the groundwork for reducing emissions from B.C.'s large emitters. Under this legislation, the government of B.C. established caps for designated GHG emitters in the province by issuing tradable compliance units corresponding to given periods. The cap-and-trade program therefore allows polluters who successfully reduce emissions below their ceiling/cap to sell their excess capacity (quota or right) to emit to those that are over their caps (assigned amount units).

The cap-and-trade system is an opportunity for B.C. to participate in national, regional and international emission trading schemes. For instance, B.C. is a part of the Vancouver Declaration on Clean Growth and Climate Change, Under2 Coalition, Carbon Pricing Leadership Coalition, RegionsAdapt, International Zero Emission Vehicle Alliance, States & Regions Alliance, International Carbon Action Partnership, Western Climate Initiative, Pacific Coast Collaborative Climate Leadership Action Plan, B.C. & Guangdong-Memorandum of Understanding on Climate Change and Low Carbon Development) (British Columbia Federal and International Cooperation).

Because it provides an incentive for sustainable choices that yield fewer GHG emissions by either putting a price or setting a cap on emissions, B.C.'s carbon pricing framework could constitute a valuable option to reduce emissions while growing the economy. B.C.'s real GDP grew more than 17%, while net GHG emissions declined by 4.7% between 2007 and 2015 (Climate Leadership Plan 2016:12). According to statistics in B.C.'s Climate Leadership Plan, implementation of the province's low carbon fuel standard has resulted in the avoidance of over 2.3 million tonnes of emissions of GHGs between 2010-2012: the decrease in GHG emissions since 2007 could be attributed to B.C.'s policy of putting a price on carbon emissions (*Ibid*, 18).

Complementary actions to cut emissions

Tightening codes for vehicles and energy efficiency standards, among other complementary actions, can target market barriers where carbon pricing is not (timely) enough to cut emissions in the pre-2030 timeframe. The federal government's approach to decarbonising transportation includes setting and updating vehicle emissions standards and enhancing the efficiency of transportation systems. According to the Pan Canadian Framework, this would involve putting more zero-emission vehicles on the road (such as plug-in hybrids, electric vehicles and hydrogen fuel-cell vehicles, and biofuels), shifting from higher-to-lower-emitting modes (such as public transit, cycling, transporting goods by rail rather than trucks) and using cleaner fuels (advanced biofuels). The B.C. government has operationalised these standards by putting in place the following meaningful transport related policies/investments (Climate Leadership Plan, 2016:18-21):

- **Increasing the low carbon fuel standard**: B.C.'s low carbon fuel standard aims to reduce the carbon intensity of transportation fuels by 10% by 2020 relative to 2010. Planning to increase the standard to 15% by 2030 is expected to achieve up to a 3.4 million tonne reduction in annual GHG emissions.
- **Incentives for using renewable natural gas**: B.C.'s amended Greenhouse Gas Reduction Regulation is expected to boost emission reductions in transportation: it will permit utilities to double the total pool of incentives available to transform commercial fleets to natural gas. Moreover, the production of renewable natural gas resources through increased demand and encourage investments in natural gas fuelling stations at customers' facilities will be promoted.
- **Incentives for purchasing a clean energy vehicle (CEV)**: B.C.'s CEV program is projected to facilitate the use of zero-emission vehicles (ZEVs) in B.C. Buyers or lessees of a qualifying new ZEV will be eligible for B.C.'s SCRAP-IT program (to get older/higher emission vehicles off the road) and incentives off the pre-tax sticker price for fuel cell electric, plug-in hybrid electric, battery electric and hydrogen fuel cell vehicles.
- **Supporting vehicle charging development for ZEVs**: B.C. is committed to promoting this innovation by developing regulations that can encourage the installation of infrastructure for electric vehicle charging and electric vehicle charging stations in strata buildings and developments.

- **10-year plan to improve the transportation network in B.C.**: the plan is a comprehensive set of strategies for transitioning to low carbon fuels such as increasing the number of B.C. public buses and fuelling stations that run on compressed natural gas (CNG). Encouraging ferries/vessels to run on either ultra-low sulphur diesel or liquefied natural gas (a low-carbon content fuel), promoting the (expansion/) construction of new rapid transit in Vancouver and Surrey, reducing congestion by replacing the George Massey Tunnel to reduce idling and optimize movement through Canada's Pacific Gateway are additional strategies under the province's 10-year plan.

Adaptation and Climate Resilience

Canadian governments have identified actions that can strengthen resilience and adaptation to the effects of extreme weather events among other climate change impacts in Canada. Actions constitute the establishment of a Canadian Centre for Climate Services (to help improve access to authoritative and foundational information) and the building of regional adaptation capacity and expertise (by working with regional and Canadian governments/partners). Implementing scientific data and traditional knowledge, building climate resilience through infrastructure, protecting and enhancing human health and well-being, supporting regions that are vulnerable to the dramatic and permanent impacts of climate change, and reducing disaster risks and climate-related hazards in the country, including addressing impacts related to failures in winter roads are additional actions to ensure that Canadians thrive in a changing climate (Pan-Canadian Framework, 2016).

The government of B.C. has partnered with the Pacific Climate Impacts Consortium, Engineers and Geoscientists British Columbia, and Engineers Canada and their Public Infrastructure Engineering Vulnerability Committee Protocol and undertaking other initiatives to address potential effects of climate change on roads and bridges. To further ensure the resilience, effectiveness, efficiency, and reliability of B.C.'s transportation infrastructure, and adaptability to climate conditions, B.C. has developed best practice guidance. It is expected to address likely climate change impacts on the highway infrastructure and adapt the transportation system to extreme weather, among other effects (British Columbia Adapting Transportation).

Clean Technology, Innovation, and Jobs

The federal government has released its Mid-Century Long-Term Low-Greenhouse Gas Development Strategy, and it remains committed to meeting its climate change goals and creating economic opportunities in Canada by investing in clean technology. This strategy is intended to bring new and in-demand Canadian technologies to expanding global markets and enhance the cost-effectiveness and efficiency of mitigation and adaptation measures while equipping the nation's workforce with the knowledge and skills to succeed. The federal government is committed to supporting B.C., among other provinces and territories (with investments in clean technologies, among other emission-reduction opportunities) in this regard through the following investments (Government of Canada, 2016:47-48):

- $62.5 million for the deployment of charging infrastructure for electric vehicles, natural gas and hydrogen refuelling stations, and demonstration of next-generation recharging technologies;
- $82.5 million over two years for research and development of clean energy technologies;
- $100 million/year from the Regional Development Agencies to support clean technology; $50 million over four years for supporting new climate change and air quality technologies;
- $125 million over two years including for projects that reduce emissions of GHG;
- $81 billion over 11 years for investments in public transit, transportation that supports trade and green infrastructure;
- $1 billion, over four years, to help promote clean technology in different sectors of the economy
- $1.9 billion in the order of $50 million in clean energy and technology, $831 million for clean transportation, $300 million for transportation infrastructure, $24 million to improve the energy

efficiency of homes and businesses and $704 million for clean electricity infrastructure.

An Overview of Regulatory Approaches Controlling Transportation in Sweden

World Bank statistics indicate that per capita emissions in Sweden dropped from 6.6 in 1960 to 4.5 in 2014 (World Bank Group). Between 1990 to 2015 Swedish transport emissions, where road transport with cars and heavy-duty vehicles dominate, fell by 25% from (from 19.3 to 18.2 MT CO_2 equivalent in 2015), mainly a result of policies encouraging a switch from petrol-powered to diesel-powered cars (Government of Sweden, 2017:14). Reduced Climate Impact, one of 16 environmental quality objectives that the Riksdag (Swedish Parliament) adopted, is the basis for climate action in Sweden. To live up to the Paris Agreement and implement this objective, the Riksdag, in 2017, passed a 3-pillar climate policy framework: Climate Act, national climate targets and a Climate Policy Council.

The Climate Act legislates that the Swedish government should, every fourth year, develop a climate policy action plan that is grounded on its national climate targets: the action plan should contain planned policies/measures to achieve emission reductions. The goal is for the Swedish government to (i) by 2045, have no net emissions into the atmosphere and should thereafter achieve negative emissions; (ii) by 2030, reduce emissions from domestic transport, excluding domestic aviation (by at least 70% compared with 2010); (iii) by 2030, reduce emissions in sectors covered by the EU Effort Sharing Regulation (ESR) (by at least 63% lower than in 1990); and (iv) by 2040, reduce emissions in the sectors regulated by the EU ESR (by at least 75% lower than in 1990) (*Ibid*, 11-12). To meet these targets in a timely fashion and make Sweden 'one of the world's first fossil-free welfare state,' Sweden has adopted the following cross-sectorial and sector-specific policy instruments.

Cross-sectoral policy instruments

Carbon pricing: the EU Emissions Trading System (EU ETS), established in 2005 by Directive 2003/87/EC to cost-effectively reduce emissions of GHG and combat climate change, works on the cap-and-trade principle and in many aspects is part of Sweden's Climate policy. It regulates emissions of carbon dioxide from combustion installations and energy-intensive industries (mineral oil refineries, coke ovens, iron and steel industry, pulp and paper industry, and mineral industry) and emissions of nitrous oxide and perfluorocarbons (Directive 2003/87/EC). Applicable in Sweden through the Emissions Trading Act (2004:1199) and the Emissions Trading Ordinance (2004:1205), some 760 Swedish installations are included in the EU ETS system (*Ibid*, 43).

Sweden introduced energy and carbon dioxide taxes in 1991 as the nation's strategy to cut CO_2 emissions in sectors that are not covered by the EU ETS system. The level of a carbon dioxide tax is influenced by the content of the fossil carbon in the fuel: the higher the carbon content, the higher the fee, meaning that non-fossil fuels such as ethanol and other biofuels are not subject to these taxes (carbon pricing). Carbon dioxide tax had increased from SEK 0.25/kg CO_2 in 1991 to SEK 1.13/kg CO_2 in 2017. Energy tax, levied on carriers of energy (petrol and diesel) used by engines and for heating, was introduced in 1924 and 1937, respectively, with fuel used for heating and electricity made subject to an energy tax in the 1950s and in January 2016. The energy tax on diesel was raised by SEK 0.52/litre and on petrol by SEK 0.47/litre (Government of Sweden, 2017:44).

Therefore, an energy tax on fuels depends on whether it is used as motor fuel or heating fuel or between industry, households and the energy sector. Tax reduction applies for sustainable fuels and varies depending on the quantity of biodiesel blended in diesel and ethanol blended in petrol. So, depending on whether it is used for low blending in petrol, high blending in petrol (E_{85}), or high blending in diesel (ED_{95}), ethanol has 88 to 100% exemption from energy tax. The deduction is 36% of the regular energy tax for FAME in diesel and 100% (both CO_2 and energy taxes) for hydrogenated vegetable and animal oils and fats (HVO), including other biofuels classified as gasoline or diesel (*Ibid*).

Local Climate Investment Programme (LCIP): also known as the Climate Leap, the LCIP is a local investment program that the Swedish government introduced in 2015 to assist certain local and regional investments/organisations (those that are not covered by the EU ETS) to reduce their GHG emissions. The annual budgetary allocation for this program has been growing: from SEK 600 million/year in 2016 to SEK 1300 million in 2019. The Swedish government, during September through June 2017, made decisions on 1035 investments totalling SEK 4.65 billion, of which grants covered 43%. The expectation is that investments that were granted up until 2017, June 20th will generate a reduction of nearly 0.7 Mt CO_2 equivalent/year during the technical life span of these investments (*Ibid*, 45).

Sweden's Environmental Code and planning legislation: Sweden's Environmental Code and planning legislation contain general rules that must be observed in all proposed projects and programs that are significantly hazardous to the environment and climate, and requirements to use the best available technology. Under the Environmental Code, permits are needed before the establishment of substantial environmentally hazardous activities, with emissions of GHG constituting a significant portion of the environmental impact assessment procedure in the country. The Planning and Building Act also direct planning measures (*Ibid*).

Climate change communication: this policy measure is intended to equip Swedes with the tools and knowledge needed to mitigate and adapt to climate change, including other sectoral climate policy instruments/measures. Sweden's Environmental Protection Agency and Meteorological and Hydrological Institute have the mandate to, among others, gather and communicate climate change information, and provide training, funding, and platforms for dialogue and cooperation between key climate actors. The Fossil-free Sweden, the Strategic Innovation Partnership Programs and Smart Industry are additional initiatives within which dialogue and collaboration with stakeholders also take place in Sweden (Government of Sweden, 2017:46-54).

Research and development (R&D): the government has made available SEK 620 million for energy and climate-related research and development for 2017-2020 as a way of creating better preconditions to achieve its emission reduction targets. The overarching objective of energy research and innovation is to enable the fulfilment of Sweden's climate and energy objectives and other energy-related environmental objectives. In 2017 the Swedish government proposed an expansion of the amount of contributions to energy development and research with some SEK 620 million for 2017-2020 (*Ibid*, 46-54).

Sector-specific (Transport) policy instruments

In addition to the above cross-sectorial policies, the government of Sweden has adopted the following sector-specific policy instruments: aviation tax, fuel change, requirements for renewable fuels at filling stations, EC Fuel Quality Directive (Directive 2009/30/EC), emission performance standards for new vehicles, differentiated vehicle tax, super-green rebate, lower benefit value on cars with advanced environmental technology, electrical bus premium, bonus-malus-system for new light vehicles, electric vehicle premium, charge at home-grant, research and demonstration, eco-bonus system for heavy transports and Fossil-free transport solutions (*Ibid*, 51-54).

Aviation tax: as of 1 April 2018, flights leaving from Swedish airports pay an added charge of 6-39 euros (60 - 400 kronor), depending on the destination. Air travel tax aims to diminish the carbon footprint of flights. The aviation tax is governed by the Aviation Tax Act and EU ETS (as per EU Regulation No. 421/2014 of the European Parliament and of the Council of 16 April 2014 amending Directive 2003/87/EC).

Fuel Change: fuel change is an emission reduction obligation that was introduced on 1 July 2018. Suppliers of petrol and diesel are obligated to reduce emissions from petrol and diesel by increasing biofuel blending. With the indicative target to 2030 to reduce emissions by at least 40% (a share of biofuels of about 50%), fuel change is crucial for the phasing out of transport fossil fuels in Sweden.

Requirements for renewable fuels at filling stations: in Sweden, it is a legislative requirement for filling stations with sales of petrol and diesel above 1,500 m^3/year to supply not less than a renewable fuel.

EC Fuel Quality Directive (Directive 2009/30/EC): this low carbon fuel standard introduces conditions for suppliers of fuel to cut down the GHG intensity of energy supplied for road transportation and establishes sustainability criteria for biofuels if they are to be counted towards the duty to cut down GHG intensity.

Emission performance standards for new vehicles: under EU regulations setting emission performance standards, new vans and passenger cars are part of the Community's approach to reducing emissions of CO_2 from light-duty vehicles: new passenger cars must not emit an average of over 130g CO_2/km by 2015 and not above 95g CO_2/km by 2021. Furthermore, new vans should not emit an average of over 175g CO_2/km by 2017 and 147gCO_2/km by 2020.

Differentiated vehicle tax: Swedish law stipulates that vehicle owners pay an annual vehicle tax that is differentiated concerning the vehicle's CO_2 emissions/km (with CO_2-related vehicle tax set at SEK 22/g CO_2 /km beyond 111 g CO_2 /km in mixed driving). The vehicle tax aims to encourage car buyers to go for low climate impact cars. The tax for cars adapted for ethanol and gas is lower: SEK 11/g CO_2 /km beyond the first 111 g CO_2 /km, etc.

Super-green rebate: the Super-green rebate policy was intended to contribute to technological development and deployment such as reducing obstacles for a large-scale introduction of hybrid and electric vehicles in Sweden. Swedish buyers of passenger cars that meet EU exhaust conditions—Euro 5 or Euro 6—and emit not more than 50grams of CO_2/km are entitled to a super-green car rebate: this rebate is set at SEK 20,000 for private buyers of electric cars and 35 or 17.5% of the cost difference between the price of a super-green car and a non-super-green car of a similar type for non-private buyers.

Lower benefit value on cars with advanced environmental technology: this incentive was designed to encourage private use of company-registered cars with sustainable technologies. Company-registered cars in Sweden receive comparatively favourable tax treatment through the reduction of their benefit value. Also, the benefit value of plug-in hybrids, electric cars powered by natural gas (but for liquified petroleum gas) receive an extra 40% discount until 2020.

Electrical bus premium: this bus premium applies to electrical busses for public transportation use in Sweden. Contingent on the number of passengers and whether the bus runs uniquely on electricity or is a hybrid, regional public transportation agencies can apply for this premium, and SEK 350 million for 2016-2019 has been allocated in this regard.

Bonus-malus-system for new light vehicles: vehicles with low CO_2 emissions in Sweden are eligible for a bonus at purchase, but those with high emissions of CO_2 will be highly taxed within the first three years.

Electric vehicle premium: this premium was introduced to reduce dependency on cars by improving commuting longer distances with electric bicycles and scooters. About SEK 350 million/year between 2018-2020 for a premium that covers up to 25% of the purchase price is available for this purpose.

Charge at home-grant: this rebate is equivalent to 50% of costs to buy/install homes and electric vehicles charging stations. About SEK 90 million/annum between 2018–2020 is available for this program to financially encourage households to switch to sustainable means of transportation.

Research and demonstration: the Swedish government finances the EU Refuel project (to develop strategies to introduce cost-effective alternative vehicle fuels) and other large-scale biofuels research projects. Funded programs include strategic vehicle research and innovation, collaboration program for renewable fuels and systems, biomass gasification research, battery funding, energy efficiency in transportation, a demonstration program for electric vehicles and innovations for a sustainable society.

Eco-bonus system for heavy transports: to motivate the transfer of freight transport by road transport to water transport, and hence reduce GHG emissions from heavy transports, the Swedish government has allocated SEK 150 million for Eco-bonus between 2018-2020.

Fossil-free transport solutions: the government assigned the sum of SEK 1 billion to promote the switch to an electrified transportation system, and development of sustainable solutions for batteries, electric cars, and biogas between the period of 2018–2023. With SEK 3 million/annum until 2019, the Swedish Energy Agency, with the assistance of the Swedish National Board of Housing, Building and Planning, the Swedish Environmental Protection Agency, Transport Analysis, the Swedish Transport Administration and the Swedish Transport Agency will be coordinating and preparing a strategic plan for the transition to a fossil-free transportation sector.

Conclusion

The research attempts to inform transport policy in Canada's British Columbia and Sweden, two of the 15 jurisdictions that received the 2018 United Nations Momentum for Change Climate Action Award. With a focus on the transport sector, the aim was to offer a framework upon which Africa can translate laws to reduce emissions and strengthen national adaptive capacity into action in a way that will not compromise the prospects for holding global temperature increases well below 2° C.

Both governments have adopted the objective to make their territories one of the world's first fossil-free states: to that end, they have launched fossil-free initiatives and taken climate actions. Drawing from the experience of British Columbia and Sweden, a successful climate policy should have the following elements: information on climate change impacts; data on emissions of GHGs in the jurisdiction; ambitious GHG emissions targets against a baseline year, including a net-zero GHG emissions targets; and a climate action plan to implement audacious GHG reduction targets.

Pricing carbon pollution; promoting adoption of and innovation in clean vehicles and fuels; creating new clean tech jobs; and working to direct the development of dependable and safe transportation infrastructure that is constructed to withstand extreme weather events are significant pillars of their climate strategies. If these strategies have put Sweden and British Columbia top of the list of jurisdictions that are doing the most to save the climate system, there's no excuse for failing to follow suit and pass climate laws to cut GHG emissions far beyond what other governments have done and yet enjoy robust economic growth and promote in Africa.

References

Ajulor, O.V. (2018) 'The Challenges of Policy Implementation in Africa and Sustainable Development Goals', in *PEOPLE: International Journal of Social Sciences* Vol.3 No.3, 1497-1518.

Awojobi, O. (2017) 'The Impacts of Climate Change in Africa: A Review of the Scientific Literature', in *Journal of International Academic Research for Multidisciplinary* Vol. 5 No.11, 39-52.

British Columbia, (n.d) 'British Columbia's Carbon Tax.' Online: https://www2.gov.bc.ca/gov/content/environment/climate-change/planning-and-action/carbon-tax

British Columbia, (n.d) 'Adapting Transportation Infrastructure to Climate Change.' Online https://www2.gov.bc.ca/gov/content/transportation/transportation-environment/climate-action/adaptation

British Columbia, (n.d) 'Federal and International Collaboration.' Online: https://www2.gov.bc.ca/gov/content/environment/climate-change/planning-and-action/government-collaboration.

Chirisa, I., *et al.,* (2015) 'Transport and the environment: a critical review for Africa', in *Chinese Journal of Population Resources and Environment* Vol. 13, 4309-319.

Clark, K. (2018) 'The Paris Agreement: Its Role in International Law and American Jurisprudence', in *Notre Dame Journal of International & Comparative Law* Vol.8 No. 2.

Decision 1/CP.21, Adoption of the Paris Agreement, Report of the COP on its 21st session, held in Paris from 30 November to 13 December 2015, addendum, FCCC/CP/2015/10 Add.1 (29 January 2016)

Directive 2003/87/EC of the European Parliament and of the Council

Edenhofer, O., *et al.* (eds.) (2014) 'Summary for Policymakers' in *Climate Change 2014: Mitigation of Climate Change. Contribution of Working Group III to the Fifth Assessment Report of the Intergovernmental Panel on Climate Change,* Cambridge, IPCC

Eriksen, S., K. O'Brien and I. Rosentrater (2008) 'Climate Change in Eastern and Southern Africa: impacts, vulnerability and adaptation', in Global Environmental Change and Human http://www.bvsde.paho.org/bvsacd/cd68/climafrica.pdf

Government of British Columbia (2016) *Climate Leadership Plan*, Vancouver, Government of British Columbia.

Government of Canada (2016) *Pan-Canadian Framework on Clean Growth and Climate Change*m, Ottawa, Government of Canada

Government of Canada (2018) *National Inventory Report 1990-2016: Greenhouse Gas Sources and Sinks in Canada, Canada's Submission to the United National Framework Convention on Climate Change*, Gatineau, Government of Canada.

Government of Sweden (2017) *Sweden's Seventh National Communication on Climate Change* Stockholm: Naturvårdsverket

Ivanova, M. (2017) 'Politics, Economics, and Society' in Klein, D., *et al. The Paris Agreement on Climate Change: Analysis and Commentary.* Oxford: Oxford University Press.

Kahsay, F. A., and L. G. Hansen (2016) 'The effect of climate change and adaptation policy on agricultural production in Eastern Africa", in *Ecological Economics* Vol. 121, 54-64

Levin, K., *et al.* (2012) 'Overcoming the tragedy of super wicked problems: Constraining our future selves to ameliorate global climate change', in *Policy Sciences* Vol. 45 No. 2 123–152.

Masson-Delmotte, V., *et al.* (2018) 'Summary for Policymakers' in *Global Warming of 1.5°C: An IPCC Special Report on the impacts of global warming of 1.5°C above pre-industrial levels and related global greenhouse gas emission pathways, in the context of strengthening the global response to the threat of climate change, sustainable development, and efforts to eradicate poverty.* Geneva, IPCC.

Matthews, J.B.R. (ed.) (2018) 'Annex I: Glossary' in Masson-Delmotte, V., *et al.* (eds.) *Global Warming of 1.5°C. An IPCC Special Report on the impacts of global warming of 1.5°C above pre-industrial levels and related global greenhouse gas emission pathways, in the context of strengthening the global response to the threat of climate change, sustainable development, and efforts to eradicate poverty.* Geneva: IPCC.

Nachmany, M. *et al.*, The 2015 Global Climate Legislation Study, A Review of Climate Change Legislation in 99 Countries: Summary for Policy-makers. Online:

http://www.lse.ac.uk/GranthamInstitute/wp-content/uploads/2015/05/Global_climate_legislation_study_20151.pdf

Protocol to the United Nations Framework Convention on Climate Change (Kyoto), 37 ILM (1998) 22.

Rosen, A.M. (2015) 'The Wrong Solution at the Right Time: The Failure of the Kyoto Protocol on Climate Change', in *Politics and Policy* Vol. 43 No.1, 30-38, 30.

Serdeczny, O., *et al.* (2016) 'Climate change impacts in Sub-Saharan Africa: from physical changes to their social repercussions', in Regional Environmental Change

UNFCCC, Conference of the Parties (COP) 15th session, Agenda item 9 (High-level segment), Draft Decision -/CP.15, Copenhagen, FCCC/CP/2009/L.7, 7-18 December 2009, para.1.

United Nations Framework Convention on Climate Change, 31 ILM (1992) 851 [UNFCCC].

World Bank Group, (n.d) "CO_2 emissions (metric tons per capita): Sweden." Online: https://data.worldbank.org/indicator/EN.ATM.CO2E.PC?name_desc=true

World Bank, (2019) CO_2 emissions from transport (% of total fuel combustion) (2019). Online: https://data.worldbank.org/indicator/en.co2.tran.zs

World Health Organization (2019) 'Health and sustainable development.' https://www.who.int/sustainable-development/transport/health-risks/climate-impacts/en/

Worldometers (2019) 'Current World Population.' Online: http://www.worldometers.info/world-population/#table-forecast

Chapter Thirteen

Global Warming and Climate Colonialism/Imperialism: Appraising Decolonisation

Nkwazi Nkuzi Mhango

Introduction

Currently and ominously, the world faces many manmade threats such as global warming, hunger, poverty, nuclear proliferation and wars resulting from the looting, plunder and scarcity of resources. However, one phenomenon, namely global warming, poses one of the greatest threats to the world. Many countries have already been adversely affected. Due to global warming, sea levels are now rising; hurricanes are as well increasing not to mention, for the first time, the creation of climate or environmental refugees (Dun & Gemenne, 2008; 2011; Hartmann, 2010; Morrissey, 2012; and Gemmenne, 2015). Global warming has a lot to do with most of the conflicts, hunger, poverty and insecurity that haunt many people of the world as it affects almost everything mainly resources (Scheffran & Battaglini, 2011; and Scheffran, Brzoska, Kominek, Link & Schilling, 2012), be they, human or material. Therefore, in no way can one address, think about or talk about global problems without touching on global warming, globalisation, colonisation and imperialism. Of all problems facing the world, global warming happens to be the thorniest due to the fact that it affects almost everyone and every country and every sector, although in different ways and magnitudes which are contingent on histories of colonialism, globalism and imperialism.

This chapter interrogates global warming, particularly how it started, and how it is affecting poor countries that comparably have very little, if any, culpability in respect of the phenomenon. Importantly, the chapter connects global warming to colonialism (Newell & Paterson, 2010; Premalatha, Abbasi, Abassi & Abbasi,

2011; and Paterson, 2016) and imperialism (Sealey-Huggins, 2017). The chapter proposes the need to decolonise global warming and the international superstructure that buttresses climate-change-global-apartheid. The idea is to ensure that states that are responsible for global warming become accountable and responsible for their crimes. Instead of coloniality and hegemony, the international community needs true accountability, collegiality and sincerity in addressing global warming and its ramifications.

As the world seeks to address global warming, Mhango (2018a) also explores ways in which global warming plays out with exigencies of unity in collectively addressing the problem. On this note, I view global warming as a uniting force, whether positive or negative. I further submit that global warming, if openly and seriously dealt with, is likely to be the opportunity for the world to see the big picture. Collective discussions would allow the victims of global warming to air their grievances and the solutions instead of being bulldozed and hoodwinked by rich countries cum-big polluters as is currently the case. This means that every country, regardless of how big or small, must have the right to participate in addressing this phenomenon. In so doing, the process must be truly owned by all stakeholders and not by states that have global veto powers or financial muscles. The possibility of winning the war against global warming is only through equality, unity and the decolonisation of the international mechanisms currently in place. Since the world became aware of global warming, global colonial domineering, arrogance, individuality, national interests as opposed to bona fide international engagements have taken a centre stage.

In principle, global warming can be blamed on carbon colonialism (Billett, 2010), toxic imperialism (Attfield, 2009) and sham efforts to address climate change. Without bona fide international efforts to decolonise the environments many innocent countries, particularly poor ones, are likely to suffer. This chapter offers the example of how the US contaminated the Marshal Islands in ways that harmed the citizens. The chapter will begin by shedding light on how global warming is being handled at the international level.

The Handling of Global Warming Issues at the International Level

Before going into details of global warming, we need to briefly define it. Fisher, Hales, Wang, Ko & Sze (1999) cited in Shine (2009) define global warming as "the ratio of the surface temperature change due to a sustained emission of a gas, relative to the temperature change due to a sustained emission of CFC-11" (p. 468) or chlorofluorocarbon 11 (Ravishankara, Daniel & Portmann, 2009); which means a certain type of ozone-depleting gas (Newman, Oman, Douglass, Fleming, Frith, Hurwitz, Kawa, Jackman, Krotkov, Nash & Nielsen, 2009) or ozone-depleting properties (Vining, 2009) whose results, among others, is global warming, which, in turn, creates a long-term hot state of Earth (James Lovelock cited in Helmreich, 2011).

Essentially, global warming, as its name goes, for the author, is an increase of world temperature to unprecedented amounts that are likely to harmfully affect all living creatures on earth. Global warming has been politicised (Oosthoek & Gills, 2013). This shows how ignorant and indifferent such major polluters are. Also, this shows the shakiness of the international system not to mention putting our scientific advancement to question. Instead of politicising global warming, it is necessary to resolve the problem (Bruce, 1999 cited in Paterson, 2013; and Tranter, 2013).

Interestingly, Public Policy Polling (2013) cited in van der Linden (2015) maintains that 37% of Americans believe that global warming is a hoax as opposed to 97% of climate scientists who have concluded that human-caused global warming is happening (Cook, Nuccitelli, Green, Richardson, Winkler, Painting, Way, Jacobs & Skuce, 2013 cited in van der Linden, 2015). I submit that it is not only the 37% who feel that global warming is a hoax. Baer & Singer (2016) note that former US President; George H. W. Bush was excited to see photos that show global warming as "a hoax perpetrated by power-mad environmentalists" (p. 20). If the President of such a powerful country – a country that was part of the G7 – has such views, why then are other smaller countries being pull into the agenda? The U.S.A which denies climate change is the one that also perpetrates atrocities globally (CNN, 2003). Thus former South African

President, Nelson Mandela is cited in the CNN (2003): "if there is a country that has committed unspeakable atrocities in the world, it is the United States of America." Thanks to the colonial nature of the international community, the same villain has been allowed to commit even more atrocities against the world. Therefore the US and other major polluters lack moral ground to lead others.

What would have been the reaction of the so-called developed world had such a person been an African President? One can refer to how the world, especially the west reacted when former South African President Thabo Mbeki questioned HIV/AIDS conventional science the west had come up with (Nattrass, 2008). While his rationale was scientifically true that AIDS was used racially as it has been *vis-à-vis* its cause, origin and how it is spread (Cullinan, 2009), Euro-America would just not have an African President questioning Eurocentric epistemologies. Despite there being evidence that the first HIV/AIDS cases were reported in Los Angeles on June, 5, 1981(Merson, O'Malley, Serwadda & Apisuk, 2008), Eurocentric scholars devised theories that attributed the origin of HIV/AIDS to Africa. The Eurocentric objective was to destroy African cultures while hiding behind the pretext of fighting the pandemic. I live in Canada. I have never seen any campaigns against HIV/AIDS that are as loud and penetrating as the ones evidenced in Africa. The point here is that it is more revealing for Africans to always unpack the latent/implicit/unsaid aims in Euro-American projects than it is to focus merely on their manifest/explicit/professed aims.

Is Global Warming a Moral, Political or Scientific Issue?

Although global warming is defined in scientific terms, it affects everyone and it is therefore a concern to everyone, including policy makers (McCright & Dunlap, 2011; (Biermann & Boas, 2010). Global warming has some elements of colonialism. Regarding colonialism, former Uruguayan President, Jose Mujica cited in Ganis (2015) posits that "by looking at the current global trends, we can say that now the whole earth planet is a colony and the colonizers come from within, trying to exploit it in their favour" (p. 20). I concur with Mujica's argument. The quote exactly fits in the current global warming discourses and practices wherein the west dominates both in pollution and in proffering lopsided solutions that further immiserate citizens of the developing states. In this regard, it is necessary to decolonise the international structure so that states are more equal. The global warming issue is a political, economic, epistemological and neo-colonial issue. The current international structure was constituted while many African countries were still under colonialism. As such, Euro-American states are unfairly forcing all other countries to bear the burden of Euro-American mischief-making on the environment.

Deetz (2010) notes that in the seventeenth century, the British cities and rivers were more contaminated and polluted than they became in the nineteenth century and beyond. In the seventeenth century, coal was used in the "principal fields for the investment of British capital investment" (Nef, 2013, p. 3); almost all British machinery at that time was powered by coal (Davis, 2012; Mathias, 2013). In this sense, the developed countries inevitably underwent pollution during the process of industrialisation. Notwithstanding the fact that Africa has not caused global warming, African states are being internationally terrorised to bear the burden of such global warming (Leader, 2003; Cooke, 2013). Under the 21st Conference of the Parties (COP21) in Paris in December 2015, "developing countries are submitting their Intended Nationally Determined Contributions (INDCs), indicating their emissions reduction commitments for the near term (to 2025 or 2030)" (Iyer, Edmonds, Fawcett, Hultman, Alsalam, Asrar, Calvin, Clarke, Creason, Jeong & Kyle, 2015). These submissions do not consider the fact that Africa did not cause global warming; the measures and contributions will also have negative ramifications on the economies in African countries. Clémençon (2016) notes that the COP21 essentially helps developed states to avert responsibility for their massive pollution of the atmosphere. Thus, Euro-America is eco-terrorising African states and other developing countries. The coercion, on developing countries, to bear the burden for global warming is an aspect of environmental terrorism or the unlawful use of force against environmental resources with the intention of harming certain individuals or deprive populations of environmental benefits in the name of social or political objectives (Gleick 2006). This is what developed countries are replicating by trying to avoid historical accountability on issues surrounding global warming.

How Global Warming, Colonialism and Neocolonialism are Tied Together

Colonisation (Grovogui, 2016; and Schmidt, 2016), created poverty that caused environmental destruction. Therefore, global warming must be understood as an aspect of colonialism, neo-colonialism and neoimperial terrorism.

Apart from causing global warming, the US is abusing and misusing nuclear power on other countries. It stops other countries from developing nuclear power even as it possesses and uses the same nuclear power (Kim, 2014; Gerson, 2009; Lutz & Enloe, 2009; and Jacobs, 2013). Surprisingly, despite being the only country that twice misused nuclear power against innocent citizens of other countries, the US is still allowed by the international community to lead the war against global warming. The key question is where the US gets the moral ground to stop others from polluting the world.

Apart from causing global warming (Gore, 2016), the US conducted nuclear experiments on Marshall Island as Rudiak-Gould (2013: 100-101) states: "…the most applicable of which was the testing of nuclear weapons conducted by the United States from June 30, 1946 to August 18, 1958. During that time, the United States ran a total of 67 nuclear tests, the most powerful of which was the "Bravo" shot which was the equivalent of 1,000 Hiroshima bombs". Baracca (2018) also notes that, up until 1963, the Pacific Ocean saw 105 nuclear tests performed on it. How much harm did such tests cause to the environment, both acquatic and terrestrial? Here, we are talking about the Marshall Island. How many birds, fish and sea life were destroyed? If this single example is devastating, what of other cases of nuclear stockpiles all over the world? To address all such dangers needs international commitment and understanding based on the decolonisation of the world system, in order to enable it to serve the interests of all humankind.

Despite committing such horrendous environmental terrorism, the US has never been taxed to redress the travails of Marshall Islands. This is simply because the US is hegemonic in the world

(Paterson, 2013). The industrialised countries are using climate capitalism which revolves around large scale exploitation of fossil fuels (Kahn & Yardley, 2007; Stearns, 2018; Newell & Paterson 2010), yet Donald Trump so much puts America first that he refuses even to buy into the climate change agenda (Politico Staff, 2017 cited in Croucher, 2018). Chinese leaders have also already flatly rejected accountability for global warming, by any means (Kahn & Yardley, 2007). In this regard, global warming is tied to global militarism.

Global Warming and Global Militarism

Due to US unclear experiments, citizens of Marshall Islands have confirmatory omens on the land, in the air and in the sea, including about cancers, deaths, environmental hazards, loss of habitat as a result of the environmental terrorism (Jetnil-Kijiner, 2014; McElfish, Hallgren & Yamada, 2015; Barker, 2012; Wartofsky, 2010; Richards, Berge, Pinca & Wallace, 2008). The question here is about how the US can possibly address the citizens of Marshall Islands about the threat of global warming when it has already subjected them to nuclear experiments.

What transpired in the Marshall Islands shows that:

1) There is human greed motivated by arrogance and ignorance. When the US duped the Marshallese, apart from exhibiting greedy and arrogance, it exhibited ignorance of the interconnectivity and intersectionality of the humankind. Debris from Japan's Fukushima Daiichi Nuclear Power Station (F1NPS), TEPCO—which produced about 250 million tons of rubble and debris (Norio, Ye, Kajitani, Shi & Tatano, 2011)—not to mention radioactive isotopes that have already been detected in China and North America - (Qiao, Wang, Zhao, Zhao, Dai, Song & Song, 2011; Ten Hoeve & Jacobson, 2012; and Trappe, Minc, Kittredge & Pink, 2014) have been detected in the U.S.A. This shows how deadly greed and ignorance can be to humankind. Additionally, there is no way we can ignore what transpired in the former USSR at Chernobyl on 26 April, 1986 when a nuclear plant exploded and spewed over 50 tons of nuclear fuel in the atmosphere, 70 tons of other fuels and 700 tons of radioactive graphite that settled near the site (Oosthoek & Gills, 2013).

2) Another thing exhibited is the eminent dangers nuclear poses to humankind. Japan also thought its nuclear plants were safe. Yet Ohtsuru, Tanigawa, Kumagai, Niwa, Takamura, Midorikawa, Nollet, Yamashita, Ohto, Chhem & Clarke (2015) note that the Chernobyl nuclear disaster caused acute radiation syndrome (ARS).

3) There is no international mechanism that can force Japan and other countries, whose nuclear reactors have already proved to be unsafely lethal, to close them down.

As indicated in the case of Marshall Islands, the US does not know that, in the near future, the unguarded and unsecured Runit dome (Gerrard, 2015) under which nuclear remnants are superficially buried may leak and start contamination as is currently happening in the case of Fukushima whose isotopes are detected in China and North America.

Culture and Space Exploration and their Contributions to Global Warming

Another area we need to consider and explore critically is the whole issue of exploration of space. Since the US and the then Union of Soviet Socialist Republic (USSR) started their races to the moon and later the space (Deese, 2009), how many rockets and spaceships were used to reach their goals; and how much smoke plumes did they release in the atmosphere ever since they started such nefarious adventures? Knowing how rockets that propel spaceships to the space consume millions of tonnes of fossil fuels, we can imagine how much global warming such races have caused not to mention millions of debris they left in the atmosphere. There is no way a spaceship can blast to the space without a rocket to push it up to target. Rockets, for decades, have been spewing millions if not billions of tons of gases in the atmosphere and stratosphere mainly black carbon (Friedberg, 2013) which in turn affects the atmosphere so as to directly bear on environmental degradation, which results in global warming.

As it is in the case of space exploration, there is no way we can address global warming without addressing toxic cultures that exacerbate it. For example, how much smoke do fireworks globally spew into the atmosphere during Christmas, Diwali, New Year and other occasions that use fireworks? Excluding Asian countries, African countries do not have any culture of using fireworks despite the fact that they recently joined this toxic culture that contributes to global warming. No doubt that the festivals mentioned above use excessive fireworks which cause pollution (Pandve, 2008; Palaneeswaria 2012). If we can remind ourselves how many tonnes of fireworks, for example, Asian countries use annually, we might be able to grasp how much such cultures contribute to global warming. Useful in countering global warming is the Rastafari "green philosophy"; Ubuntu ethics of care (Sibanda, 2017; Chuwa, 2014; Ramose, 2015; Mawere, 2012))

Consumerism as a Contributor to Global Warming

Former Uruguayan President Jose Mujica says that if all humans would consume as much as an average American consumes, we need three planets (*Al Jazeera*, 2013). To put it in this context, the US has always been defined by big things from buildings to vehicles. At an individual level, thanks to its capitalistic nature and race towards gigantism (Dezalay, 2005), everybody would like to have bigger things from big houses and mansions to bigger oil guzzlers and yachts for the superrich under the American dream. Consider the mansion American stars live in. If the citizens of the US and the like can reduce their taste for gigantism, how much can they serve? Try to imagine the greenhouse gas such mansions, oil guzzlers spew to the atmosphere pointlessly. How much water do such people use without regard for others? I live in North America. When I go to school to pick my children up, I see how children open water taps and leave water gushing while teachers and parents are just watching, in many occasions, as if they have nothing to do with this endemic and systemic abuse. How much energy is used to pump such water? Electric Power Research Institute (2008) cited in Mielke, Anadon & Narayanamurti (2010) notes that energy accounts for 27% of all water consumed in the United States outside the agricultural sector. Such power consumption does not involve the water consumed and abused. So, too, this does not involve resources such as food that are as well abused. As it is in the case of water, if we consider the power used annually to light Christmas and New Year in the Northern hemisphere, one can understand the nonsense behind accusations that it is developing countries that are causing climate change.

Further, to gauge how much resources, especially electricity and water the North American consumes, add the amount of electricity and water used in shale oil production in Canada and the US (Mielke, Anadon & Narayanamurti (2010). The situation is poised to become bleak soon. Elcock (2010) notes that by the year 2030, for example, in the US, domestic consumption of fresh water is expected to increase by 7% while water consumed for energy production is expected to increase by nearly 70%, and water consumed for biofuels (biodiesel and ethanol) production is expected to increase by almost 250%. So, Africa needs to be compensated by the polluters in the global north (Mhango, 2018b: 181). While Africa and other poor countries do not contribute substantial amounts of greenhouse gases, Holbrooke (2008) notes that the United States produces 19.4 tons of carbon dioxide per person per year; China (5.1 tons) trails not only the United States but also Russia (11.8 tons) and the countries of Western Europe (8.6 tons). India checks in at only 1.8 tons per capita (p. 3). Thus, there must be a mechanism to avoid burdening African citizens who do not cause global warming (Prins & Rayner, 2007). Euro-America must compensate Africans; they must invest clean technology [not old used technology] to Africa; they must avoid shifting the burden to Africans (Dennis, 2006; Razali, 2012). This can be easily done by increasing investment in clean energy sources, exporting new technology to Africa instead of exporting the old and polluting ones as is currently the case. Instead of allowing them to set the rules that shift the blame to poor countries, the states of the global north must compensate Africans.

Conclusion

As argued in this chapter, global warming has not yet received deserved attention. Much still needs to be done at individual, national and international levels. Most importantly, it has been argued that nothing can be achieved currently without decolonising the international status quo as far as colonialism and neocolonialism are concerned. Thus, if the international community is sincere and serious about global warming, the first step towards addressing and arresting it is for them to accept the blame for creating it. Colonial powers created and benefited from global warming. The door to finding the solution primarily lies with decolonising the international superstructure (Wendt, 1995) that is responsible for the phenomenon. For, if the international community does not embark on the decolonisation of the international superstructure, nothing positive will be achieved. It is the current neocolonial global superstructure created and espoused by colonial powers that shaped almost every problem the world is facing today. Had they not done this, there was no way the world would have been grappling with this phenomenon. It is for this reason that I have categorically argued in this chapter that, the first step to finding solutions for global warming lies in practical and true decolonisation of all current international mechanisms and structures. As noted above, for colonial powers which use other poor and weak countries to conduct their nuclear experiments as I have demonstrated with the Marshall Islands case wherein the US conducted many nuclear tests, such countries need to be brought to book so that they compensate the victims.

The second step is for countries responsible for global warming to accept the blame. Therefore, instead of politicking and politicising global warming, culprits need to come clean on the phenomenon so that they can have a moral ground to lead others in the fight against global warming. Culprits should commit themselves to the law that prohibits them from recidivism as far as global warming is concerned.

Thirdly, all powerful countries that hugely benefited from colonialism and later global warming, as the product of colonialism, must unconditionally and urgently compensate the victims so that the world can move forward collectively without any bitter feelings arising from historical wrongs. Victims of global warming would also have to be compensated.

Acronyms

ARS	Acute Radiation Syndrome
AIDS	Acquired Immune Deficiency Syndrome
CF	Chlorofluorocarbon
COP21	21st Conference of the Parties
F1NPS	Fukushima Daiichi Nuclear Power Station

G7	Group of Seven
HIV	Human Immunodeficiency Virus
INDCs	Intended Nationally Determined Contributions
TEPCO	Tokyo Electric Power Company
UN	United Nations
US	United States
USSR	Union of soviet Socialist Republic

References

Al Jazeera. (2013). Jose Mujica: 'I earn more than I need'-Talk to Al Jazeerahttps://www.youtube.com/watch?v=hteGnL-8SeU. (Accessed December, 2018).

Allen, R.C. (2009). *The British industrial revolution in global perspective* (Vol. 1). Cambridge: Cambridge University Press.

Attfield, R. (2009). Mediated responsibilities, global warming, and the scope of ethics. *Journal of Social Philosophy*, 40(2), pp.225-236.

Baer, H. and Singer, M. (2016). *Global warming and the political ecology of health: Emerging crises and systemic solutions*. Routledge.

Baracca, A. (2018). The unsustainable legacy of the Nuclear Age. *arXiv preprint arXiv:1812.02332*.

Barker, H. (2012). *Bravo for the Marshallese: regaining control in a post-nuclear, post-colonial world*. Nelson Education.

Biermann, F. and Boas, I. (2010). Preparing for a warmer world: Towards a global governance system to protect climate refugees. *Global environmental politics*, 10(1), pp.60-88.

Billett, S. (2010). Dividing climate change: global warming in the Indian mass media. *Climatic change*, 99(1-2), pp.1-16.

Chuwa, L.T. (2014). *African indigenous ethics in global bioethics: Interpreting Ubuntu* (Vol. 1). Springer.

Clémençon, R. (2016). The two sides of the Paris climate agreement: Dismal failure or historic breakthrough?

CNN. (2003). *Mandela: U.S. wants holocaust* (1) 30.

Cooke, S. (2013). Animal rights and environmental terrorism. *Journal of Terrorism Research*.

Croucher, S. (2018). *Globalization and belonging: The politics of identity in a changing world.* Rowman & Littlefield.

Davis, R. (2012). *The rise of the English shipping industry in the seventeenth and eighteenth centuries* (No. 48). Oxford University Press.

Deese, R. S. (2009). The artifact of nature: 'Spaceship Earth 'and the dawn of global environmentalism. *Endeavour, 33*(2), pp.70-75.

Deetz, J. (2010). *In small things forgotten: an archaeology of early American life.* Anchor.

Dennis, C. (2006). Promises to clean up industry fail to convince. https://www.google.co.za/search?source=hp&ei=Y3DlXMfA E8zgkgWkzI9o&q=Promises+to+clean+up+industry+fail+to +convince&oq=Promises+to+clean+up+industry+fail+to+co nvince&gs_l=psy-ab.12...0.0..5988...0.0..2.0.0.......3....2..gws-wiz.....0.

Dezalay, P.B.Y. (2005). Introduction: professional competition and the social construction of transnational markets. In *Professional competition and professional power* (pp. 15-36). Routledge.

Dun, O.V. and Gemenne, F. (2008). Defining 'environmental migration'. In Forced Migration Reviews vol 31: 10 - 11

Elcock, D. (2010). Future US Water Consumption: The Role of Energy Production 1. *JAWRA Journal of the American Water Resources Association, 46*(3), pp.447-460.

Friedberg, J. (2013). Bracing for the impending rocket revolution: how to regulate international environmental harm caused by commercial space flight. *Colo. J. Int'l Envtl. L. & Pol'y, 24*, p.197.

Gade, C.B. (2012). What is Ubuntu? Different interpretations among South Africans of African descent. *South African Journal of Philosophy, 31*(3), pp.484-503.

Ganis, A. (2015). José Mujica's Speech at the UN: a Post-colonial Look at a Neo-colonial Issue.

Gemenne, F. (2011). Why the numbers don't add up: A review of estimates and predictions of people displaced by environmental changes. *Global Environmental Change, 21*, pp.S41-S49.

Gemenne, F. (2015). One good reason to speak of 'climate refugees'. *Forced Migration Review, 49*, pp.70-71.

Gerrard, M.B. (2015). America's forgotten nuclear waste dump in the Pacific. *SAIS Review of International Affairs, 35*(1), pp.87-97.

Gerson, J. (2009). US foreign military bases and military colonialism: Personal and analytical perspectives. *The bases of empire: The global struggle against US military posts*, pp.44-70.

Gleick, P.H. (2006). Water and terrorism. *Water policy*, 8(6), pp.481-503.

Gore, A. (2006). *An inconvenient truth: The planetary emergency of global warming and what we can do about it.* Rodale.

Greene, B. P. (2007). *Eisenhower, science advice, and the nuclear test-ban debate, 1945-1963.* Stanford University Press.

Grovogui, S. (2016). *Beyond Eurocentrism and anarchy: memories of international order and institutions.* Springer.

Gunter, L. (2011). No saviours in sight for Somalia: The UN is toothless and the West is stretched too thin to help. *National Post, 11.*

Hartmann, B. (2010). Rethinking climate refugees and climate conflict: rhetoric, reality and the politics of policy discourse. *Journal of International Development: The Journal of the Development Studies Association, 22*(2), pp.233-246.

Helmreich, S. (2011). From spaceship earth to Google ocean: Planetary icons, indexes, and infrastructures. *Social Research, 78*(4), pp.1211-1242.

Holbrooke, R. (2008). The next president: Mastering a daunting agenda. *Foreign Affairs*, pp.2-24.

Inikori, J.E. (2002). *Africans and the Industrial Revolution in England: A study in international trade and economic development.* Cambridge University Press.

Iyer, G.C., Edmonds, J.A., Fawcett, A.A., Hultman, N.E., Alsalam, J., Asrar, G.R., Calvin, K.V., Clarke, L.E., Creason, J., Jeong, M. and Kyle, P. (2015). The contribution of Paris to limit global warming to 2 C. *Environmental Research Letters, 10*(12), p.125002.

Jacobs, J.M. (2006). A geography of big things. *Cultural Geographies, 13*(1), pp.1-27.

Jacobs, R. (2013). Nuclear conquistadors: military colonialism in nuclear test site selection during the Cold War.

Jensen, M.C. (1993). The modern industrial revolution, exit, and the failure of internal control systems. *The Journal of Finance, 48*(3), pp.831-880.

Jetnil-Kijiner, K. (2014). *IEP Jaltok: A history of Marshallese literature* (Doctoral dissertation).

Kahn, J. and Yardley, J. (2007). As China roars, pollution reaches deadly extremes. *New York Times, 26*(August), p.A1.

Kim, K.H. (2014). Examining US news media discourses about North Korea: A corpus-based critical discourse analysis. *Discourse & Society, 25*(2), pp.221-244.

Leader, S.H. and Probst, P. (2003). The earth liberation front and environmental terrorism. *Terrorism and Political Violence, 15*(4), pp.37-58.

Lohr, S. (2006). The cost of an overheated planet. *The New York Times, 12*(December).

Lutz, C. and Enloe, C. (eds.) (2009). *The bases of empire: The global struggle against US military posts.* NYU Press.

Mathias, P. (2013). *The first industrial nation: The economic history of Britain 1700–1914.* Routledge.

Mawere, M. (2012). â€˜ Buried and Forgotten but Not Deadâ€™: Reflections on â€˜ Ubuntuâ€™ In Environmental Conservation in Southeastern Zimbabwe. *Global Journal of Human-Social Science Research, 12*(10-B).

McCright, A.M. and Dunlap, R.E. (2011). The politicization of climate change and polarization in the American public's views of global warming, 2001–2010. *The Sociological Quarterly, 52*(2), pp.155-194.

McElfish, P.A., Hallgren, E. and Yamada, S. (2015). Effect of US health policies on health care access for Marshallese migrants. *American journal of public health, 105*(4), pp.637-643.

Merson, M.H., O'Malley, J., Serwadda, D. and Apisuk, C. (2008). The history and challenge of HIV prevention. *The lancet, 372*(9637), pp.475-488.

Mhango, N. (2018). *Jokey Horse-Jockey North-South Rapport: Diagnostic-cum-Prognostic-Academic Perspectives on Who Truly Depends on Whom.* Langaa RPCIG.

Mhango, N.N. (2018). *Decolonising Colonial Education: Doing Away with Relics and Toxicity Embedded in the Racist Dominant Grand Narrative.* Langaa RPCIG.

Mhango, N.N. (2018). *How Africa Developed Europe: Deconstructing the His-story of Africa, Excavating Untold Truth and What Ought to Be Done and Known*. Langaa RPCIG.

Micheletti, M. and Stolle, D. (2008). Fashioning social justice through political consumerism, capitalism, and the internet. *Cultural Studies*, *22*(5), pp.749-769.

Mielke, E., Anadon, L.D. and Narayanamurti, V. (2010). Water consumption of energy resource extraction, processing, and conversion. *Belfer Centre for Science and International Affairs*.

Mora, C., Tittensor, D.P., Adl, S., Simpson, A.G. and Worm, B. (2011). How many species are there on Earth and in the ocean? *PLoS biology*, *9*(8), p.e1001127.

Morrissey, J. (2012). Rethinking the 'debate on environmental refugees': from 'maximalists and minimalists' to 'proponents and critics'. *Journal of Political Ecology*, *19*(1), pp.36-49.

Muxe Nkondo, G. (2007). Ubuntu as public policy in South Africa: A conceptual framework. *International Journal of African Renaissance Studies*, *2*(1), pp.88-100.

Nattrass, N. (2008). AIDS and the scientific governance of medicine in post-apartheid South Africa. *African affairs*, *107*(427), pp.157-176.

Nef, J.U. (2013). *The rise of the British coal industry*. Routledge.

Newell, P. and Paterson, M. (2010). *Climate capitalism: global warming and the transformation of the global economy*. Cambridge University Press.

Newman, P.A., Oman, L.D., Douglass, A.R., Fleming, E.L., Frith, S.M., Hurwitz, M.M., Kawa, S.R., Jackman, C.H., Krotkov, N.A., Nash, E.R. and Nielsen, J.E. (2009). What would have happened to the ozone layer if chlorofluorocarbons (CFCs) had not been regulated? Atmospheric Chemistry and Physics, 9(6), pp.2113-2128.

Norio, O., Ye, T., Kajitani, Y., Shi, P. and Tatano, H. (2011). The 2011 eastern Japan great earthquake disaster: Overview and comments. *International Journal of Disaster Risk Science*, *2*(1), pp.34-42.

Ohtsuru, A., Tanigawa, K., Kumagai, A., Niwa, O., Takamura, N., Midorikawa, S., Nollet, K., Yamashita, S., Ohto, H., Chhem, R.K. and Clarke, M. (2015). Nuclear disasters and health: lessons learned, challenges, and proposals. *The Lancet, 386*(9992), pp.489-497.

Palaneeswaria, T. (2012). A study on attitude of fireworks manufacturers in Sivakasi towards eco-friendly fireworks. *International Journal of Trade and Commerce.*

Pandve, H.T. (2008). The Asian brown cloud. *Indian journal of occupational and environmental medicine, 12*(2), p.93.

Paterson, M. (2013). *Global warming and global politics.* Routledge.

Paterson, M. (2016). Global warming. *The Ethical Dimensions of Global Change*, p.181.

Premalatha, M., Abbasi, T., Abbasi, T. and Abbasi, S.A. (2011). Energy-efficient food production to reduce global warming and ecodegradation: The use of edible insects. *Renewable and sustainable energy reviews, 15*(9), pp.4357-4360.

Prins, G. and Rayner, S. (2007). Time to ditch Kyoto. *Nature, 449*(7165), p.973.

Qiao, F., Wang, G., Zhao, W., Zhao, J., Dai, D., Song, Y. and Song, Z. (2011). Predicting the spread of nuclear radiation from the damaged Fukushima Nuclear Power Plant. *Chinese Science Bulletin, 56*(18), p.1890.

Ramose, M. (2015). Ecology through Ubuntu. *Emerging from Cultures and Religions of the ASEAN Region*, pp.69-76.

Ravishankara, A.R., Daniel, J.S. and Portmann, R.W. (2009). Nitrous oxide (N2O): the dominant ozone-depleting substance emitted in the 21st century. *Science, 326*(5949), pp.123-125.

Razali, W.W. (2012). Guest Editorial: Blame The Forests for Environmental Degradation and Biodiversity Loss: in Defence of the Tropical Forests. *Journal of Tropical Forest Science*, pp.437-439.

Rimmer, M. (2014). 'We are here to make history': The United Nations climate summit 2014. *Medium.*

Rudiak-Gould, P. (2013). *Climate change and tradition in a small island state: the rising tide.* Routledge.

Scheffran, J. and Battaglini, A. (2011). Climate and conflicts: the security risks of global warming. *Regional Environmental Change, 11*(1), pp.27-39.

Scheffran, J., Brzoska, M., Kominek, J., Link, P.M. and Schilling, J. (2012). Climate change and violent conflict. *Science, 336*(6083), pp.869-871.

Schmidt, B.C. (2016). *Political Discourse of Anarchy, The: A Disciplinary History of International Relations*. SUNY Press.

Sealey-Huggins, L. (2017). '1.5° C to stay alive': climate change, imperialism and justice for the Caribbean. *Third World Quarterly, 38*(11), pp.2444-2463.

Shine, K.P. (2009). The global warming potential—the need for an interdisciplinary retrial. *Climatic Change, 96*(4), pp.467-472.

Sibanda, F. (2017). Praying for Rain?: A Rastafari Perspective from Zimbabwe. *The Ecumenical Review, 69*(3), pp.411-424.

Stearns, P.N. (2018). *The industrial revolution in world history*. Routledge.

Ten Hoeve, J.E. and Jacobson, M.Z. (2012). Worldwide health effects of the Fukushima Daiichi nuclear accident. *Energy & Environmental Science, 5*(9), pp.8743-8757.

Thanekar, S.A. and Thanekar, S.S. (2011). Role of a Common Indian Man in Solving Global Warming. In *Proceedings of International Conference on Life Science and Technology (ICLST 2011)*.

Tranter, B. (2013). The great divide: Political candidate and voter polarisation over global warming in Australia. *Australian Journal of Politics & History, 59*(3), pp.397-413.

Trappe, M.J., Minc, L.D., Kittredge, K.S. and Pink, J.W. (2014). Cesium radioisotope content of wild edible fungi, mineral soil, and surface litter in western North America after the Fukushima nuclear accident. *Canadian journal of forest research, 44*(11), pp.1441-1452.

van der Linden, S. (2015). The conspiracy-effect: Exposure to conspiracy theories (about global warming) decreases pro-social behaviour and science acceptance. *Personality and Individual Differences, 87*, pp.171-173.

Vermeij, G.J. (2016). Gigantism and its implications for the history of life. *PLoS One, 11*(1), p.e0146092.

Vining, C.B. (2009). An inconvenient truth about thermoelectrics. *Nature materials, 8*(2), p.83.

Wartofsky, L. (2010). Increasing world incidence of thyroid cancer: increased detection or higher radiation exposure? *Hormones, 9*(2), pp.103-108.

Wendt, A. (1995). Constructing international politics. *International security*, *20*(1), pp.71-81.

Chapter Fourteen

Moving Beyond Neoimperial Lamentations over Decolonising African Land and Environments: The Model of Zimbabwe as the Future

Tom Tom & Clement Chipenda

Introduction

Land is an essential component of the environment, including climate. Discourses on the environment and climate are incomplete without interrogation of issues on land ownership and control. Accordingly, environment, including climate (change), policies are premised on land ownership and control. All the socioeconomic and political activities of societies are based on or relate to the land in one way or the other. Land and, more broadly, natural resources are the main livelihood sources that need prioritisation. Control of land by the indigenes implies their ownership of the environment. Popular land movements by the 'Black' indigenous people of Africa would help in repossessing land, space and livelihoods. The proliferation of discourses on decolonisation and decoloniality has helped to put necolonial practices and ideologies on the spotlight.

The colonialists created an introverted Zimbabwe (the then Rhodesia) and deliberately sought to decimate traditional ownership, rights, knowledge and practices on land and other facets of the environment and climate. This reconfiguration was experienced in all other states of Africa, and generally the Global South. Super-imposition of 'modern and formal' knowledge, policies and practices was the norm under the colonial administration and it remains a covert and overt strategy under neo-colonialism. The traditional ways of knowing and addressing environment and climate issues were (and are) essentially key components of unwritten social policy interwoven in multiple African cultures. However, these cannot be relegated or discarded in the name of 'alien modernity' or 'alien modern social policy'.

371

Significant contributions to post-colonial theory and the decoloniality agenda are a major force for the emancipation and empowerment of the Global South. Several scholars spearheaded decoloniality (Nhemachena, 2018; Mawere and Nhemachena, 2018; Nhemachena, Warikandwa and Amoo, 2018; Nhemachena and Dhakwa, 2018; Nhemachena, Mlambo and Kaundjua, 2016; Benyera, 2018; Gatsheni-Ndlovu, 2016; 2013a; 2013; 2012; 2011, 2007b; Gatsheni-Ndlovu and Benyera, 2015; Mawere, 2012; 2014; 2015; Boehmer, 1995; Said, 1978; Fanon, 1967). In addition, renowned social policy scholars (Adesina, 2007; 2011; Mkandawire, 2004; 2006; 2011) and other African scholars call for reconsideration of social policy in a pro-African and development context.

The wider vision of social policy calls for major shifts in understanding and applying social policy, particularly from predominantly social protection (mono and narrow) to multi-tasking of social policy. Such a shift implies that social policy should be considered broadly in terms of social protection, redistribution, production, reproduction and social cohesion. The wider vision of social policy has a transformative orientation and blends smoothly with the decolonial agenda. Informed by such an agenda, the chapter interrogates critical questions pertaining to the foundations, latent and manifest fissures and biases, application and efficacy of colonial and neo-colonial land policies, and generally environment and climate policies in Zimbabwe. The chapter seeks to revamp policies pertaining to the environment and climate change within the ambit of decolonial approaches, methods and practice.

Colonialism, Alienative Land Tenure and the Social Question in Zimbabwe

There is consensus among scholars on land and agrarian reforms that land is a key socioeconomic resource whose appropriate utilisation leads to sustainable socioeconomic transformation of any country. Accordingly, the social, economic and political development of any country cannot be de-linked from land ownership, control and use. Ownership and use of land create and guarantee sources of wellbeing, freedom, power, security, income, livelihoods and so on (Moyo, 2012; Kariuki, 2009; Cousins, 2005; Jill, 2005). The crosscutting value of land places it on national and international agendas (Moyo and Chambati, 2013). Given the importance of land to individuals and groups, land is at the core of conflicts and contestations (Moyo, 2011; Sadomba, 2013). The history of Zimbabwe is in part a struggle over key resources such as land (Moyo, 2011).

In Zimbabwe, where agrarian systems were racially-skewed and controlled by few Whites, a land question emerged (Moyo, 1995; 2000; 2001; 2011; 2013; Moyo and Yeros, 2005a; Moyo and Chambati, 2013; Sachikonye, 2005a). Such a question signifies a quest for inclusive development. The key literature on Zimbabwe's land reform reiterates the existence of a land question. Our point of departure is that the existence of a land question implies the existence of a social question. Land dispossession by the British colonialists from 1890 to 1980 shaped the land question in Zimbabwe (Moyo, 2011; 2012; Sachikonye, 2005a).

Zimbabwe was integrated, subordinately, into the world capitalist system since colonisation in the late 19th Century (Moyo, 2011). Such integration was achieved "mainly through the settler colonial mode of political rule and social production, based largely on unequal and repressive agrarian relations that defined the character of the state" (Moyo and Chambati 2013). The land question in Zimbabwe therefore lies in colonial accumulation by dispossession and the failure by post-colonial government to address the alienative agrarian structure. British colonialists used various overt and covert strategies of dispossessing the Black majority of their prime land supported by social and economic policies of racial exclusion and alienation.

Exclusionary and oppressive laws to "force the black Zimbabweans off the prime land were vehemently implemented" (Martin and Johnson, 1981). The instruments that were used include the Rudd Concession, Native Reserve Order in Council of 1898, "Native Reserve Areas of 1915, Land Apportionment Act of 1930, Maize Control Act of 1931, Cattle Levy Act, Land Acquisition Scheme, Land Husbandry Act of 1951" (Utete, 2003); and the Land Tenure Act of 1969 (Utete, 2003; Mukanya, 1991; Gundani, 2002). These led to state-supported unequal and repressive agrarian relations between the Blacks and Whites (Moyo, 2011; Moyo and Chambati, 2013; Weiner, 1988; Bush and Cliffe, 1984; Amin, 1972;

373

Yeros, 2002; Moyana, 2002). Land dispossession coupled with "extra economic regulations and taxes turned Zimbabwe into a labour reserve economy, while repressing the peasantry and small scale rural industry and commerce without creating full-scale proletarianisation" (Bush and Cliffe, 1984; Yeros, 2002; Weiner, 1988; Amin, 1972;). These measures were intended to suppress the wellbeing of the Black majority. Accumulation from below was deliberately relegated while spearheading accumulation by the few Whites.

At independence, "6 000 white farmers owned 15.5 million hectares; 8 500 black farmers operating on a small scale held about 1.4 million hectares; and approximately 4.5 million communal farmers held 16.4 million hectares" (Gundani, 2003). Land for the Whites was mostly located "in the high rainfall agro-ecological regions where the potential for agricultural output is greatest while the drier, highly marginal agro-ecological areas with poor soils and inadequate rainfall were reserved for the majority of the black population" (Ruswa, 2007: 3). Most of the communal land was located in the periphery and margins of the country where the soil fertility was very poor and rainfall was very low therefore, were prone to droughts (Utete, 2003). Sadomba (2013) summarises the "land question in Zimbabwe as relating to the cross-cutting importance of land to social, economic and political development for all groups; colonial accumulation by dispossession of the black; the centrality of land in the anti-colonial armed struggles; the post-colonial ideological and constitutional constraints on attempts to reverse the colonial land ownership structure and the subsequent land movements". Accordingly, land was among the key demands of the Black masses during the three liberation struggles (Moyo, 2011).

Post Colonial Land Question and Neo-Colonial Machinations

The demand for land and structural change were not adequately realised particularly in the first two decades after independence. The "post-independence policies failed to resolve the national questions of broad-based development, social inclusion and national integration" (Moyo and Chambati, 2011; Moyo and Yeros, 2009). Part of the failure is "due to the constraints of the Lancaster House Agreement of 1979" (Mlambo, 2010: 59). This Constitution side-lined land redistribution to the majority of Blacks while maintaining the colonial land tenure structure.

The Lancaster House Agreement emphasised the supremacy of market-based land reform. There had to be a willing seller "for the government to purchase land for resettlement" (Moyo, 1995). In addition, "the adoption of the Economic Structural Adjustment Programme (ESAP) in the 1990s further moved the majority of the blacks from key resources and led to increased poverty" (Moyo and Yeros, 2005a; Moyo and Chambati, 2013). Ownership of land by the Whites became more entrenched. The result was a reinforcement of historical alienation of land and other key resources from the majority, especially the Blacks. Both the neo-liberal agenda of ESAP and constraints of the Lancaster House Agreement stood against broader ownership of land by the Black majority. Consequently, land movements increased as the Black masses sought to restore their ownership and control over land (Moyo, 2000).

The "government of Zimbabwe adopted three post-colonial land reform and resettlement programmes to correct the colonial imbalances in access to and use of prime land" (Musemwa and Mushunje, 2011). Core principles of such reforms included equity and empowerment through land acquisition and redistribution, and agrarian support (Sachikonye, 2005b; Moyo, 2002; Utete, 2003; Mukanya, 1991). Important to note is that post-colonial reforms transcended land issues and were extended to other areas of social policy including education, health, housing and employment.

The Land Issue, Afro-rooted Social Policy and Decoloniality

There is broad consensus on the view that Africa was decentred, de-rooted, otherised, subjugated, peripheralised and alienated through colonialism. In the contemporary era, Africa and the broader Global South are grappling with neo-colonialism and neo-imperialism. In such a context, broad intellectual reengineering (Mkandawire, 2001); introverted development (Moyo and Yeros, 2007); covert and overt neo-colonial efforts (Mamdani, 2008; Borras, 2006); and out of context social policies (Mkandawire, 2004; 2006; 2011; Adesina, 2007; 2011) are among the various problems Africa should proactively address. Land and appended natural resources were the targets of colonialists and they remain an indelible mark in neo-colonial and neo-imperial interests.

Broadly, the Global South is haunted by policy paradigms and instruments that are out of context and trivialisation or non-recognition of policy instruments emanating from this part of the world. For example, land reform is not acknowledged or supported as a social policy instrument by organisations with hegemonic presence in global social policy, development and governance such as the Organisation for Economic Cooperation and Development (OECD). Moreover, production, reproduction and social protection benefits the 'Black' land beneficiaries are accumulating are not acknowledged. Yet land grabbing by international capital due to its socioeconomic value and or that of the natural resources appended to the land is increasing. Decoloniality is a broadening field of study, new thinking and platform for action in the Global South. Several scholars and practitioners have contributed to this important area. Overall, all the contributors to decoloniality reveal how the colonised and formerly colonised are presented as inferior compared to the colonisers; so the inferiorised are hailing their presence and identity, and reclaiming their past that was either lost or distorted due to colonialism.

Through enslavement and colonial processes, Africans were viewed as synonymous with animals; mercilessly exploited and alienated (Nhemachena, 2018). A corpus of racially skewed values, policies and practices that were crafted by western states to militate against the emancipation, empowerment and development trajectory of indigenous Africans are increasingly being questioned and deconstructed (Nhemachena, Warikandwa and Amoo, 2018:1; Nhemachena and Dhakwa, 2018: 73). Accordingly, Nhemachena, Mlambo and Kaundjua (2016: 15) argue for the need to research, write and publish Africa in ways that herald its importance as a social, economic and political force in the global order. The decolonial drive is evident in various contributions. Africans should articulate and celebrate their identity and shift from viewing the west as superior and as the standard in all spheres (Ndlovu-Gatsheni, 2007b, 2011; 2012; 2013; 2013a; Ndlovu-Gatsheni and Benyera, 2015). For this reason, when the westerners steal or rob from Africans, this is politely but wrongly addressed as accumulation or alienation or centralisation. They are seldom addressed in literature as having stolen from Africans – but they are inaccurately addressed as having "accumulated", as having "alienated", "appropriated" and as having "centralised" resources (Nhemachena, Warikandwa & Amoo, 2018).

In other crucial contributions, Benyera (2018:121) characterises colonial relations between the west and its colonies as parasitic and based on various modalities of theft. Power relations that remain tilted in favour of the colonising nations and against the colonies are questioned in a context where diversity of both the colonising and colonised nations is acknowledged. Central to Benyera's (2018) contribution is the acknowledgement of 'modalities of theft' as having barely changed after colonialism and the need to view and practice decoloniality as the endeavour to unmask and jettison the various manifestations of forms of power relations and domination (Benyera, 2018: 121).

Post-colonial theory and decolonial attempts can be noted in earlier contributions by scholars including Frantz Fanon (1967). Fanon (1967) queries explicit promotion of White racial superiority over non-white colonial peoples; and how such division has led to 'otherisation' of the colonised and most of the colonised being alienated from their cultures. It is only when colonised nations are free that the formerly colonised can reclaim and reconstruct their own history and culture (Fanon, 1967). In a similar context, Said (1978) interrogates stereotypes and the colonial assumptions that are inherent in western representations of the *Orient* - a term that the west uses to refer to the Arab world, whose spatial spread is in North Africa and the Middle East. The *Orient* is considered and represented as inferior, strange, bizarre, odd and irrational to the *Occident* (the west) that is always presented as superior, modern, dominant and as the source of all history. Boehmer (1995:63) questions binary oppositions between the coloniser and colonised or formerly colonised. How these affect identity, representation and development in colonies and former colonies occupies Boehmer's (1995) contributions. Rodney (1985) delves into how Europe developed Africa while several other scholars focused on former colonies, dependence, underdevelopment and prospects for change (Amin, 1972; Ashcroft, Griffiths and Tiffin, 1995).

The Wider Vision of Social Policy – Transformative Social Policy

Comprehensive social policy with a development agenda performs production, redistribution, reproduction, protection and social cohesion/nation building tasks/functions (the wider vision of social policy). Transformative Social Policy (TSP) focuses on returning to the wider vision of social policy and moving away from the neoliberal approach (Tekwa and Adesina, 2018). The TSP gives primacy to the wider vision of social policy with its diverse functions (production, redistribution, social protection, social reproduction, social cohesion and nation building (Yi, 2015; Hujo, 2014; Adesina, 2009; Mkandawire, 2004). Working within TSP, Adesina (2009: 38) views TSP as the collective public efforts of securing people's wellbeing while Mkandawire (2004) emphasises that TSP as the collective interventions in the economy to influence access to and the incidence of adequate and secure livelihood outcomes. Transformative social policy emphasises policy linkages and the inseparability of the social from the economic. The economy is conceived as being embedded in society where diverse social, economic and political relations and structures interact through processes of exclusion and adverse incorporation, preventing the poor from benefiting from development policies and market changes (Tekwa and Adesina, 2018; Mkandawire, 2004; Hulme, Moore and Shepherd, 2001).

Against a background of reduction of social policy to social assistance in dominant social policy literature (by the OECD); and mono tasking of social policy (primarily social assistance as mainstream social protection) under neoliberalism (as evidenced by structural adjustment programmes introduced by the International Monetary Fund and World Bank in Africa), TSP emphasises the "importance of a holistic approach to deal with the economic, social and political relations, policy linkages and the comprehensiveness of social policy interventions to transform the existing unequal and unjust social, economic and political relationships to enhance the wellbeing of the people" (Yi, 2015; Mkandawire, 2004). TSP is diagrammatically represented in Figure 1 below.

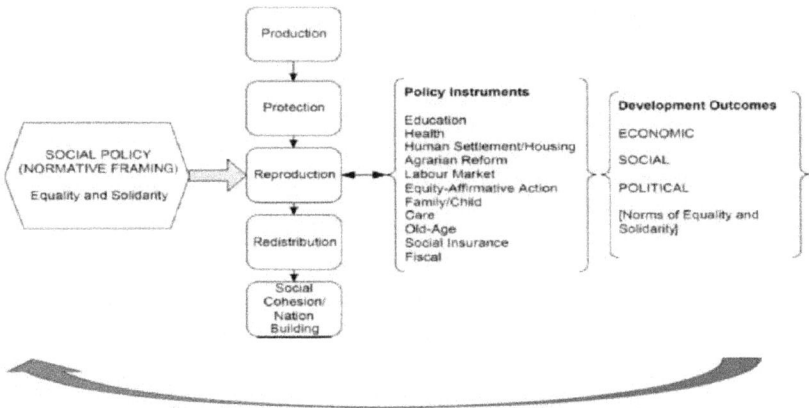

Figure 1: Transformative Social Policy Conceptual Framework
Source: Adesina (2011: 463)

Central to TSP is the deliberate challenge of underlying structural risks and their longer term implications for vulnerability and poverty and inequalities. These deliberate efforts are missing in current safety nets and social protection programmes including those by the International Monetary Fund (IMF), World Bank (WB) and other institutions. Despite emphasis on transformative social protection by Sabates-Wheeler and Devereux (2008) and other scholars, such an approach falls short of addressing the underlying socioeconomic and political structural factors that create and sustain inequality and poverty. TSP has potential to transform racialised, ethnicised, gendered and other forms of inequality and poverty which according to Shields (2008), are manifestations emanating from the intersections of these social identities and categories. Common ground can be established between TSP and decoloniality in interrogating the position of land in environment and climate discourses. Both question the basis and reproduction of inequalities, have broader instruments and are transformative.

Land, the Wider Vision of Social Policy and Decoloniality

The need to decolonise land, space and livelihood sources within the overall environment and climate discourses and the wider vision of social policy is articulated in this section on the basis of selected themes.

Redistribution

Land redistribution is the major outcome of Zimbabwe's fast track land reform. Compared to the first two land reforms, the fast track land reform had major impact on disrupting colonial and post-colonial interests. At independence, Zimbabwe inherited a racially-biased system of land tenure in which 1 % of the population (approximately 6 000 White large scale commercial farmers) had owned 15.5 million hectares of prime agricultural land compared to 700 000 African households who were restricted to 16.4 million hectares of largely unproductive and peripheral land (Moyo, 1995).

The fast-tracked land reform radically changed a bimodal agrarian structure that was created and sustained through colonial accumulation by dispossession and racially-skewed support systems that in their diversity covertly and overtly worked against the Black population. The fast-tracked land reform led to the acquisition of 13 million hectares and resettlement of 180 000 families in just over a decade (Hanlon, Manjengwa and Smart, 2014; Scoones *et al.*, 2015). Such an extent of land redistribution is significant considering that previous phases of land reform in the early 1980s, Zimbabwe achieved minimum success as evidenced by the resettlement of 70 000 families on 3.4 hectares of land against a set target of 162 000 families (Moyo, 2013: 32).

In various study sites (including Zvimba, Goromonzi, Shamva, Kwekwe, Hwedza, Chiredzi and Mangwe), redistributive outcomes of the fast-tracked land reform are not restricted to the land. The land beneficiaries now have access to appended natural resources (fauna and flora) that were hitherto a preserve for the British colonialists and foreign tourists. The colonialists protected their areas through trespass laws to the disadvantage of the indigenous population. In essence, the indigenous groups were excluded from utilising and controlling their ancestral land and space, and livelihoods derived from using the land and appended natural resources. The fast-tracked land reform also fast tracked access to land, fauna and flora across Zimbabwe. However, sustainable utilisation of fauna and flora is essential in the aftermath of the land reform. Revival or strengthening of indigenous knowledge systems (IKS) in environmental protection and sustainability are necessary. Important to understand is that the colonisers trivialised IKS, and characterised such knowledge systems

380

as backward and anti-modern. The colonies were covertly and overtly engineered to embrace Western Knowledge Systems (WKS).

Land use and production

Dispossessing the colonisers of God and ancestral given land, and efforts to defend land rights against neo-colonial land grabbing are commendable achievements in Zimbabwe. However, the initial phase of occupation by the 'new farmers' in the early 2000s, land use and the production of all major crops (maize, wheat and tobacco) and livestock severely declined. For example, James (2015) conducted a comparative study of new resettlements, old resettlements and communal areas and noted that communal area households used much more land in 2011-2012 than their counterparts in A1. In that case, most A1 farmers used 3 hectares in 2011-2012 compared to 2 hectares in old resettlement areas and between 0.4 and 0.8 in communal areas. Just over 20 percent of new farmers failed to even use half of their land in 2011-2012 (James, 2015). Moyo *et al.* (2009) and Dekker and Kinsey (2011) reported low land utilisation in A1 resettlements compared to communal areas. However, caution on concluding low land use in fast track farms is essential due to variations in reporting land use by both farmers and scholars.

Suggestions for improving land use have been proffered by many scholars and practitioners (Scoones, 2017; 2018; 2019; Shonhe, 2015; 2017; 2018; Scoones, Marongwe, Mavedzenge, Murimbarimba, Mahenehene and Sukume, 2010; 2011; 2012; Hanlon, Manjengwa and Smart, 2014). For land reform Zimbabwe's land reform as a decolonial project and as a transformative social policy tool to be successful, production and market constraints should be aggressively addressed by government, land beneficiaries and other stakeholders. Proactive breakthroughs and support for availability of affordable agricultural inputs and penetration of lucrative markets are urgent needs.

Social protection

The fast track land reform as a movement to attain control over land and space, by the Black majority, has social protection outcomes. Social protection is one of the major tasks/functions of social policy with a transformative agenda (Adesina, 2011; Mkandawire, 2006). Achieved or potential social protection outcomes are greater than social assistance or safety nets under the neoliberal approach.

Zimbabwe's land reform is an *ex ante* social protection 'tool' whose protective benefits are widely heralded across fast track farms; and can be improved especially if production and market constraints are addressed. Diverse study sites reveal that ownership and use of prime agricultural land complemented by on and off farm activities in some cases has better social protection outcomes than narrow social assistance (Chipenda, 2018; Chibwana, 2016; Tekwa and Adesina, 2018). Despite land reform not being recognised as a social policy instrument by the OECD, food production, availability and consumption and sovereignty are reported to be increasing in the fast track farms in a context of declining need for food aid.

Social reproduction

Transformative social policy goes beyond protection, vulnerability, destitution and short-term vulnerability analysis (Adesina, 2011). Social reproduction is an essential function of the fast track land reform, particularly from the standpoint of decoloniality and the need for Africa to control its environment and climate. Despite contestations in understanding social reproduction, the fast track land reform has broadened sources of income for household reproduction through both farm and off farm activities, enhanced the likelihood of having more siblings (biological reproduction) as spouses become more secure due to ownership of land and improved social organisation and agency against socioeconomic problems demanding collective effort. However, increasing the prospects for youth to take over and improve farming, reducing and/or eliminating production and market challenges and improving social services (schools and clinics) among other considerations will enhance social reproduction.

Social cohesion/nation building

Land reform has potential for enhancing social cohesion and nation building particularly when it transforms the structural bases of inequality and paves a new trajectory of equity and broad-based development. In Zimbabwe, particularly the fast tracked land reform transformed the racialised bimodal agrarian structure to a trimodal arrangement (James, 2015; Mkodzongi, 2013; Moyo and Chambati, 2013). Redistributing land reform satisfied the goals of the liberation struggles (the first and second *Chimurengas*) and post-independence land movements. Among other concerns the first and second *Chimurengas* were a struggle for lost land, livelihoods and dignity. The masses supported the liberation among other things to get back land stolen from them by the British colonialists. Among the indigenous 'Black population' of Zimbabwe, land reforms addressed racial issues in land tenure. However, conflicts between Blacks and Whites were escalated. Moreover, Zimbabwe suffered international isolation and sanctions due to the fast track land reform.

Indigenous Knowledge Systems (IKS)

The indigenous knowledge systems of Africa, in their diversity, define who we are as Africans and our ownership of the environment and climate. The indispensability of IKS has been emphasised by many scholars and practitioners, and often presented as the missing link in Africa's development (Mawere, 2015; 2014; 2012). Along with colonial accumulation by dispossession, was a scurrilous attack on IKS as unscientific, illogical, anti-development and unGodly (Mawere, 2015: 57). Yet indigenous communities found and still find value in it. Paradoxically, after ages of demonising IKS, the West is now emphasising the importance of such knowledge in agriculture, medicine and other areas.

Increasing calls have been made at national and international levels for communities to preserve, learn, exchange IKS and maximise the exploitation of IKS. In essence, IKS is a development tool. With the advent of the fast tracked land reform, exploitation of flora with medicinal qualities has increased as the indigenous people enjoy broader access to flora in various parts of Zimbabwe. Such flora includes *gavakava, mupfura, muroro, rukato, mutunduru, mufuta* and many more. Moreover, due to production constraints, mainly emanating from unavailability, shortage or exorbitant prices of agricultural inputs, most A1 land beneficiaries are utilising organic fertiliser, and crop rotation and intercropping (longstanding IKS in agriculture to enhance soil fertility). Without use of IKS, agriculture would be very expensive or even unaffordable particularly in Zimbabwe where there are economic challenges. In Zimbabwe, there were challenges like dwindling local production capacity, low bilateral support and roll back of major donors after their masters' capitalist interests were frustrated by the fast track land reform. These problems are largely colonial residues. Current use of IKS in the fast track farms is not being done on a large scale. Enhancing use of both IKS in a context where their comparative advantages are combined and utilised is essential.

Spirit Mediums and Traditional Leadership

Spirit mediums and traditional leadership play essential roles in the lives of the indigenes of Zimbabwe and broadly Africa. Through colonial accumulation by dispossession, the indigenous groups did not only lose quantifiable resources such as land and mineral deposits. The qualitative aspects of their culture were eroded, decentred and weakened. Colonial hegemony led to peripheralisation, trivialisation, demonisation and attempts to wipe out spirit mediums and the entire traditional leadership. Local structures that shaped social life in terms of religion, gender, age, identity, access to resources and so forth were represented as inferior, suppressed and superseded by Christianity – a religion that paved way, pacified the indigenous population and justified various colonialists' modalities of theft in Zimbabwe and other parts of the Global South.

Through colonial land dispossessions, the indigenous people were not only alienated from land as a factor of production, but also from the sacred places and areas of worship where they conduct ceremonies pertinent to their culture, communicate and reunite with their ancestors. In the Zvimba study site in Mashonaland West Province, for example, the Manjinjiwa lineage under the headship of Matibiri-Magaramombe chieftainship was forcibly removed by the British from the area now converted to Dalkeith and Noordt gate farms in 1919 (Murisa, 2009). The majority of the lineage members were resettled in Kasanze in Murombedzi, some moved to Hurungwe while very few were retained on the farms. Their original area was more than an area of residence and livelihood source but it was also an ancestral territory. Evicting them to pave way for Whites' commercial agriculture disrupted connections of the Manjinjiwa with their ancestors. The Manjinjiwa spirit was further unsettled and decentred after independence when one of the clan members (also the spirit medium of the Manjinjiwa) unsuccessfully agitated to return to their ancestral land. Some members of the lineage moved to Makonde communal area. The Manjinjiwa spirit (*svikiro*) was unsettled in the spiritual world because it resided far from its sacred land.

The need to return to the centre of their spiritual territory and reconnect with their ancestors motivated the repossession of land. At Dalkeith farm repossession of White-owned large-scale commercial farms was led by "traditional leaders - spirit mediums and chiefs - and ordinary people from neighbouring communal and urban areas" (Murisa, 2009, 245). Unlike the common rhetoric pertaining to the processes of occupying 'White lands', in Zvimba, war veteran activity was limited and they worked on the basis of the leadership of spirit mediums and chiefs in mobilising people from communal areas to occupy large-scale commercial farms. In the fast track farms, the position of chiefs as a vital cog of traditional leadership is not appropriately recognised. In the context of fast track farms, their role was reconfigured after the land reform and they do not have a mandate as is the case in communal areas as outlined in the Traditional Leaders Act (25/1998 modified by S. I. 430A/1999, 22/2001).

Conclusion

Land is an essential component of the environment and climate. Policies pertaining to land reforms, and environment and climate change are in essence social policies. Ideally the crux of these policies is the people and their wellbeing. The chapter considers Zimbabwe's land reforms in a broader context of a decolonial agenda in environment and climate discourses. Decoloniality has been blended with the Transformative Social Policy conceptual framework. TSP ties well with attempts to decolonise land tenure in Zimbabwe and broadly the Global South. Land reform and all other policies within and outside environment and climate change have a social component. Land reform in particular is a policy tool that is intended for transforming livelihoods. Thus, land use and production should be enhanced through multi-stakeholder support to the land beneficiaries with greater emphasis on agricultural inputs, farm mechanisation and penetration of lucrative markets. A vibrant locally owned agricultural sector is essential for indigenous people to control the environment. Indigenous people cannot be expected to care for an environment which they do not own and control: their ownership and control of the environment must be recovered and then this will be part of the motivation for them to care deeply for their African environment.

References

Adesina, J. (2007). *Social policy in sub-Saharan African context: In search of inclusive development.* Basingstoke: Palgrave.

Adesina, J. (2009). Social policy in sub-Saharan Africa: A glance in the rear-view mirror. *International Journal of Social Welfare,* 18(1): S37-S51.

Adesina, J. (2010). *Return to a wider vision of development: Social policy in reframing a new agenda.* Keynote Address delivered at the 48th Session of the UN Commission for Social Development (3 February). New York: UN Headquarters.

Adesina, J. (2011). *Towards a new global anti-poverty agenda: Wider vision, broader instruments.* New York: UNRISD.

Amin, S. (1972). Underdevelopment and Dependence in Black Africa: Origins and Contemporary Forms. *Journal of Modern African Studies,* 10(4): 503-524.

Ashcroft, B., Griffiths, G. and Tiffin, H. (1995). *The Post-Colonial Studies Reader.* London: Routledge.

Benyera, E. (2018). Colonialism, the Theft of History and the Quest for Africa. In: Nhemachena, A., Warikandwa, V. and Amoo, S. K. (eds.), *Social and Legal Theory in the Age of Decoloniality: (Re-) Envisioning African Jurisprudence in the 21st Century* (pp. 121-164). Bamenda: Langaa RPCIG.

Benyera, E., Mtapuri, O. and Nhemachena, A. (2018). The Man, Human Rights, Transitional Justice and African Jurisprudence in the Twenty-First Century. In Nhemachena, A., Warikandwa, V.

and Amoo, S. K. (eds.), *Social and Legal Theory in the Age of Decoloniality: (Re-) Envisioning African Jurisprudence in the 21st Century* (pp. 187-218). Bamenda: Langaa RPCIG.

Boehmer, E. (1995). *Colonial and Post-Colonial Literature.* Oxford: Oxford University Press.

Borras, S. Junior. (2005). Can Redistributive Land Reform be achieved via Market-Based Voluntary Land Transfer Schemes?: Evidence and Lessons from the Philippines. *Journal of Development Studies,* 40(1): 90-134.

Bush, R. and Cliffe, L. (1984). Agrarian policy in labour migrant societies: Reform or transformation in Zimbabwe? *Review of African Political Economy,* 11(29): 77-94.

Chibwana, M. W. T. (2016). *Social Policy Outcomes of Zimbabwe's Fast Track Land Reform Programme (FTLRP): A case of Kwekwe District.* PhD diss., University of South Africa.

Chipenda, C. (2018). *After land reform: What about the youth?* Conference presentation delivered at the International Conference on Authoritarian Populism and the Rural World organised by the Emancipatory Rural Politics Initiative (ERPI), International Institute of Social Studies (ISS), The Hague, Netherlands, 17-18 March 2018.

Fanon, F. (1967). *Black Skin, White Mask.* London: Grove Press Incorporated.

Fanon, F. (1968). *Black Skin, White Mask.* London: Pluto Press.

Gundani, P. H. (2002). The land crisis in Zimbabwe and the role of the churches towards its resolution. *Studia Historiae Ecclesiasticae* xxviii(2): 123-169.

Hanlon, J., Manjengwa, J. and Smart, T. (2014). *Zimbabwe takes back its land.* Sterling: Kumarian Press.

James, G. (2015). *Transforming rural livelihoods in Zimbabwe: Experiences of Fast Track Land Reform, 2000-2012.* PhD thesis, The University of Edinburgh.

Mawere, M. (2015). Indigenous knowledge and public education in Sub-Saharan Africa: *Africa Spectrum,* 50(2): 57-71.

Mawere, M. (2014). *Culture, indigenous knowledge and development in Africa: Reviving interconnectedness for sustainable development.* Bamenda: Langaa RPCIG.

Mawere, M. (2012). *The struggle of African indigenous knowledge systems in an age of globalisation: A case for children's traditional games in south-eastern Zimbabwe*. Bamenda: Langaa RPCIG.

Nhemachena, A. & Mawere, M. (2018). The Development of (Neo-) imperial sacrifice, global atavism and African insecurities: An introduction. In Mawere, M. & Nhemachena, A. (eds.), *Rethinking Securities in an Emergent Technoscientific New World Order: Retracing the Contours for Africa's Hi-jacked Futures*. Bamenda: Langaa RPCIG.

Mawere, M. and Mwanaka, T. R. (2015). Good governance, democracy and sustainable development in Africa: An introduction. In: Mawere, M. and Mwanaka, T. R. (eds.), *Democracy, Good Governance and Development in Africa* (pp. Vii-xiv). Bamenda: Langaa RPCIG.

Mkandawire, T. (2007). Transformative social policy and innovation in developing countries. *The European Journal of Development Research*, 19(1), pp. 13-29.

Mkandawire, T. (2011). Welfare regimes and economic development: Bridging the conceptual gap. In: Fitzgerald, V., Heyer, J. and Thorp, R (eds.), *Overcoming the Persistence of Poverty and Inequality* (pp. 149-171). Basingstoke: Palgrave.

Mkandawire, T. (ed.) (2001). *Social policy in a development context (No. 25 Ed.)*. Geneva: United Nations Institute for Social Development.

Mkandawire, T. (ed.) (2004). *Social policy in a development context*. Basingstoke: Palgrave Macmillan.

Mkandawire, T. (ed.) (2006). *African intellectuals: Rethinking politics, language, gender and development*. London: Zed Books.

Mkodzongi, G. (2013). *Fast tracking land reform and rural livelihoods in Mashonaland West Province of Zimbabwe: Opportunities and constraints, 2000-2013*. PhD Thesis, the University of Edinburgh.

Mkodzongi, G. (2016). I am the paramount chief, this land belongs to my ancestors: The reconfiguration of rural authority after Zimbabwe's land reforms. *Review of African Political Economy*, 43(51), 99-114.

Mkodzongi, G. & Spiegel, S. (2018). Artisanal gold mining and farming: Livelihood linkages and labour dynamics after land reform in Zimbabwe. *The Journal of Development Studies*

Mkodzongi, G. (2011). *Land occupations and the quest for livelihoods in Mhondoro Ngezi Area, Zimbabwe*. Huntingdon: Mimeo.

Moyo, S. and Yeros, P. (eds.) (2005). *Reclaiming the land: The resurgence of rural movements in Africa, Asia and Latin America.* London: Zed Books.

Moyo, S. and Sukume, C. (2004). *Agricultural sector and agrarian development strategy.* Paper prepared for the World Bank, Zimbabwe Country Office.

Moyo, S and Yeros, P. (2005b). Land occupations and land reform in Zimbabwe: Towards the National Democratic Revolution. In Moyo, S and Yeros, P. (eds.), *Reclaiming the land: The resurgence of rural movements in Africa, Asia and Latin America.* London: ZED Books.

Moyo, S and Yeros, P. (2007a). Intervention, the Zimbabwe Question and the Two Lefts. *Historical Materialism*, 15(3), pp. 171-204.

Moyo, S and Yeros, P. (2007b). The radicalised state: Zimbabwe's interrupted revolution. *Review of African Political Economy*, 34(111), pp. 103-121.

Moyo, S. (1985). *The Socio-economic status and needs of ex-combatants: The case of Masvingo Province.* ZIDS Consultancy Report prepared for the Lutheran World Federation. Harare: ZIDS.

Moyo, S. (1986). The land question. In: Mandaza, I. (ed.) (1986). *Zimbabwe: The Political Economy of Transition 1980-1986.* Dakar: CODSERIA.

Moyo, S. (1994). Economic nationalism and land reform in Zimbabwe. Harare: SARIPS.

Moyo, S. (1995). *The land question in Zimbabwe.* Harare: SAPES Trust.

Moyo, S. (2000). *Land reform under structural adjustment in Zimbabwe: Land Use Change in the Mashonaland Provinces.* Uppsala: Nordiska Afrika Institutet.

Moyo, S. (2001). The land occupation movement and democratisation in Zimbabwe: Contradictions of Neoliberalism. *Millennium Journal of International Studies*, 30(2), pp. 310-330.

Moyo, S. (2002). Peasant organisations and rural civil society: An introduction. In: Romdhane, M and Moyo, S. (eds.) *Peasant organisations and the democratisation process in Africa.* Dakar: CODESRIA.

Moyo, S. (2003). The interactions of market and compulsory land acquisition process with social action in Zimbabwe's land reform.

In: Mandaza, I. and Nabudere, D. (eds.) *Pan-Africanism and Integration in Africa.* Harare: SAPES Books.

Moyo, S. (2004). *Overall impacts of the Fast Track Land reform Programme, AIAS monograph Series 02/2004.* Harare: AIAS.

Moyo, S. (2005). *Land policy, poverty reduction and public action in Zimbabwe. ISS/UNDP Land, poverty and public action paper No. 11.* The Hague: ISS.

Moyo, S. (2007). *Emerging land tenure issues in Zimbabwe, AIAS Monograph Series, 1/2007.* Harare: AIAS.

Moyo, S. (2008). *African land questions, the state and agrarian transition: Contradictions of neoliberal land reforms.* CODESRIA Green Book Series, Dakar: CODESRIA.

Moyo, S. (2011). Three decades of agrarian reform in Zimbabwe. *Journal of Peasant Studies,* 38(3): 493-531.

Moyo, S. (2013). Land reform and redistribution in Zimbabwe since 1980. In: Moyo. S. and Chambati, W. (eds.), *Land and Agrarian Reform in Zimbabwe: Beyond White-Settler Capitalism* (pp. 29-78). Dakar: CODESRIA.

Moyo, S. and Chambati, W. (2013). Introduction: Roots of Fast Track Land Reform. In: Moyo, S. and Chambati, C. (eds.), Land *and Agrarian Reform in Zimbabwe: Beyond White-Settler Capitalism* (pp. 1-28). Dakar: CODESRIA.

Moyo, S. and Yeros, P. (2007b). The radicalised state: Zimbabwe's interrupted revolution. *Review of African Political Economy,* 34(111): 103-121.

Moyo, S., Chambati, W., Murisa, T., Siziba, D., Dangwa, C. and Nyoni, N. (2009). *Fast Track Land Reform Baseline Survey in Zimbabwe: Trends and Tendencies, 2005/06.* Harare: Africa Institute for Agrarian Studies.

Moyo, S., Helliker, K. D and Murisa, T. (eds.) (2008). *Contested terrain: Land reform and civil society in contemporary Zimbabwe.* Pietermaritzburg: S&S Publishers.

Murisa, T. (2009). *An analysis of emerging forms of social organisation and agency in the aftermath of Fast Track Land Reform in Zimbabwe.* PhD Thesis, Rhodes University, South Africa.

Ndlovu-Gatsheni, S. J. (2013a). *Coloniality of Power in Postcolonial Africa: Myths of Decolonisation.* Dakar: CODESRIA

Ndlovu-Gatsheni, S. J. 2016. *The Decolonial Mandela: Peace, Justice and the Politics of Life*. New York: Berghahn.

Ndlovu-Gatsheni, S. J. (2007b). In search of common ground: Oral history, human rights and the United Nations (UN) Council on Human Rights. Keynote presentation delivered at the International Conference on Human Rights and Social Justice: Setting the agenda for United Nations Human Rights Council, organised by the University of Winnipeg (Global College) as part of Human Action Week, 23-25 February.

Ndlovu-Gatsheni, S. J. (2011). *The Logic of Violence in Africa. Ferguson Centre for African and Asian Studies Working Paper No 2*. Milton Keynes, UK.

Ndlovu-Gatsheni, S. J. (2013). *Empire, Global Coloniality and African Subjectivity*. New York: Berghahn Books.

Ndlovu-Gatsheni, S. J. and Benyera, E. (2015). Towards a framework for resolving the justice and reconciliation question in Zimbabwe. *African Journal on Conflict Resolution,* 15(2): 9-34.

Nhemachena A. and Dhakwa, E. (2018). Beyond Eurocentric Human Rights Jurisprudence and Towards Animality? Humanoid Robots and the Decomposition of African Humanism and Personhood: In: Nhemachena, A., Warikandwa, V. and Amoo, S. K. (eds.), *Social and Legal Theory in the Age of Decoloniality: (Re-) Envisioning African Jurisprudence in the 21ˢᵗ Century* (pp. 73-120). Bamenda: Langaa RPCIG.

Nhemachena, A., Warikandwa, V. and Amoo, S. K. (2018). Identity, Originality and Hybridity in Jurisprudence and Social Theory: An Introduction. In: In: Nhemachena, A., Warikandwa, V. and Amoo, S. K. (eds.), *Social and Legal Theory in the Age of Decoloniality: (Re-) Envisioning African Jurisprudence in the 21ˢᵗ Century* (pp. 1-72). Bamenda: Langaa RPCIG.

Nhemachena, A., Mlambo, N. and Kaundjua, M. (2016). The Notion of the 'Field' and the Practices of Researching and Writing Africa: Towards Decolonial Praxis." *Africology: The Journal of Pan African Studies,* 9(7): 15-36.

Rodney, W. (1985). How Europe Underdeveloped Africa. *Journal of Black Studies,* 16(2): 115-130.

Ruswa, G. (2007). *The golden era? Reflections on the first phase of land reform in Zimbabwe. Occasional Research Paper Series*. Harare: African Institute for Agrarian Studies.

Sachikonye, L. M. (2005a). *The promised land: From expropriation to reconciliation and jambanja*. Harare: Weaver Press.

Sachikonye, L. M. (2005b). The land is the economy: Revisiting the land question. *African Security Review*, 14(3): 31-44.

Sadomba, Z.W. (2013). A Decade of Zimbabwe's Land Revolution: The Politics of War Veteran vanguard. In: Moyo, S. and Chambati, W. (eds.), *Land and Agrarian Reform in Zimbabwe: Beyond White-Settler Capitalism* (pp. 79-122). Dakar: CODESRIA.

Said, E. (1978). *Orientalism*. New York: Pantheon.

Scoones, I. (1998). *Sustainable rural livelihoods: A framework for analysis. IDS Working Paper Series Number 72*. Brighton: IDS.

Scoones, I. (2009). Livelihoods perspectives and rural development. *Journal of Peasant Studies*, 36(1): 1-47.

Scoones, I. (2010). 'Zimbabwe's Land Reform: Challenging the Myths.' *The Zimbabwean, Weekly,* 21 October 2010.

Scoones, I. (2017). Zimbabweland, How are the children of Zimbabwe's land reform beneficiaries making a living? http://www.theZimbabwean.co/2017/04/children-zimbabwe-land-reform-beneficiaries-making-living/ (Accessed 12 May 2019).

Scoones, I. (2018). *Land reform in Zimbabwe: Challenges for policy*. s.l: Kindle Edition.

Scoones, I., Marongwe, N., Mavedzenge, B. and Murimbarimba, F. (2010).*Zimbabwe's land reform: Myths and realities*. Oxford: James Currey Press.

Scoones, I., Marongwe, N., Mavedzenge, B. and Murimbarimba, F. (2011). Zimbabwe's land reform: Myths and realities. *Africa Today*, 57(4): 125-139.

Scoones, I., Marongwe, N., Mavedzenge, B., Murimbarimba, F., Mahenehene, J., and Shonhe, T. (2018). *The political economy of agricultural commercialisation in Zimbabwe*. Working Paper 12. University of Cape Town: Centre for African Studies.

Shonhe, T. (2017). *Reconfigured agrarian relations in Zimbabwe*. Bamenda: Langaa RPCIG.

Shonhe, T. (2015). *Global commodity circuits, finance and markets and the new farmers in Zimbabwe: A case study of Hwedza district.* Presentation to the Centre for Civil society at the University of KwaZulu-Natal, South Africa, 20 November 2015.

Shonhe, T. (2015). *Tractors and agrarian transformation in Zimbabwe: Insights from Mvurwi.* Working Paper 21. Agricultural Research Policy in Africa (ARPA).

Sukume, C. (2012). Livelihoods after the land reform in Zimbabwe: Understanding processes of rural differentiation. *Journal of Agrarian Change*, 12(4): 503-527.

Scoones, I., Marongwe, N., Mavedzenge, B., Murimbarimba, F., Mahenehene, J., and Sukume, C. (2011). *Zimbabwe's land reform: A summary of findings.* Brighton: Institute of Development Studies.

Tekwa, N. and Adesina, J. (2018). Gender, Poverty and Inequality in the Aftermath of Zimbabwe's Land Reform: A Transformative Social Policy Perspective. *Journal of International Women's Studies,* 19(5): 45-62.

Thebe, V. (2018). Youth, agriculture and land reform in Zimbabwe: Experiences from communal areas and resettlement scheme in semi-arid Matabeleland, Zimbabwe. *African Studies*, 77(3): 336-353.

United Nations Research Institute for Social Development (2006). *Transformative social policy: Lessons from UNRISD Research. UNRISD Research and Policy Brief No. 5.*Geneva: UNRISD.

Yi, I. (2015). *New challenges for and new in social policy.* Geneva: United Nations Institute for Social Development.

www.ingramcontent.com/pod-product-compliance
Lightning Source LLC
Chambersburg PA
CBHW060020030426
42334CB00019B/2109